THE ART OF
Blue Sky
STUDIOS

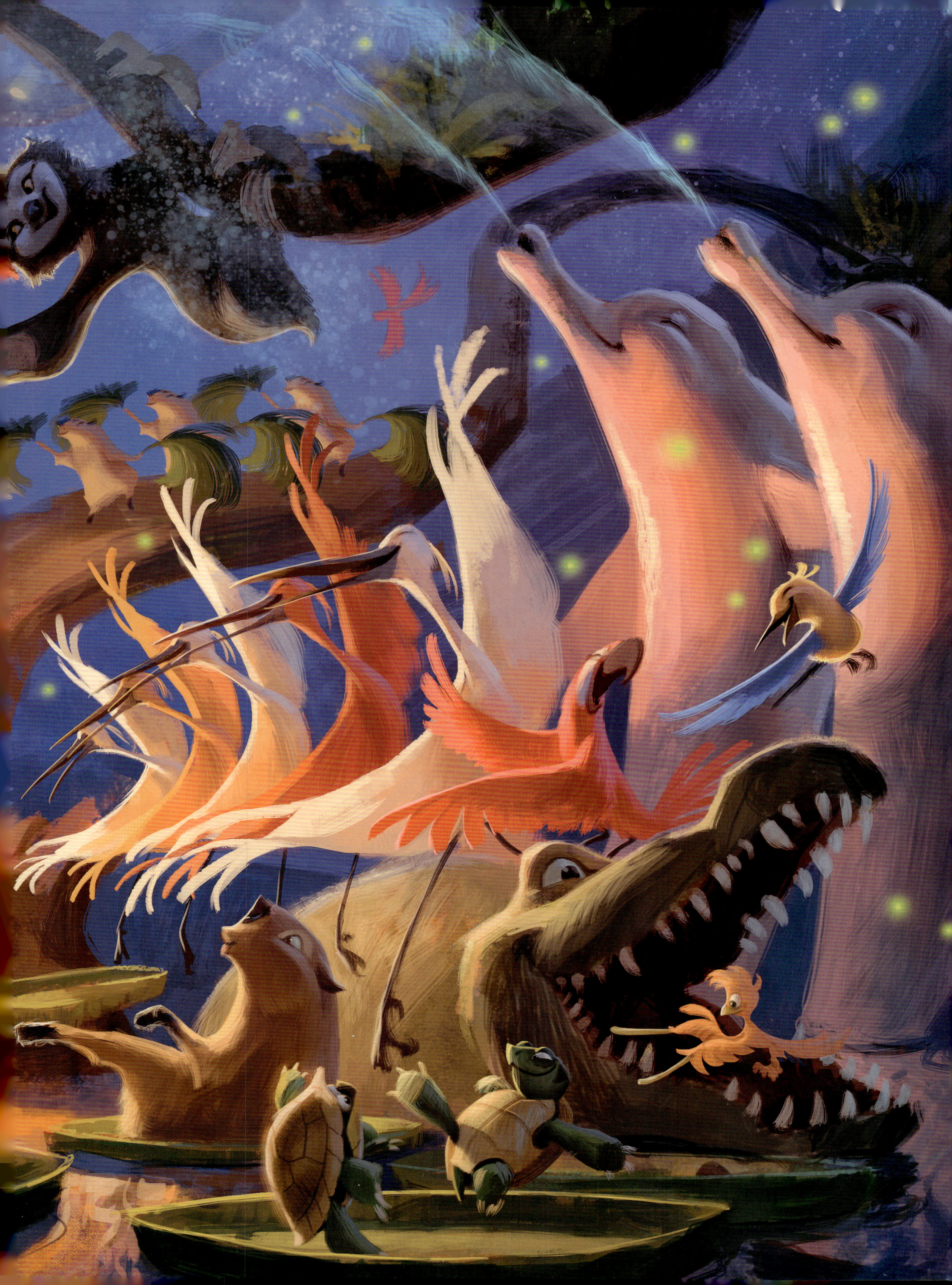

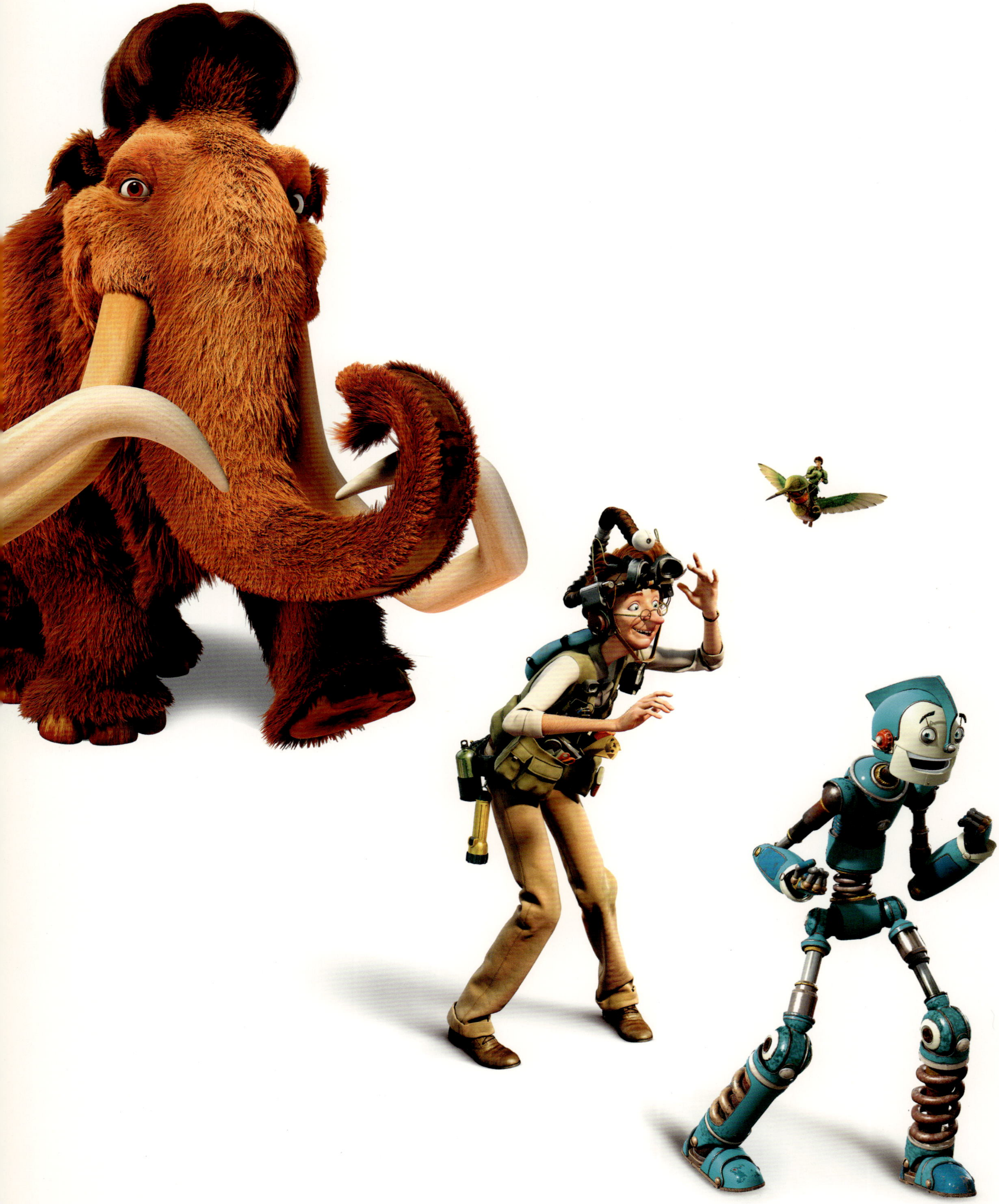

THE ART OF Blue Sky™ STUDIOS

WRITTEN BY
JAKE S. FRIEDMAN

TITAN BOOKS
London

CONTENTS

Foreword   11

The Beginning   12

CHAPTER 1
Ice Age
17

CHAPTER 2
Robots
55

CHAPTER 3
Ice Age: The Meltdown
83

CHAPTER 4
Dr. Seuss' Horton Hears a Who!
107

CHAPTER 5
Ice Age: Dawn of the Dinosaurs
145

CHAPTER 6
Rio
175

CHAPTER 7
Ice Age: Continental Drift
209

CHAPTER 8
Epic
239

CHAPTER 9
Rio 2
275

Epilogue   301

Acknowledgments   304

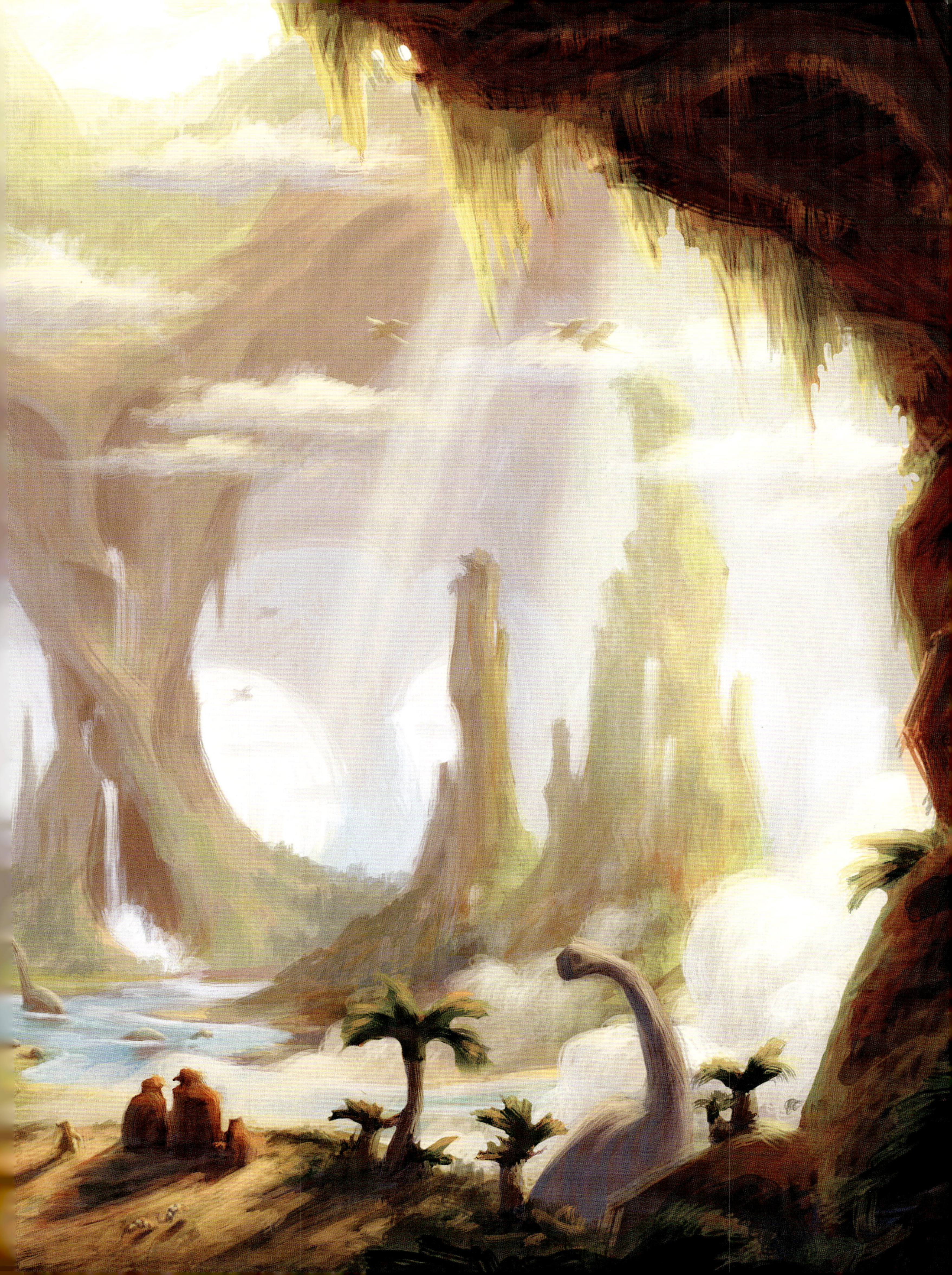

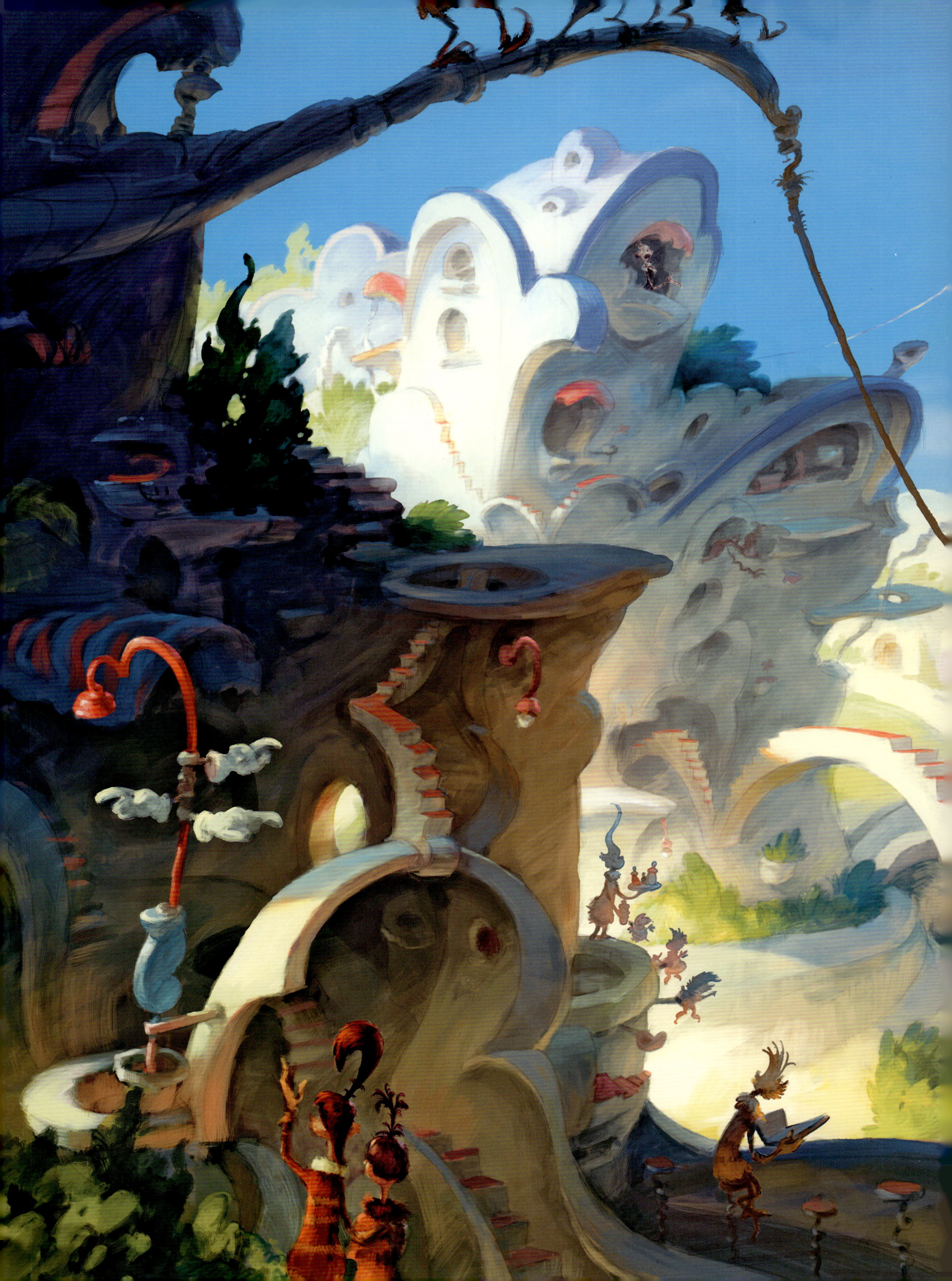

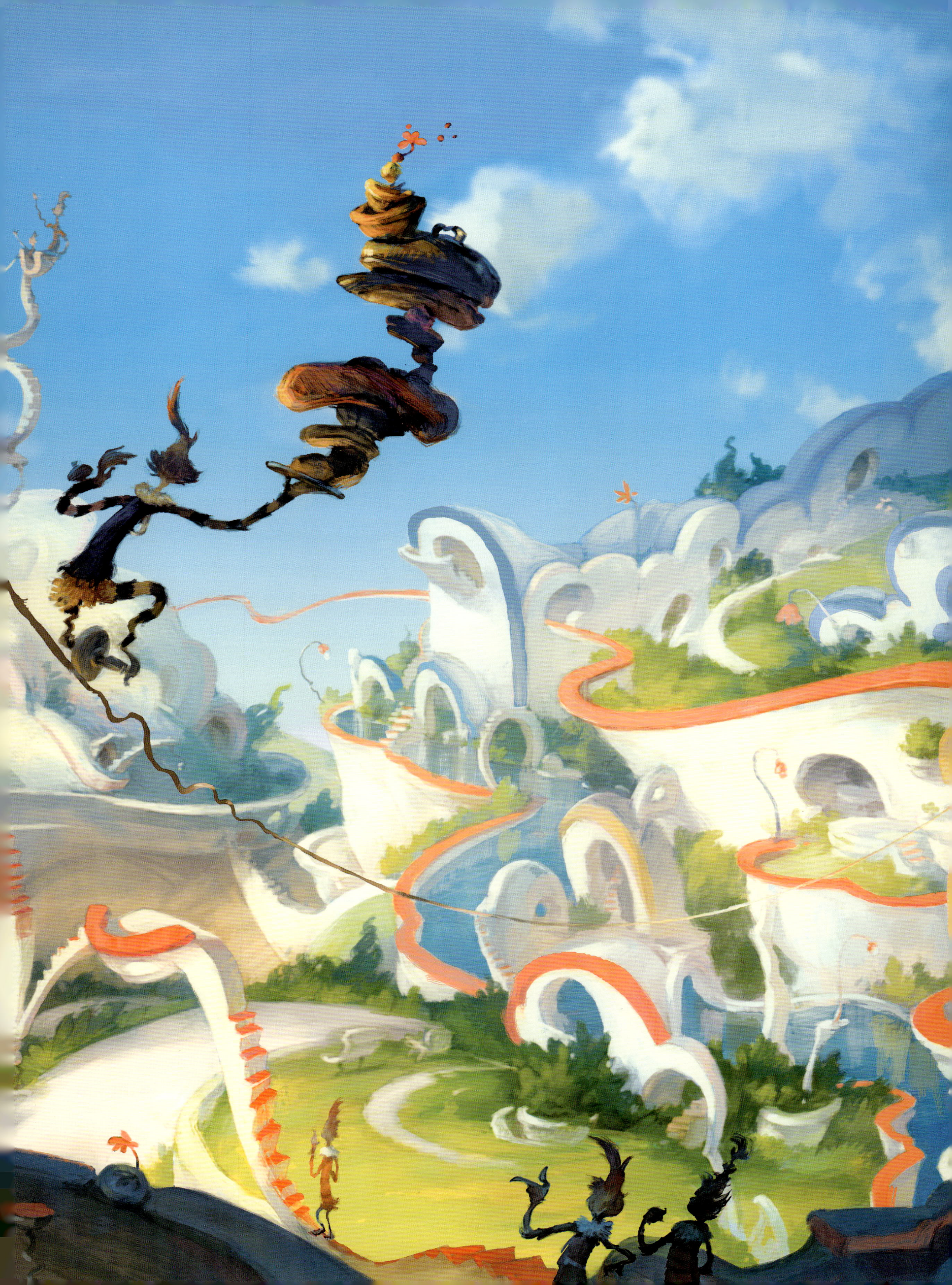

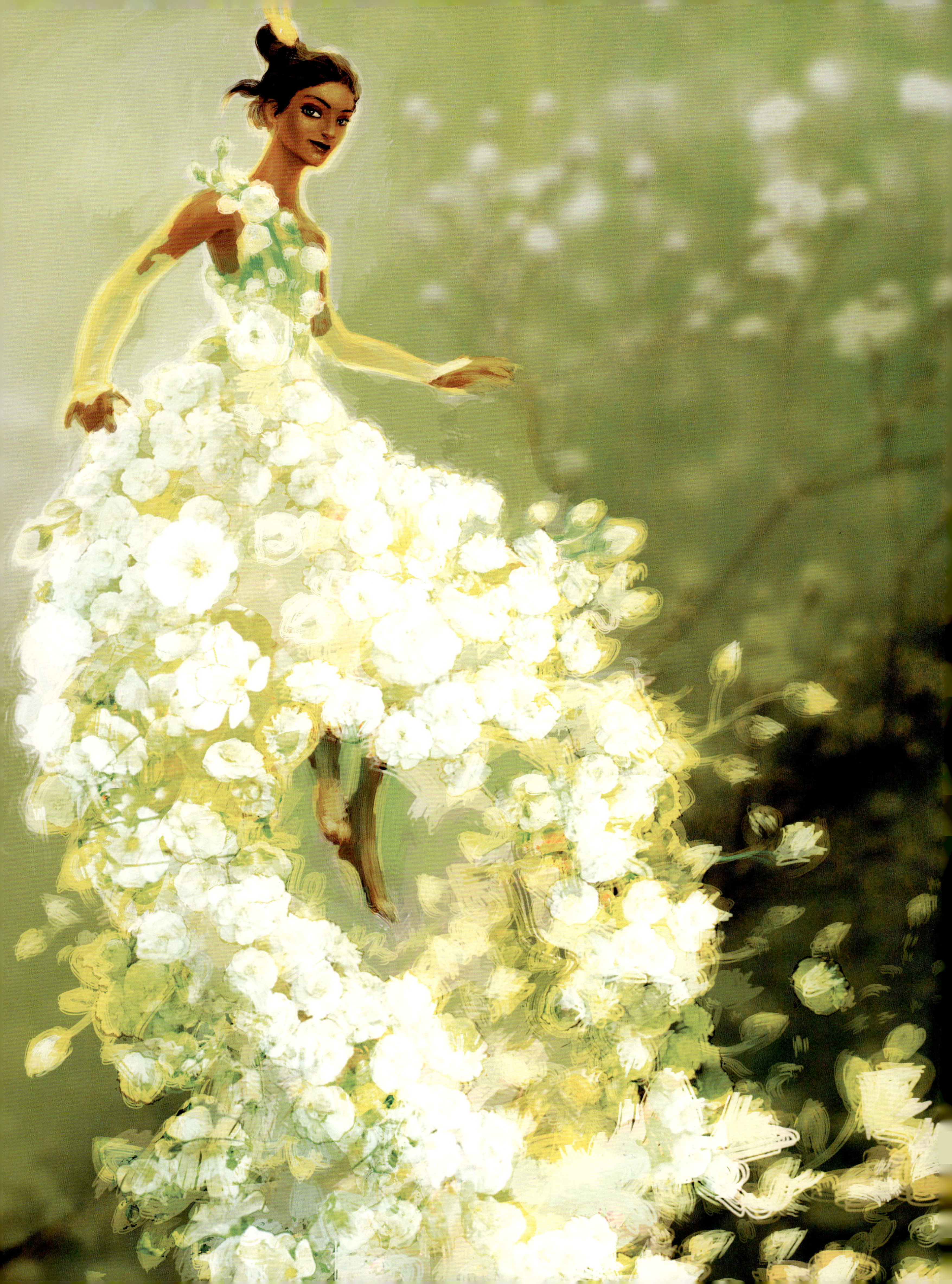

FOREWORD

• ◆ •

In 1987, computer animation was a new frontier with endless possibilities. We had little money, little business experience, and no evidence that a company like ours had ever succeeded. But we were infected.

So much lay ahead of us: so many dreams; so many hours, weeks, and years; so many goals that seemed too distant to reach. We struggled to look not at where we were, but where we were headed. We wanted to make movies. It was about visual storytelling, and each of us saw our role in achieving that objective.

As we moved forward, we attracted others who were similarly infected, and Blue Sky grew. As we grew in size, we also grew in breadth of talent. Ideas flowed from everywhere. Every person perceived each challenge from his or her own perspective. It was a rich environment. Most of all, it was FUN!

One step always led to the next, and in time, we were accomplishing our dreams and going beyond them. One after another, our goals fell behind us and in their place manifested a future that none of us could have anticipated.

From six of us to 600. From laxative commercials to applause on the Oscar stage. From animating a "feature presentation" graphic for a regional theater chain to our own film premieres in Radio City Music Hall and Rio de Janeiro, and film franchises embraced by audiences around the globe.

Our proudest accomplishment by far is the community of caring and talented people who have come together to carry the dream to fruition and beyond. It is to them we owe every success, and it is from them we take our inspiration for the future.

—Carl Ludwig, Eugene Troubetzkoy, Chris Wedge,
cofounders of Blue Sky Studios

(Opposite) **Epic: Queen Tara's lilac dress** – concept art • Michael Knapp
(Top) **Robots: Lug** – concept art • Bill Joyce
(Bottom) **Ice Age: Dawn of the Dinosaurs: Scrat and Scratte** – concept art • Peter de Sève

THE BEGINNING

• ◆ •

"The very beginning was geeky and fun, and there were no commitments to anyone but ourselves to make this stuff cool."
—CHRIS WEDGE

In a 400 square-foot space in Briarcliff Manor near Ossining, New York, six people conspired to change the art of computer graphics. The small team was attempting to do something remarkable and believed that they each brought something to the table that no one else could.

Michael Ferraro was a programming whiz able to compose the digital language that made things run. Dr. Eugene Troubetzkoy specialized in computer-generated geometrics. Carl Ludwig could mathematically determine how light rays affect different materials on surface faces. Chris Wedge came from a background of character animation by various methods, including the burgeoning new media of computer animation. Alison Brown had the marketing contacts. David Brown (no relation) was the financial backbone of the group and the head of the small organization.

Up until that point, 3-D computer images still appeared entirely graphic, reminding the audience that they were watching a digitally rendered picture. The team knew that the key to simulating real life lay in the secret of light rays. If shadows were not simply painted on, but rather scientifically determined through algorithmic computation, the most remarkable graphics could appear as tangible as a photograph. No program had ever come close to replicating the properties of light on a real-life object, and if it succeeded, it would revolutionize computer animation forever. Their efforts would eventually lead to the creation of a game-changing new renderer known as CGI Studio.

Chris Wedge had always loved character animation and as a child had made his own stop-motion animated films. When he was still an undergrad studying film at Purchase College in the late 1970s, he "completely tripped" into a job at MAGI, one of the very first computer animation companies.

MAGI (or Mathematical Applications Group, Inc.) had been founded in 1966 to develop early computer software that measured rays of nuclear radiation. Working on government contracts, MAGI built its software to simulate the laws of physics and called the product "SynthaVision." It was at MAGI that Wedge met Dr. Eugene Troubetzkoy, a longtime employee of the company.

Born in Paris, Troubetzkoy had earned a PhD in theoretical physics from Columbia University and had been one of the first people to work in computer animation. Indeed, in the late 1970s, computer animation was still in its infancy. The programmers at MAGI were producing beautiful images and had developed a complex language to animate computer graphics, yet they lacked the skill to artfully bring them to life.

Wedge started applying his knowledge of animation to MAGI's technology to help produce animated television commercials. As a result of MAGI's success in TV, in 1980 the company was given the opportunity to create the computer animation for Disney's *Tron* (1982). Michael Ferraro was brought on as a systems architect, and Carl Ludwig, an electrical engineer who had worked on NASA's Lunar Module, was hired to build the color digital film recorder that put *Tron* on celluloid.

Tron proved to be one of the most innovative computer-animated films ever committed to the screen, its groundbreaking visuals pointing the way to a new digital age. Unfortunately, even with its moderate success, MAGI began to struggle. To try to keep the company afloat, MAGI hired David Brown, a CBS/Fox Video marketing executive who would help run the New York sales end of the studio; they also hired Alison Brown as managing producer. Wedge took the opportunity to step back from production and enrolled in a master's program at Ohio State University, as he says, "to study how to apply the new language of computer programming to the decades-old art form of animation."

In the mid-1980s, MAGI shut down for good. Nevertheless, Wedge, Ludwig, Ferraro, and Troubetzkoy still saw incredible untapped potential in the medium and decided to form their own computer animation studio. Also on board were Alison Brown, who had valuable connections with potential clients, and David Brown, who had experience managing companies. In the spring of 1987, the six partners launched Blue Sky Studios, with the goal of creating revolutionary computer animation.

Ferraro began building a programming language that was custom-made to utilize their specific software. "We just started writing code," says Ludwig, "and we had all these great dreams and all these great ideas, and off we went. And by the fall of '87, when we were actually making our first simple pictures, we thought we could raise some money."

DESPITE THEIR HUMBLE BEGINNINGS, Blue Sky had an ace in the hole. CGI Studio was a renderer based more on physics than the scan-line renderers of its competitors. Competing renderers required the graphic designers to paint in the shaded effects—every light and every shadow. This required a whole team of digital artists to replicate authentic lighting on digitally animated graphics. It was rarely done convincingly.

Blue Sky was attempting to create a renderer that produced realistic lights and shadows automatically. It required not only a scientific understanding of the properties of light, but an artist's approach to when and how that light should be used. Ludwig studied the light refraction index of properties like water, ice, and crystal and would then input those values directly into the programming code. This allowed the artists who used the renderer to work as intuitively as photographers.

"Intuition is very, very important," says Ludwig. "People's time is the thing you value the highest. And you have to give them something they can do naturally."

Unfortunately that October, the stock market crashed, and the little company suddenly found itself without any potential revenue.

(Opposite) The six founders of Blue Sky Studios: *(left to right)* Michael Ferraro, Carl Ludwig, Alison Brown, David Brown, Chris Wedge, Eugene Troubetzkoy. *(Top)* Carl Ludwig helped pioneer Blue Sky Studios' groundbreaking use of light rays. *(Left)* An early digital test by Carl Ludwig showcases radiosity on different surfaces.

THE BEGINNING   13

THROUGHOUT THESE TURBULENT TIMES, the team was continually developing the rendering techniques of CGI Studio. In particular, they were working on engineering a ray tracer, a complex computer program that, at the time, was not commercially available or widely desirable. On the surface, it seemed impractical to run a program so complex and memory-heavy, but the key to Blue Sky's success lay in its potential.

In essence, a ray tracer traces light rays between a simulated light source, an object, and the camera's eye. When Ludwig used it to render a digital image of a glass of red wine near a chrome sphere, the ray tracer calculated the index of refraction of light through the glass, the reflection of the sphere on the glass's bottom, and the absorption of light as it passed through the wine and cast a subtle burgundy shadow. There were numerous other attributes that came into play to create the final image, and they were all done with algorithms. In digital terms, Blue Sky's shadows were "real."

It took two years for Blue Sky Studios to find their first client: a company that wanted their logo animated so it would be seen flying over the ocean in front of a sunset. The studio rendered a single beautiful frame and, fortunately, they were awarded the job.

"But that single frame took two days to render," says Wedge, "so we realized we were in big trouble because we had nowhere near enough time to produce the whole piece of animation." At their wits' end, Blue Sky approached a local graphics studio that generously allowed them to use their computer processors to render the job. In the end, the client was pleased, and it led to more work. "The very beginning was geeky and fun, and there were no commitments to anyone but ourselves to make this stuff cool," says Wedge.

To further grow the company, Blue Sky created animations for pharmaceutical commercials, which showed the inner workings of time-release capsules. Slowly the studio began picking up other jobs that involved more complex computer graphics and animation, working for clients including Bell Atlantic, Rayovac, Gillette, PBS (producing the "Mathman" segments for TV's *Square One*), and Braun—an endeavor that won the studio a CLIO advertising award.

With the growing success of the renderer, the team could afford to be a little more picky about their jobs. "It's kind of like steering a freighter," says Wedge. "We slowly and painfully turned it over a couple of years. We got to the point where we could maybe do a character in a commercial, then maybe a whole commercial. Finally we managed to put a reel together that was mostly about character performance and less about time-release capsules."

By the mid-'90s, Blue Sky was producing commercials starring talking coffee beans for Chock full o'Nuts and the first computer-generated M&M's. They also animated network IDs for MTV, a gig that led to a pivotal relationship between the small animation studio and the music television network.

In 1992, MTV had produced a live-action short film called *Joe's Apartment* about a young hipster living with friendly, stop-motion-animated cockroaches. The short was a hit, and the network decided to spin it into its first feature film. Blue Sky created some test animation of computer-generated cockroaches and was hired to create the supporting cast of digital insects.

The film was a cult hit and drew the attention of Hollywood studios. The studio soon expanded, landing the CG character work for *A Simple Wish* (1997), *Alien: Resurrection* (1997), *Mousehunt* (1997), *Star Trek: Insurrection* (1998), *Fight Club* (1999), and the memorable talking fish from the second season finale of *The Sopranos*.

"We had a tremendous advantage over other people doing the work," says Ludwig. "Our guys would go out there to the film set, take a white sphere and a chrome sphere, set it up where it was being shot, and that would show them where all the lights were. We would then essentially do the same thing digitally, set up lights exactly like they had them on the set, and we would render it, and the stuff would match beautifully. When we did the alien in *Alien: Resurrection*, you really couldn't tell the difference. It was perfect."

Alien: Resurrection was Twentieth Century Fox's first involvement with Blue Sky, and it began a cooperative business venture that would mature in the years to come. In the meantime, Wedge had been developing something on his own, a project that could finally marry this groundbreaking technology with his love of filmmaking.

AROUND 1990, NATIVE BRAZILIAN CARLOS SALDANHA was a graduate student at New York's School of Visual Arts. Wedge was his thesis advisor, and Saldanha was Wedge's star pupil. "Chris said, 'We have this great idea to do a short,'" says Saldanha, "and he showed me a few storyboard panels for *Bunny*."

Wedge had started developing *Bunny* in 1990 as a way to showcase the capabilities of CGI Studio. Working on it in his spare time, he honed the story over several years, and *Bunny* evolved into a powerful fable of love, loss, and rebirth. In the short, a relentless moth irritates a lonely rabbit widow. At the end of the story, the moth beckons her toward a heavenly glow, reuniting her with her husband. The titular character performs her actions entirely in pantomime, weaving a narrative that makes us laugh and cry within a span of just seven minutes..

After his graduation, Saldanha was brought on as an animator, and while Wedge moved over to work on the CG elements in Blue Sky's feature projects, Saldanha ended up directing some of the commercials. "Everybody worked a little bit on *Bunny*," says Saldanha, "but everyone worked off-hours on the side, so *Bunny* took quite a while."

In 1996, Blue Sky producer Nina Rappaport realized that *Bunny* would be an exceptional showpiece for the studio. She placed Wedge on *Bunny* full time, with a goal of completing it in two years. The models for *Bunny* included surfaces of fur, glass, metal, and several other materials that were beyond the capabilities of standard rendering technology. Fortunately, Blue Sky's renderer, CGI Studio, was able to accurately configure what those surfaces would look like when they interacted with light coming from sources as small as a swinging light bulb and as expansive as an ethereal cloudscape.

"Some of the fun of *Bunny* started as us exercising the technology," says Wedge. "Carl would sit in his corner, dreaming up bells and whistles for the renderer, and one of his ideas was the extension of the ray tracer that we call 'radiosity.'" Radiosity not only tracks rays to the first surface from the light source but also collects the reflected light from surfaces that surround those objects, creating colored highlights and toned shadows that are convincingly realistic.

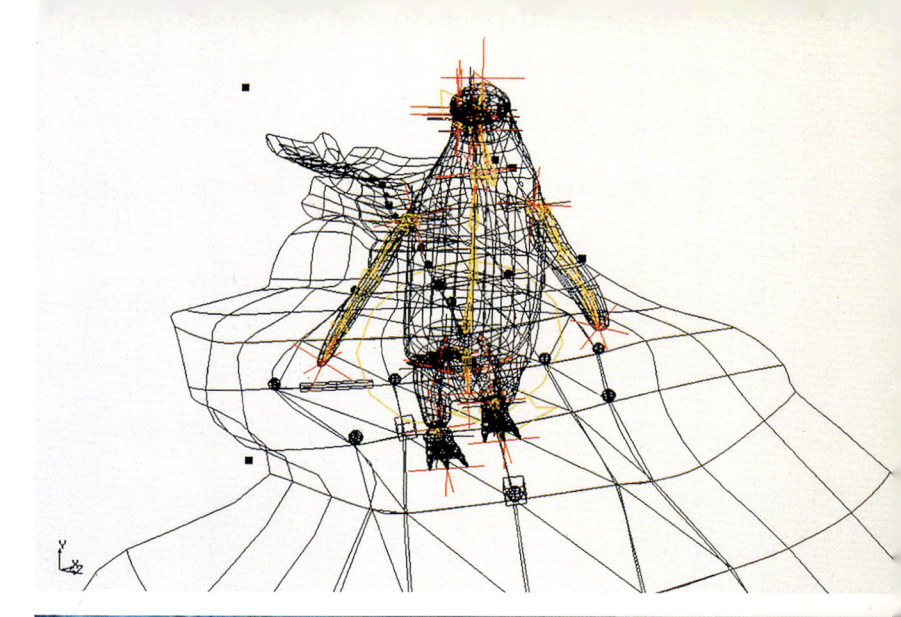

Bunny was finally completed in 1998 and went on to win the Academy Award for Best Animated Short. "That got us the cred that really greased the wheels for our involvement with Fox," says Wedge.

Fox saw great potential in the little Oscar-winning animation studio and offered Blue Sky a chance to make a feature film of its own, with Wedge set to direct. Lori Forte, a producer for Fox Animation in Los Angeles, had been developing an animated film about the mammals of the Ice Age. The world, characters, and tone of the film were all there in black and white, and Blue Sky Studios was the perfect candidate to bring it to the screen.

(Opposite top) Another early test by Ludwig showing radiosity and refraction through differently shaped surfaces.
(Opposite bottom) A swimming Xenomorph from *Alien: Resurrection* (1997) before and after realistic lighting effects are applied.
(Top and above) The iconic penguin spirit animal in *Fight Club* (1999) in wireframe and final render.

THE BEGINNING   15

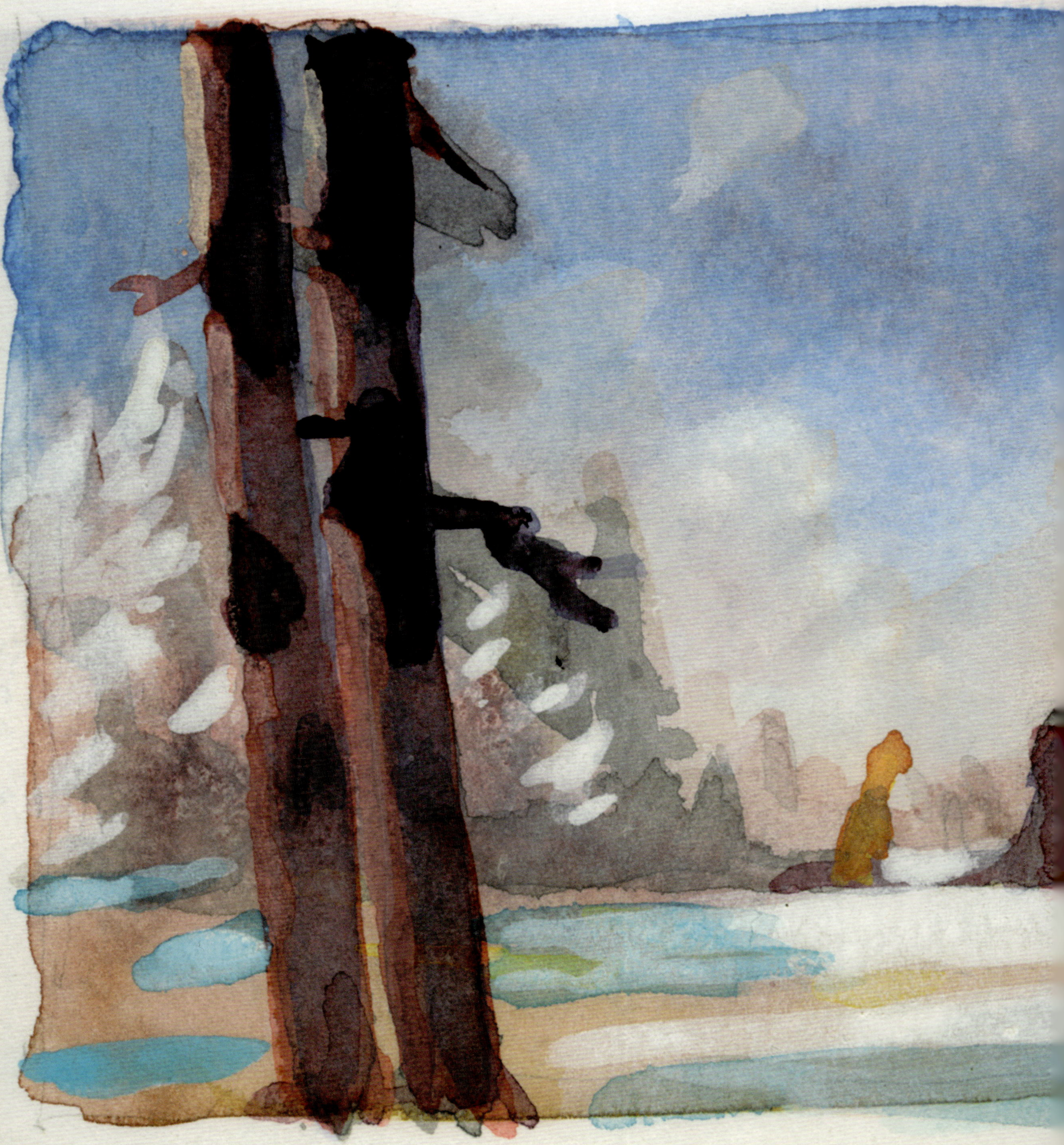

CHAPTER 1 · *Ice Age*

*"I don't know about you guys, but
we are the weirdest herd I've ever seen."*

—SID

Even after the success of *Bunny*, Blue Sky Studios needed a hit to prove its chops in the competitive arena of commercial cinema. Fortunately, Fox producer Lori Forte was composing a universal story in a setting that had never been tackled in a motion picture before.

"I was developing ideas and stories for Fox Animation in LA," she says, "and one of the ideas that came up was to do a movie set in the Ice Age. I had grown up with dinosaur movies, but I always loved the mammals from the Ice Age. We hadn't seen anything with them before in animation, and I wanted to give them their due."

Forte enlisted the help of writer Michael J. Wilson, who was instrumental in creating the core group of heroes: Manny the mammoth, Sid the sloth, and Diego the saber-toothed tiger. He also created Soto, the villain and head of Diego's pack. Writer Michael Berg also pitched in to help create the tone of the movie, and the three developed the initial script, outlining the trio's adventures.

When Fox approached Chris Wedge with the first draft of the script, it played like a typical journey movie, taking the characters from a starting point to an end point with outlandish encounters in between. Fox wanted Blue Sky to make the movie, but only if Wedge would bring to it the kind of pathos and character-driven humor that made his short animation so memorable. "They gave us the script for a very straight-ahead, talking animal adventure movie and said, 'We'll make this film if you can make it a comedy,'" says Wedge. "That was the challenge. I said, 'Let's dig in.'"

(Previous pages) **Watercolor trio** – color key • Greg Couch
(Top) **Trio in profile** – early character sketch • Peter de Sève
(Opposite) **Baby and heroes** – early concept art • Greg Couch

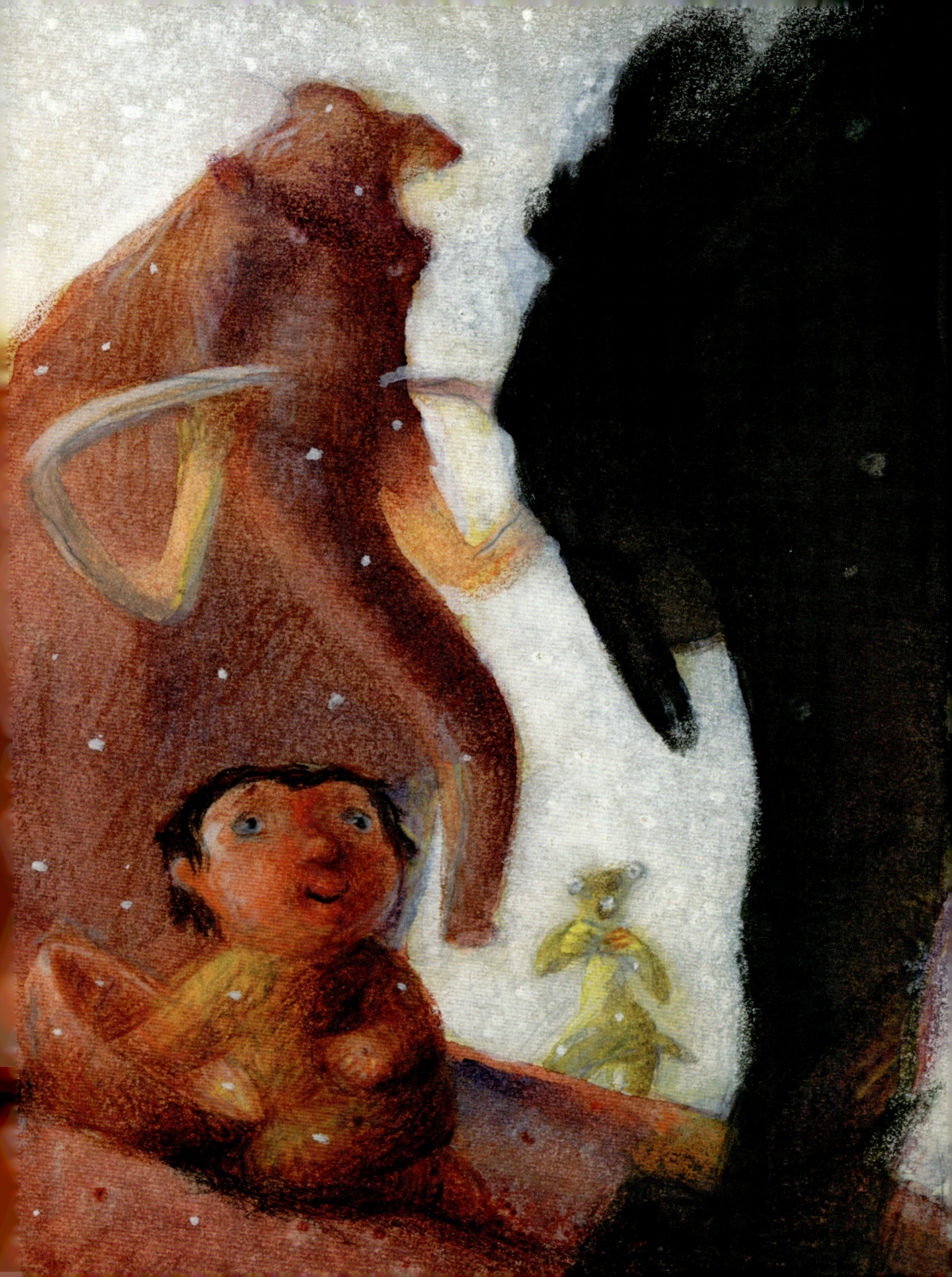

THE INITIAL ICEBREAKER

Although he would later be joined by codirector Carlos Saldanha—his former student—at the start of the project, it was entirely up to Wedge to decide how to translate the script for the screen. "From the beginning we knew we weren't going to make a movie just featuring animals talking in front of a white background," says Wedge. "The script called for it to start in the fall, and I tried to enforce the idea that as the movie got colder and colder, Manny's heart would get warmer and warmer."

Prior to *Ice Age*, Blue Sky's art direction was entrusted to one artist alone. For a project of this magnitude, however, the crew had to specialize in order to optimize the workflow. Peter Clarke, an artist known as "the creator of worlds" for his lush illustrations of make-believe environments, was brought in to design the backgrounds of *Ice Age* and give the universe its personality. Wedge hired illustrator Peter de Sève to design the characters. De Sève and Clarke found that their styles complemented each other's, their illustrations looking as though they could exist within the same universe from the start. Mary GrandPré, known for the striking cover and chapter illustrations she created for the US versions of the Harry Potter novels, provided designs that helped influence the appearance of the prehistoric humans.

Because the filmmakers had not chosen a final look for the film, de Sève was given free rein to invent the entire cast of characters from scratch. "When I design a character," says de Sève, "I don't approach it thinking, 'What does this character look like?' I ask myself, 'Who is this character?' If you don't know who he is, you can't do the character designs; you can only do drawings of someone

(Opposite top) **Scrat** – character sketch • Peter de Sève
(This page and opposite bottom) **Manny in various glacier landscapes** – set designs • Peter Clarke
(Right) **Diego** – character sketch • Peter de Sève

ICE AGE 21

"When I'm searching for a character, it's about not only what they look like but how they act. Context is everything."

—PETER DE SÈVE

(From top left clockwise) **Aardvark, Piranha, Starts, Freaky Mammal** – early character sketches • Peter de Sève
(Opposite) **Cave drawing showing shovel mouth with bird** – early character sketch • Peter de Sève

22 THE ART OF BLUE SKY STUDIOS

ICE AGE 23

who looks like a hero or a villain. You have to know what's going on in the character's head, behind the eyes. So when I'm searching for a character, it's about not only what they look like but how they act. Context is everything."

Just because a character looks complete on paper doesn't necessarily mean it translates seamlessly to 3-D space. For instance, de Sève designed Soto with what he described as "flames of fur" protruding out from his cheekbones. One of the CG artists complimented de Sève on the front-facing drawing but asked what the character's head looked like from the side. "That was my first challenge," says de Sève. "It was like the gauntlet was laid down. I learned that I could have a good drawing, but I would have to be able to defend its volume in 3-D."

Similarly, Manny didn't quite find his final form until Mike Defeo and the Modeling department sculpted him in clay. As expressive as a character could be, it still had to be formed in a CG model that could be rigged with a working skeleton. If an arm wasn't long enough to scratch a character's own nose, it went back to the drawing board. "We knew we were going to encounter restrictions with the technology," says Wedge, "but the one place where we didn't want to restrict ourselves was character."

The art director on *Ice Age*, Brian McEntee, provided the overall flow of color throughout the film, setting parameters for how the visual language of each scene and shot would appear. Greg Couch, a color stylist, was one of the artists whose job it was to create inspirational production paintings for the movie. Without knowing for certain what the finished film was going to look like, Couch created acrylic paintings exploring lighting, staging, and a sense of emotion. Each painting that realized a moment of the script became a "color key."

"Everyone had a pile of books at their desk," says Couch. "I had a book of photos of the Arctic Circle in Norway, and the colors were just amazingly saturated. Because of the area's location on the globe, the sun's always low, and it's always magic hour. So it's always orange against deep purple, yellow against cobalt blue–colored skies."

The color design of each scene was influenced by both physical and emotional elements: the kind of light illuminating the digital set and the mood Wedge wanted to convey. It gave the film a visual outline that spans the entire spectrum, even though it all takes place against a backdrop of ice.

"There's a lot more color in *Ice Age* than white," says Wedge. "To my eye and my sensibility, the backgrounds had to be as distinct as the protagonists. I wanted the environment, the Ice Age itself, to be its own character. And that's why the movie opens with an anthropomorphic glacier chasing a hapless little guy into the valley."

(Top and opposite center) **Inside cave** – concept art • Greg Couch
(Opposite bottom) **Cave paintings** – concept art • Brian McEntee

ICE AGE 25

26 THE ART OF BLUE SKY STUDIOS

(Opposite) – **Ice bridge** – color exploration • Greg Couch, *(Top)*, **Diego with night sky** – concept art • Greg Couch, *(Center)* **Manny and Sid** – concept art • Greg Couch, *(Bottom left)* – **Ice Age animals** – concept art • Greg Couch, *(Bottom right)* **Diego** – early character sketch • Peter de Sève

ICE AGE 27

Manny

"I WANTED TO UNRAVEL MANNY as we went through the first movie," says Chris Wedge. "The script had him waking from a nightmare where he saw his family set upon by human hunters, but I thought that was front-loading the story. I wanted him to be a bit more enigmatic, like a troubled character where you wonder, 'What is wrong with this guy?' The more we thought about it, the more we felt that that sequence belonged deep in act two. When we understood what made him tick, it would deepen our relationship with him. You have a lot of respect for him for the sacrifice that he's making."

(Opposite top) **Manny** – early character sketch • Peter de Sève, *(Opposite bottom)* **Manny side view** – concept art • Mary GrandPré, *(Top)* **Manny and Sid** – concept art • Steve Blevins, *(Left)* **Manny and Sid** – concept art • artist unknown, *(Below)* **Manny** – early character sketch • Peter de Sève

(Top) **Manny, Sid, Diego, and Baby** – concept art • Greg Couch
(Above) **Manny in the cave** – concept art • Steve Blevins
(Left) **Manny** – early character sketch • Peter de Sève
(Opposite top left) **Manny amongst other animals** – concept art • Greg Couch
(Opposite top right) **Manny walking** – early character sketch • Peter de Sève
(Opposite bottom) **Manny walking** – early character color exploration • Greg Couch

ICE AGE 31

(Above) **Northern lights** – early concept art • Greg Couch

STARTING FROM SCRAT

The opening of the film introduced the world to Scrat, the scraggly, bug-eyed rodent scrambling from a fast-approaching Ice Age, beleaguered as much by the threat to his acorn as to his scrawny little life. He has since become not only the mascot of the franchise but iconic of the whole studio. And he wasn't even in the original script.

In the draft delivered to Wedge, the story began with Manny waking from a dream about his family and then encountering the animals' migration through the autumnal landscape. This march across the fall foliage might have been disorientating to an uninitiated audience who paid to see the age of ice.

"I didn't think that it was original or engaging enough," says Wedge. "I wanted a sequence at the beginning that would set the audience's expectations, to get the tonal range and scope of action that they were in for, and encapsulate it in five minutes. 'Now that you can understand what our movie's about, you can enjoy it.' I still believe that it's a great way to start a movie."

The idea was to anthropomorphize the Ice Age itself and create a struggle between the global natural disaster and a tiny character—but what sort of character? De Sève was sharing a studio office with McEntee at the time and had a board covered in drawings inspired by a company field trip to New York's American Museum of Natural History.

"I was just riffing on prehistoric creatures," says de Sève, "mostly looking at stuff from the museum, sort of staying scientifically accurate. I was approached by Wedge, and he said, 'We need some kind of a rodent who is going to start a cataclysm.' I had a whole bunch of drawings on the board, and I was constantly adding to them. And a picture on the left-hand corner was a drawing of a kind of mouse, but with saber teeth. And he said, 'That's him!'"

The job of storyboarding the pivotal introductory sequence was entrusted to artist Bill Frake. A veteran of the '70s Disney training program, Frake studied under Eric Larson—one of Disney's famed Nine Old Men—and was an artist on *Who Framed Roger Rabbit*, *Hercules*, *Fantasia 2000*, and many other films. "The Disney artists taught me to feel emotion like an artist and insert that into the environments," says Frake, "and then the environment would create an emotion with the character, so it becomes a partner. The camera is the third objective viewer, so if there's only one figure on the set, you actually have three characters there: the figure, the background, and the camera."

"I think the beauty of Scrat is the simplicity and the purity of him. He represents the essence of animation—the indestructible characters who could live forever, who are over the top and funny. He has flaws, and he's the underdog. And his scenes are entirely visual, pure pantomime. It's an animator's dream and a director's dream as well."

—CARLOS SALDANHA

(Opposite) **Scrat** – earliest character sketch • Peter de Sève
(This page) **Scrat expressions** – early character sketches • Peter de Sève

ICE AGE   35

36   THE ART OF BLUE SKY STUDIOS

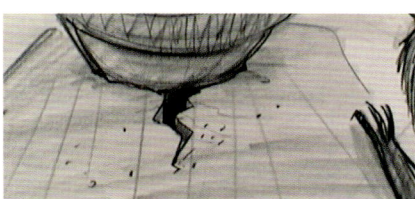

Frake took the intro sequence assignment home over the weekend, but an unusual impediment stood in his way. "We were renting a home at the time, and the owner told us to be sure to feed this wild squirrel a peanut," Frake recalls. "I was sitting down trying to do my work and there he was, literally banging on the sliding glass door for his peanut. I decided I wasn't going to open the door until I finished my work, but he was banging so hard I kept losing my concentration. Finally I opened the door and gave him a pizza crust, and after I closed the door he just looked at it, then at me. Then he jumps onto one of the deck chairs and begins ripping the stuffing out, staring at me and chattering up a storm. I thought the little guy was crazy! He didn't want pizza or anything, just that nut."

Frake turned that squirrel into a tragic hero, a character who spends his time organizing things to be just right, becoming increasingly irate as all of his well-laid plans go up in smoke. Frake returned to Wedge on Monday morning and pitched a hundred panels of storyboard gags. "We tried to boil things down to the simplest thing it could possibly be," says Wedge, "and that's what I think makes the Scrat character so emblematic of the everyman. It's the Sisyphean quest for something he'll never attain, even if it's as simple as eating an acorn."

"It was wordless, and the audience was completely riveted," remembers de Sève. "They had no idea what it was, and it ended up being the perfect trailer. Whenever it would come on, people would watch this thing and go silent. It was its own little animated film, and it would end with [the title] 'Ice Age,' and everybody wanted to see the movie." Though Scrat doesn't speak, Wedge ended up voicing the character's noises. (The sounds were an expression, he jokes, of the pressure the studio was feeling at the time.)

The audience response was greater than Blue Sky had anticipated, and it became necessary to insert Scrat into the film periodically, this new addition proving to be a stroke of brilliance. The cutaways from the main dramatic plot allowed the audience to relax and laugh again, while letting the filmmakers swiftly move the main characters through the expansive territory on their long journey.

Scrat was perhaps cinema's first lead character to operate completely outside the main plot of a film, hardly interfering with the continuity of the other three main characters and still managing to steal the show. "It created a movie language that had never been done before," says codirector Carlos Saldanha. "I think Scrat was the trigger for the avalanche—no pun intended. He was the guy who put us on the map."

(Top) **Scrat on beach** – color key • Daisuke Tsutsumi, (Bottom) **Ice Age opening sequence** – storyboard thumbnails • Bill Frake, (Right) **Scrat** – early character sketch • Peter de Sève

Sid

"SID IS REALLY THE one character who is consistent all the way through," says Lori Forte. "He wears his heart on his sleeve. He's the conscience of the group; he tries to do what's best, even if it goes awry, even though he's made fun of, and he's the butt of a lot of jokes. He's pretty much the one who really doesn't have to change, because he has a solid moral code himself, though it doesn't seem like that at times. In cinema, the 'fool' is such an important character because he's always the clown and made fun of, but he's the one who is the wisest. And I sort of brought a little bit of that to Sid."

(Opposite top) **Sid with flower** – final frame, *(Opposite bottom)* **Sid** – early character sketches • Peter de Sève,
(Top left) **Sid** – early concept art • artist unknown, *(Top right)* **Sid** – early character sketch • Peter de Sève,
(Bottom) **Sid in barren landscape** – color key • Greg Couch

(Top) **Sid wading in pond** – color key • Greg Couch, *(Bottom)* **Sid with female sloths** – color key • H. B. Lewis, *(Bottom corner)* **Sid sticks his neck out** – early character sketch • Peter de Sève, *(Opposite top left)* **Sid** – early character art • H. B. Lewis, *(Opposite top right)* **Sid strolling** – early character sketch • Peter de Sève, *(Opposite bottom)* **Sid evolution** – concept art • Peter de Sève (design) and Daisuke Tsutsumi (painting)

40 THE ART OF BLUE SKY STUDIOS

ICE AGE 41

Diego

"DIEGO'S ARC WAS REALLY a discovery of friendship and family in the herd versus the tiger pack, which is based on hierarchy and doing everything for one leader," says Lori Forte. "Diego started out as a cold, heartless assassin who was sent to get the baby for Soto, but at the last minute he had forged a friendship with Manny and Sid, and he stood up against his own kind to save his friends. It's heroic and miraculous that someone could change that much. It shows that change is possible—that you don't have to be just one thing, that you can control your fate. Diego had only known the pack mentality. Then he got to know more about others who are different from him, and he learned that they also share the same heart. I think that was so wonderful about the character—he reminds us that people everywhere may be different from us, but we share similarities that unify us."

(Top) **Diego** – early character sketch • Peter de Sève, *(Above)* **Diego on the prowl** – concept art • Peter de Sève, *(Opposite top)* **Diego sitting** – color key • Greg Couch, *(Opposite bottom)* **Diego poses** –character sketches • Peter de Sève

42 THE ART OF BLUE SKY STUDIOS

"Diego reminds us that people everywhere may be different from us, but we share similarities that unify us."

—LORI FORTE

ICE AGE

44 THE ART OF BLUE SKY STUDIOS

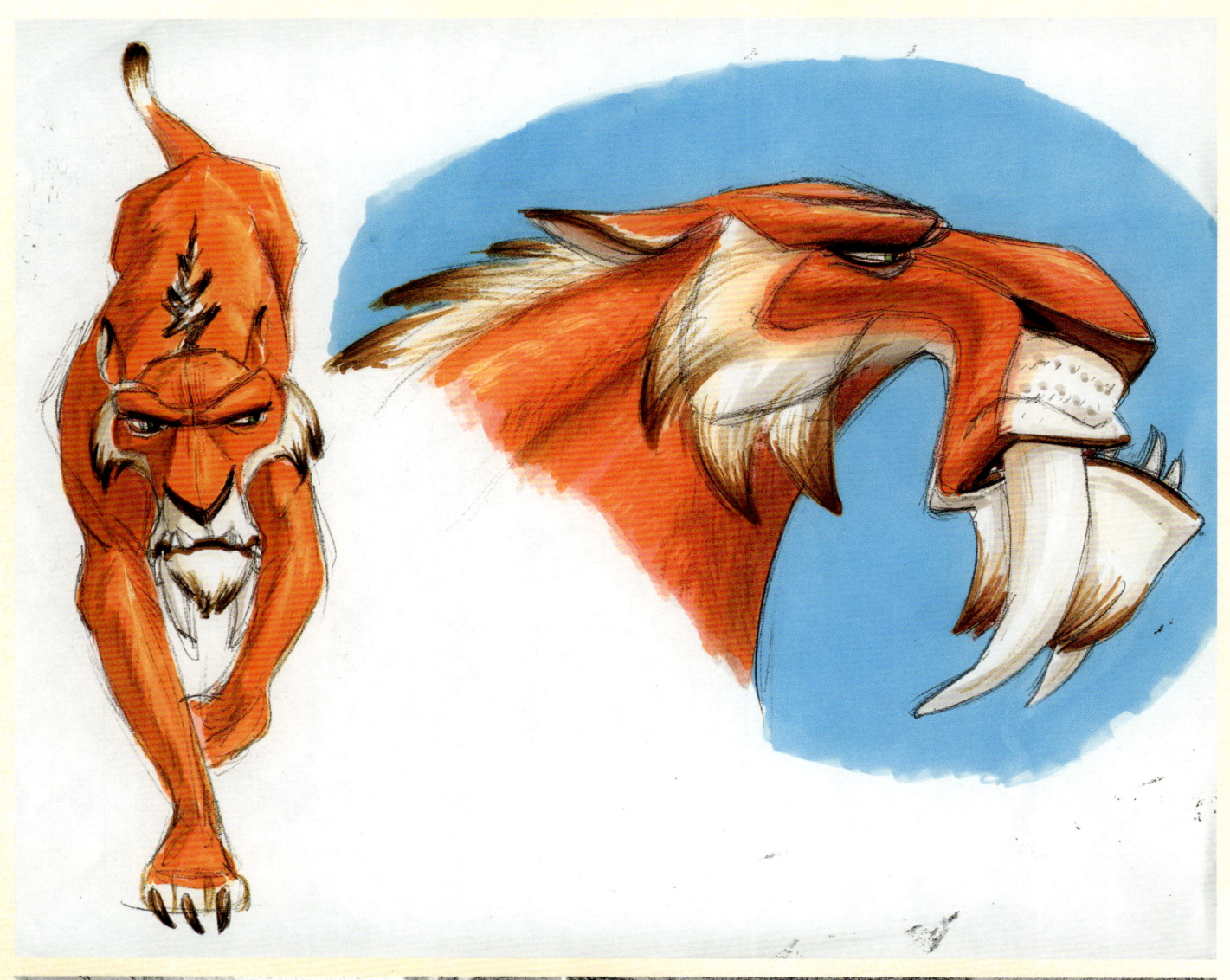

(Opposite top) **Diego** – early character art • artist unknown, *(Opposite bottom)* **Tiger attack** – concept art • Peter Clarke, *(Top)* **Saber pack** – concept art • Greg Couch, *(Bottom left)* **Diego** – final frame, *(Bottom right)* **Diego** – early character sketch • Peter de Sève

ICE AGE 45

"I tried to make the humans feel as much like the background as the environment did. Except for the baby—he was designed to be rounder and more appealing."

—CHRIS WEDGE

DIRECTING THE SUPPORTING CAST

When Saldanha was brought on to codirect *Ice Age*, there were 150 employees to manage. While working with the animators every day to further develop the characters' personalities and actions, he developed a special fondness for Scrat.

"The best communication is when you don't have to talk," says Saldanha. "If you can get what's going on without dialogue, then the actors and the directors are doing good work. I always felt that way with the Chaplin and Buster Keaton movies. Usually the story is so simple, you could tell it in just a couple of words. So Scrat was, for me, that representation. At the time there were a lot of movies coming out with smart dialogue and funny jokes, and Scrat just squeaked. It felt fresh."

Because Scrat only had gestures to express himself, his range of movements had to be nearly limitless. Before the filmmakers knew it, Scrat had become a major landmark in CG character animation, his rubberized stretchiness recalling the zany cartoons of the past, yet situated within a tangible 3-D universe. Through Blue Sky's revolutionary work, Scrat became a technological breakthrough, bringing a 2-D flavor to CG animation previously thought unattainable.

Conversely, the human tribe seen in *Ice Age* was animated in a more stylized way. "I wanted the motion of the humans to be kind of a two-and-a-half-dimensional look," says Wedge, "like Egyptian hieroglyphics. I wanted to make sure our main characters were front and center, and I didn't want anything to distract from that. I tried to make the humans feel as much like the background as the environment did. Except for the baby—he was designed to be rounder and more appealing."

At the end of the film, the herd returns this appealing bundle to his people. But as they disappear into the sunset, Manny, Sid, and Diego have done more than just deliver a lost child. They have led us through an unforgettable story of adventure, comedy, and pathos that breaks the boundaries of what was thought possible in animated film.

Ice Age was released March 15, 2002, and its huge success gave the animation studio the creative freedom to move ahead with a film devised completely in-house. The basic outline of *Ice Age* was delivered to Blue Sky, but for several years at the studio, Wedge had been cooking up an original idea of his own. It was a conceit that went back to the playful roots of his childhood. And as a kid, he had loved robots.

(Opposite top) **Baby** – early concept art • Peter de Sève, *(Opposite bottom)* **Baby** – color key • Daisuke Tsutsumi, *(Top)* **Father** – color concept art • Michael Rose, *(Above)* **Trio in forest** – color keys • Greg Couch

ICE AGE 47

48 THE ART OF BLUE SKY STUDIOS

(Opposite top) **Trio in cave** – color key • Greg Couch, *(Left and bottom)* **Color script portion** • artist unknown, *(Above and top)* **Female sloths** – character sketches • Peter de Sève, *(Middle)* **Baby** – character art • Mary GrandPré (design) and artist unknown (painting)

ICE AGE 49

The Herd

"WE WANTED THE CHARACTERS to come from different places in the animal kingdom and all be alienated from their group somehow, and ultimately come together as a family," says Lori Forte. "The message, if there is one, is you don't have to be related to become family. And I think in today's world, and the world of 2002 when the movie came out, it's always an important theme—that you can find family anywhere."

50   THE ART OF BLUE SKY STUDIOS

(Opposite top) **Trio with baby** – character sketch • Peter de Sève, *(Opposite center)* **Baby walking** – final frame, *(Opposite bottom)* **Campfire** – color key • Greg Couch, *(Top)* **Baby in cave** – color key • Greg Couch, *(Bottom)* **Trio with baby** – final frame, *(Right)* **Trio in profile** – character sketch • Peter de Sève

ICE AGE 51

(Top) **Diego, Manny, and Sid running** – color key • Greg Couch
(Bottom) **Manny saves Diego** – color key • Greg Couch

BLUE SKY SHORTS
Gone Nutty (2002)

ONCE *ICE AGE* WAS COMPLETED, and with no other films yet in the pipeline, Blue Sky retained only a small coterie of animation artists, and all were eager to start their next project. It was decided that a short film based on the *Ice Age* universe would be the perfect DVD bonus feature, and so Carlos Saldanha pitched the idea for a four-minute cartoon about Scrat. It would make use of the remaining studio artists, as well as the digital elements that had been designed for the *Ice Age* film.

"After we finished the first movie, I thought that the little guy deserved more," says Saldanha. Having come up with a wealth of Scrat ideas that never made it into the original movie, Saldanha took these concepts and worked them into *Gone Nutty*, which pits Scrat against gravity—and his own greed.

"We were looking for things we hadn't done in the movie, like the skydiving concept," he says. "We pushed a lot in the animation and facial expressions, moving a little bit out of our comfort zone in terms of what we could do with Scrat. Shorts are great because you get to experiment and explore things that are out of the box that you sometimes can't do in the movie. In doing so, you learn and get better and find new tricks for making the character appealing, while advancing the personality and body motion."

Gone Nutty wound up earning an Academy Award nomination, and it was included on the *Ice Age* DVD.

(Top, center, and bottom) **Scrat in** *Gone Nutty* – final frames

ICE AGE 53

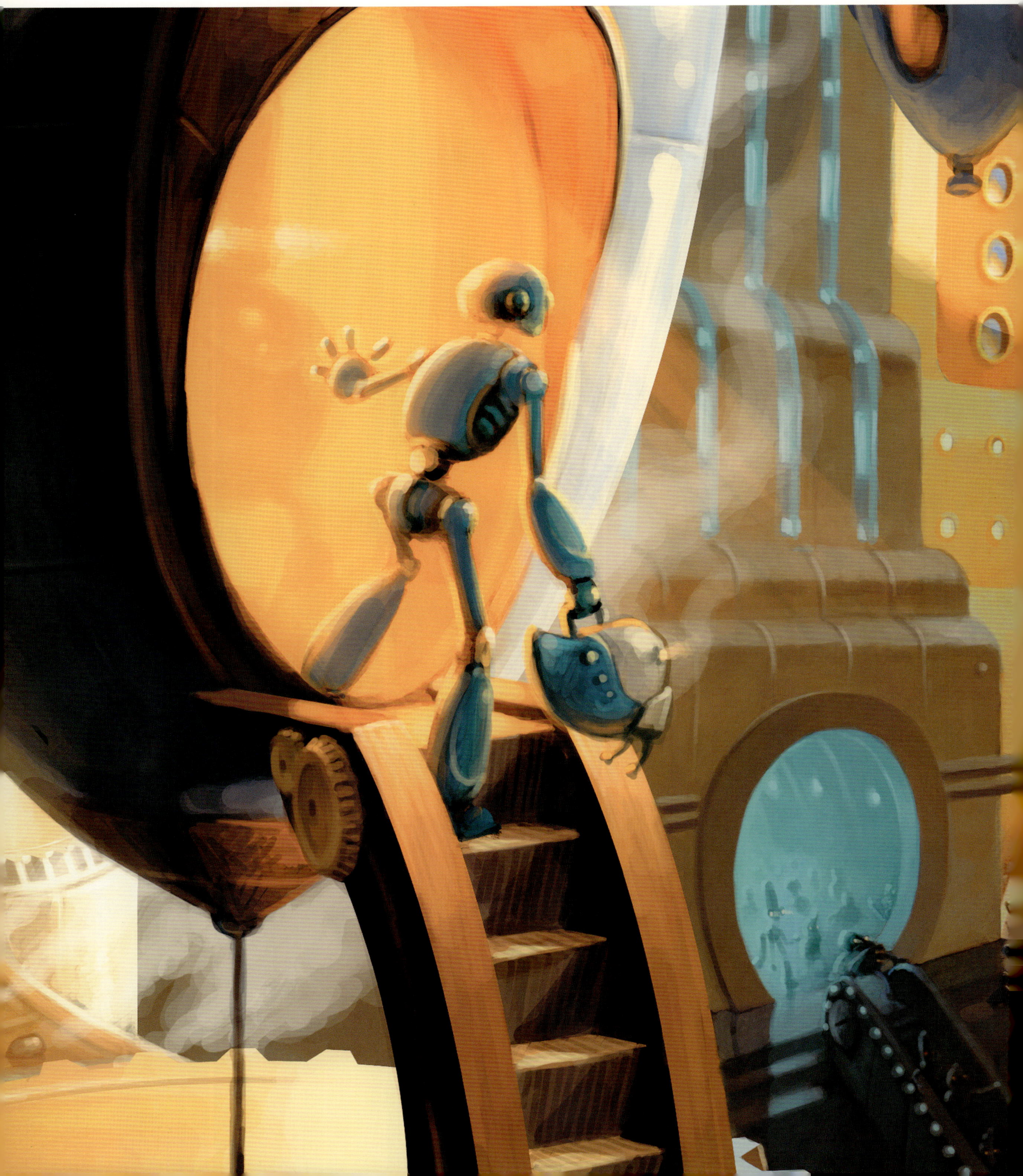

CHAPTER 2 · **Robots**

*"This is our moment to shine,
to show them what we're made of!"*

—RODNEY COPPERBOTTOM

Until the theatrical release of *Ice Age*, Blue Sky's future as a feature film studio was uncertain. A few months after it hit theaters and proved to be a huge hit, that all changed. "[Fox] said, 'That film you want to make about robots that you've been talking about for three years? You can start it now,'" remembers Wedge.

"Which meant we had five years' worth of work to do in about two and a half years."

Wedge had shared the vision for a robot movie with William Joyce, a prolific children's book author/illustrator who also worked in animation as a production designer in both television and film. Joyce had collaborated with Pixar on *Toy Story* and *A Bug's Life*. "John Lasseter had been telling me for a long time that I had to meet this guy Chris Wedge, that he and I would really get along," says Joyce.

Joyce and Wedge finally met when Fox brought them both together to try to adapt Joyce's children's book *Santa Calls*. The project never came to fruition, but the two remained friends and began brainstorming a movie they could produce together.

"We just thought robots were cool, ever since we were kids," says Joyce. The chance to explore story ideas came when opportunity took them hostage. It was during a party in Joyce's home state of Louisiana that he and Wedge took a midnight canoe ride in their tuxedoes and became stranded in the fog. In the hours they spent trying to find the shore, they outlined the plot of the movie they would make—assuming they would survive the night.

Rather than going down the tried-and-tested dramatic route that pits robots against humanity, they approached the story from an angle of fun and whimsy. They would create a parallel world of mechanical entities in which every single thing is made up of metal parts. There would not be just one type of robot, but the sleek among the clunky, the cogs at odds with the mainframes, living in one big smelting pot of class strata.

(Previous pages) **Rodney's arrival in Robot City** – concept art • Michael Knapp, *(Top)* **Four-year-old Rodney** – concept art • Greg Couch, *(Opposite)* **Rodney** – early concept art • Greg Couch (design) and Michael Knapp (painting)

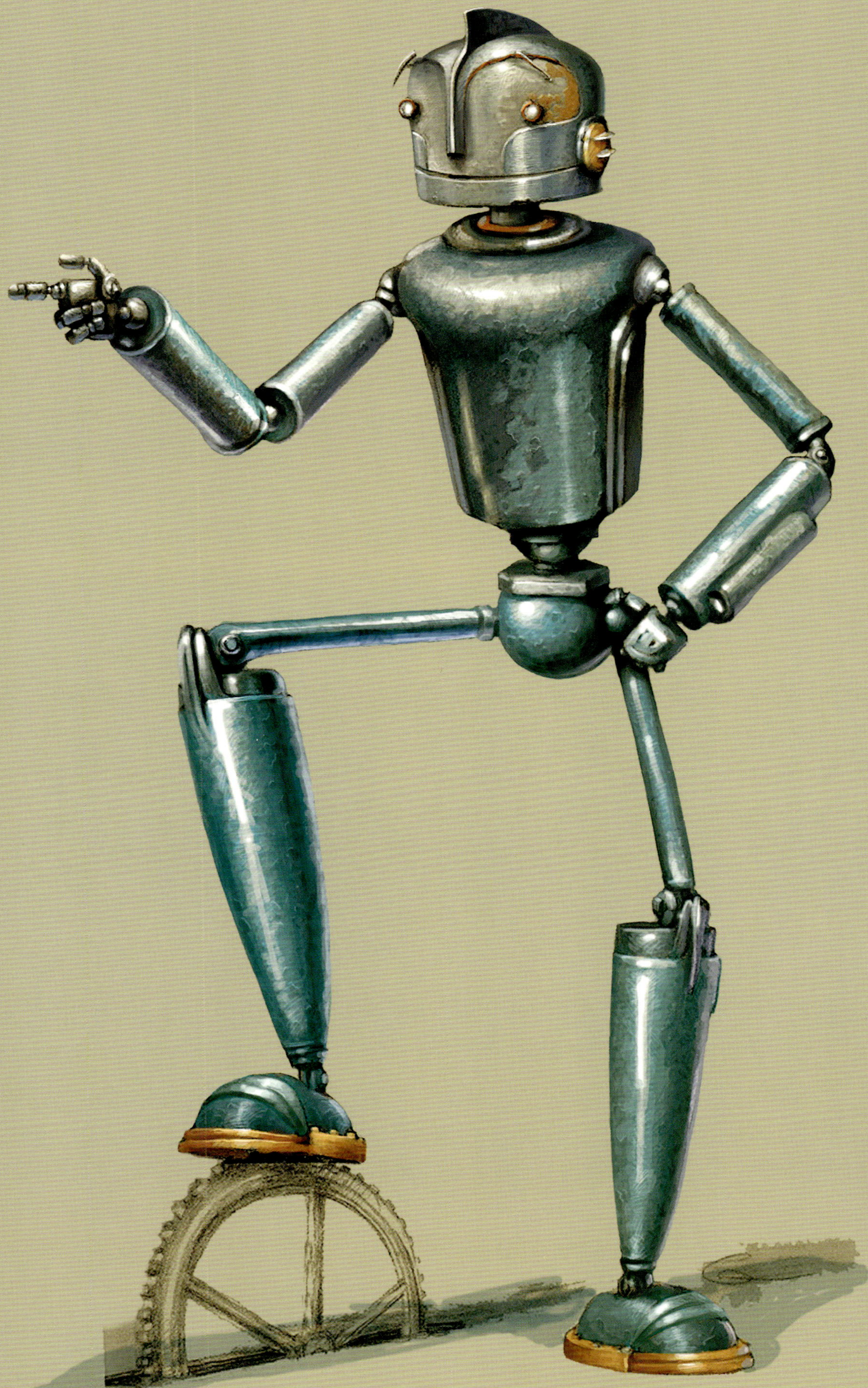

According to Wedge, it would hinge on a fundamental allegory. "The movie combats the whole 'planned obsolescence' thing that pervades our market today," he says. "The idea is just because you're old doesn't mean you're useless and that you can't improve yourself."

ONE MAN'S JUNK IS ANOTHER MAN'S MOVIE

Wedge began the project by steering the artists away from a space-age vision and toward an approach of kinetic gears and moving parts. It was exactly in line with what Joyce had imagined, and he next embarked on creating a scale model of an eclectic, Rube Goldberg–esque city for robots: "One day we just went to a bunch of junk shops down in Louisiana and bought every kind of weird, old mechanical thing from the 1930s: a pressure cooker, a toaster, a canister, an oilcan, gears, and pulleys . . . even a cow-milking machine! We made a metal city diorama, using all this machinery as our architecture and gluing all the springs and bits for windows and other details."

Wedge was set to direct the film with Joyce producing and acting as the sole production designer, but the team also needed an art director. Thirteen years earlier, when Wedge was getting his master's in computer graphics at Ohio State University, he had met a young computer graphics artist named Steve Martino. Martino had completed the same graduate program and was working at a small local company in Columbus at the time. Wedge was impressed by Martino's creativity and his steady attitude, and when it came time to begin *Robots* in 2002, he brought him aboard to art direct.

58 THE ART OF BLUE SKY STUDIOS

(Top) **Robot City at night** – concept art • Greg Couch, *(Left)* **Robot City** – found object composition mock-up • Bill Joyce and Brandon Oldenburg, *(Opposite center)* **Train station clock** – concept art • Bill Joyce, *(Opposite bottom)* **High-end city area** – concept art • Michael Knapp

ROBOTS   59

(Top) **Big Weld Plaza** – color key • Thomas Cardone, *(Bottom)* **Big Weld workshop** – concept art • Michael Knapp and Bill Joyce, *(Opposite top)* **Big Weld gates** – concept art • Steve Martino

They immediately started searching for more visual references and developed an acute eye for mechanical detail. "Once you get your head into that space," says Martino, "you look at the world in a totally different way. You drive into work, and you're like, 'Wow, look at the rust on the back of that truck!' Or you see a big piece of machinery, like a big backhoe, and the way the joint moves, and you think, 'That would be really cool to put in a character somewhere.'"

Joyce had created several works of art meant to capture the scope, spirit, and details of the robot world. These "moment paintings" were interpreted by Martino and communicated to the rest of the design team. Joyce's illustration style had two distinct qualities that the filmmakers found essential in laying the foundation of a robot world. For one, Joyce's use of roundness in his art gives the imagery a child-safe friendliness. Hence the headquarters for Bigweld Industries is a giant sphere, as are the gates at the entrances and Mr. Bigweld himself. The mechanics of the Crosstown Express are all large, round shapes in the form of wheels and balls that create a visually dynamic contrast against the verticals of the Robot City skyscrapers. Additionally, Martino discovered a second trait in Joyce's art that was integral to the scope of Robot City.

"He has a rhythm that I call Big-Little-Tiny," says Martino. "If you look at his illustration, he's got a wonderful way of leading the eye. He'll always leave a very giant shape as a restful place in the composition—that's the 'Big.' Then there's the 'Little,' something that gives you a little more detail. And then there's the 'Tiny,' some textural element, which is a fine, minuscule detail that informs your understanding of the scale of that big, quiet area. One little detail down at the bottom tells you that all the gear-works you understood to be small are actually *enormous*."

When the Modeling and Set Dressing departments were translating Joyce's artistic rhythm to 3-D shapes, they were bound by limited resources and an extremely tight schedule. "Sometimes it might be more cost effective to make everything simple and not put in that tiny detail," adds Martino. "But we needed a balance of those tiny details to inform the scale of what the world is. So it was important that we maintain that rhythm in building the city. That even if we pare back, we don't lose those tiny details, because the world would then fall apart. That's just Bill's style."

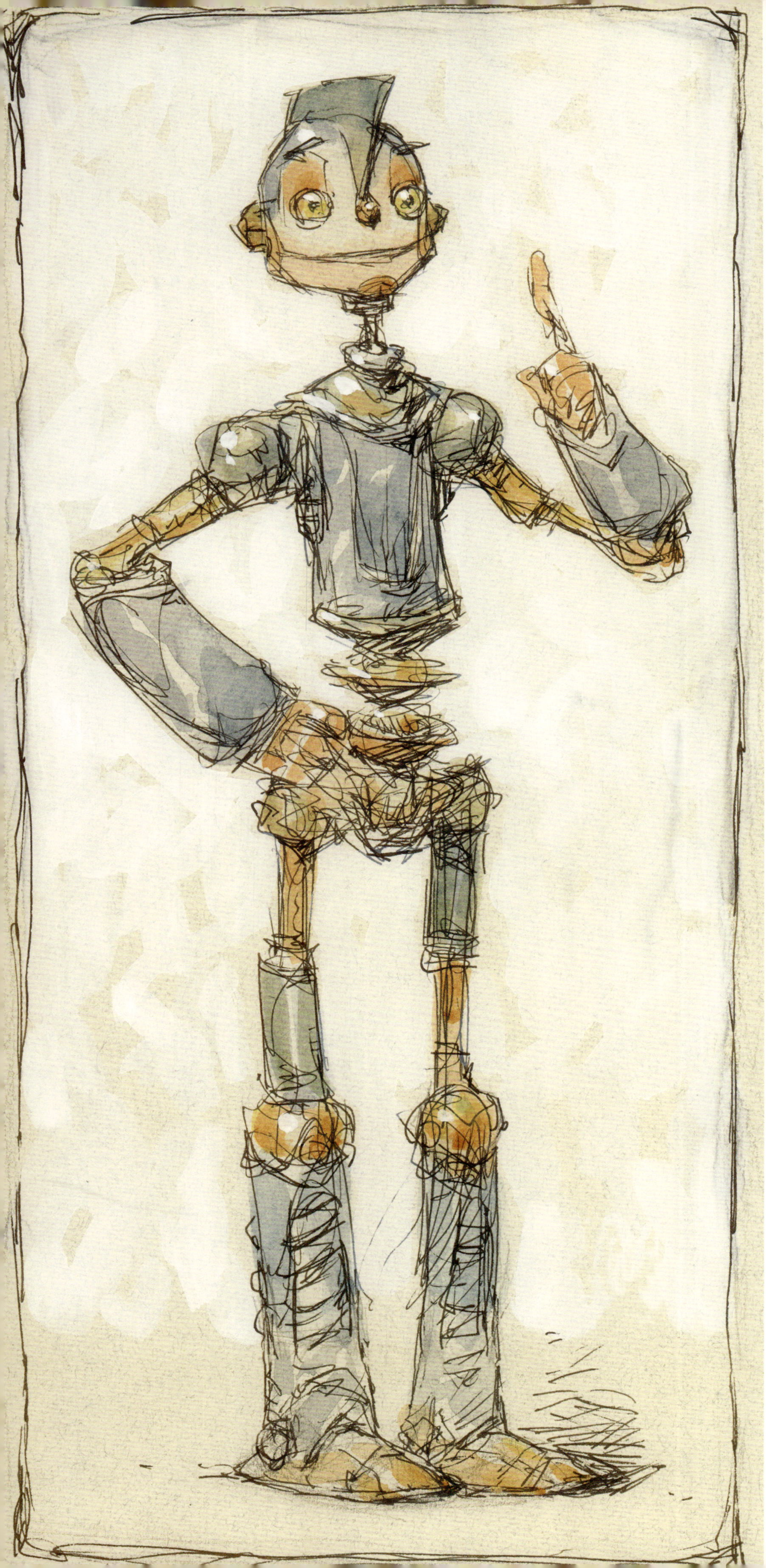

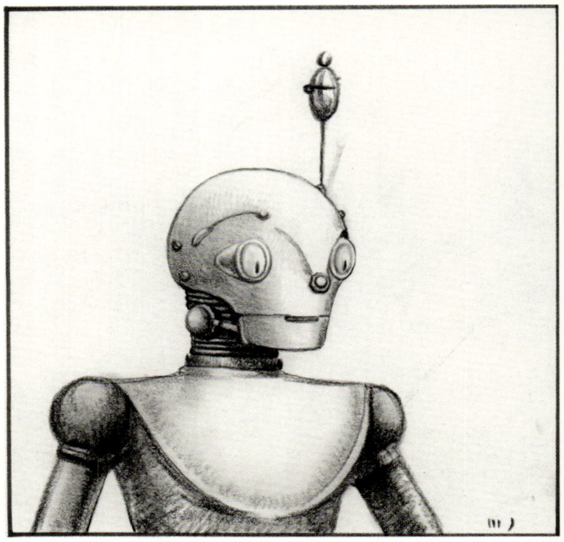

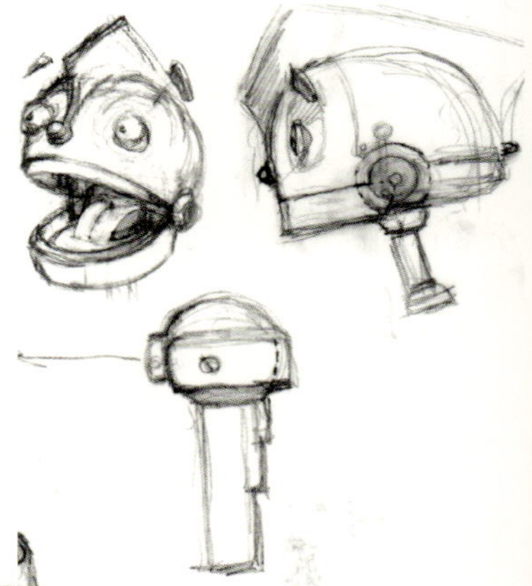

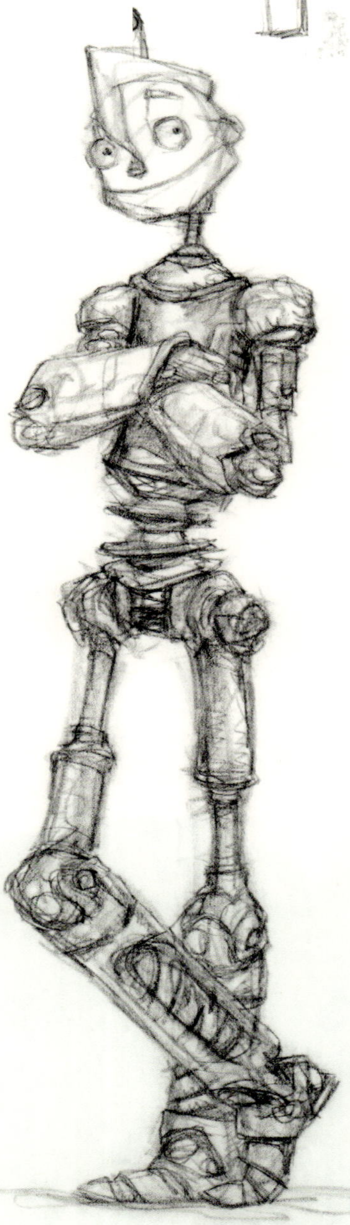

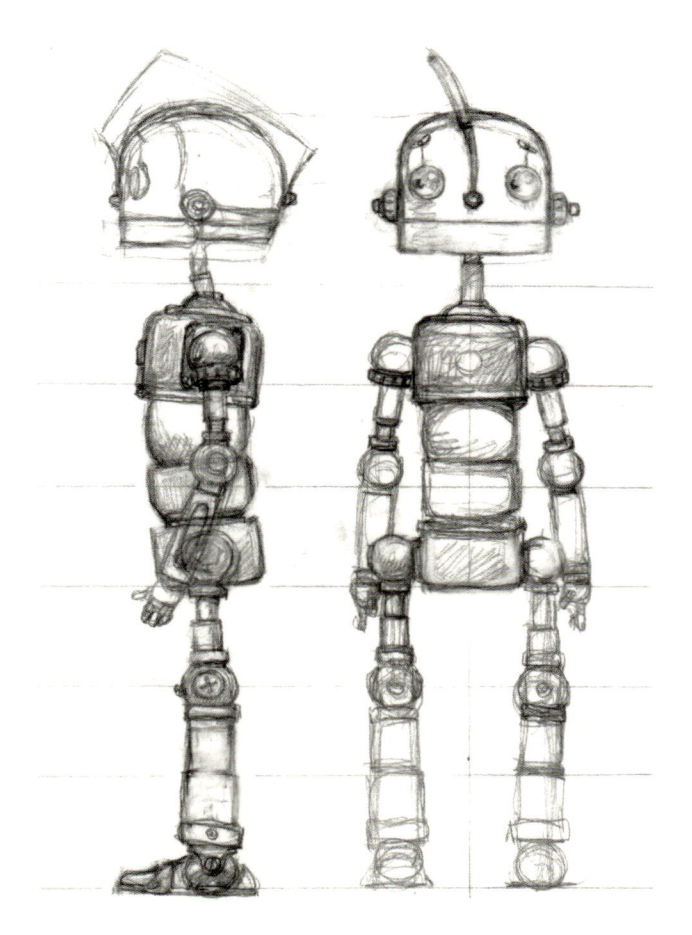

A LEADING METAL MAN

Adding scale and personality to the environment was essential, but the characters had to be designed to not only fit in but also to stand out to the audience.

Wedge found inspiration for the hero Rodney in a combination Volkswagen minibus and his grandfather's old Evinrude outboard motor. Somewhere in those objects lay his leading man. Staff artists tried for months to find the character, piling up sketch after sketch.

"Characters are hard to crack, and the leads are always the hardest," says Joyce. "It's like you're designing a movie star, and you have to give them the strange alchemic appeal that movie stars have but you can't quite pinpoint. They're not always the prettiest people, but they're amazing to look at, and you don't want to take your eyes off them. That's what we're trying to build."

The groundwork for Rodney's design was already done, but he was still missing that certain special something. Wedge handed the character off to Peter de Sève.

"I think what I brought to the character was imperfection—the everyman thing," says de Sève. "The original designs were too heroic, and I didn't necessarily see him as a perfect specimen. I brought to him a little of my own slouched build, a loose-limbed lankiness. So one of the most important things of that design was to make his torso a broken cylinder, so he could bend or slouch instead of being a rigid form." De Sève also added an element of asymmetry to Rodney. If you look closely, the pistons of his upper arms are reversed, and one of his lower legs is missing its casing over a now-bare steel rod.

(Opposite left) **Rodney** – character sketch • Peter de Sève, *(Opposite top right)* **Rodney** – concept art • Bill Joyce, *(Opposite middle right)* **Rodney** – breakout drawings • Greg Couch, *(Opposite bottom right)* **Rodney** – character sketch • Peter de Sève, *(Top left)* **Rodney building the Wonderbot** – animation sketch • Mark Behm, *(Top right)* **Seven-year-old Rodney** – breakout drawing • Greg Couch, *(Above)* **Rodney** – character sketch • Peter de Sève

ROBOTS 63

(Top) **Robot City at night** – concept art • Greg Couch, *(Bottom left)* **Ratchet** – concept art • Bill Joyce, *(Bottom center)* **Cappy** – concept art • Greg Couch, *(Bottom right)* **Cappy formal** – concept art • Bill Joyce, *(Opposite bottom)* **Big Weld** – concept art • Greg Couch

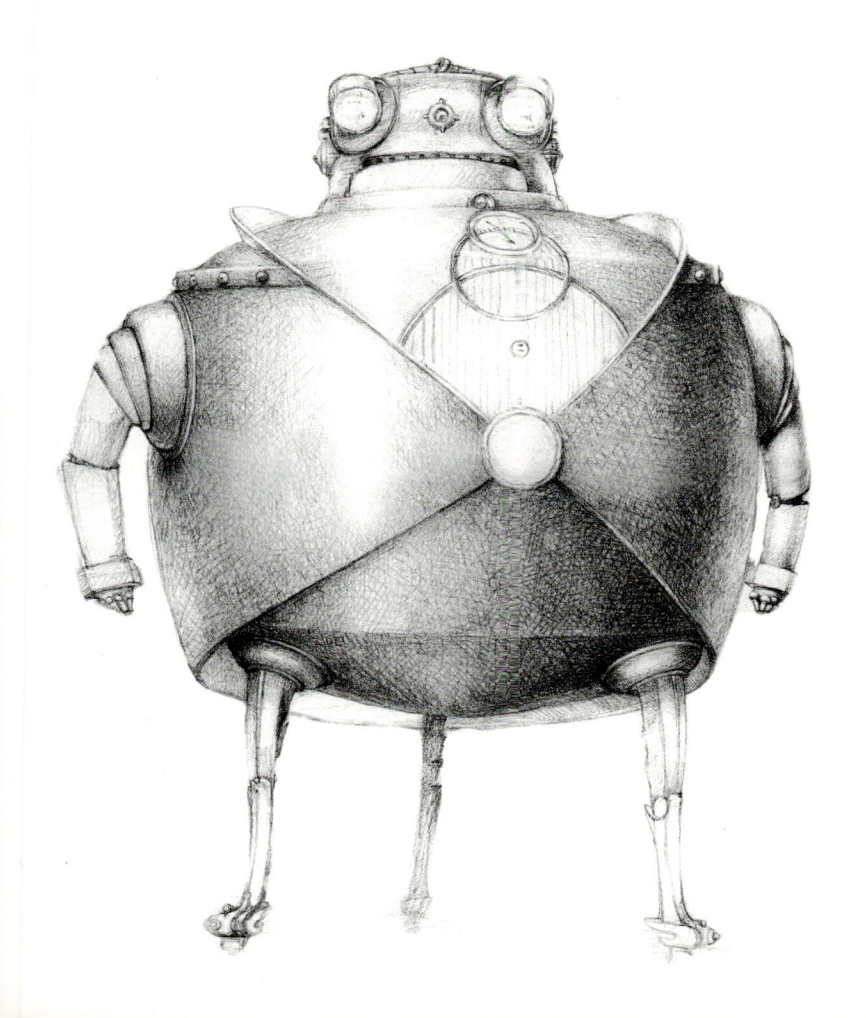

ROBOT CITY PLANNING

The film showcases the various types of robo-architecture, from the quaintness of 1930s Rivet Town to the many facets of Robot City. Robot City in particular was stratified to show the evolution of its machinery from the ground up.

"The bowels of the city came from the Industrial Revolution," says Wedge. "They were made of cast iron, and they had rivets on them, and they belched sparks and smoke. The middle of the city was Internal Combustion, mid-twentieth century. It was a little old-fashioned, from a time when you could get replacement parts. And the top of the city was more electrical, sleeker and quieter, like computers today."

The characters who inhabited each of these levels of Robot City were given different design qualities to fit that stratum. The high-enders like Ratchet and Cappy were given a palette of cool metallic blues and appear to be made up of alloys and carbon-composite materials. They represent the most ambitious socialites of the robot race, designed to look like speed bikes and top-of-the-line computers. They thrive in the boardroom, where sporting a newly buffed shine is as essential as a tailored, pinstriped suit in our world. "They have curvilinear shapes," says Martino, "as if they were CAD [Computer-Aided Design]-constructed. You saw less of the inner mechanics. They were made up of complex forms that come together perfectly, like a beautiful watch or a Porsche."

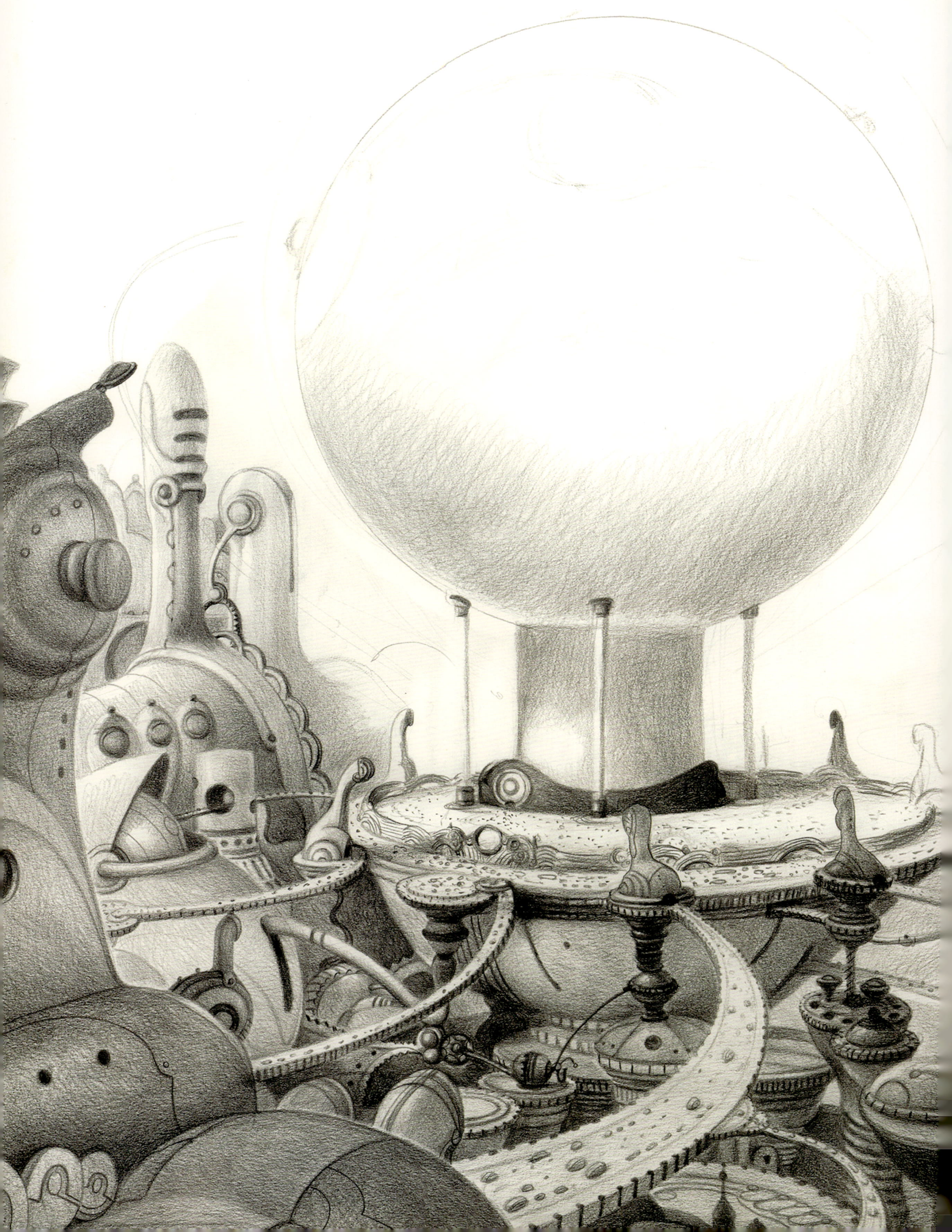

"The bowels of the city came from the Industrial Revolution. They were made of cast iron, and they had rivets on them, and they belched sparks and smoke. The middle of the city was Internal Combustion, mid-twentieth century. It was a little old-fashioned, from a time when you could get replacement parts. And the top of the city was more electrical, sleeker and quieter, like computers today."

—CHRIS WEDGE

(Top) **Party set** – color key • Daisuke Tsutsumi, *(Above)* **Robot City sketch** – concept art • Greg Couch, *(Right)* **Cappy** – concept art • Greg Couch, *(Opposite)* **Big Weld Industries/Plaza** – concept art • Bill Joyce

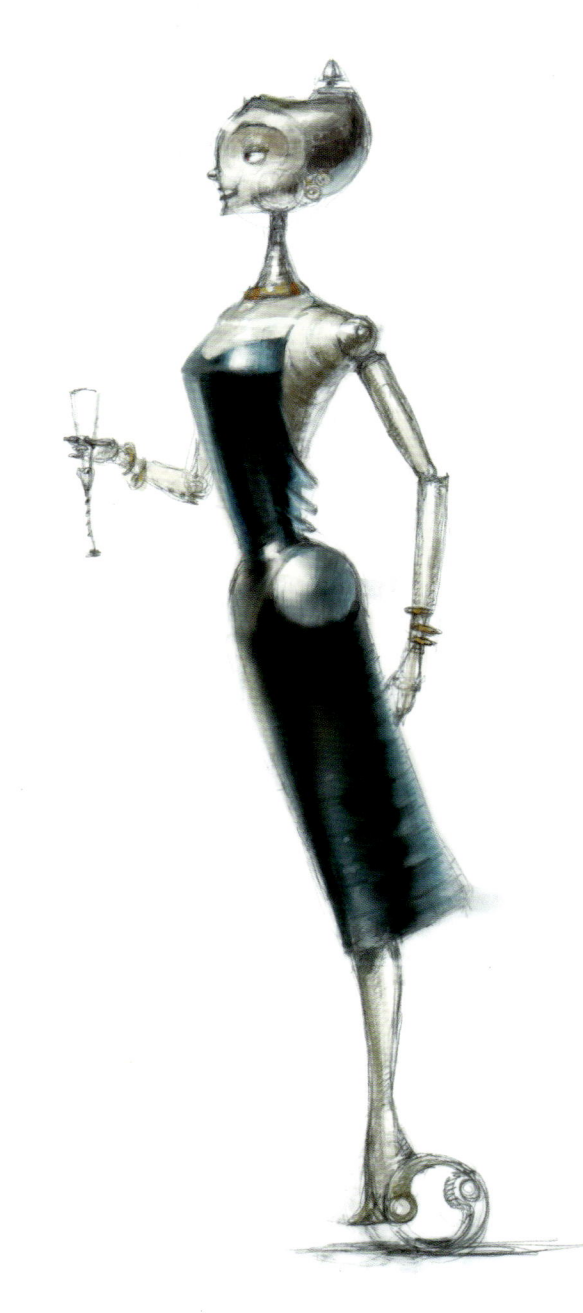

ROBOTS 67

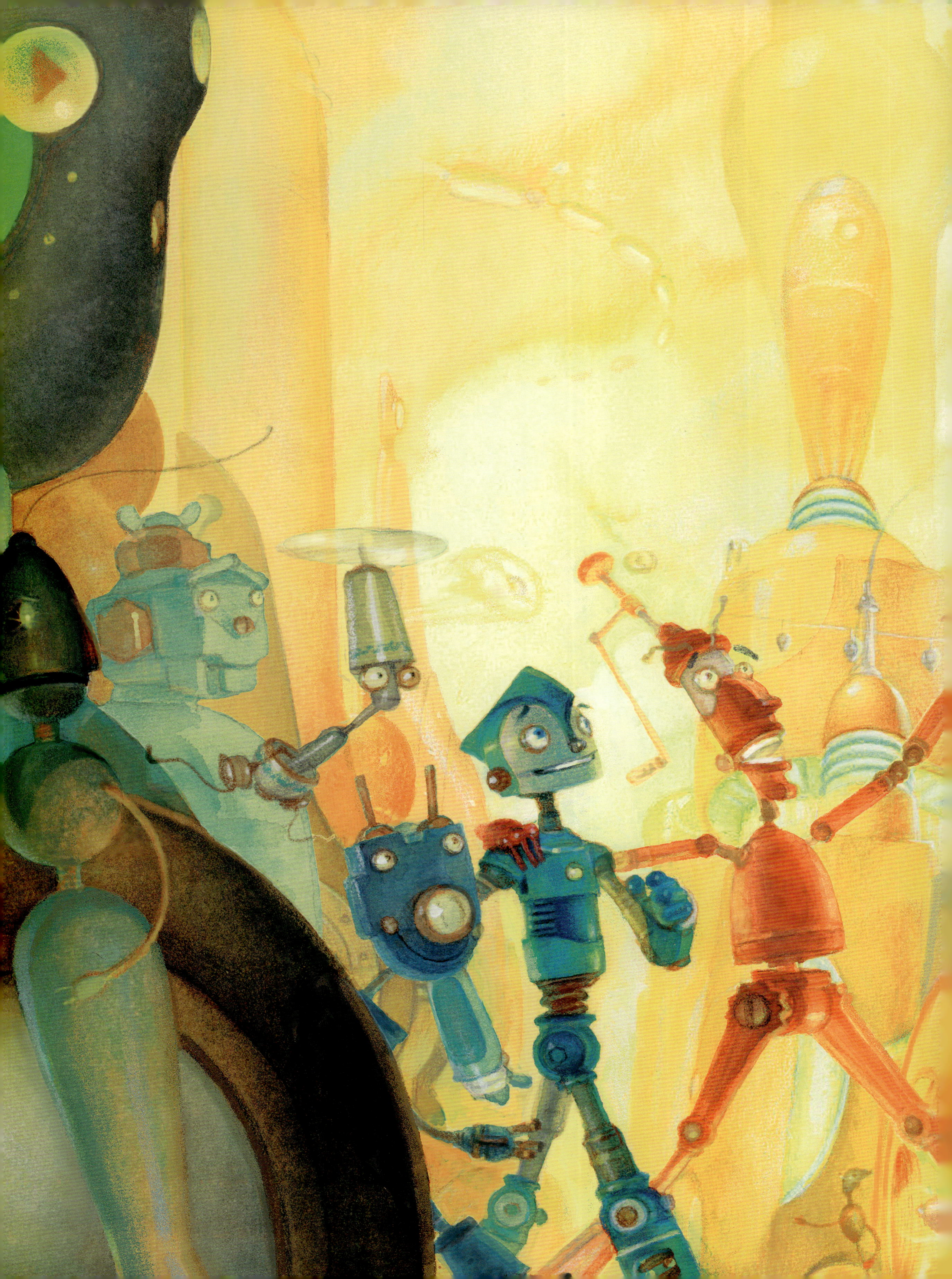

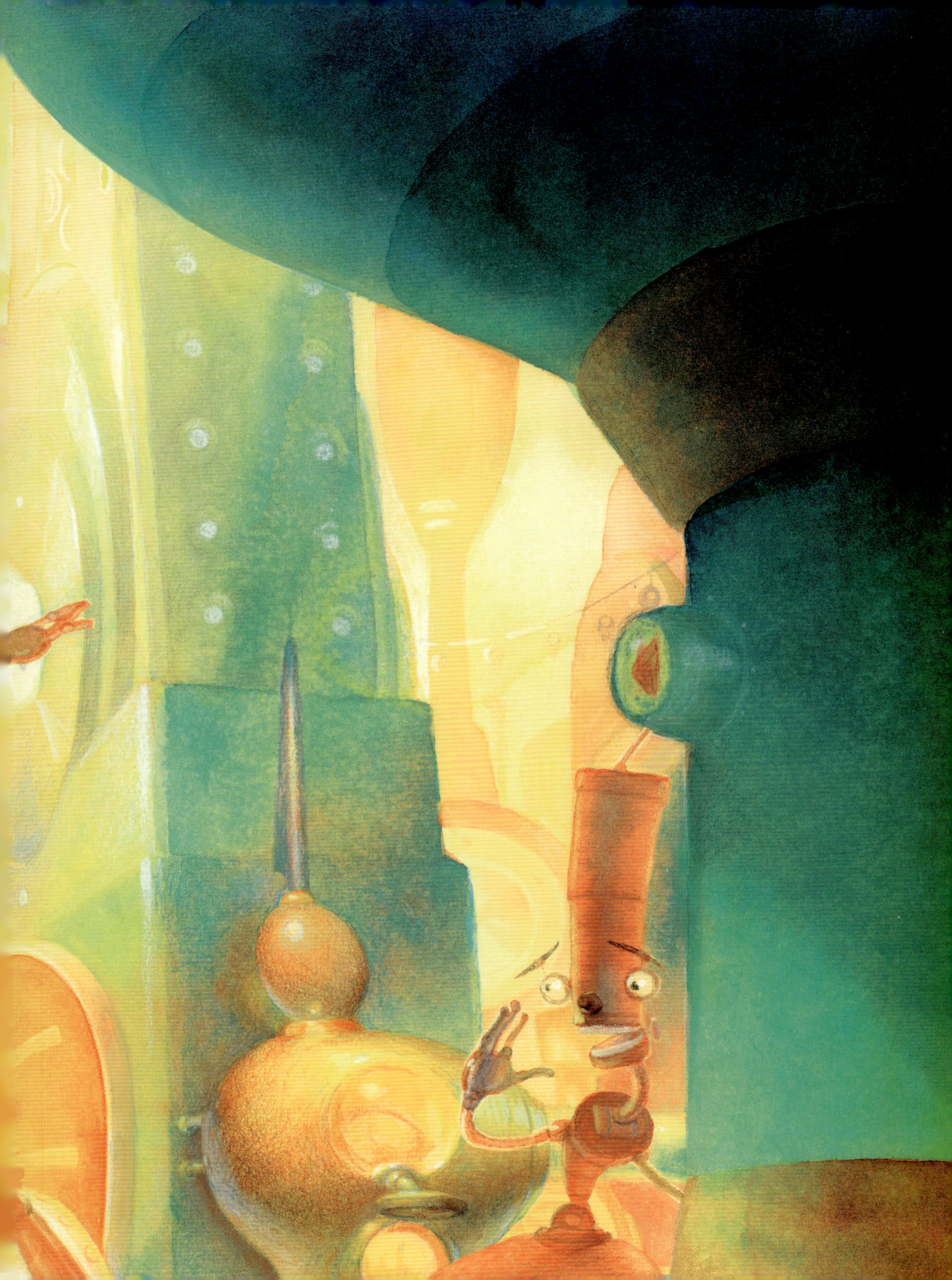

ROBOTS WITH EMOTION

The residents who live in the middle of the city, the Rusties, are representative of a more culturally diverse population. They are more expressive and emotive, evoking a more vibrant way of life; hence the saturated colors of our five main Rusties: Fender (red), Piper (yellow), Diesel (blue), Crank (orange), and Lug (green—and originally called "Lugnut"). "The Rusties are of that period when you painted things," says Martino, "so they had chipped and peeling paint. They were made up of cogs and various mechanical components that do not fit together within their form quite so perfectly."

To replicate natural wear on the Rusties, a new algorithm was developed for the studio's proprietary renderer, CGI Studio. The program determined the places on the Rusties' bodies where rust and chipped paint were most likely to occur and how the rust would look depending on the material on which it had formed. It then randomized the effect, chipping away at the sleek look of the initial Rusties' models. The result was natural-looking wear on the corners of surfaces and angles of joints. It gave the Rusties a less polished and more outmoded charm, and the effect was entirely automated through the renderer.

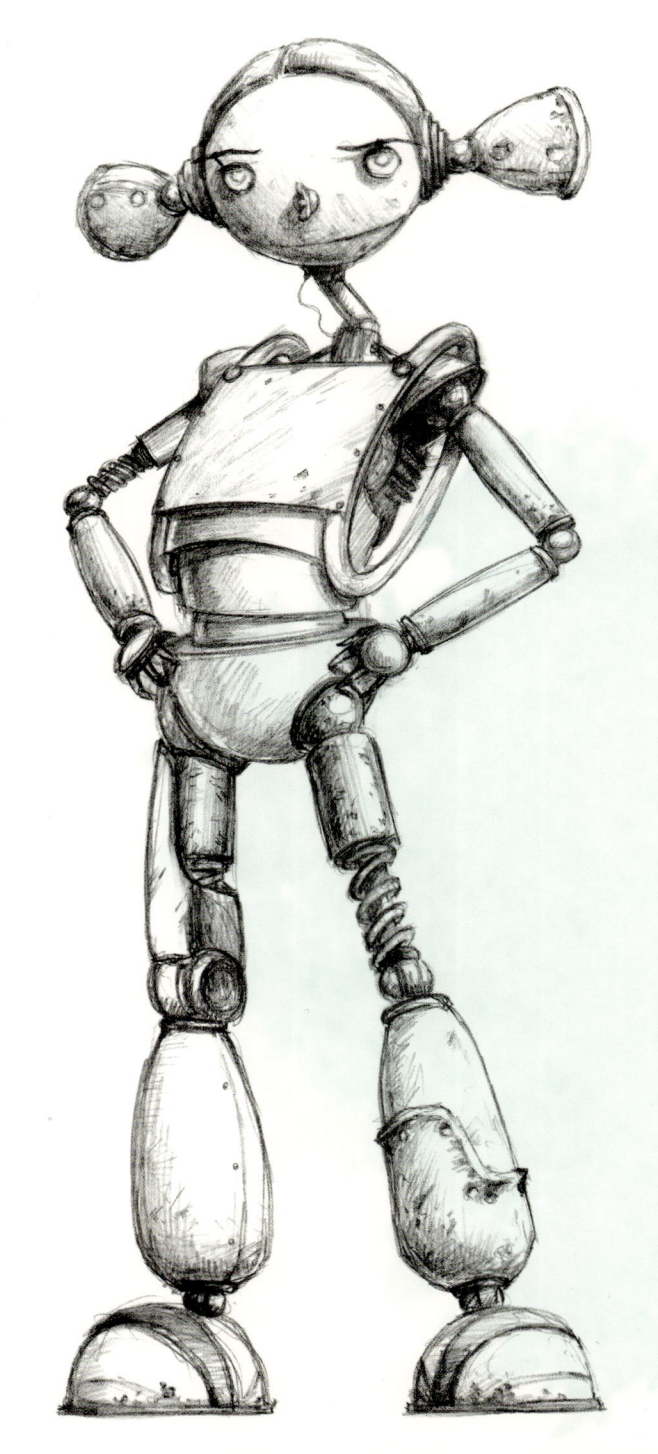

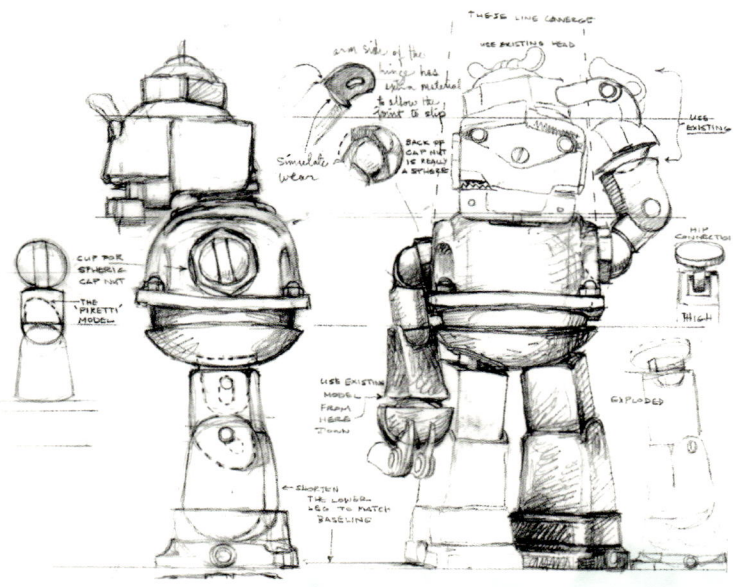

The designers and animators wanted the audience to believe that each character was made up of heavy metals. As such, they had to be very careful not to let their surfaces squash and stretch, compress or expand, like regular organic cartoon characters. "We assumed the philosophy that if you bent the metal it would look like rubber stretching, and it would destroy the effect," says Wedge. The team needed to find ways of "cheating" to ensure their protagonists had the performance range of fleshy humans within the confines of their metallic construction. "A lot of the work on *Robots* was figuring out how they retain a rigid shape while only using a little slight of hand," says Martino. "There was a little bit of squash, but you always wanted the audience to feel that they could knock on that material and it would be rigid and that the joints and pieces moved like machines did."

(Previous pages) **The Rusties show Rodney the city** – concept art • Greg Couch, *(Opposite top)* **Rodney and the Rusties** – concept art • Daisuke Tsutsumi, *(Opposite bottom left)* **Diesel** – concept art • Shaun Cusick, *(Opposite bottom right)* **Piper** – concept art • Michael Knapp, *(Top left)* **Lug** – breakout drawing • Greg Couch, *(Above)* **Fender** – concept art • Bill Joyce (design) and Shaun Cusick (painting), *(Bottom)* **Piper, Rodney, and Fender** – final frame

ROBOTS 71

(Above) **Building the baby** – concept art • Greg Couch

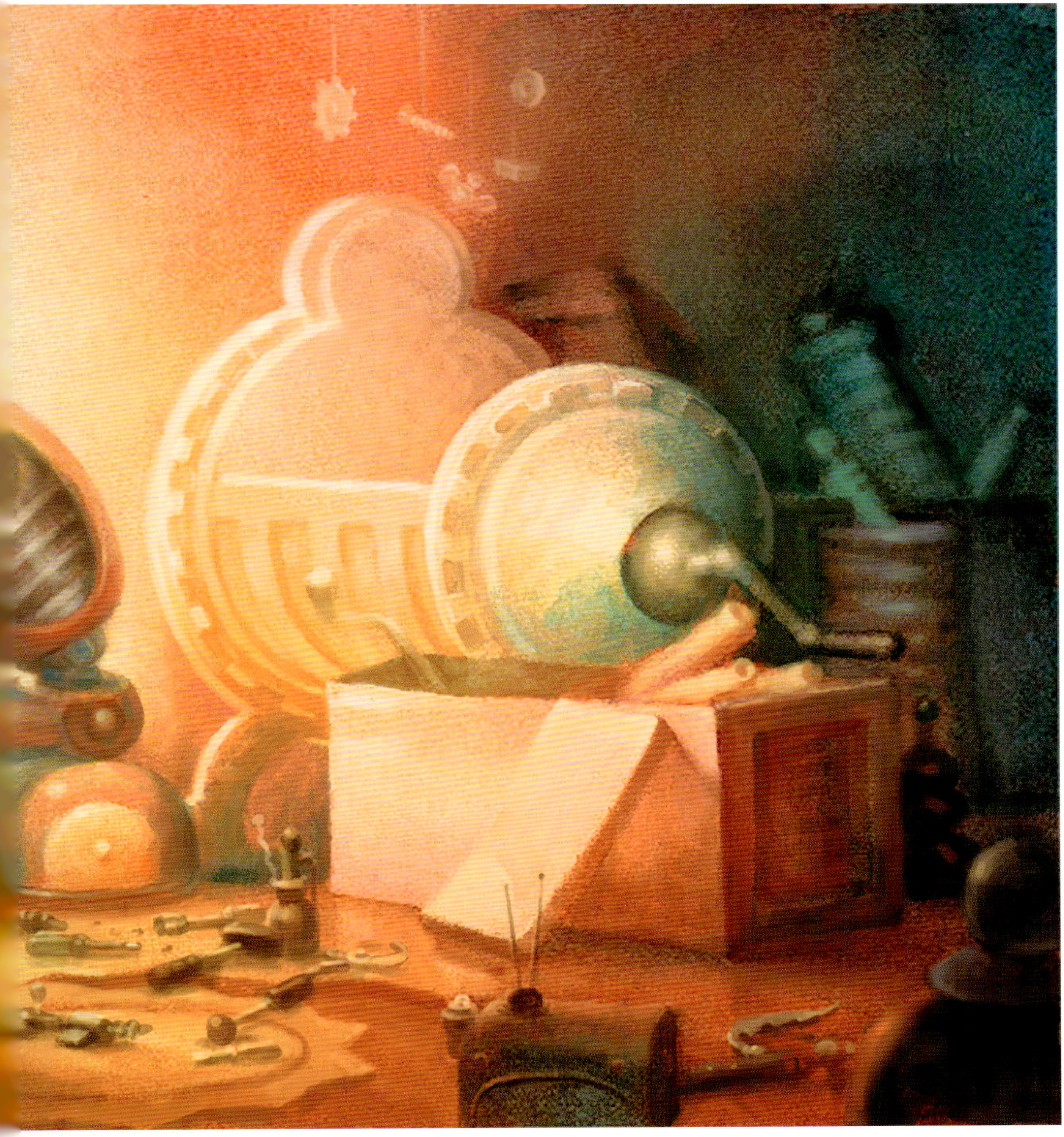

SMALL TOWN CHARM

The overarching tone of the movie was devised through a color script. The filmmakers had to take into account the way the scenes would play out visually and how the environments, characters, and mood of the film would all factor into the final image. Martino, who grew up in Ohio, knew a lot of small towns that were the inspiration for Rodney's home of Rivet Town. Every place in the film had to have a corresponding location in our world, and Rivet Town was designed after a Midwestern town with short buildings, a Main Street, and a single town hall. He and Wedge discussed the tones of the different locations, comparing Rivet Town to the nouveau skyscrapers of Robot City. They agreed it was important that each one had its own sizes and shapes and evoked a distinct feeling.

74 • THE ART OF BLUE SKY STUDIOS

(Opposite top) **Copperbottom home** – concept art • Michael Knapp, *(Opposite bottom left)* **Copperbottom home** – concept art • Bill Joyce, *(Opposite bottom right)* **Mr. Copperbottom** – color callout • Greg Couch (design) and Daisuke Tsutsumi (painting), *(Top)* **Copperbottom family** – concept art • Greg Couch, *(Above)* **Rodney's room** – color key • Thomas Cardone

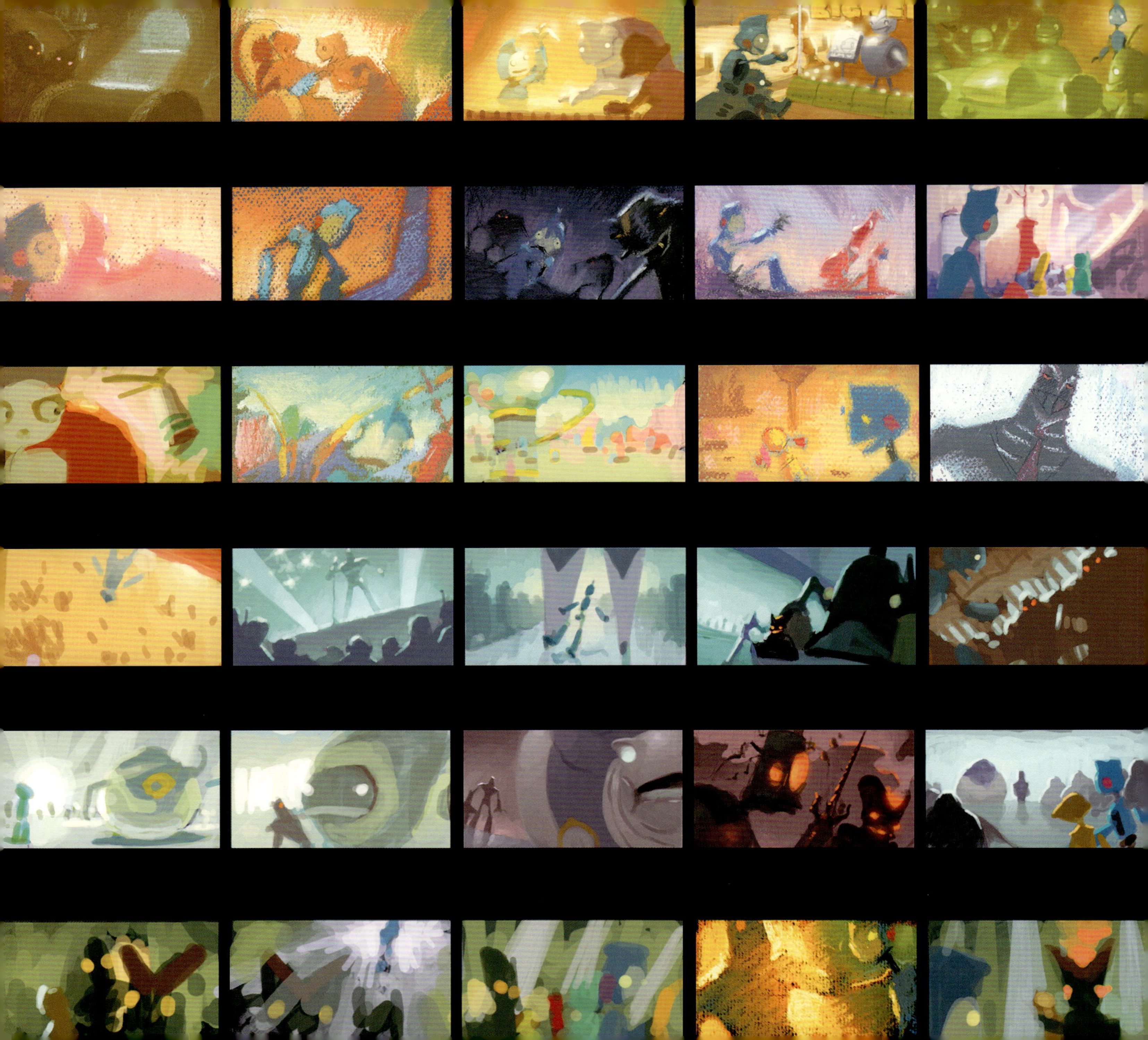

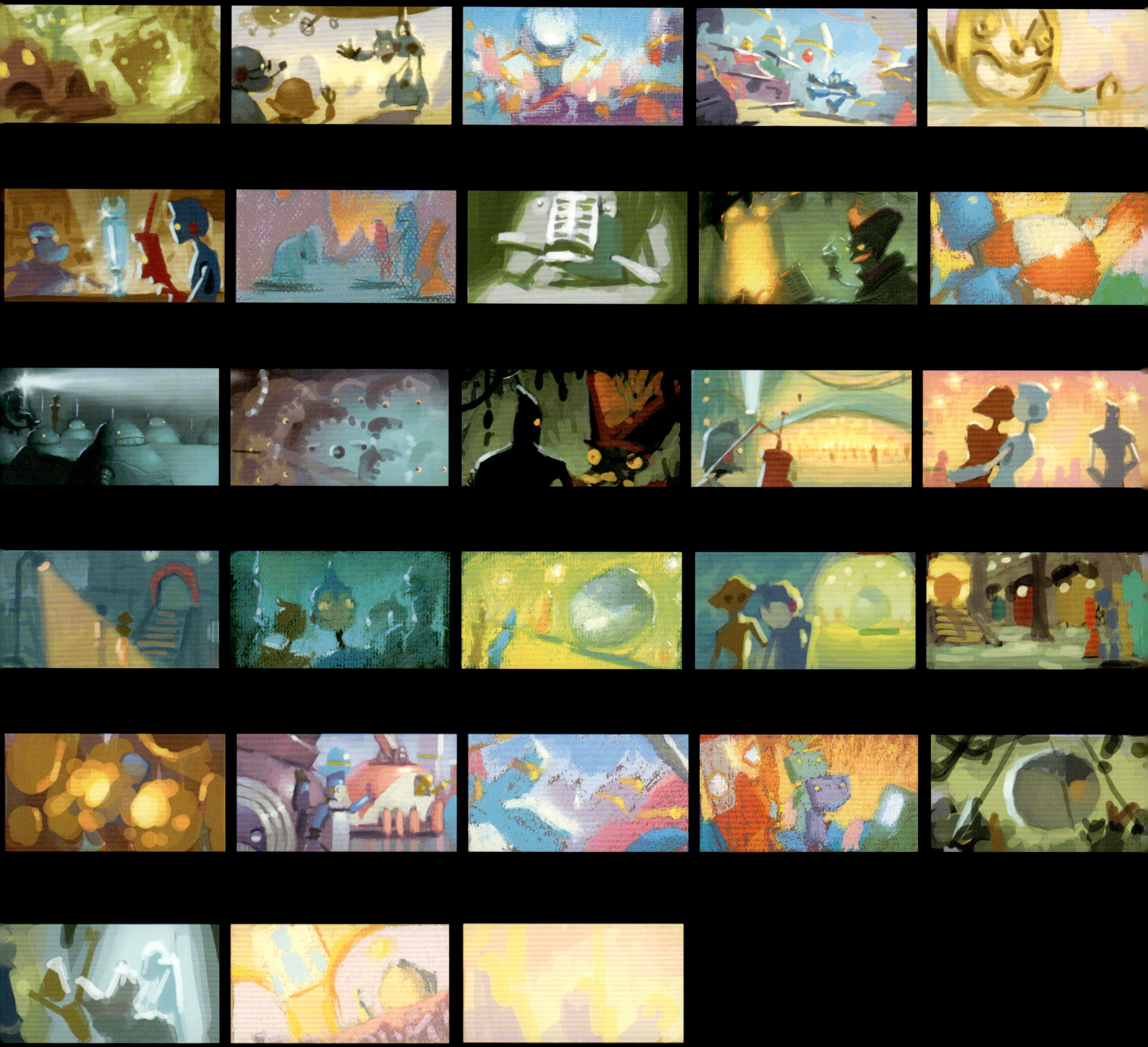

78　THE ART OF BLUE SKY STUDIOS

But it was more than just architecture that would evoke an emotional response. "Each sequence would have a tone or emotion," says Martino, "so you're taking not only the color space of those characters but also the emotion of that scene. So even if you're with the highly saturated Rusties and you're in a dangerous place, we might throw cool light onto them. We might knock the warmth and saturation out of their color because of the emotion of that particular moment."

Generally, all the metal provided a very cool palette, but the intensity of the Chop Shop evoked an imminent danger. For the climax at the Chop Shop's furnace inferno, the characters were lit with warm light and placed in a darkened environment. Their contours were aglow with rim-lighting, a subtle but striking way of pushing the tension of the scene. "So you have all these shots with this wonderful warm light rimming the characters so things are more dramatic," says Martino. "We had the characters playing in a little more shadow, a space that had a lot of cool against warmth just to create danger and that kind of emotion for the scene."

With a renderer as powerful as CGI Studio, the filmmakers were able to have the characters play in different types of light, giving them different realistic sheens on their metallic bodies. As a result, the film delivers a convincing and imaginative robot world in which audiences can easily lose themselves. "It was really fun to work on that kind of scale, just totally delightful," says Joyce. "And I think visually it was so far past what I thought we were able to achieve."

"From an art director's perspective, it was a blast, a dream," says Wedge. Compared to the sparse tundra and minimal cast of *Ice Age*, *Robots*, on its release in 2005, revealed an expansive universe that begged to be explored further. But the fan base for *Ice Age* was hungry for more, and Fox thought better than to let the property get cold (so to speak). It was time to return to the prehistoric world, but this time Blue Sky would have more resources at its disposal. The production team was given the chance to make an *Ice Age* movie more beautiful and believable than they had ever thought possible, but they soon discovered that this would entail building everything from scratch. Again.

(Previous pages) **Robots color script** • Daisuke Tsutsumi, *(Opposite far left)* **Chop Shop exterior** – concept art • Daniel López Muñoz, *(Opposite left)* **Chop Shop grinder** – concept art • Daniel López Muñoz, *(Opposite center)* **Madame Gasket** – concept art • Bill Joyce, *(Opposite bottom left)* **Minions** – concept art • Bill Joyce, *(Opposite bottom right)* **Dr. Veyizmir** – concept art • Greg Couch, *(Below)* **Ratchet and Madame Gasket** – concept art • Greg Couch (design) and Daisuke Tsutsumi (painting)

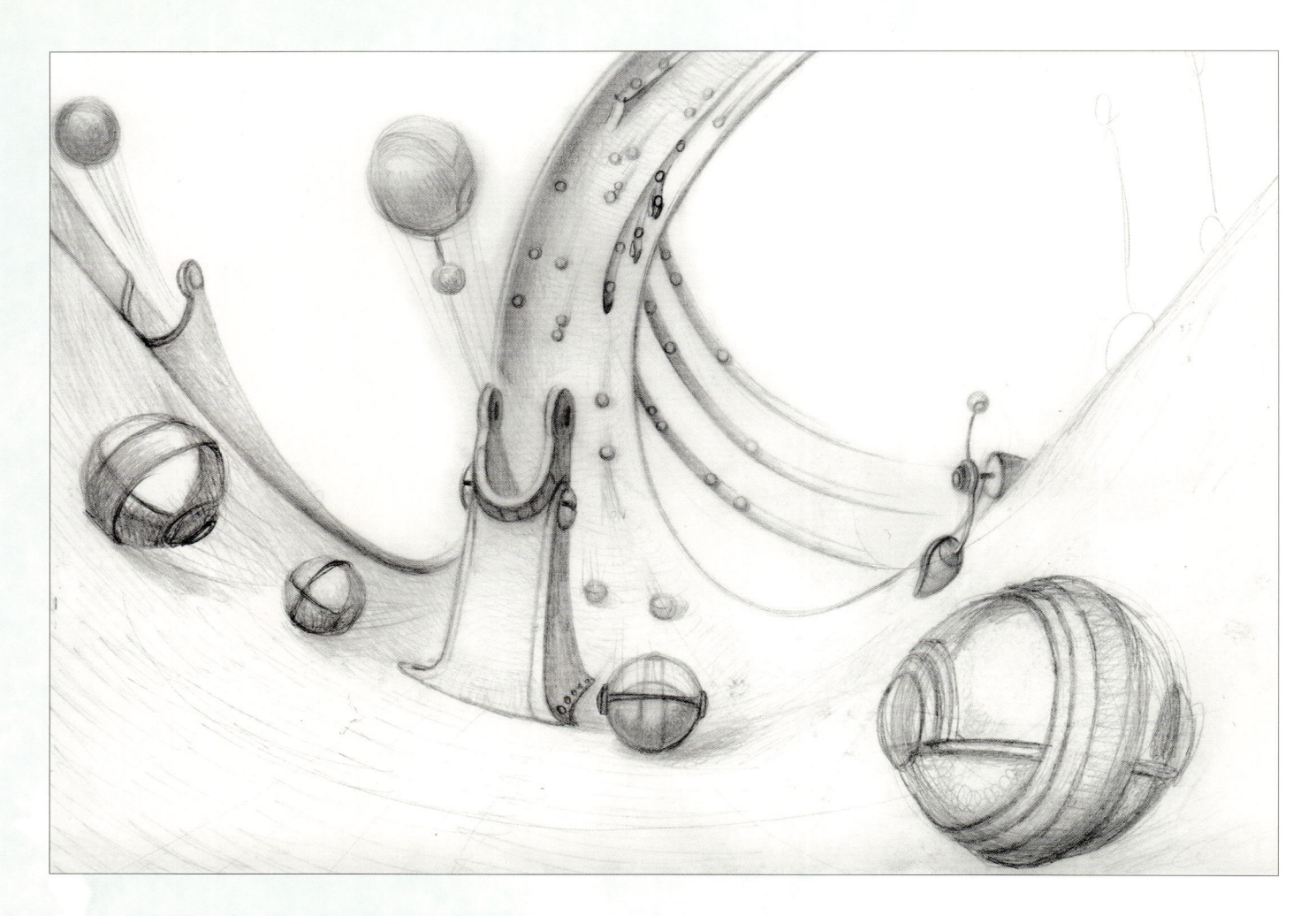

Crosstown Express

"FOR ME, ONE OF THE MOST fun parts of *Robots* was the Crosstown Express scene when Rodney first gets into town," says Joyce. "It started with one line in the script, something like, 'And then they get on the Crosstown Express.' And Chris Wedge said, 'Make us something cool for this.' So I sat with some of the artists, and we thought of the different games we liked playing when we were kids."

The discussion over games from marbles to Mouse Trap led to a series of sketches of kinetic doodads that were then storyboarded by Bill Frake. "I worked as a fireman after hours," says Frake, "and they have this little Fireman's Fair every year with really fun rides. I thought it would be fun for the characters of Robot City to commute to work on carnival rides. I learned that if you use stuff from your own experiences to put in your work, you will definitely have something no one has ever seen before. It will be something uniquely your own."

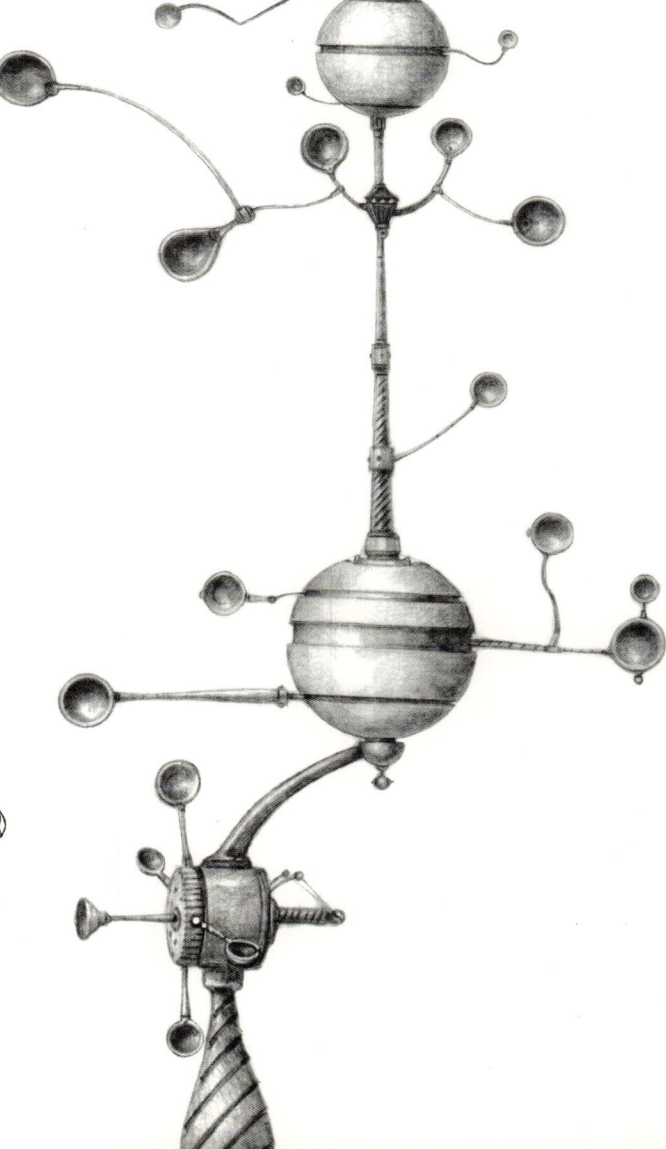

80 THE ART OF BLUE SKY STUDIOS

BLUE SKY SHORTS
Aunt Fanny's Tour of Booty (2005)

AN ADDITIONAL PEEK INTO ROBOT CITY, this short gave audiences a second glimpse at the mechanical beings that live in this strange universe.

Directed by Chris Gilligan, *Aunt Fanny's Tour of Booty* was supposed to be a simple visual guide focusing on safety in Robot City. The initial idea was to utilize previously created test animation, but the concept grew into what the short film calls Fanny's "big behind . . . the scenes tour," with new animation and characters that were not center stage in the original film. Tammy, Hacky, Zinc, and others return for this curtain call, and there is new pantomime performed by Fender.

Actress Jennifer Coolidge reprised her role as the matronly hostess leading a group of tourists through Robot City's train station, where the luggage, toilets, and vending machines are just as lively as the travelers. It captures the whimsy of the Bill Joyce–inspired movie, with a bit more slapstick thrown in. The best part about robot violence is that the victims lack nerve endings, and *Aunt Fanny's Tour of Booty* throws everything at them from flammable canisters to electric jolts at the Juice Bar. (Don't forget to ask for extra nuts.)

The short was included on the *Robots* DVD. Keep your eyes peeled for the switchboard signaling trains to White Planes—a pun on White Plains, New York, the location of Blue Sky Studios at that time.

(Top right) **Aunt Fanny** – final digital render, *(Right)* **Vending machine bot** – concept art • Michael Knapp, *(Below)* **Vending machine bot graphic** • Michael Knapp, *(Opposite top)* **Pod travel study** – concept art • Bill Joyce, *(Opposite bottom left)* **Crosstown Express diagram** – Steve Martino and Carlos Saldanha, *(Opposite bottom right)* **Transit hub** – concept art • Bill Joyce

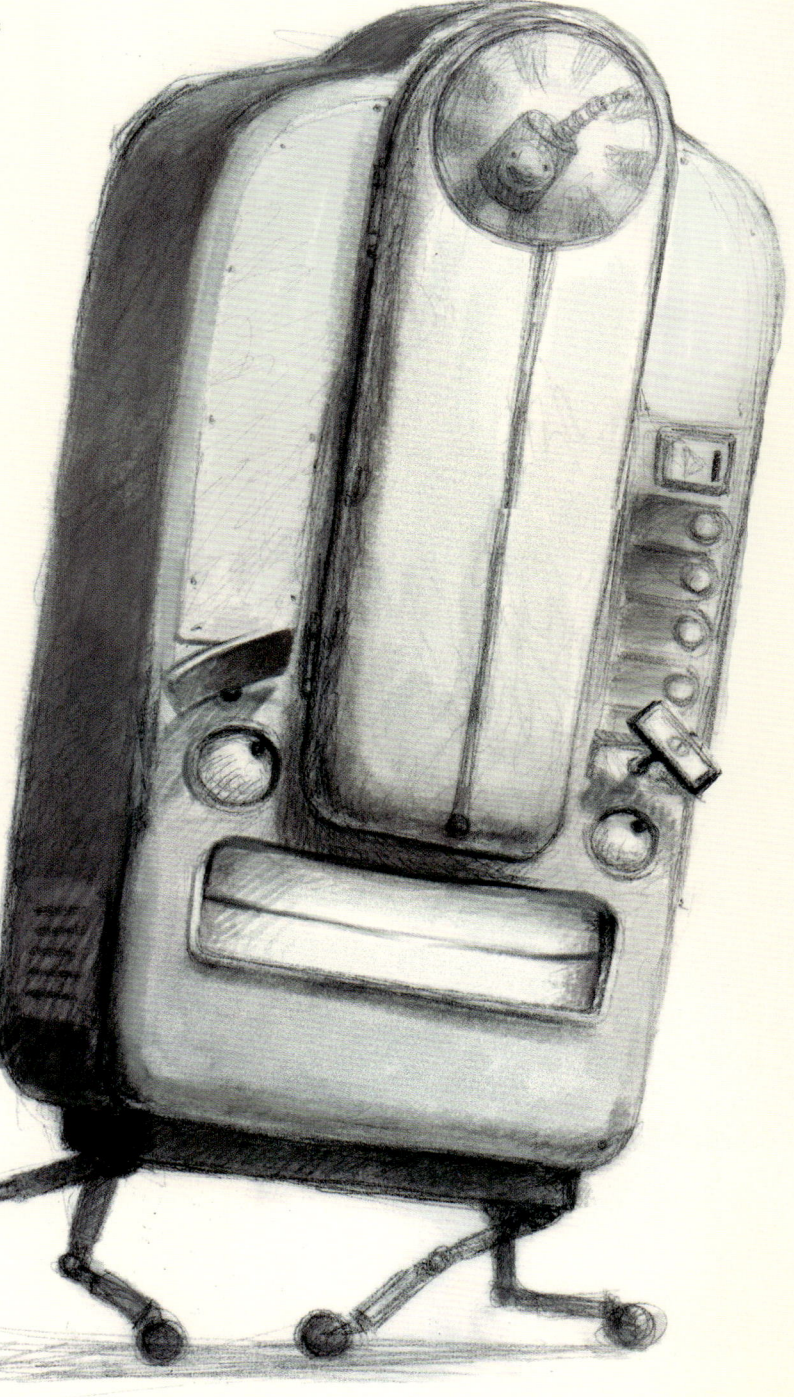

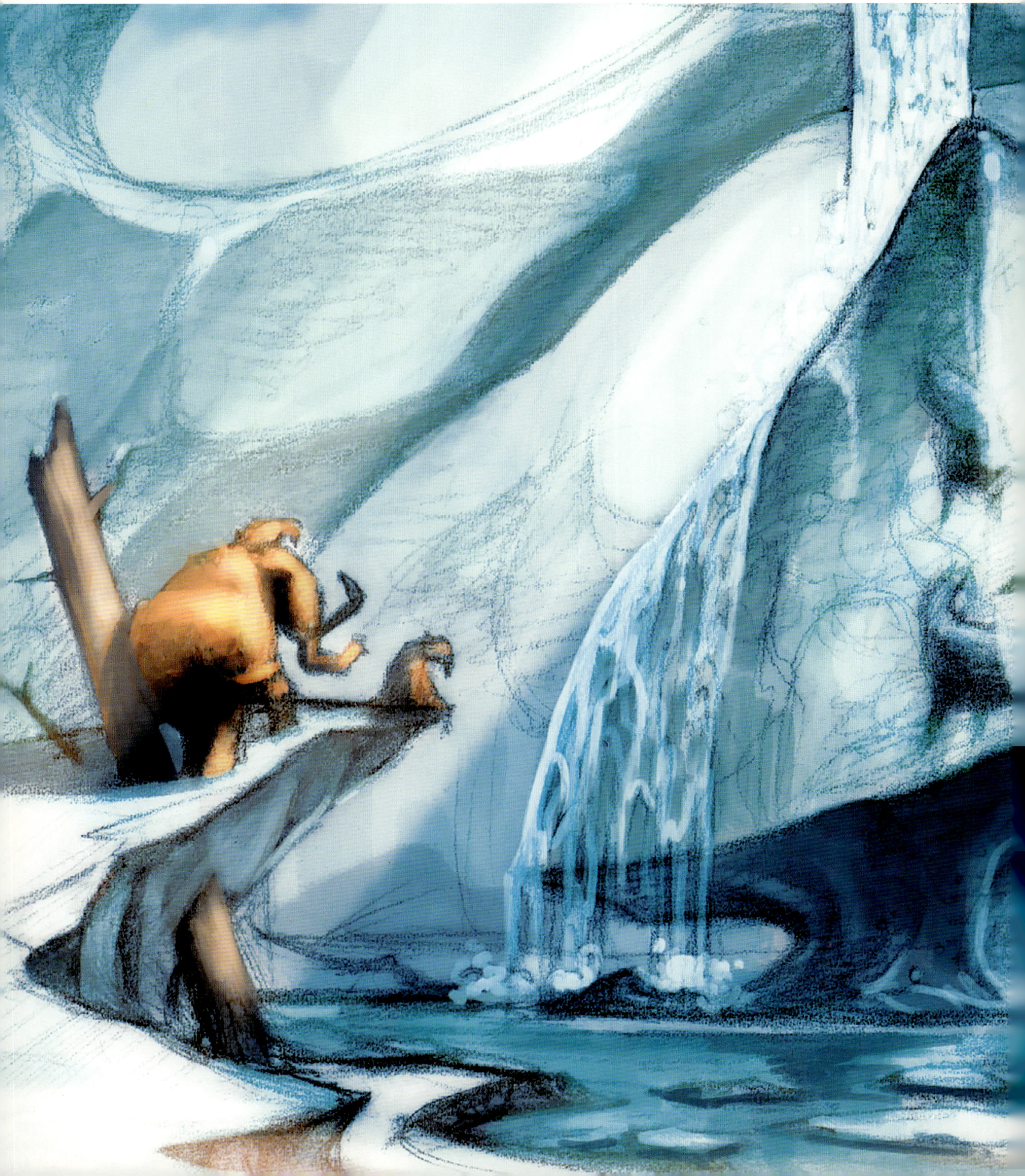

CHAPTER 3 · *Ice Age: The Meltdown*

"Like it or not, we're going to be one big happy family. I'll be the daddy, Ellie will be the mommy, and Diego will be the uncle who eats the kids who get on my nerves. Now let's move it before the ground falls out from under our feet."

—MANNY

The time was ripe for the heroes of *Ice Age* to return to the screen. Fox was aware that too much time away from the public wasn't good for a growing franchise, and besides, there were many more stories to tell in the *Ice Age* universe. *Ice Age: The Meltdown* would bring back Manny, Sid, Diego, and, of course, Scrat, and introduce a broader cast and environment. New characters would join the herd, and new landscapes would crop up throughout the tundra. And the single plot device that would instigate both of these events would be a whole new natural disaster. The glaciers are melting, and our heroes—along with their new friends—have to make it to safety before the ice dam breaks and floods the valley. Once more it's the end of the world, and if the dysfunctional group is going to survive, they'll have to work together.

The rising tide, however, was as much of a challenge for the filmmakers as the characters. There was relatively little flowing water in the first *Ice Age*, but in its sequel characters needed to swim across the surf, dive to the depths, and sail on the waves. Water was to be as much a villain as any movie character, and for the audience, it had to be a believable threat. Additionally, the fact that most of the characters were covered in fur meant that their hair had to interact more dramatically and realistically than it ever had before. This required a whole new set of CG models that could handle an epic amount of H_2O.

SOMETHING OLD, SOMETHING NEW

It's not easy to make a sequel that lives up to the first installment. From the get-go, *Ice Age: The Meltdown* was ordained to be more complex in every aspect of its production. It required additional lead characters, more complex environments, and a complete reformatting of effects. It was also the solo directorial debut of Carlos Saldanha.

(Previous pages) **Frozen threat in the waterpark** – concept art • Michael Knapp, *(Top)* **Scrat** – character sketch • Peter de Sève, *(Opposite)* **Campfire at night** – concept art • Peter Clarke (design) and Xiangyuan Jie (painting)

THE ART OF BLUE SKY STUDIOS

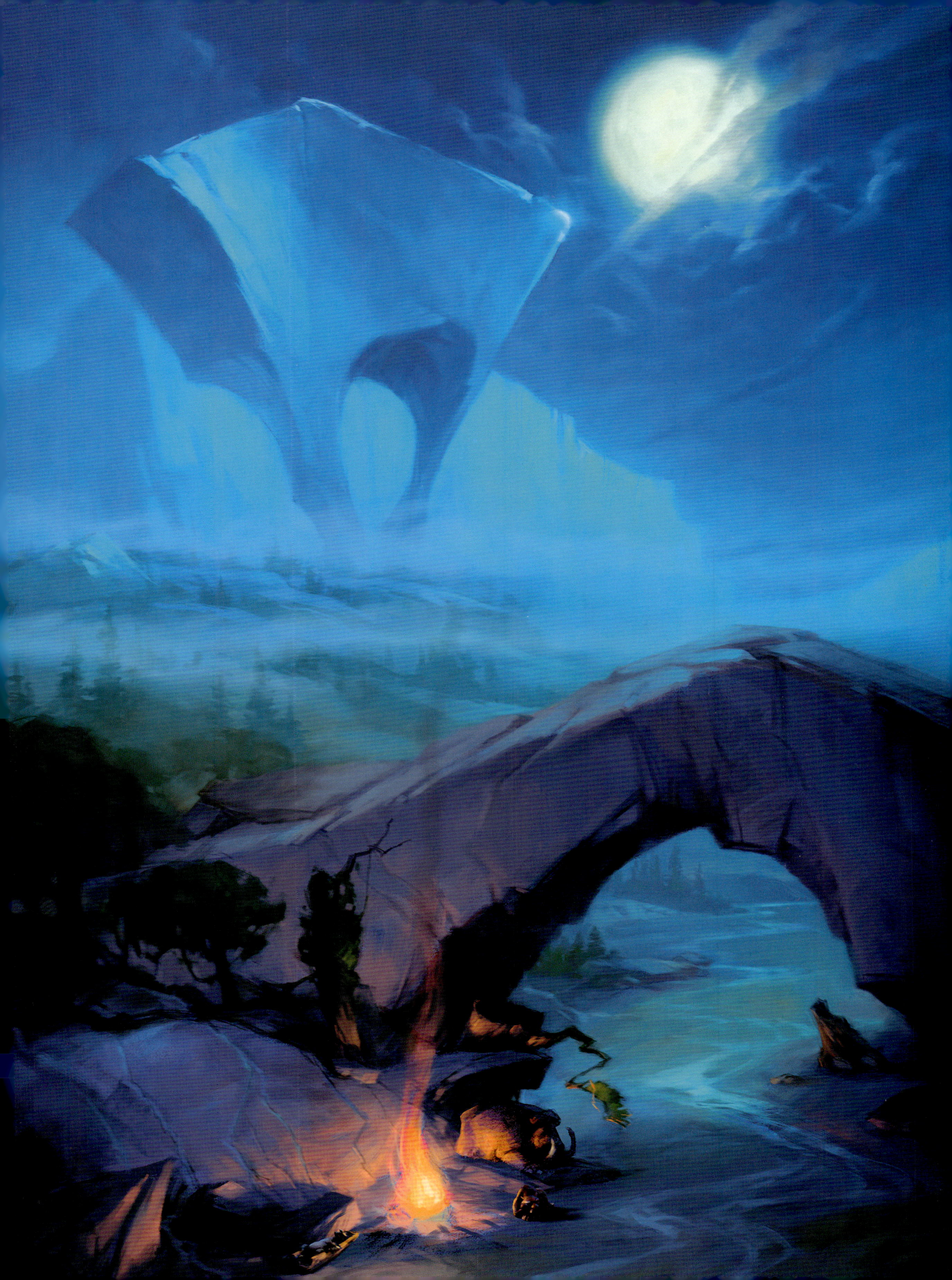

"The trick about sequels is how to make it different but also feel the same," says Saldanha. "We have to keep the essence of what we've done in the first film but make it feel that we're moving the story forward and making something unique."

The premise for the film came from the question, "What would be the opposite of an ice age?" If the temperature is beginning to increase, the ice begins to thaw and the environment starts to change. A catastrophic event is imminent, and after a massive deep-freeze, nature's next natural disaster is a worldwide meltdown, which gives rise to an enormous flood.

Tom Cardone was enlisted as the art director on the sequel. Cardone, a native New Yorker, was recruited by Disney in 1990 and was trained there as a traditional background artist, working on a range of projects, including supervising the Background department on *Hercules* and co–art directing *The Emperor's New Groove*. In 2003, he returned to the East Coast to work with Blue Sky on *Robots*. Although he was an experienced art director, Cardone experienced a new challenge when faced with an animated force of nature.

"As part of the threat, there's an increasing presence of water as the film progresses," says Cardone, "so we see a lot of mud and rain and a softening of the environment." While the first film was dominated by glaciers, *Ice Age: The Meltdown* had emerging forests, lakes, rivers, and puddles. The environments were more lush and organic, and the simple ice shapes began to make way for the more complex contours of nature.

The sharp edges of the ice were part of the sensibility of the first movie, and that was clearly changing in *Ice Age: The Meltdown*. "Water is fluid, and the ice when it melts gets smoother, so for *The Meltdown* we introduced more curves," says Saldanha. "But we were starting to rethink how to create a visual language based off the language of the first movie. We had the curves, but we also had the sharp edges of the chiseled rocks throughout the film. There are always things here and there that keep the language of the first movie."

The overarching theme of the landscape is scale. Every aspect of the environment feels like it could overpower and engulf the characters at any moment. Even a mammoth, the largest creature on Earth, is vulnerable to this tumultuous world.

(Top left) **Scrat expressions** – character sketches • Peter de Sève,
(Top right) **Ice waterpark** – concept art • Robert MacKenzie,
(Above) **Manny hit with snowball** – concept art • Michael Knapp

ICE AGE: THE MELTDOWN 87

(Above) **Glacier crumbling** – concept art • Peter Clarke (design) and Xiangyuan Jie (painting)

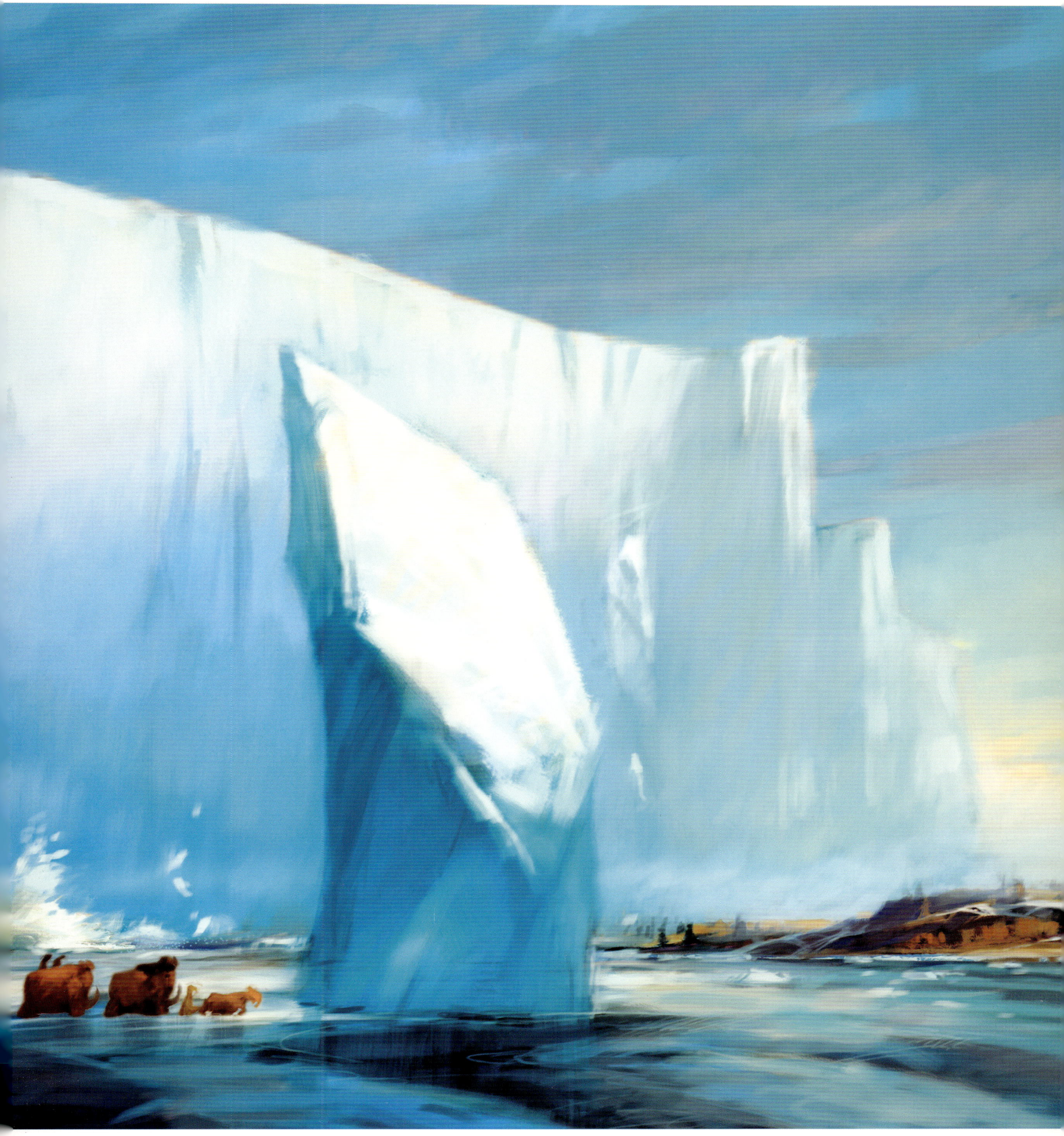

The Squeak Heard Around the World

THE RETURN OF THE SCRAT character was inevitable for the sequel, but for this installment, Saldanha knew that the rodent would be instrumental to the plot. "When I was developing the story of the meltdown," says Saldanha, "I thought that if something happens to the world, like a big dam breaking, the only character who could either cause it or stop it would be Scrat."

In the first movie, Scrat existed entirely outside of the main plot. Any overlap of his story with that of the main characters was purely circumstantial. Saldanha and his team approached the sequel with the premise that Scrat would both set the meltdown into motion and later save the valley from the flood. During the film's opening, Scrat gingerly taps his acorn onto a glacier and sets off the catastrophe. At film's end, his trail of acorn holes breaks open the valley walls, emptying it of the flood. Scrat plummets miles to earth and cheats death when he receives mouth-to-mouth resuscitation from Sid.

Saldanha believes that while the main characters struggle to survive, Scrat is incapable of truly being destroyed. As insignificant as he seems, the power to destroy—or save—the world seems to rest in his paws. "The only character who could potentially do anything about it was Scrat," he says. "That's when we developed Scrat more and integrated him more into the story. He became part of the main cast from that point on."

(Top left) **Scrat on the run** – character sketch • Peter de Sève, *(Right)* **Melting glacier** – concept art • Michael Knapp, *(Opposite)* **Scrat caught between glaciers** – concept art • Peter de Sève (design) and Xiangyuan Jie (painting)

90 THE ART OF BLUE SKY STUDIOS

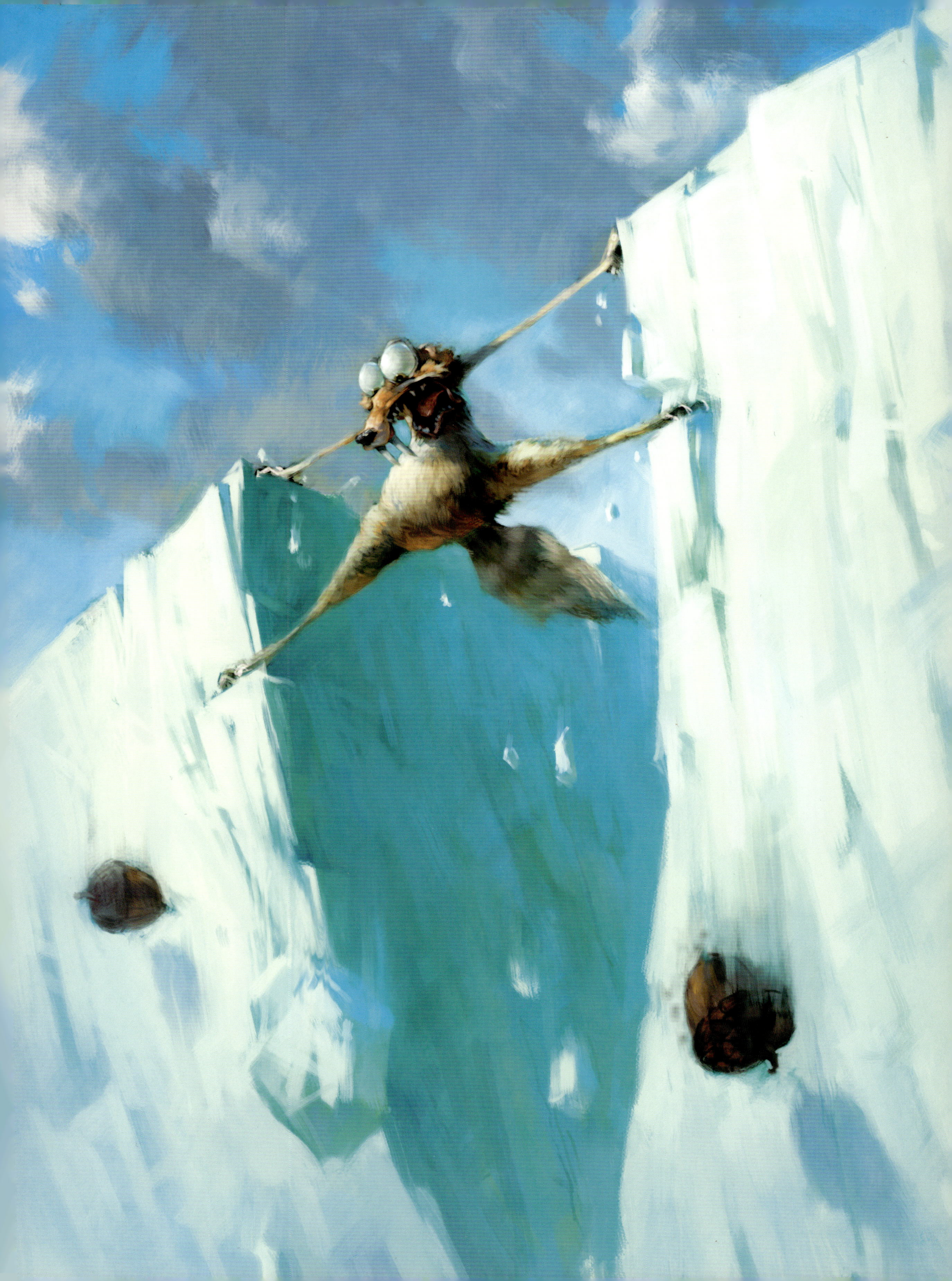

AND INTRODUCING...

As with all the *Ice Age* films, producer Lori Forte had a hand in the growth of the core group of characters. "Those characters are pretty much set in who they are," she says, "but things in their lives change for them, so they have to evolve with those new changes."

When we reencounter the characters, we find that Manny, Sid, and Diego have stuck together all these years and are currently doing their best to monitor the neighborhood children. Manny is still cantankerous, Diego is still recalcitrant, and Sid is still the desperate goofball, trying to win the respect of his diminutive protégés.

Since the first movie, our trio has matured and found community among the other prehistoric families. They've clearly retained their flaws but have also found comfort in each other, which is no small feat. And just as they have changed since the last film, so has the world around them.

"Manny thinks he's the last mammoth on earth," adds Forte, "and he lost his family in the first film so he doesn't have a lineage. Then he meets Ellie. The good news is that mammoths will not go extinct; the bad news is she thinks she's a possum. So we're always adding new twists and turns to these characters. Manny had to learn to deal with that and grow into being part of a couple."

(Top) **Ellie with possums** – concept art • Peter de Sève (design) and Thomas Cardone (painting), *(Bottom)* **Ellie hanging on branch** – concept art • Peter de Sève

92   THE ART OF BLUE SKY STUDIOS

With the addition of Ellie the mammoth and her possum brothers, Crash and Eddie, the original herd doubled in size and quadrupled in chaos. "We wanted a character with a lot of attitude who would be very sure of herself," says Saldanha, "even if she is a little kooky and fights it till the end. And we wanted funny and strong little characters to have a comedic element, so Crash and Eddie were born." In searching for the design of Ellie, Peter de Sève provided a sketch of a lady mammoth hanging by the tail on a branch that was sagging from her weight. In that single drawing, the character was born.

As a mammoth experiencing an identity crisis, Ellie insists she, Crash, and Eddie need the protection of the herd. Manny fights his growing affection for her, still hurting from the loss of his family. He struggled with opening his heart in the first film; now Manny has to learn to love again.

(Top) **Crash and Eddie** – concept art • Peter de Sève, *(Center left)* **Possum** – concept art • Peter de Sève, *(Center right)* **Ellie with Crash and Eddie** – concept art • Peter de Sève, *(Bottom)* **Manny and Ellie** – concept art • Peter Clarke

(Above) **Intimate moment between Manny and Ellie** – concept art • Peter Clarke

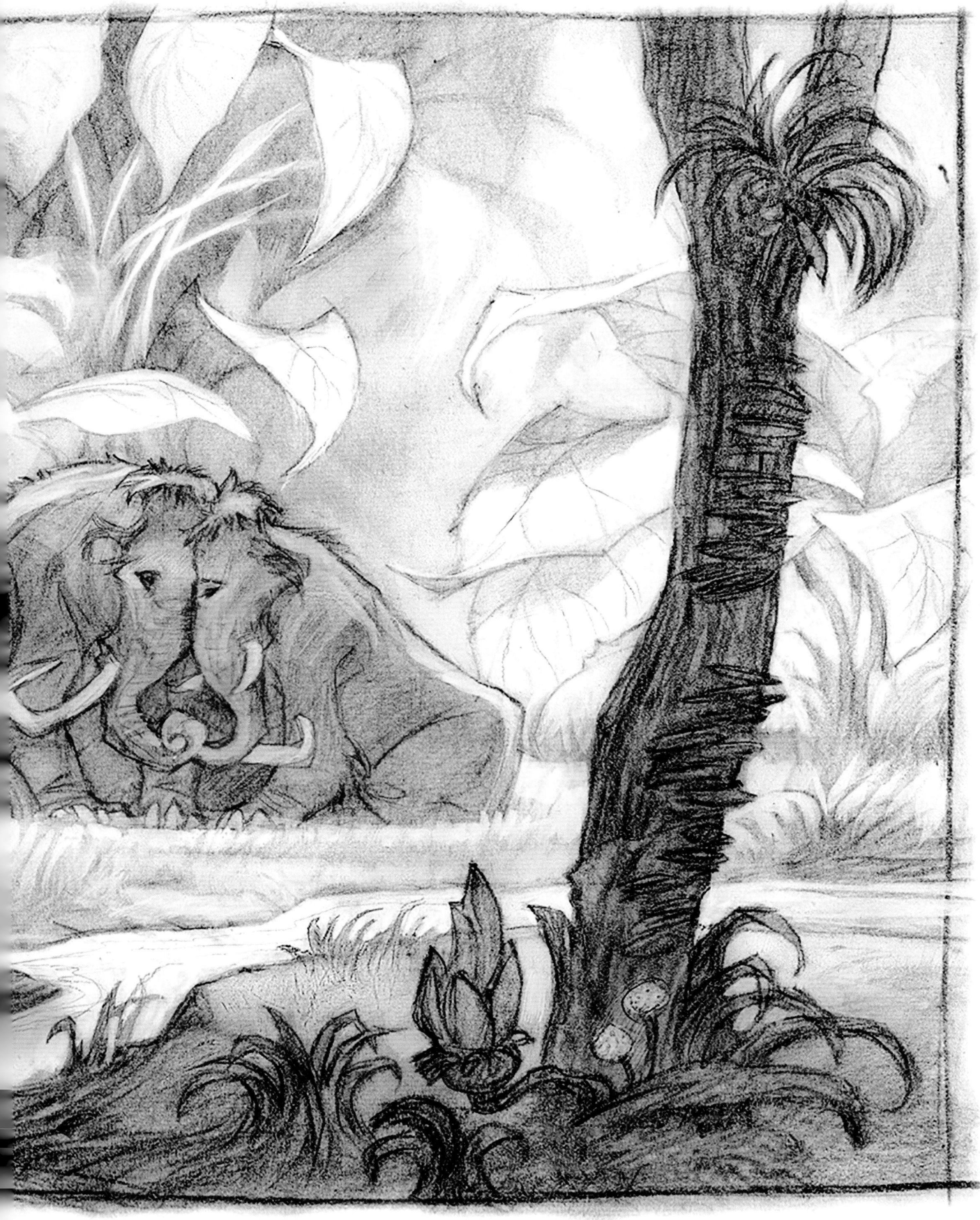

HAIRY SITUATIONS

The technological limitations of the first film necessitated clumpy fur. For *Ice Age: The Meltdown*, the fur technology was entirely new and more versatile. With new fur came new ways to make the characters look more tactile and cuddly, as well as options to groom their hair. In the original *Ice Age*, each CG character model was painstakingly covered in what the artists called "cards," which resembled overlapping tiles. Every card was texture mapped, meaning it was painted with the digital appearance of hair. As a result, the only type of fur available was clumpy in appearance, and its interaction with wind and other elements was extremely limited. Additionally, if the animators curved a part of the characters' bodies too much, the cards would cease to overlap and would reveal hairless patches of skin.

For *Ice Age: The Meltdown*, Manny, Sid, and Diego had to be completely remodeled and rerigged to look and move exactly as they did in the first movie, but with a superior fur texture. Even the clumpy nature of the trio's fur—their visual trademark in the first film—was replicated for the second film. The new characters, however, were more attractively groomed. "In *Ice Age: The Meltdown*, we could interact their fur with wind, snow, and water," says Saldanha. "And for designing the fur of the new characters, we took liberties. We wanted them to feel like they're in the same world as the first movie, but to look better."

"We didn't want to break the recognition of the characters with the new technology," says Cardone. "Everything had to relate to what was there before, but this was the first time we could actually go in there and start grooming. For instance, we worked out Ellie's

96   THE ART OF BLUE SKY STUDIOS

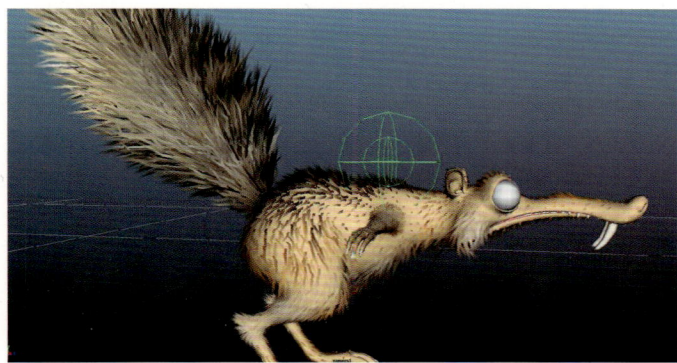

hairdo and eyelashes and gave her a soft fur collar." Each character was given a different quality of fur for each of its different body parts, and a specific decision was made on where the hair was to be longer, shorter, thinner, coarser, rougher, smoother, or any combination of those traits.

A single character in *Ice Age: The Meltdown* has many different types of hair on a variety of body parts. Crash the possum, for instance, is groomed fully and lushly around his torso, making him look soft and cuddly (the same is true of Eddie). However, the hair on his face is finer and more closely groomed to the contour of the face so as not to interfere with expression. To communicate the properties of these differing types of hair and textures, the art director collected visual references known as "callouts" that related Crash's fictional fur to something tangible in our world. Full-body paintings and details were created, and a photo of a shar-pei's nose was used as reference for the fine hair on the bridge of Crash's muzzle. It was these kinds of visual tools that allowed the artists to stay on the same page as they plunged ahead.

(Opposite top) **Manny** – fur cards to be replaced with fully rendered fur • Keith Cormier, *(Opposite center)* **Angry Manny** – final frame, *(Opposite bottom)* **Manny and Ellie** – final frame, *(Top and center)* **Scrat** – fur progression • Sheldon Chow, *(Right)* **Eddie the possum** – final frame

Scrat Heaven

FOR A FEW PRECIOUS MINUTES, Scrat encounters Heaven, where piles of beautiful acorns wait for him. As he approaches the pearly gates, he walks upright, like a human character. It is the first time he breaks from his regular four-legged scramble. The filmmakers behind the later *Ice Age* movies point to this pivotal scene as being a key turning point for the character.

"It kind of tweaked the character a little bit so he wasn't just a rodent," says Mike Thurmeier, director of the short *No Time for Nuts* and codirector of the two successive *Ice Age* films. "He was more anthropomorphic and sort of had a little more personality, which I think opened the door for him having a girlfriend in *Ice Age: Dawn of the Dinosaurs* and following a map in *Ice Age: Continental Drift*. It was an interesting moment in his development."

(Top) **Scrat at the Pearly Gates** – color key • Daniel López Muñoz, *(Left)* **Scrat Heaven sequence** – color keys • Xiangyuan Jie, *(Opposite bottom)* **Scrat** – final digital art

ICE AGE: THE MELTDOWN

ROCKING THEIR WORLD

The animated characters in *Ice Age: The Meltdown* may be better coiffed, but the animated landscape is more dangerous than ever. This time around, the very earth itself is threatening to destroy life on the surface. With toppling rocks, volcanic mounds, and explosive geysers, land dwellers are at the mercy of the elements. And sea monsters only have to bide their time.

"If the world is changing and collapsing," says Saldanha, "all the set pieces are about natural phenomena. In some way they are all catastrophic. At the same time, you can't just have action for the sake of action. You need to have a character-driven motive in there. So finding that character motivation, and at the same time creating the same big, action-packed sequence with camera movements, is fairly complex."

It's a principle at Blue Sky that broad action is not nearly as challenging as subtle acting, rich in personality. What makes an action sequence compelling is a well-defined character backdrop. A case in point is the scene in which our heroes find themselves on precarious rocks balancing over a chasm. Manny's tactless romantic advances to Ellie have backfired, and she is utterly unforgiving. As they attempt to cross a rock bridge, pieces tumble out from under their feet, and Manny, Ellie, Sid, Diego, Crash, and Eddie are each left holding on for dear life on a different balancing boulder. Manny and Ellie have to put their differences aside, lock trunks, and become the stable center of gravity that gives them all the chance to escape. "If it was just rocks

(Opposite top) **Balance set** – set design • Daniel López Muñoz, *(Opposite bottom)* **Cliffs from below** – storyboard panel • Daniel López Muñoz, *(Above)* **Balance sequence** – color keys • Robert MacKenzie, *(Right)* **Balancing rock** – concept art • Daniel López Muñoz

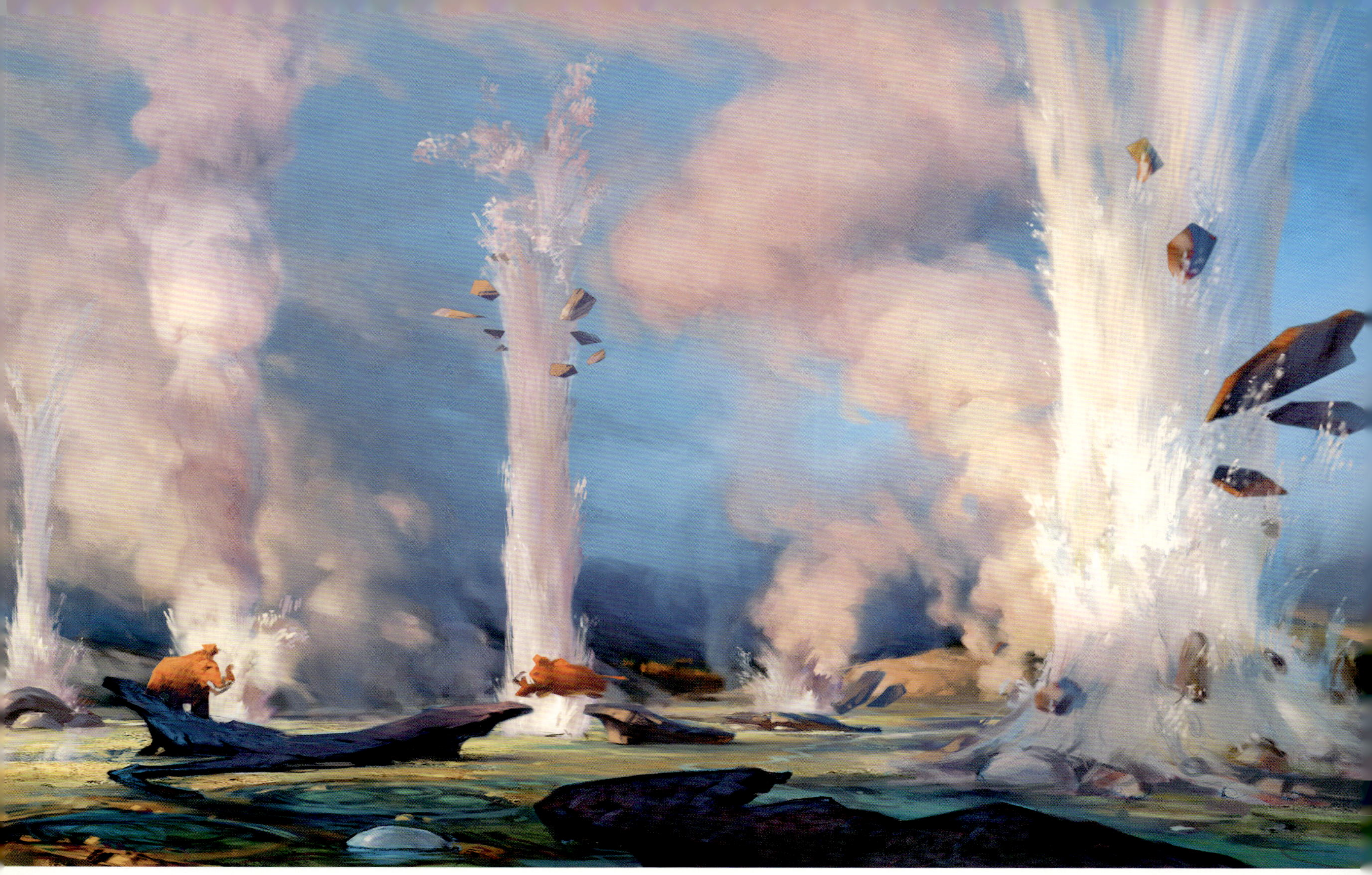

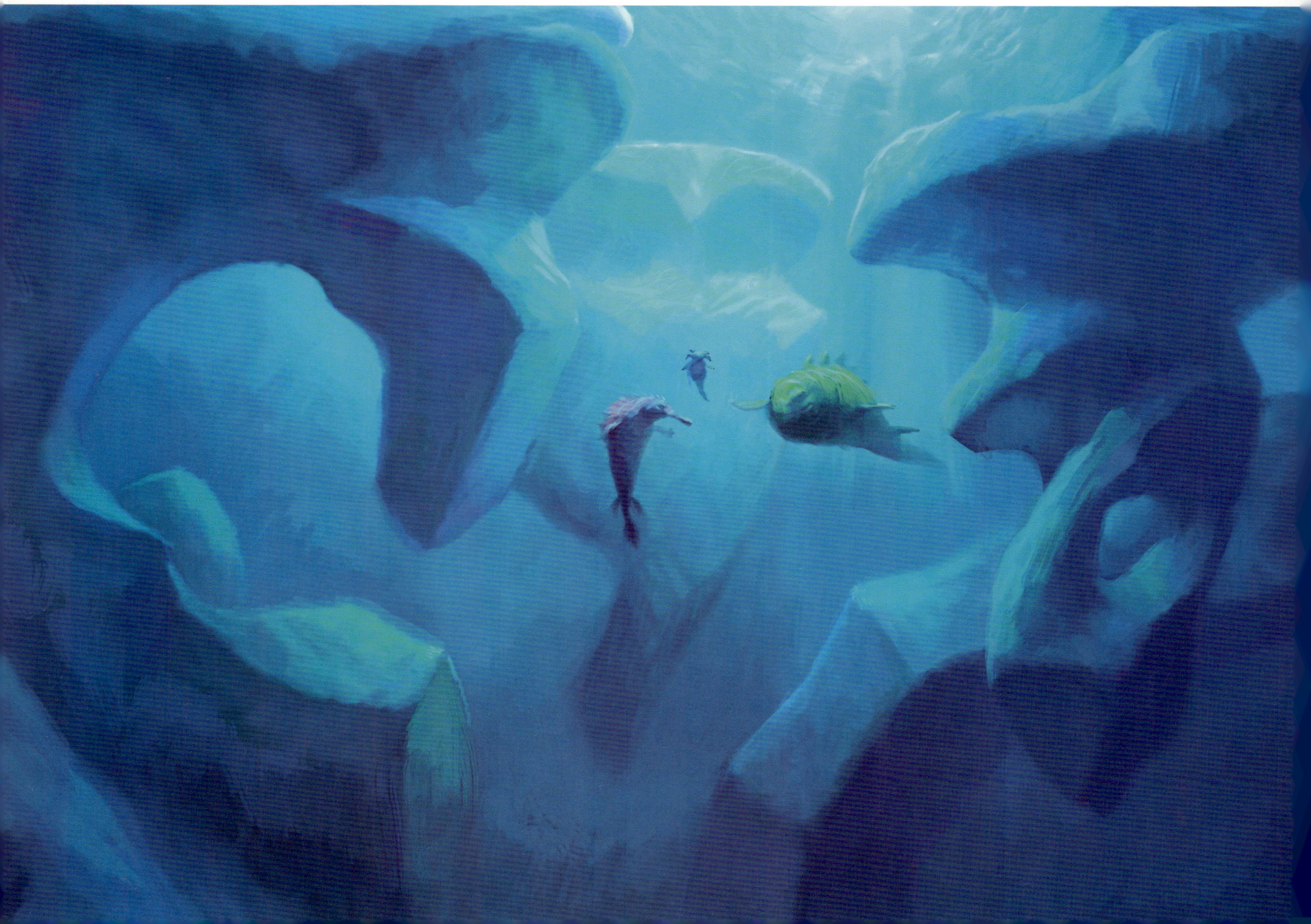

swinging around and the characters trying to survive, it would not be as interesting as having a conflict on top of that," says Saldanha. "Now Manny and Ellie have to solve their conflict on those rocks if they want the herd to stay alive."

It's this interplay between action and character that ups the ante throughout the film. When Sid is kidnapped by mini-sloths, his need for respect almost gets him tossed into an active volcano. Diego's fear of water almost costs the lives of his herd. Manny's stubbornness nearly gets him destroyed in the geyser field, and Ellie's obstinacy traps her in an ever-flooding cave at the mercy of two prehistoric leviathans.

"The sea creatures came from the much earlier days of Earth," says Saldanha, "so they're not as evolved, and so we decided not to give them dialogue. Early on they had some lines, but we felt it diminished from their personality, and they'd be more menacing if they didn't talk." When Manny takes them on to save Ellie, it's not only his brains against theirs; he's combatting his own melancholy for a chance at happiness with her. Character, as always, is key.

THE FINAL MELTDOWN

In March 2006, *Ice Age: The Meltdown* became the second-highest grossing non-holiday, non-summer release of all time. It went on to make upwards of $650 million worldwide, solidifying the *Ice Age* franchise as a global favorite.

Having tackled original stories, Blue Sky was now leaning toward an adaptation of a popular book. The studio had developed different original worlds and characters and pushed them far past their expectations. It would soon find, however, that its advances in fur technology and character animation were just beginning to scratch the surface.

(Opposite top) **Exploding geysers** – concept art • Peter Clarke (design) and Xiangyuan Jie (painting), *(Opposite bottom)* **Underwater ice formations** – concept art • Robert MacKenzie, *(Top)* **Surviving the flood** – concept art • Peter Clarke (design) and Thomas Cardone (painting), *(Above)* **Crash and Eddie rescue Diego and Sid (three images)** – color keys • Xiangyuan Jie

BLUE SKY SHORTS
No Time for Nuts (2006)

"THIS WAS A FILM THAT WAS CLOSE TO ME," says producer Lori Forte, "because we asked some of our storyboard artists to pitch us ideas for a Scrat short. Then we selected a pitch by one of our top storyboard artists at the time, Chris Renaud."

Not only did Renaud storyboard the short, he also joined Mike Thurmeier as a director on the project. The filmmaking duo had to figure out how to tackle a production featuring several different settings with limited financial resources. "The environments were conceived very simply," says Thurmeier. "We did a lot of background paintings or still camera shots so we could customize everything to a single camera."

The short continued Scrat's journey to becoming a more humanlike character, wielding a sword and pushing mechanized buttons in his journey across time and space.

"The biggest problem was when he travels back to the first *Ice Age* movie and you see the human baby on Manny's shoulders," adds Thurmeier. "To resurrect that baby's model and rig after all those years was a challenge."

No Time for Nuts became the second Scrat short to garner an Academy Award nomination, and it was included on the *Ice Age: The Meltdown* DVD.

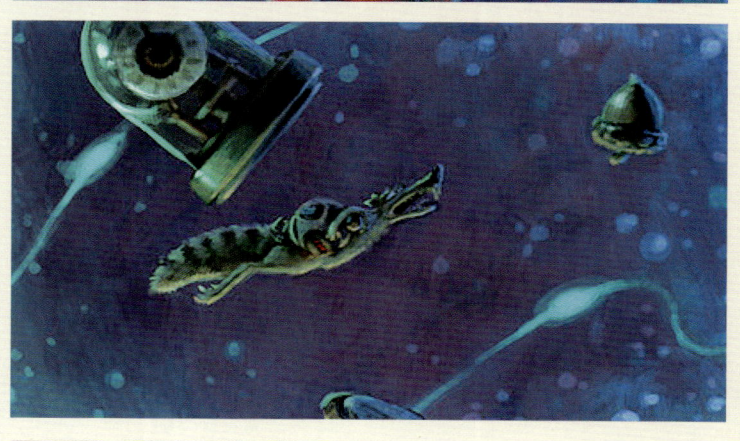

(Top) **Time machine breakdown** – concept sketches • Michael Knapp, *(Above)* **Scrat in time vortex** – color keys • Michael Knapp, *(Bottom)* **Scrat with acorn** – concept art • Michael Knapp, *(Opposite center)* **Time machine** – concept art • Michael Knapp and Nash Dunnigan, *(Opposite bottom)* **Scrat throughout history (three images)** – color keys • Michael Knapp, Vincent Di Nguyen, and Peter Nguyen

YEAR
20,000 B.C.
MONTH DAY
05 26

ICE AGE: THE MELTDOWN 105

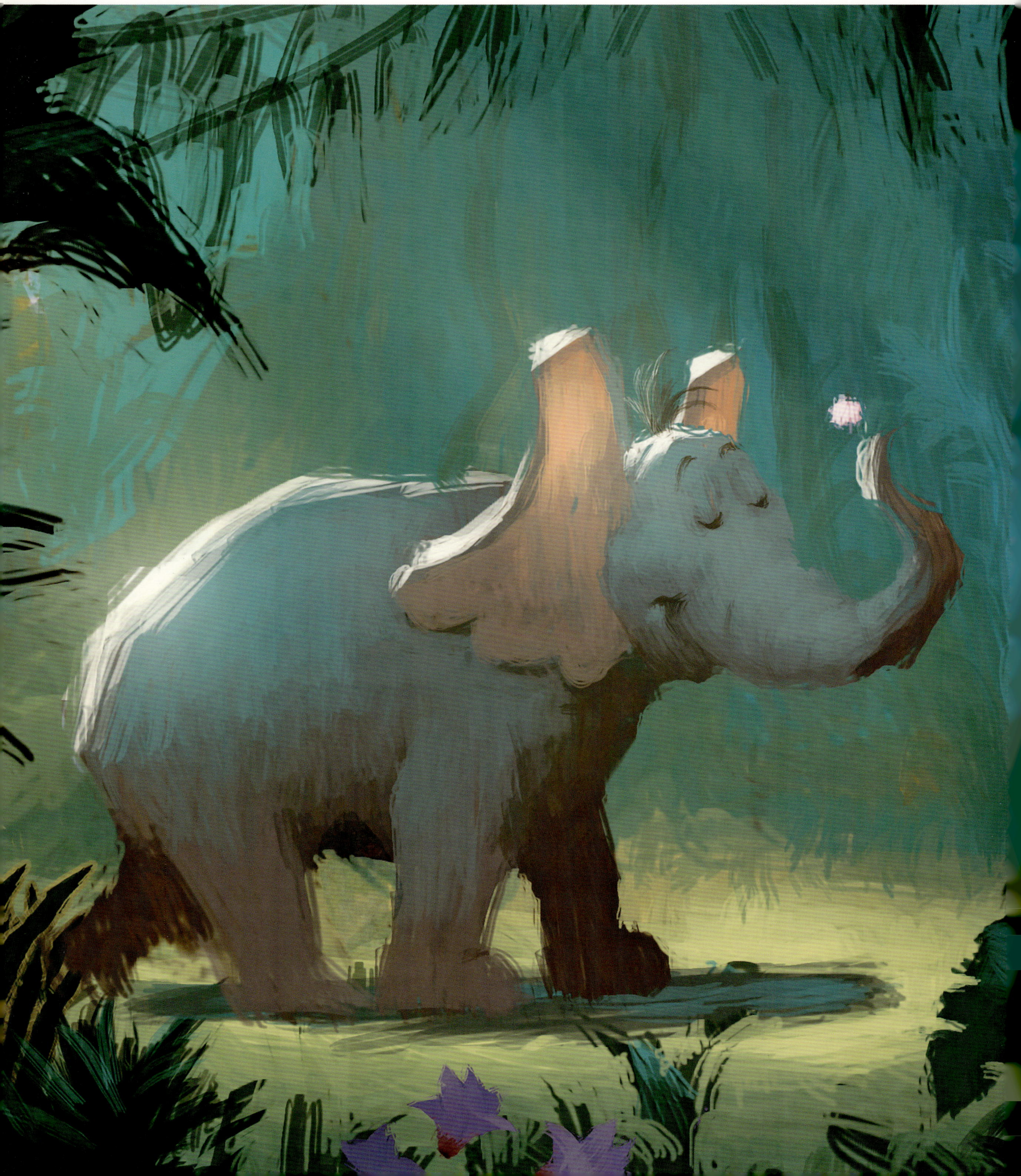

CHAPTER 4 • *Dr. Seuss' Horton Hears a Who!*

"Horton is a giant elephant in the sky! Don't bother looking, he's invisible."

—THE MAYOR OF WHOVILLE

"Essentially," says director Jimmy Hayward, "*Dr. Seuss' Horton Hears a Who!* is a whole movie about two guys on the phone." In the long history of buddy comedies, it's hard to find another movie in which the two leads never meet and still manage to change each other's lives so drastically. Horton, a pachyderm denizen of the Jungle of Nool, and the neurotic Mayor of the city of Whoville, are the only beings in their respective worlds who believe that each other's worlds even exist. When Horton's keen ears detect the sounds of Whoville atop a tiny speck, he makes it his duty to guard that speck on its clover perch. Horton is not just a good Samaritan; he's the nicest guy in the jungle. And although large and lumbering, he possesses empathy for even the tiniest of creatures.

"Every part of the story was based on the theme of the book," says director Steve Martino, "that a person's a person, no matter how small. Horton learns that, the kangaroo learns that, and the Mayor learns that about his son." It is a sentiment that has registered with young readers for generations, and the filmmakers were ready to extend its message to a moviegoing audience in a whole new way.

CARPÉ PACHYDERM

Horton the Elephant may not be as famous as Theodor Seuss Geisel's hat-wearing cat, but he possesses the same likability found in the best of the master's works. For children at heart, like Hayward, Horton has always topped the list of great Seuss characters. "It was my absolute favorite book as a kid," he says. "My mom FedExed me my copy of the book from the seventies that says 'Jimmy' on the front in marker."

Hayward hails from Vancouver and at nineteen was hired as the senior supervising animator for the first CG show on television, ABC's *ReBoot* (1994). Soon after, he went to work at Pixar as an animator

(Previous pages) **Horton with clover** – color key • Daisuke Tsutsumi, *(Above)* **The Mayor of Whoville** – concept art • Sang Jun Lee, *(Opposite)* **Close-up of Clover and Horton** – concept art • Barry Jackson

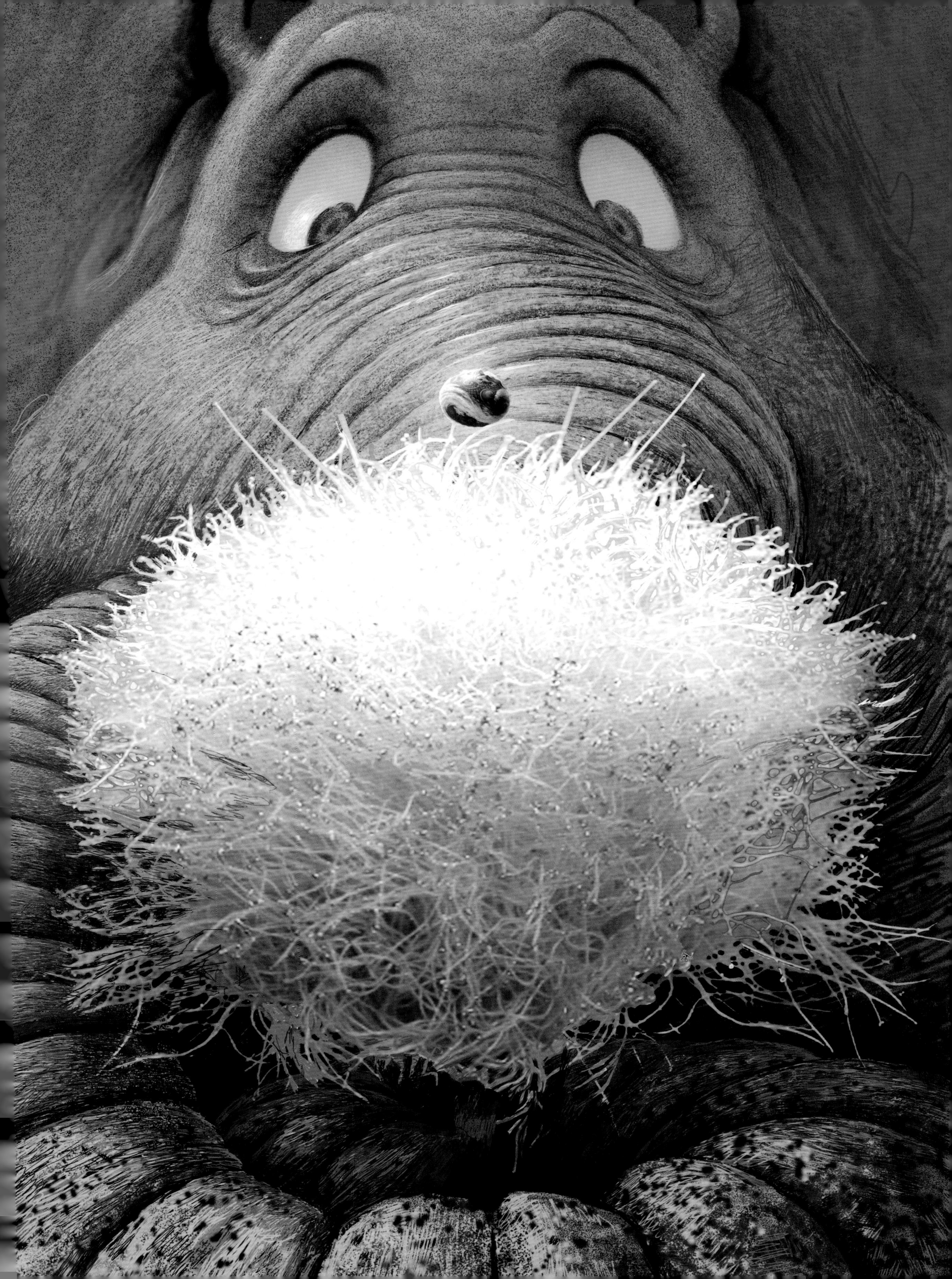

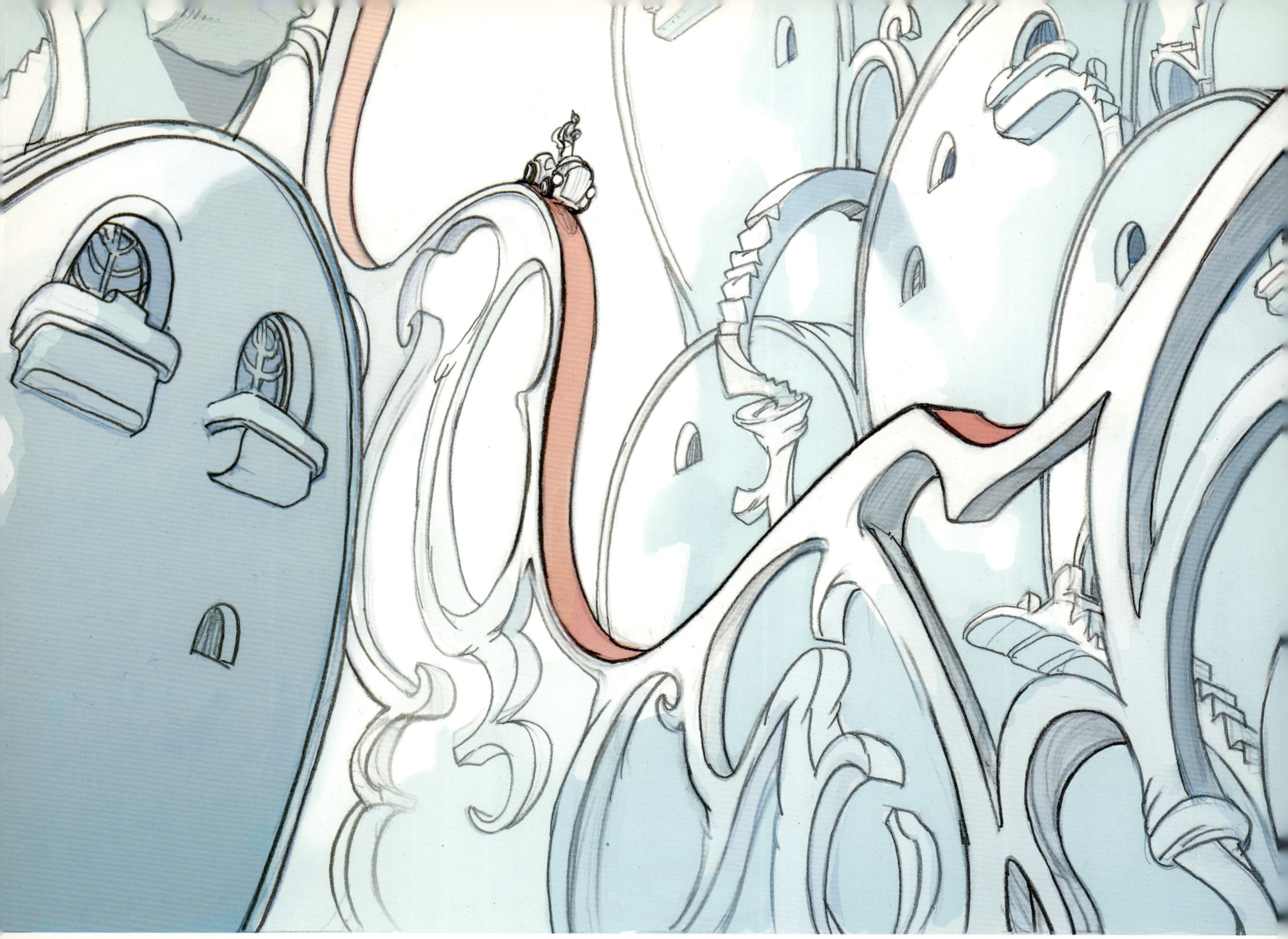

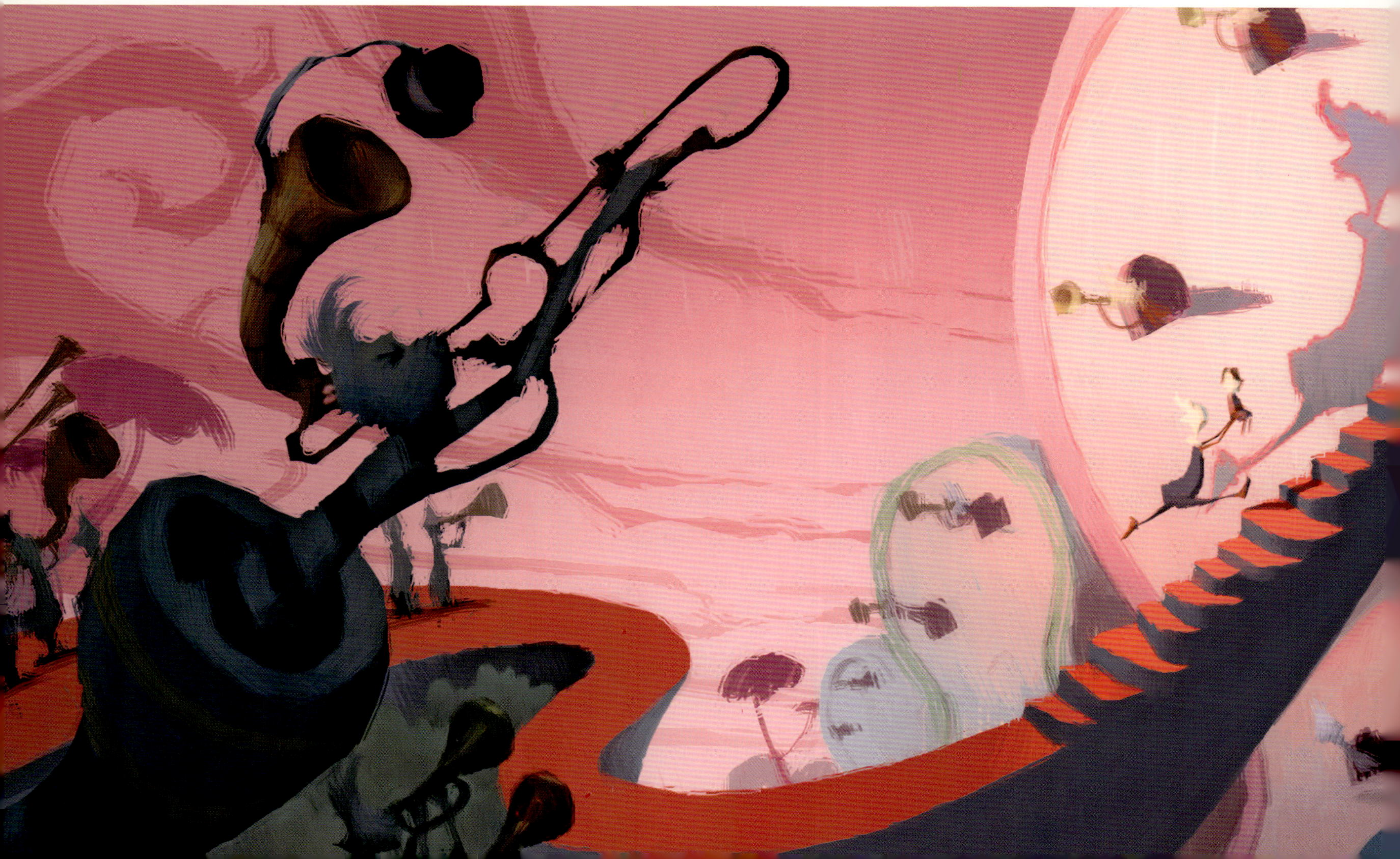

before leaving to write for Twentieth Century Fox, and then being hired by Blue Sky to carry out rewrites on Robots. His additional dialogue and scene-tweaking earned him a Director of Additional Scenes credit.

Meanwhile, Steve Martino was newly promoted from art director to director, and the two teamed up to tackle adapting a seventy-two-page picture book into a ninety-minute movie.

"Step one," says Martino, "was a promise to Audrey Geisel that we were going to uphold her late husband's work. We believed in it, and we wanted to stick to his overriding philosophy."

Martino and Hayward structured the story of the film so that it was close to that of the book. All that was original was kept intact, with some character development and ancillary characters fleshing it out into feature-film length. To show just how true they intended to stay to the original, the directors created a new version of the book for the Seuss estate, which included specially created pieces of art and verse inserted between the original pages that outlined the expanded plot of the proposed film.

"As we came into this project, the philosophy was to maximize what Seuss has created," says Martino. "We have one of the greatest illustrator-creators of imaginary worlds that has ever existed. Let's realize it in a way that lets the audience go into the book and then see what's around the corner."

FROM THE LIBRARY TO THE SCREEN

How do you create an animated Seussian universe in three dimensions when all that exists are flat drawings? Director Steve Martino and art director Tom Cardone set out to tackle this problem and define the visual style of the film. They delved into the Special Collections of the University of California's Geisel Library, where more than 8,000 pieces of original Dr. Seuss art now reside. Analyzing his pen-work, Martino studied the fat wrinkles Geisel gave everything he drew. From creatures to buildings to machines, the Seuss drawing style had a quality of playfulness that translated into organic contours. It's easy to overlook when glancing at the deft illustrations, but the Seuss style of construction includes wrinkles as predominant as the creases on our folded skin. The directors made note of this, as well as Geisel's personal taste in animation adaptation.

"I read a lot of correspondence between him and animation director Chuck Jones to understand certain things that he was very particular about," says Martino. "Architecture was one. He was very specific in his books about a certain style of architecture for that book and a different style of architecture for another, and you don't just interchange and use one for another. Whoville is taken

(Top) **Whoville roads** – concept art • Sang Jun Lee, *(Bottom)* **Who playing trombone** – concept art • Daisuke Tsutsumi

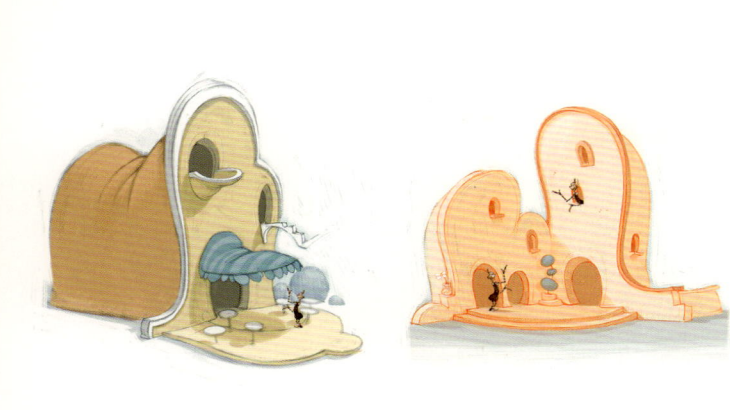

from a southwest adobe architecture approach, but it's still got his imagination running all through it."

Another key to unlocking the dimensions of Dr. Seuss' art was the original sculptures and paintings in the Geisel collection. Sculpted animal busts, mounted on wood like hunting trophies, provided important clues as to how Geisel himself visualized his creations in three dimensions. Where Geisel used a shaving brush to create a tuft of animal hair, Martino saw an accurate representation of fur in the Seuss universe. Taking in the wrinkles, architecture, fur, and everything else Seuss, the filmmakers began to shape Horton's world.

DISSECTING SHAPE LANGUAGE

Once the homework was done, art director Tom Cardone and the design team deconstructed what made a Seuss drawing distinctly Seuss. "Everyone's familiar with the style," says Cardone, "but once you start trying to copy his style, it's easy to break it." One thing Cardone noticed was Seuss drawings' distinct asymmetry. Asymmetry is not something that comes naturally with computer software.

"If we tell someone who's designing on the project to make a cylinder feel more organic and asymmetrical, they might bend it or dent it, but what makes it Seuss is to add the compression wrinkles in just the right places that make even mechanical objects feel like living, organic things," Cardone continues.

Martino used the term "bio-mechanical" to refer to the style Seuss employed to draw wrinkles on machines. To Cardone, the

(Top) **Whoville houses** – concept art • Willie Real, *(Above)* **Balcony** – concept art • Kyle Macnaughton, *(Below)* **City hall** – concept art • Willie Real, *(Opposite top)* **Mayor's front door** – painting over render • Thomas Cardone, *(Opposite center)* **Desk** – CG model • Kyle Macnaughton (design) and Edward Robbins (model), *(Opposite bottom left)* **Lamp** – CG model • Lizette Vega (design) and Brent Wong (model), *(Opposite bottom right)* **Clock** – CG model • Jake Parker (design) and Juan Chen (model)

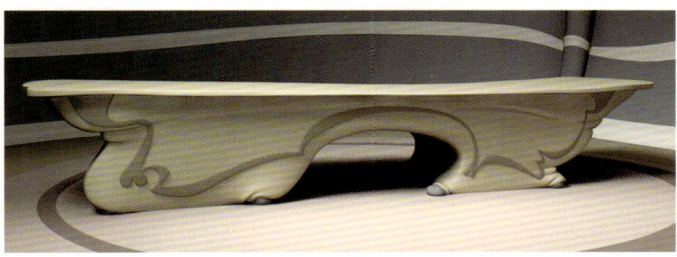

wrinkles had to be in the right place so they "made sense" structurally and graphically. Arbitrary wrinkles would break the style, and on top of that, the wrinkles had to work in three dimensions and be visualized from every angle.

"For reference we found that babies and their tight baby fat have the perfect consistency for our wrinkles," says Cardone. "But it was difficult to get that stuff into the architecture. We still have to maintain the credibility of the building or the furniture, and they can't look like they might fall over, so there's a real balance to putting different types of wrinkles where they should be."

As in true Seussian style, every object with the environment of the movie needed to be an odd shape, but it still had to feel like something you could touch in a believable environment. To achieve this, the team had to reevaluate their approach.

"As we were starting out, there was the idea that Seuss's form and shapes are very playful, so we'll have the textures be playful, and we'll have everything be playful," says Martino. But he soon discovered that this frivolous style would offer viewers little to relate to. "With these earlier explorations, your understanding had nothing to grab hold of, nothing you could connect to. If you would run into the wall, it should feel like a real wall, not like it's made out of rubber. So it was about picking and choosing some things from our reality that allow us to really 'get' this place from a scale standpoint." A turning point for the design team came when they took a 3-D render of the Mayor's house and used Photoshop to digitally paint textures over it. In it, the freeform shapes of unfamiliar architecture were matched with realistic textures like stucco and terra cotta. The uneven steps and off-kilter flowerpot might exist only in a Seuss world, but they were created from materials we could comprehend. A visit to Whoville suddenly became a much shorter commute.

DR. SEUSS' HORTON HEARS A WHO! 113

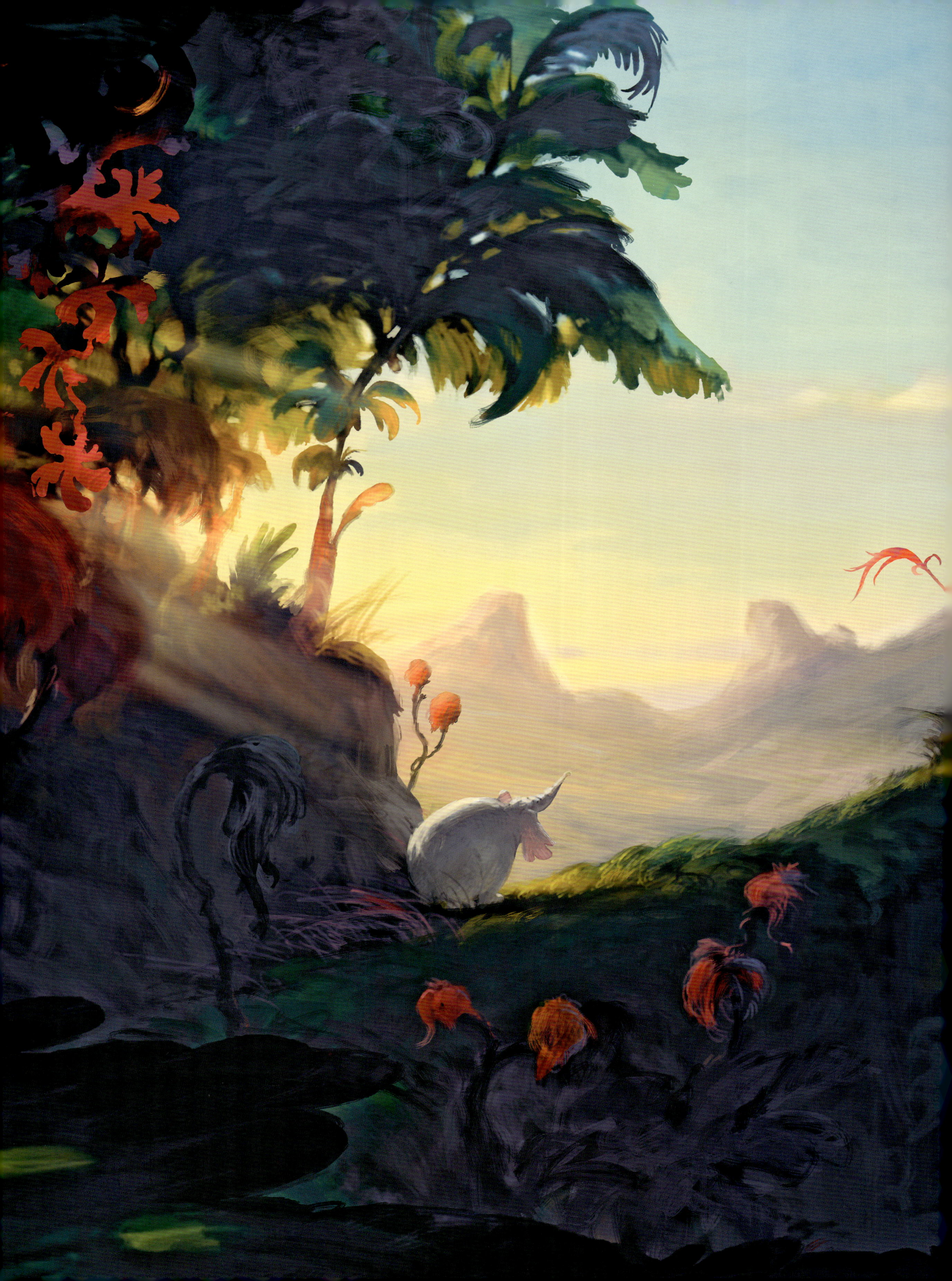

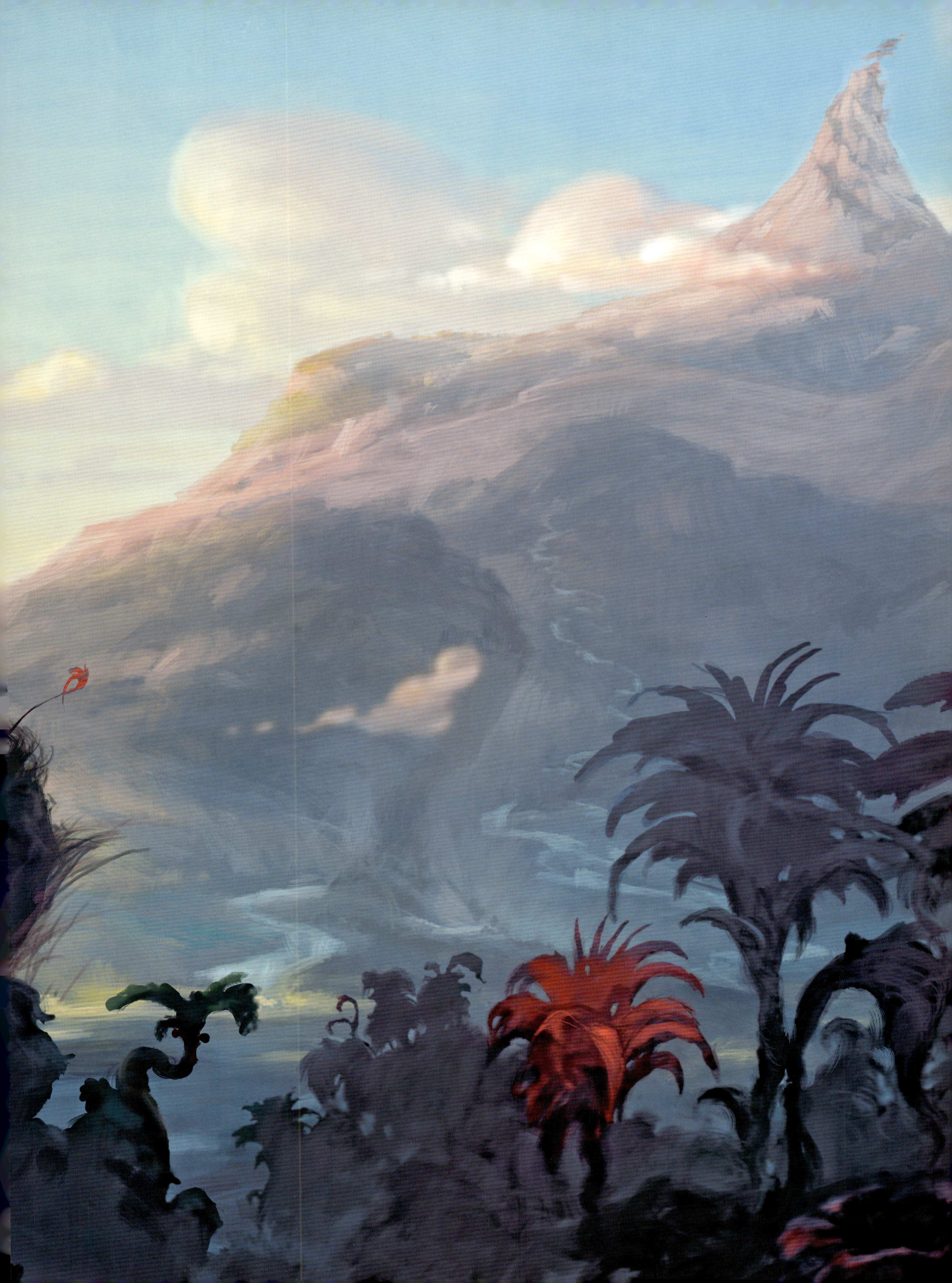

BREAKING NEW RULES

While Martino and Cardone worked with the Design team to crack the visual style, Hayward tackled the tone of the film. For that, the Animation and the Story departments started work simultaneously to figure out how the characters would be represented on screen.

"I really wanted to push the animation far," says Hayward, "and I wanted it to have the sense that the illustrations often had. I felt that the characters needed it. It wasn't squash-and-stretch in the traditional way, because that can be cheesy in CG, and I wanted to do it tastefully." To discover those boundaries, the directors attempted something never done before.

Between the design and modeling processes, models are regularly sculpted from clay or other materials to portray the character in a common pose. It gives the different CG departments a clear visualization of the character in three dimensions. On *Dr. Seuss' Horton Hears a Who!*, the leads of these various departments were called into a conference room for a meeting with the directors. In the room were a variety of sculptures covered with cloth. The

116　THE ART OF BLUE SKY STUDIOS

directors removed the cloth, and below were sculpted heads of the main characters in the most extremely squashed and stretched poses imaginable in three dimensions. The animators cheered, while the riggers stared in fright.

Constructing a realistic CG character that contorts in an anatomical way is fairly straightforward. But building one whose grinning cheeks overextend the parameters of its own head, or whose mouth opens wider than the length of its skull, is an entirely different matter. In effect, the style replicates the wildest extremes of 1940s cartoons, but instead of using pencil lines on flat paper, the artists have to manipulate geometric figures and mathematical points of intersection.

"You need a tremendous amount of control to move models like that," says Martino, "and the Rigging department has to move all the geometry around without breaking it or making it inter-penetrating. It was a huge task on their part to give animators control to move these faces into extreme poses."

The Whoville appendages were a different matter altogether. Rigging an arm that bends at the elbow is easy to do in CG. An arm that loops in a complete curve is trickier to do, and an arm that can do both on demand is the trickiest of all. In Dr. Seuss' books, the elbows are often drawn like a curve or a complete loop, and for the directors this was evocative of a very elastic animation style. But often the character needed that sharp, humanlike angle at the elbow in order to emphasize rigidity and to behave in a way that's relatable for audiences. So two sets of "Who" arm controls were built for the animators, one standard-issue arm with anatomical constraints and one that could make circular loops at the elbow. "When a character makes a point, you want firmness," says Martino, "and other times when he's very nervous, you want a flowing tube-shape. But we only wanted that to be used occasionally, as spice."

Faces and arms are far from the only character parts that change dimension in the animated world of Seuss. Entire bodies squash and stretch to the point where they go beyond anything remotely human. The Mayor had the lion's share of these odd movements between his frantic gestures and his poorly timed trip to the dentist. In some frames of animation, parts of his body were stretched three times their normal length. Once the Modeling and Rigging departments had figured out how to build these characters for animation, the next challenge was how to cover them in fur.

(Previous pages) **Horton gazes at mountain** – concept art • Kyle Macnaughton (design) and Xiangyuan Jie (painting), *(Opposite top)* **Dr. Mary Lou Larue** – character design • Jason Sadler, *(Opposite middle)* **Horton on bridge with monkeys** – concept art • Daisuke Tsutsumi, *(Opposite bottom)* **Mayor with telephone** – concept art • Daisuke Tsutsumi, *(Top right)* **Jojo** – concept art • Sang Jun Lee, *(Above)* **Jojo** – character sculpt • Sang Jun Lee (design) and Michael Defeo (sculpt), *(Right)* **Who expression sculpt** – sculpt • Sang Jun Lee (design) and Michael Defeo (sculpt)

A LOOK INSIDE BLUE SKY

Sculpting Department

TO UNDERSTAND THE DIMENSIONS of the characters, the entire team needs to be working from the same reference material. Enter the Sculpting department, tasked with translating the initial 2-D character art into tangible 3-D maquettes. The Sculpting department owes its existence to previous Blue Sky sculptors Mike Defeo, Shaun Cusick, Alex Levenson, and Andrea Blasich, who helped found and develop it, but today Vicki Saulls is the lead sculptor for every film. Her first project was *Dr. Seuss' Horton Hears a Who!,* where she had to come to grips with the extreme facial expressions of its many characters.

"We do 'expression sculpts' to know where the masses need to move," she says. "It informs the range of motion for the Rigging department, and CG modeling, and then animation. We may have a maquette in a neutral position, but if we put in all the range of motion, we may realize that its eyes need to be a little more forward, or it might need a little more mass under the cheekbones."

Every statuette begins with a designer's drawing or painting. Saulls copies the flat image by building a wire armature from clay (allowing soft parts that can be tweaked) or Magic Sculp epoxy (for sections of the sculpt that must harden quickly, like teeth, or a limb that supports weight). In the past, studio sculptors drew a grid on the maquette and digitally registered each intersection with a handheld "plotter." Nowadays Saulls simply places the sculpture on a NextEngine 3-D laser scanner.

"A lot of times in a sketch the perspective might be off," she says, "so in a sculpt you have to make sure all the proportions work out to be correct. That's something we work out dimensionally in clay before it goes into production."

At that point Saulls has to rely on her acute grasp of anatomy to understand what's happening in the character's skeleton and musculature. "I never learned caricature," she adds. "I just interpret drawings. So I guess I'm a pretty good replicator."

118   THE ART OF BLUE SKY STUDIOS

(Opposite top) **Mayor stretch expression** – character design • Sang Jun Lee
(Opposite left) **Whoville Mayor** – character sculpt • Sang Jun Lee (design) and Michael Defeo (sculpt)
(Opposite center) **Whoville council chairman** – character sculpt • Robert MacKenzie (design) and Vicki Saulls (sculpt)
(Opposite right) **Whoville council member** – character sculpt • Robert MacKenzie (design) and Michael Defeo (sculpt)
(Above) **Mayor stretch expression** – character sculpt • Sang Jun Lee (design) and Michael Defeo (sculpt)

DR. SEUSS' HORTON HEARS A WHO! 119

HAIR TECHNOLOGY

Blue Sky had redeveloped hair technology for *Ice Age: The Meltdown*, but for *Dr. Seuss' Horton Hears a Who!*, characters needed to stretch like pieces of used bubblegum, sometimes two or three times their normal length. When a model stretched to that extreme, the hair material on its surface was stretched too thin, and patches of the model's surface began to show through between the hairs.

"One of the difficulties with stretching the arm," says Hayward, "is that the hair's going to separate." The fur was groomed in layers so that when the character is stretched to the extreme, it looks just as lush as when he is at rest. "Between the Fur and Lighting departments, they really nailed it," continues Hayward.

The fur on all the Whos was very carefully groomed. Preproduction sketches depict proud Whos sporting their fashionable fur, trimmed and dyed to resemble ornate vestments. There are no clothing outlets in Whoville, just very talented hairdressers.

(Top left) **Katie** – character design • Jason Sadler, *(Top center)* **Fur hat** – concept art • Dave Catrow, *(Top right)* **Who baby carriage** – concept drawing • Dave Catrow, *(Bottom left)* **Jojo** – fur and hair • Sheldon Chow, *(Bottom center)* **Katie** – fur • Jamie Williams, *(Bottom right)* **Mayor** – fur • Jamie Williams

120   THE ART OF BLUE SKY STUDIOS

DR. SEUSS' HORTON HEARS A WHO!

(Top) **Female Whos** – character concepts • Jason Sadler (design) and Robert MacKenzie (painting), *(Bottom)* **Various Who illustrations** – concept art • Dave Catrow

122 THE ART OF BLUE SKY STUDIOS

DR. SEUSS' HORTON HEARS A WHO! 123

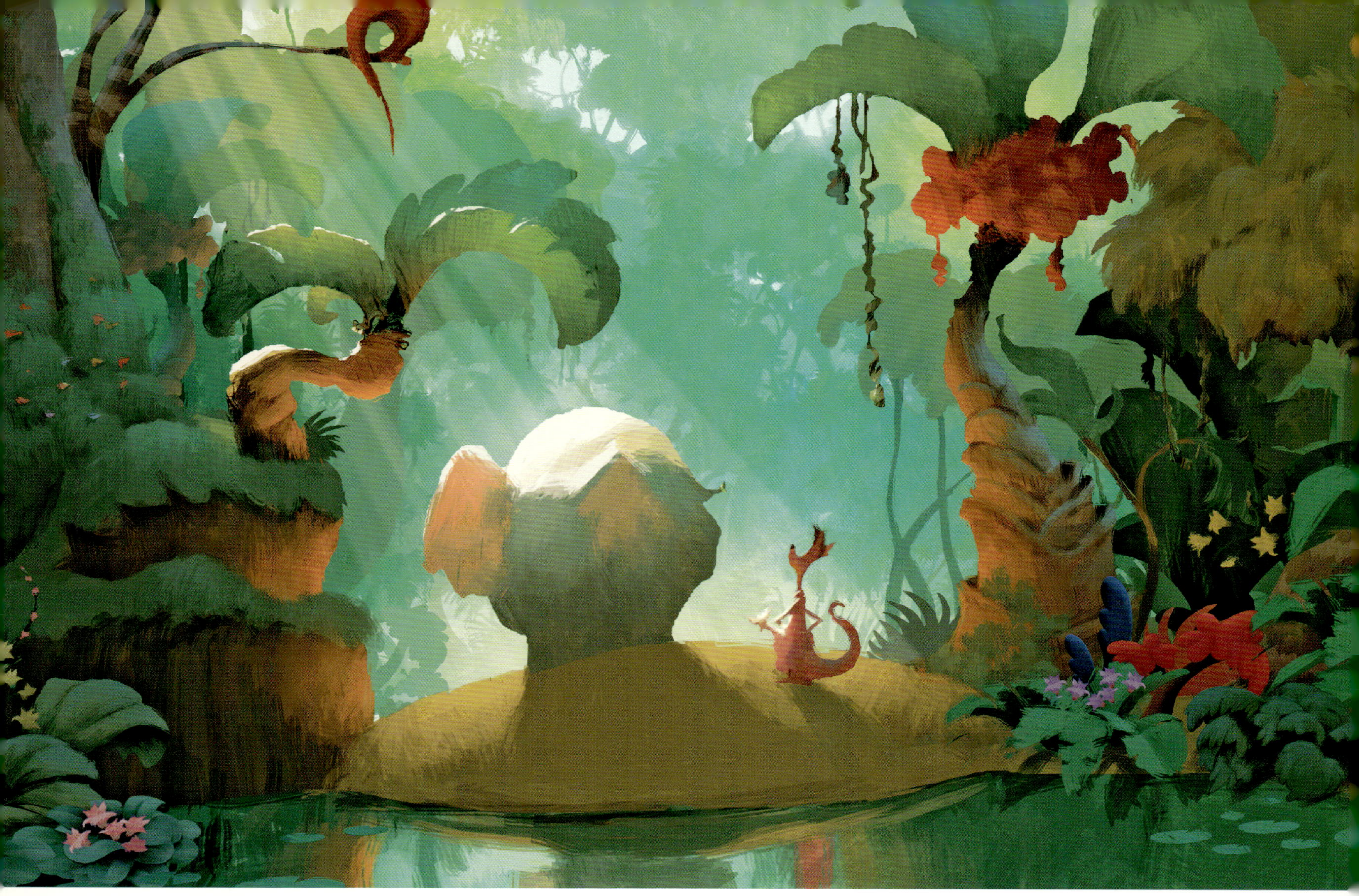

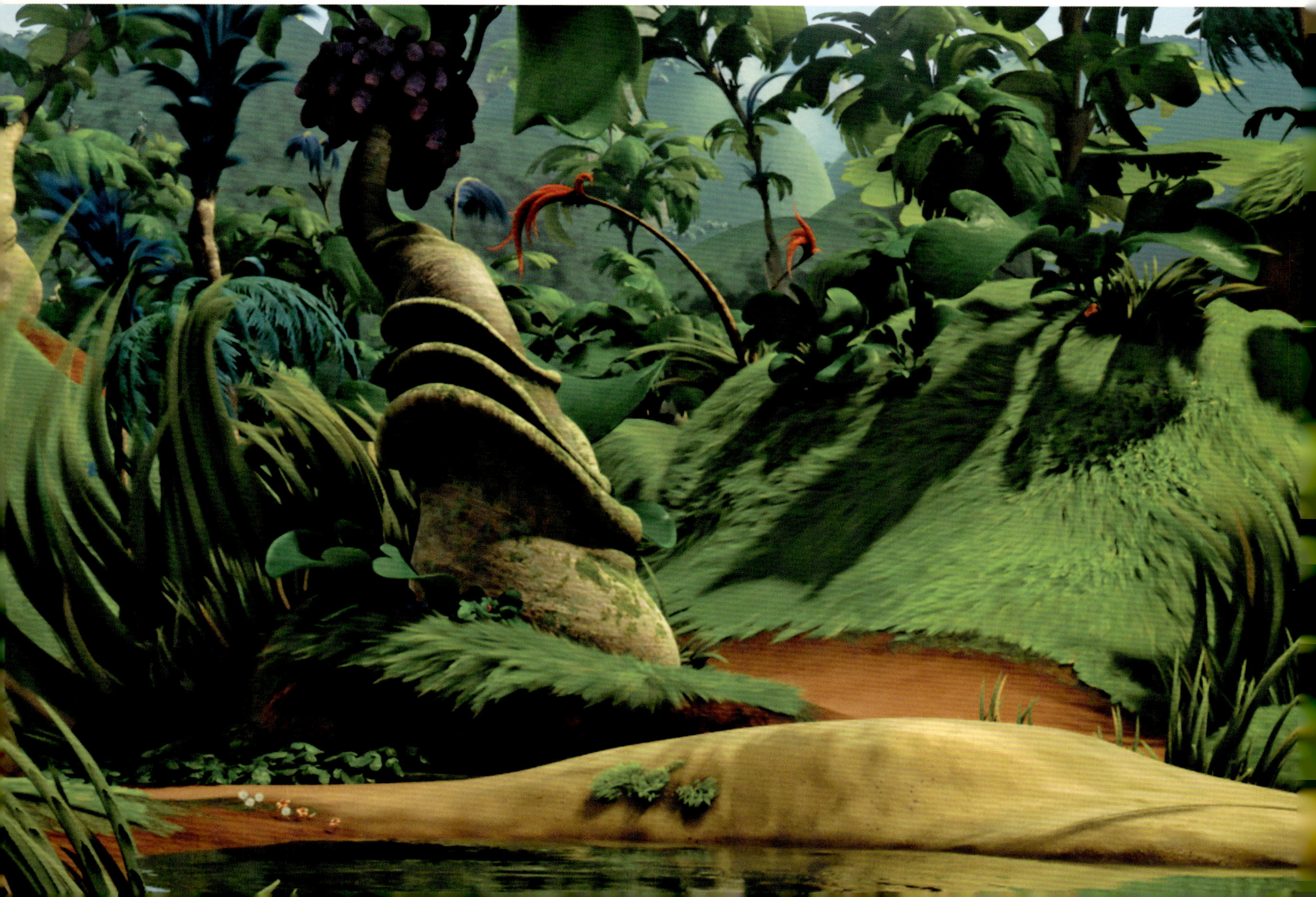

But fur plays an important part beyond the fuzzy characters. Dr. Seuss's original drawings of the Jungle of Nool depict foliage that is soft and inviting, even down to his illustration of the all-important clover. Cardone and his team designed foliage that echoes those classic drawings. He found that replacing jungle grass with green fur looked more appropriate, "but we still had to change the size of the blades, make it look softer here and there, and add clumps and variation to it." Like everything Seuss, Cardone made sure the fur was in line with the original pen style: "There was a flow and rhythm to it, just like the way he drew." Even the red clover in the movie is a patch of carefully groomed CG fur on a stem.

(Left top) **Horton and Kangaroo in jungle** – concept art • Greg Couch (design) and Daisuke Tsutsumi (painting), (Above) **Environments (two images)** – color keys • Richard Vander Wende, (Left) **Nool environment** – final rendered set, (Below) **Nool trees** – concept art • Kyle Macnaughton

DR. SEUSS' HORTON HEARS A WHO! 125

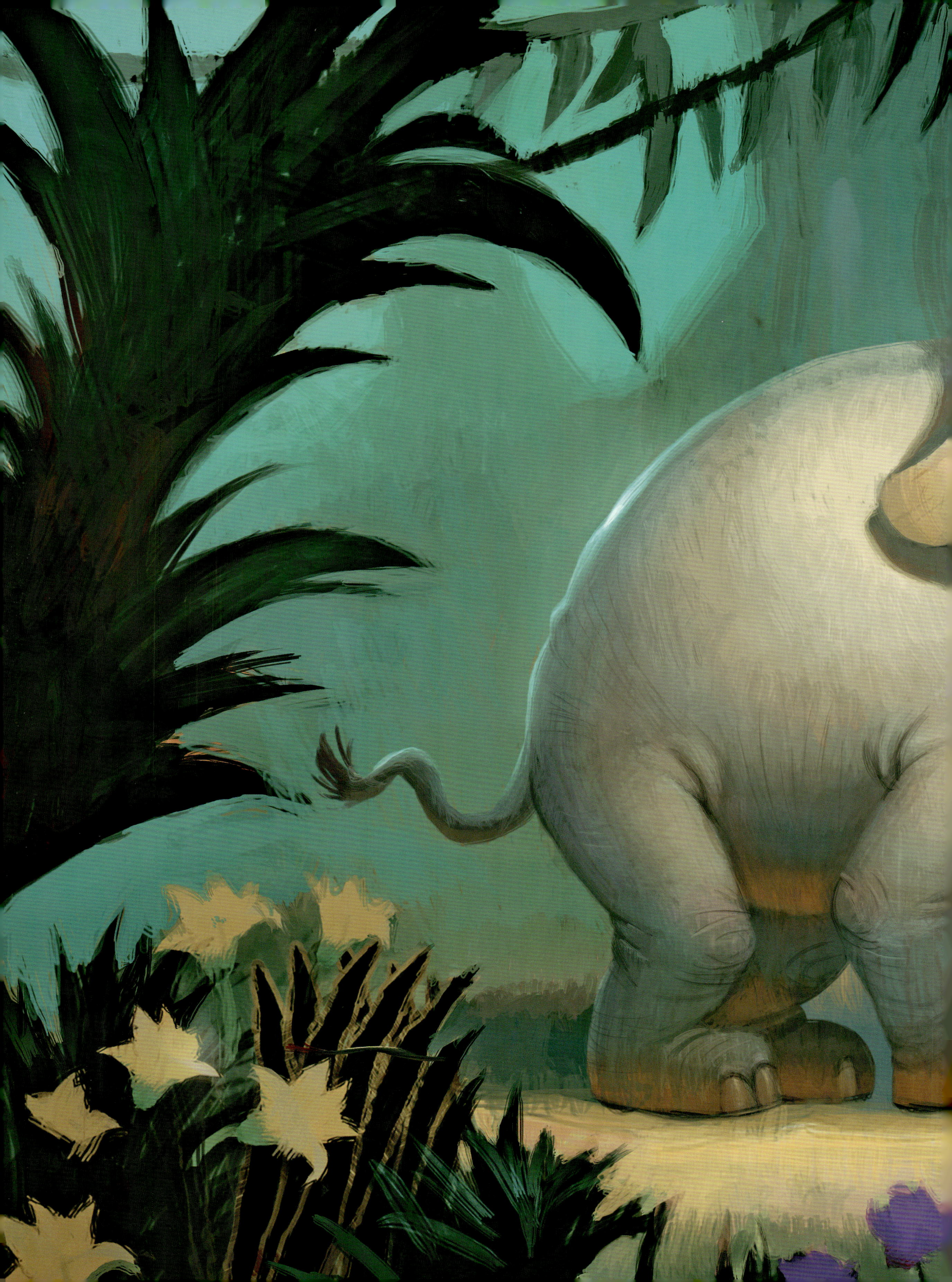

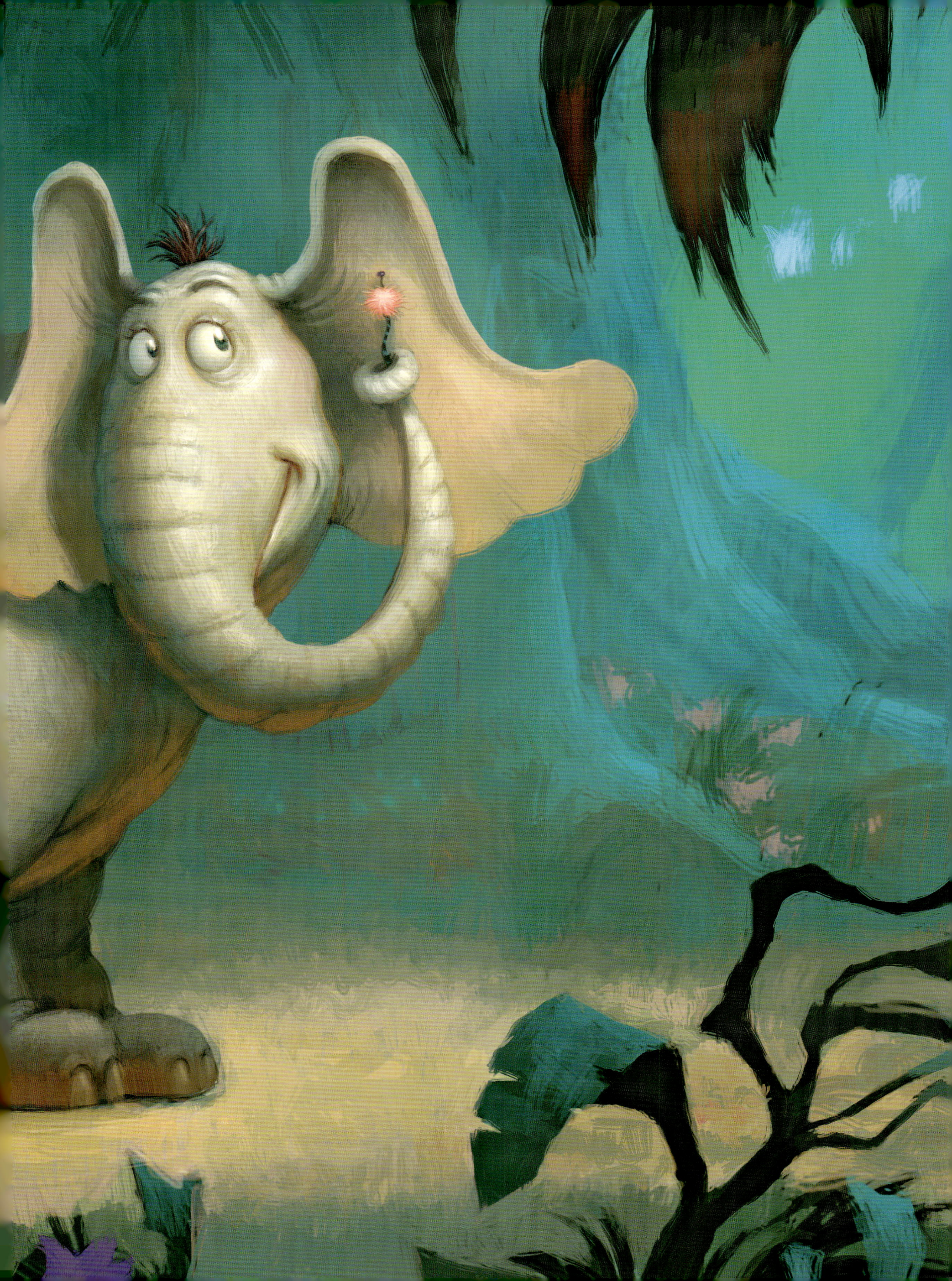

LOOKING THROUGH SEUSS-COLORED GLASSES

Whoville and the Jungle of Nool seen in the movie are accurate evocations of the color scheme from Seuss's original illustrations. "We used a very limited palette like the colors in the book," says Cardone, "and we stuck to that as much as we could. So even though the film was dimensional and had a reality to it, there's still that link to the source material."

Horton himself is the only gray animal in a world of colorful creatures and plants. The hot pink of Horton's clover stands out in the film, being the only object designated that striking hue. Tensions come to a climax when Vlad the Vulture snatches the clover from Horton and soars over a cliff with it, dropping it moments later into a vast field of pink clovers.

"When I was a little kid reading this book," says Hayward, "I'd look at that picture of Horton chasing Vlad up the mountain, and I'd flip the page to the massive clover field, and I'd gasp, 'Oh my God! How is he ever going to find it?' I wanted audiences to feel that way."

"We planned the color of the whole film based on the time of day, staging, and the emotion we were trying to communicate in

128 THE ART OF BLUE SKY STUDIOS

support of the story," says Cardone. "For example, for the couple of minutes Horton gallops up the mountain, we drained all the red from the environment. There is only a cool palette of greens and blues. When the camera reveals the endless field of pink, the impact of that complementary color hits us all the stronger."

"Horton comes to the edge of that cliff and the camera wheels around to reveal this pink field of clovers, and all of those clovers are actual animated models."

When Horton sees the endless field of clovers, there are no matte paintings. Every one of those millions of clovers is a real CG model, with its little red tuft blowing in the animated wind. As a result, each single frame of film for the scene took three arduous days to render— an impressive show of dedication to Dr. Seuss's original book.

(Previous pages) **Horton listens to clover** – concept art • Daisuke Tsutsumi (design) and Peter Nguyen (painting), *(Top)* **Horton overlooks sea of clovers** – concept art • Daisuke Tsutsumi, *(Left)* **Horton holds clover** – final frame, *(Right)* **Clover** – final digital art

FILLING IN THE GAPS

While the parts of the script derived directly from the book were immediately iconic, the filmmakers also had to make creative choices to flesh out the characters and story. The Mayor in Seuss's original book was a very small role and had to be expanded into a lead part for the film. "Our goal was to fill in the pages of the book," says Martino, "not to rewrite the story. But you've got to get into the Mayor's perspective: He's talking to an elephant in the sky. And to be the only one having that communication creates a tremendous conflict."

As a result, the Mayor was developed with the typical traits of a politician—panicked about his position in the community and terrified about his mayoral legacy. "Plus," adds Martino, "we had a character in him who was very nervous and hyperactive. We thought that would be a great way to convey his personality, and it seemed to fit with what we see in Dr. Seuss's drawing style."

(Right) **Mayor of Whoville** – concept art • Sang Jun Lee, *(Below)* **Mayor at work** – concept art • Rafael Zentil

130   THE ART OF BLUE SKY STUDIOS

DR. SEUSS' HORTON HEARS A WHO! 131

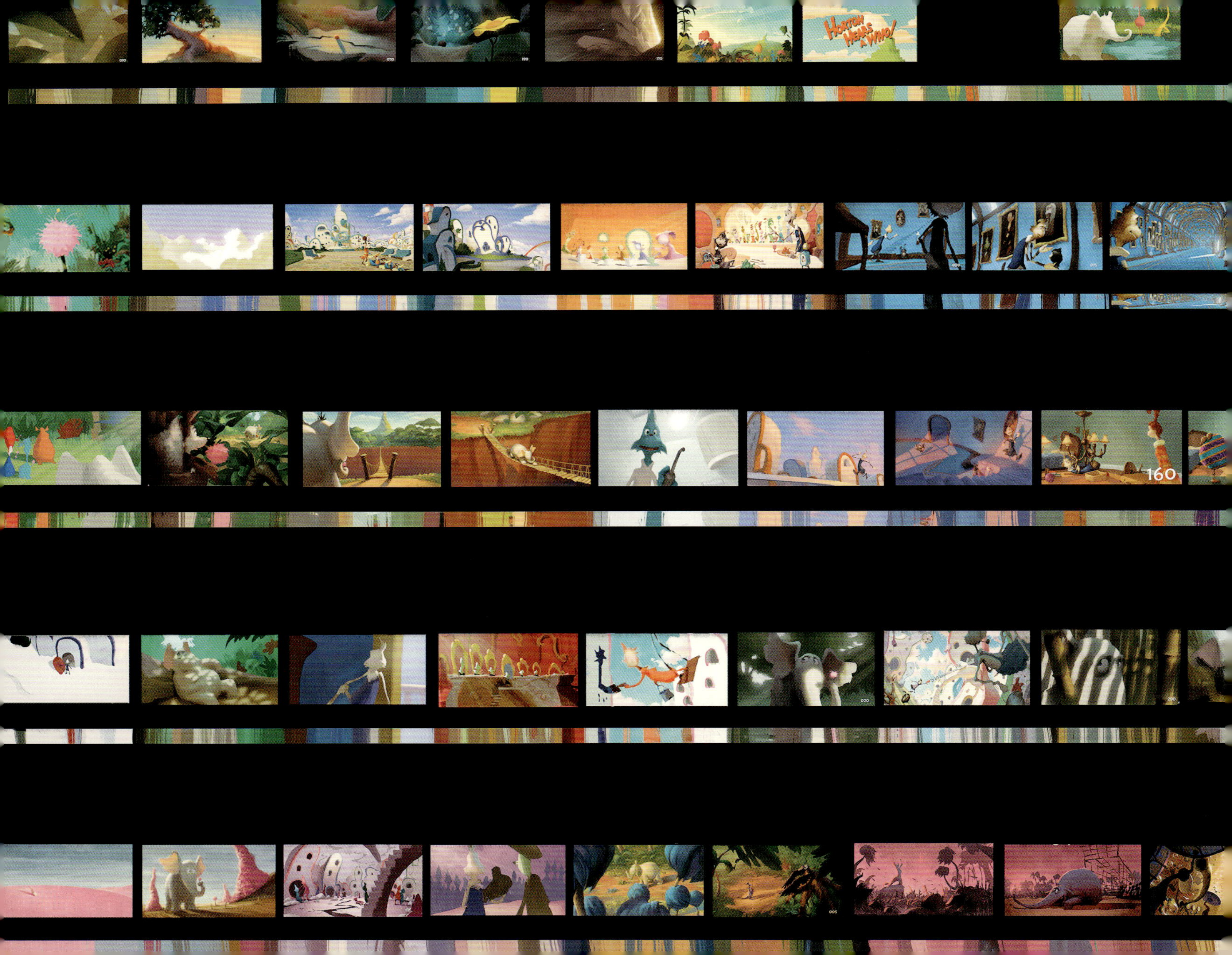
HORTON HEARS A WHO!
160

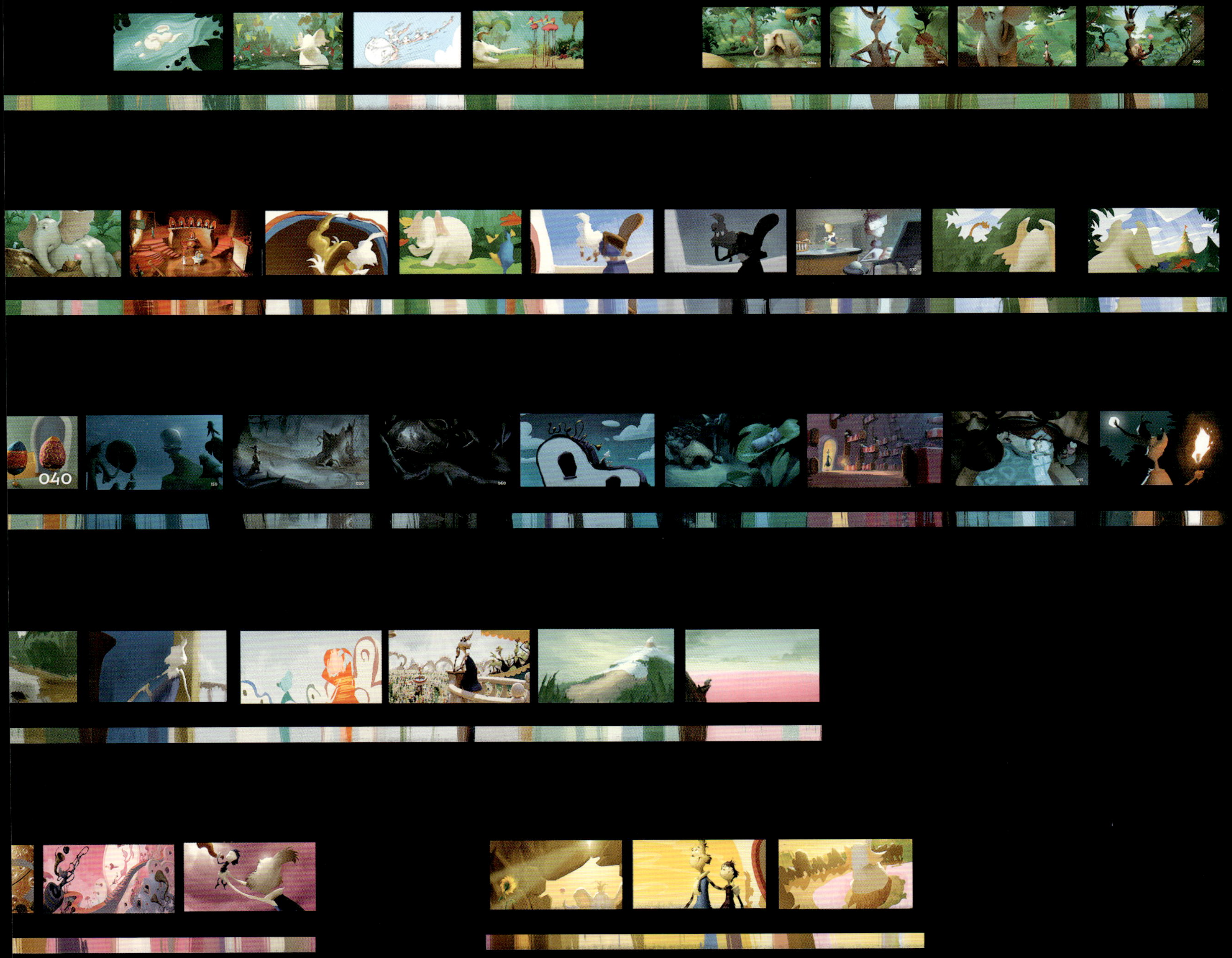
040

THE VOICES OF REASON

In contrast to the Mayor's personality and his overall character arc, Horton is a playful, kindhearted character with a staid goal all the way through the film. He does not grow or change over the course of the story, but every character who interacts with him does. Horton needed a voice that manifested that personality.

"We went to Jim Carrey as our first choice because of the sweet, polite character Horton is," says Hayward. "I wanted Jim to use his own voice, like when he plays Lloyd Christmas in *Dumb and Dumber*. That's a guy who looks at the world in a beautiful way and sees the good in everything. Jim's innocent sense of comedy is brilliant, and having Jim using his regular voice for the character was a home run."

Steve Carell was also the first choice for the voice of the Mayor, a character as misunderstood as Horton. Each has a secret they can't share with anybody in their own worlds, and the moment they try, they put themselves at personal risk.

"Steve Carell is one of the best actors for putting that kind of humanity into a voice," says Martino. "Little things he does—a stutter or a pause in his vocal delivery—add that kind of depth to the character."

(Previous pages) **Dr. Seuss' Horton Hears a Who! color script** • Daisuke Tsutsumi, *(Top)* **Smiling Horton** – concept art • Sang Jun Lee (design) and Robert MacKenzie (painting), *(Left)* **Horton with clover** – character sculpt • Sang Jun Lee (design) and Michael Defeo (sculpt), *(Opposite)* **Horton on rope bridge** – storyboard panels • Eric Favela

THE ART OF BLUE SKY STUDIOS

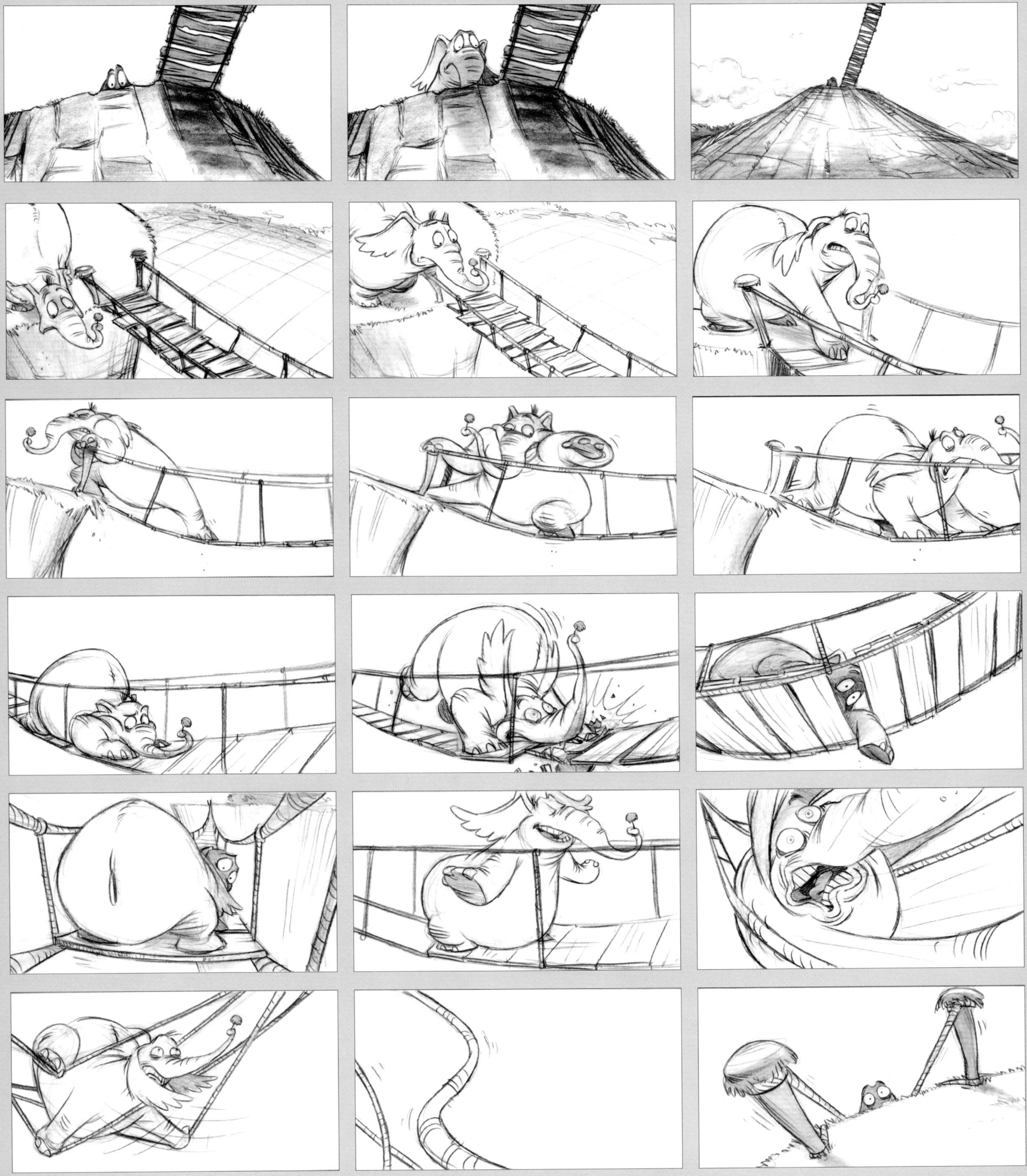

(Above) **Horton cannonball dive** – concept art • Jeff Biancalana (storyboard) and Andrew Leung (painting)

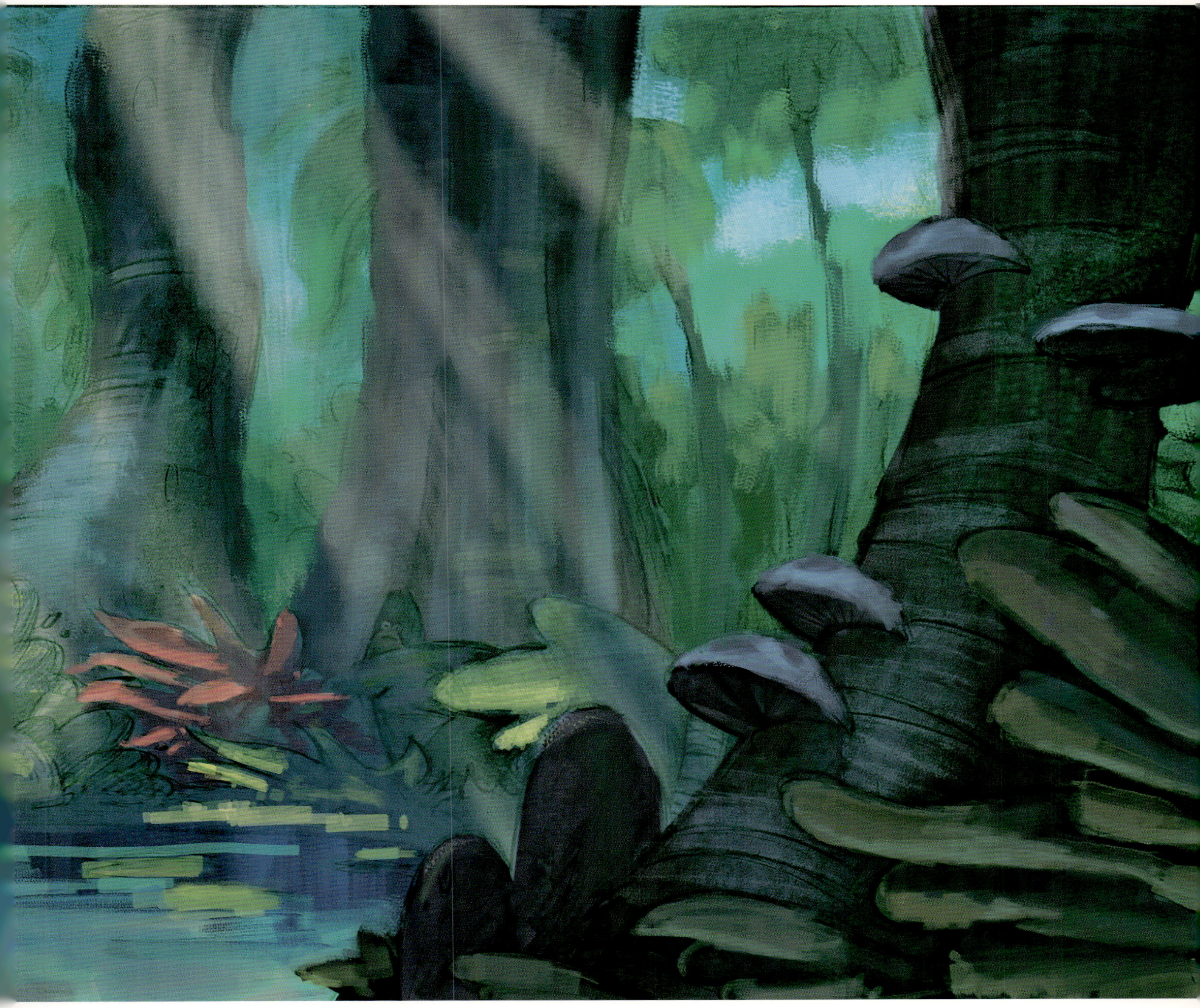

LIFE LESSONS

Together, the natural progression of the characters and the growing risk they face lead to the overriding theme of the book: A person's a person, no matter how small. The mantra is as meaningful today in a world of CG animation as it was when the book was written. In the movie, the lesson is extended to the kangaroo family as well as the Mayor's disaffected son, JoJo. It is lonely, ignored JoJo who adds the final "Yop!" that saves both Horton and Whoville from destruction.

"When I was a kid, my dad always wanted me to be like him and be into municipal politics," says Hayward. "He wanted me to go to law school, and I wanted to play in punk bands and make movies. I just naturally plugged that in the story between the Mayor and JoJo. I made JoJo a little emo dude, with his hair in his face, and he went off to a secret place and made music. None of that's in the book, but it's something very familiar to me. This kid's trying to get away from his parents, who don't understand him, and he ends up saving the world through his music."

Father and son finally come together in a powerful climax, having both experienced the same sort of rejection before finally being accepted. "It all comes back to that Seuss message," adds Hayward. "Be exactly who you are, and that's who you're supposed to be."

Dr. Seuss' Horton Hears a Who was released on March 14, 2008, to high critical praise. The varied characters and settings had pushed the studio's technology beyond expectations. Next they would return to the characters who made the studio famous and pit them against the most complicated villains and environments they had yet encountered.

(Top) **Mayor holding Jojo** – concept art • Daisuke Tsutsumi, (Opposite top) **Jojo with experiment and Jojo with plate** – concept art • Sang Jun Lee, (Bottom) **Mayor and Jojo at table** – concept art • Daisuke Tsutsumi

DR. SEUSS' HORTON HEARS A WHO! 139

(Above) **Mayor and Jojo in living room** – concept art • Sang Jun Lee

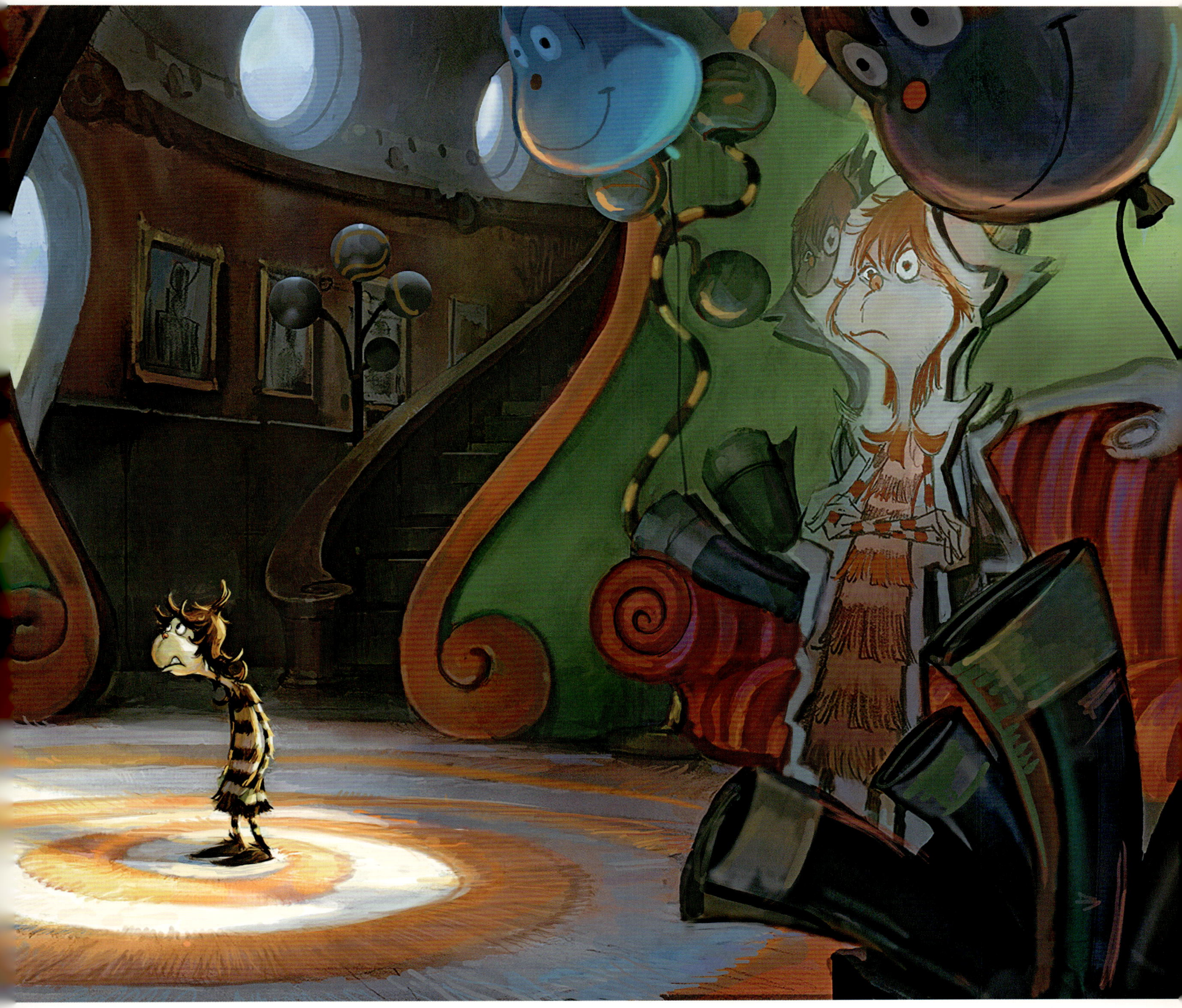

BLUE SKY SHORTS
Surviving Sid (2008)

THE ICE AGE SLOTH (as well as actor John Leguizamo) returns for a stint as a camp counselor to a group of wiseacre children. Karen Disher and Galen Chu both directed this mini-adventure; Disher came from the storyboard department while Chu came from animation.

Chu tried to stay loyal to the characters that he had previously worked with: "I had animated a lot of footage of Sid before, so most of my approach was bringing over that sensibility and that familiarity with how to pose and animate the character and his expressions and mannerisms. We tried to bring our feature sensibility into the short."

"Sid's really fun to direct," says Disher, "because he's the cartooniest of them all. Scrat, too. You can get really physical with them, you can beat them up, have them stomped on or abused, and it's funny to watch. That's why we love cartoons, because we know they're not getting hurt. It's the core of our whole hundred-year-old medium." Scrat makes a cameo appearance, too, voiced as always by cofounder Chris Wedge.

This was Disher and Chu's directorial debut and paved the way for their more prominent roles in subsequent Blue Sky projects.

Surviving Sid was included on the *Dr. Seuss' Horton Hears a Who!* DVD.

(Top and right) **Sid's leaf hat** – concept art • Nash Dunnigan, *(Bottom)* **Sid and kids with campfire** – color key • Vincent Di Nguyen

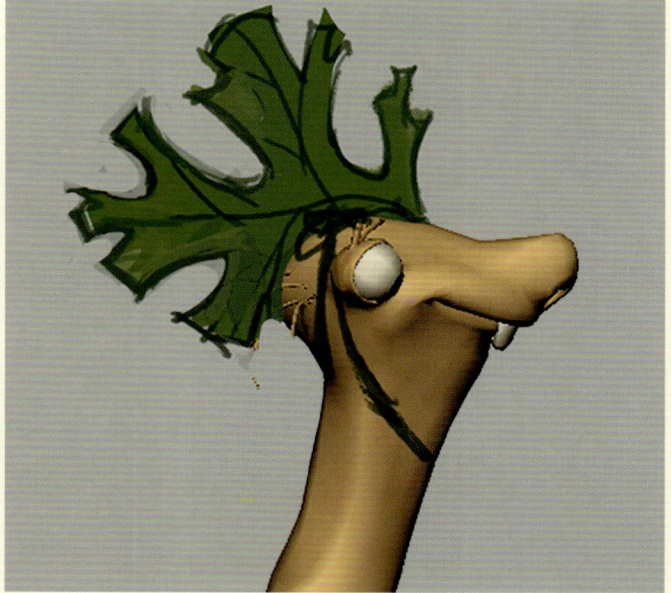

(Above) **Grand Canyon** – color key • Vincent Di Nguyen
(Right) **Camper kids** – color key • Vincent Di Nguyen
(Below) **View of set with coordinates** – environment concept • Nash Dunnigan

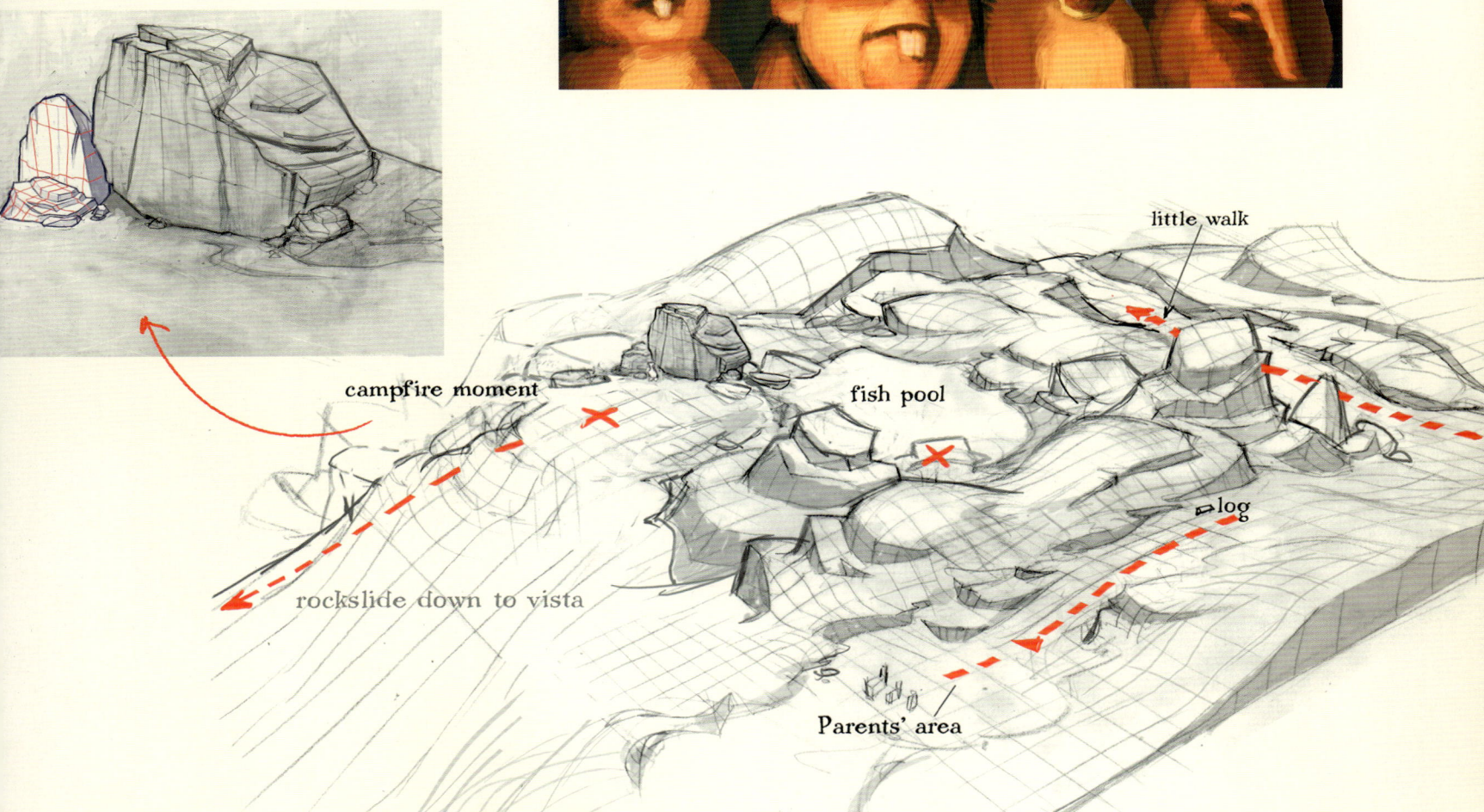

little walk

campfire moment

fish pool

log

rockslide down to vista

Parents' area

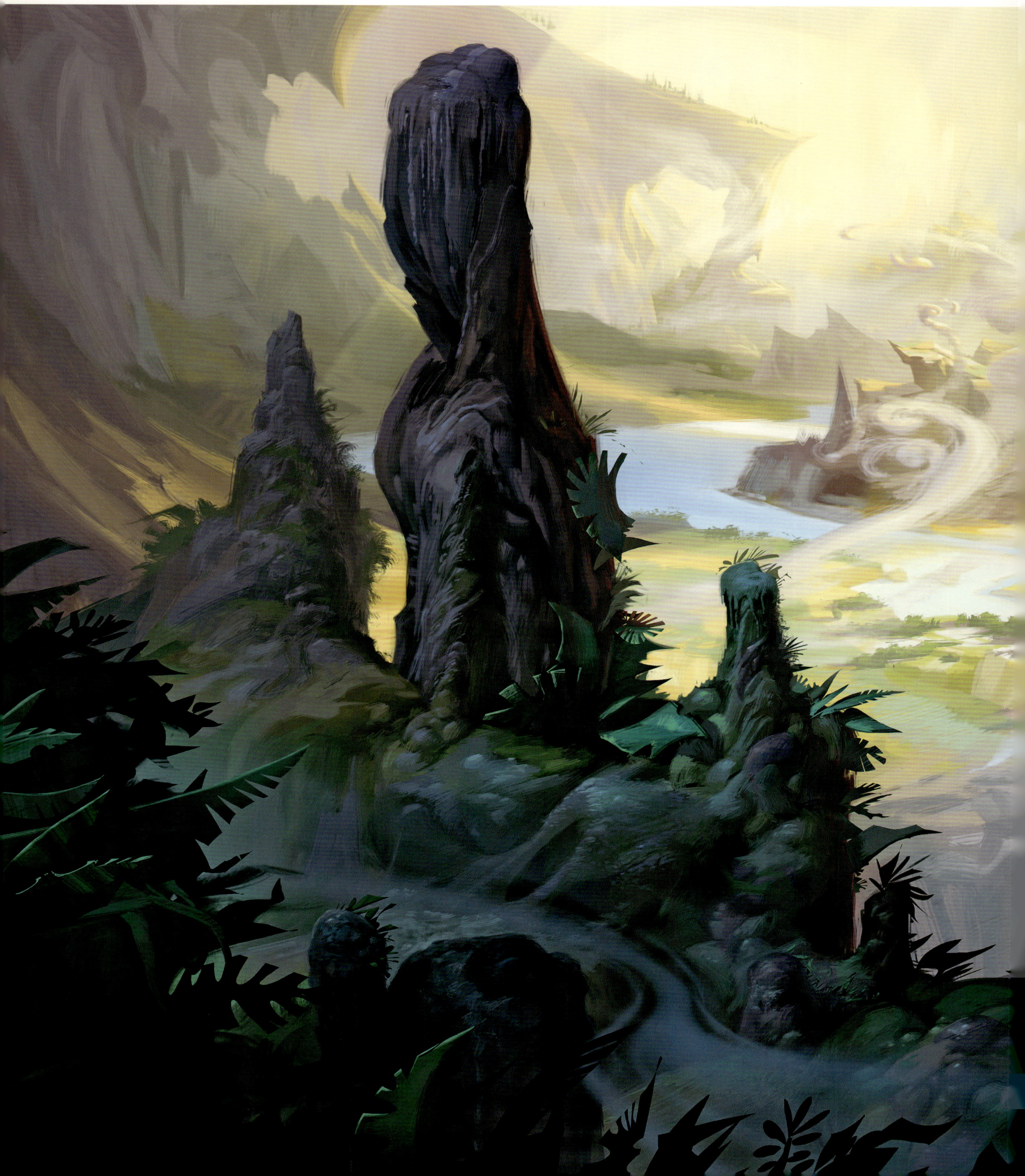

CHAPTER 5 · *Ice Age: Dawn of the Dinosaurs*

"Now then, eyes forward, back straight . . . oh, and breathe in the toxic fumes and you'll probably die."

—BUCK

Green is not a color one associates with either the Ice Age era or the *Ice Age* movies. Usually the backdrop is as stark as a snowflake, with some pine trees thrown in for good measure. In the third installment of the series, our prehistoric protagonists travel to a lost jungle with an entirely new cast of villains—creatures who have to move and behave in a very un-mammal-like way.

Dinosaurs don't move like mammoths, tigers, or any other creatures Blue Sky had previously animated. What's more, their tropical home—an entirely new scenario for our characters—needed to feel like part of the *Ice Age* universe. While these new elements would give *Ice Age: Dawn of the Dinosaurs* a new look and feel, the returning characters' personalities still had to be consistent. Any break from continuity, artistically or dramatically, would make for an unconvincing movie. The filmmakers were obliged to honor the designs and storytelling that made *Ice Age* so popular. They just needed to figure out how.

GROWING BIGGER

Carlos Saldanha had cut his teeth codirecting the first *Ice Age* and *Robots* under Chris Wedge before going on to direct *Ice Age: The Meltdown* solo. For *Ice Age: Dawn of the Dinosaurs*, Saldanha was enlisted to direct again.

The film went into production during a pivotal time at the studio. "Blue Sky started getting more complex," remembers Saldanha. "Suddenly we had about three hundred people and many projects going on at once, and it was the first time we really started to see Blue Sky as a multipicture production house. There were several groups of teams working on projects, and so the studio started to open up."

(Previous pages) **The Lost World** – concept art • Peter Clarke & Jon Townley (design) and Michael Lee (painting), *(Top)* **Buck with knife** – character sketch • Peter de Sève, *(Opposite)* **Group surrounded by dinos** – concept art • Peter de Sève (character design) and Xiangyuan Jie (painting)

146   THE ART OF BLUE SKY STUDIOS

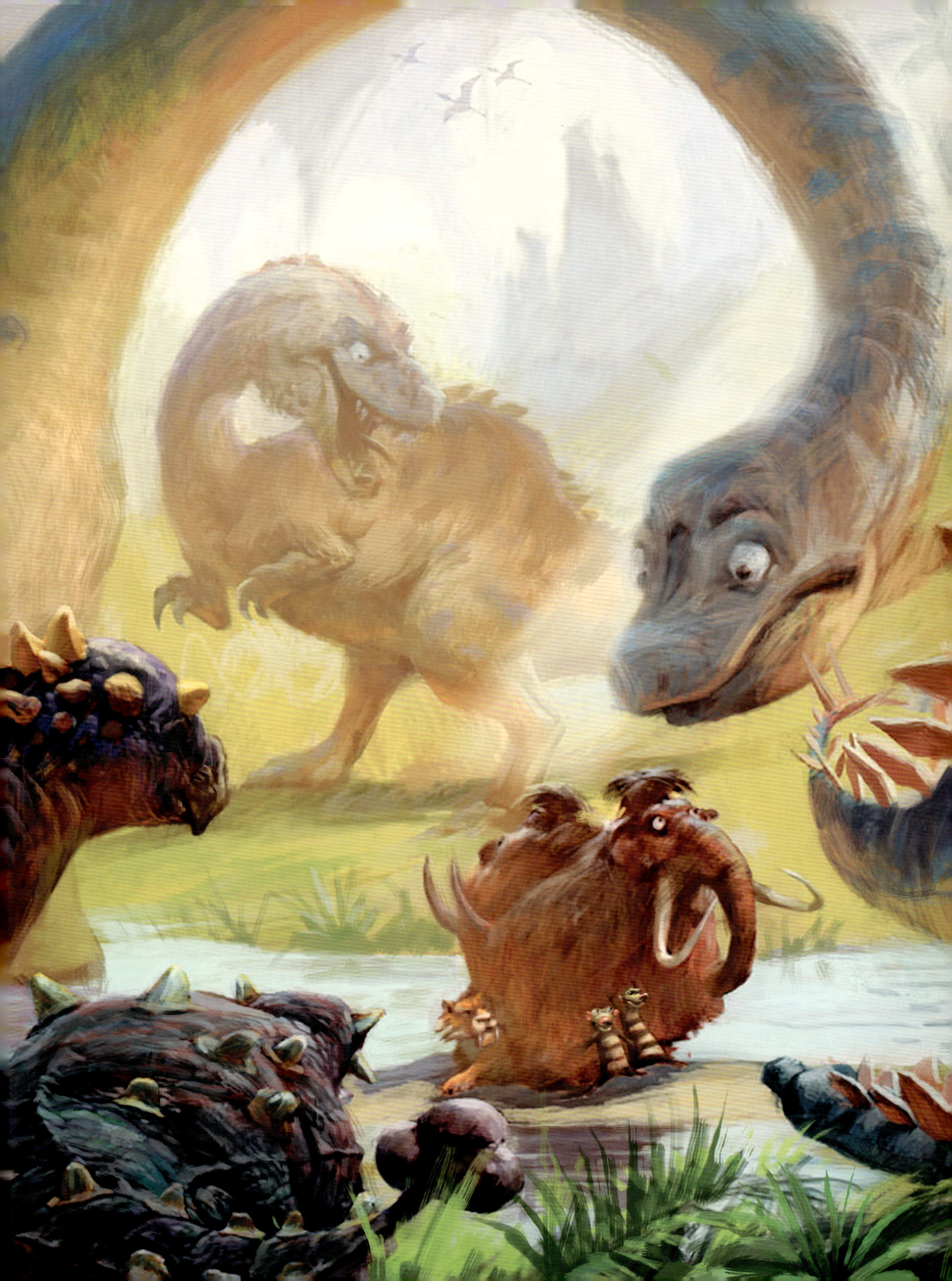

As Blue Sky looked to foster its talent pool, Michael Knapp was promoted to the role of art director on *Ice Age: Dawn of the Dinosaurs*. Before Blue Sky, Knapp had been a freelance illustrator in Pittsburgh and had recently moved to New York. He began working remotely for Bill Joyce, creating designs for a proposed animated short that would become *Rise of the Guardians*. Joyce liked his work and connected him to Wedge, who hired Knapp as a designer for the Wedge/Joyce collaboration *Robots*. He worked as a set designer and visual developer in varying capacities on subsequent Blue Sky features, until art directing the 2006 short *No Time for Nuts*.

Saldanha and Knapp began to shape *Ice Age: Dawn of the Dinosaurs*' unique look while being careful to stay true to the property's visual tone. The third *Ice Age* feature is set in its regular icy tundra for only the initial third of the story. It's an environment that is relatively easy to build in CG, and its pale backdrop makes the characters highly recognizable. However, once the gang reaches the underground dinosaur jungle and its overgrown topography, we have our first glance of them in an entirely lush setting. To the viewer, the jungle world is as breathtaking as anything the ice age had to offer, although the trick was to keep it consistent.

Knapp and his team of artists had the task of designing this new world in the original style developed by Peter Clarke. Clarke, who was the key environmental designer for the first movie, also contributed some preproduction drawings for this third installment. "The look has become a little more organic over the years," says Knapp, "but great sweeping planes and dynamic shapes are still the visual foundation."

It was Knapp's task to adapt a jungle scenario into the simple graphic shapes that belong in the *Ice Age* universe—a style that was initially established partially due to the studio's limited resources.

"It was a huge challenge," says Saldanha, "even more than *Ice Age: The Meltdown*, because it was bigger. We're talking about a world of dinosaurs. It's a subject that's been done a lot in CG, and we wanted to be funny, unique, and different."

Our heroes' quest is to rescue a kidnapped Sid, protect the pregnant Ellie, and help Buck—a survivalist weasel with a few loose screws—conquer his own personal Moby Dick in the form of Rudy, an albino *Baryonyx*. New dangers lurk behind every overgrown shrub, and the herd needs to work together if they're going to get out of this Lost World in one piece.

SAME STYLE, NEW TWIST

Some of these new dangers included towering cliffs, carnivorous plants, and toxic chasms, but this jungle world is also peppered with rocks, stumps, cracks, and land formations that echo the familiar *Ice Age* style. "We're trying to be faithful to the established shape language, while making it lush," says Knapp. "There's still a minimalist element to it, but the rhythm and frequency of the shapes became a more important factor."

It was essential to Saldanha to maintain this style, even though his attention was being divided. He carried the directing heft for the first

(Above) **Leaving cave** – concept art • Michael Knapp, *(Opposite top)* **Animal homes** – concept art • Clayton Stillwell, *(Opposite bottom)* **Lost World at night** – concept art • Peter Clarke (design) and Xiangyuan Jie (painting)

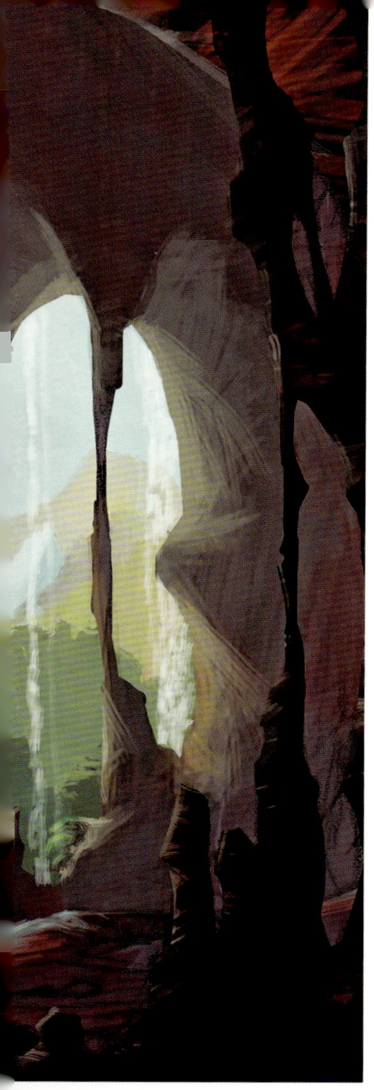
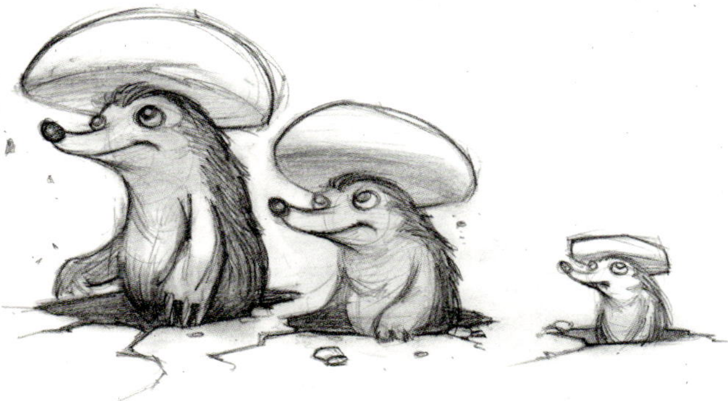
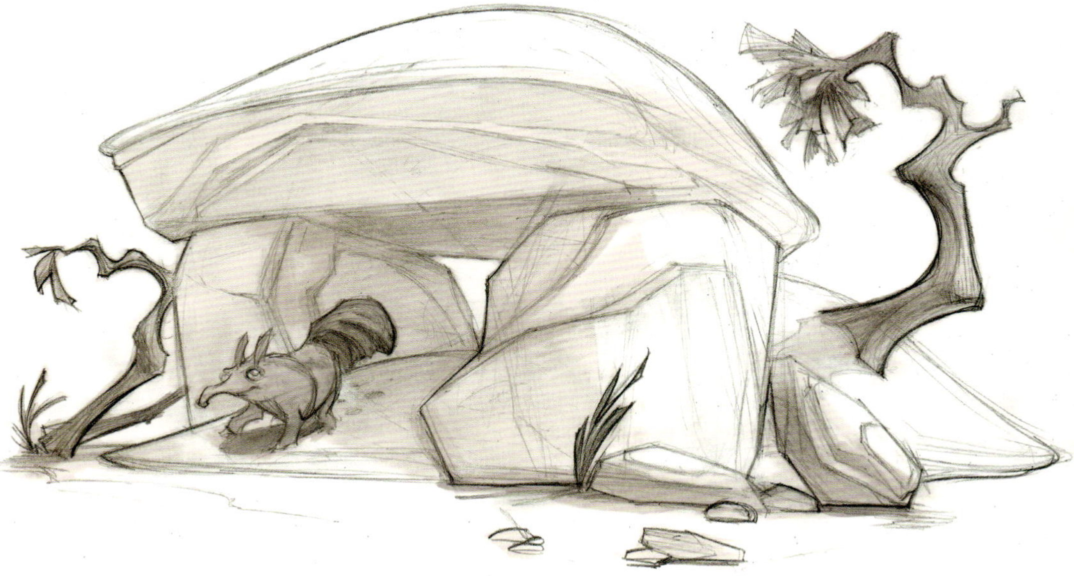
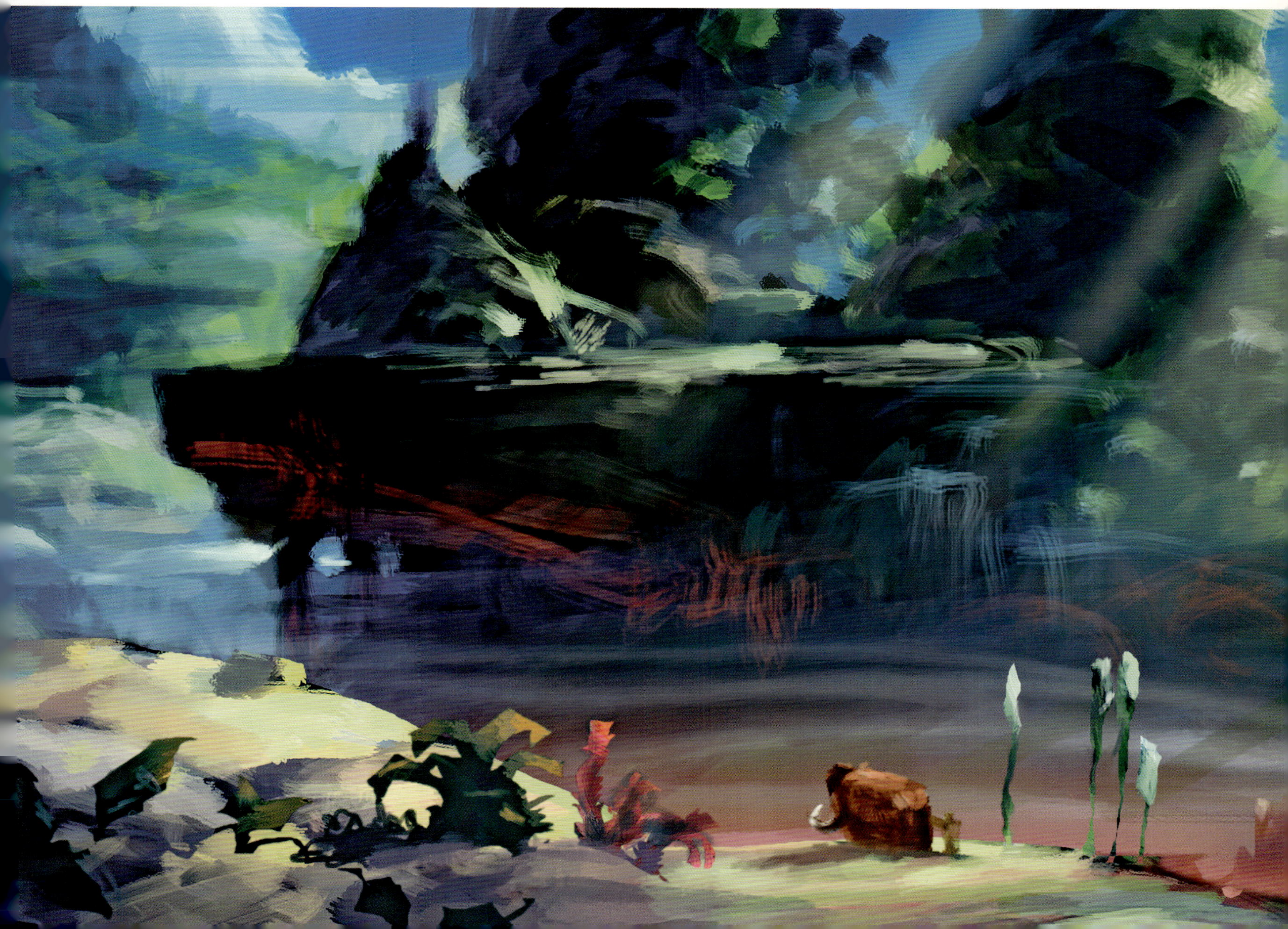

(Above) **Ellie with animals along for ride** – concept art • Michael Knapp

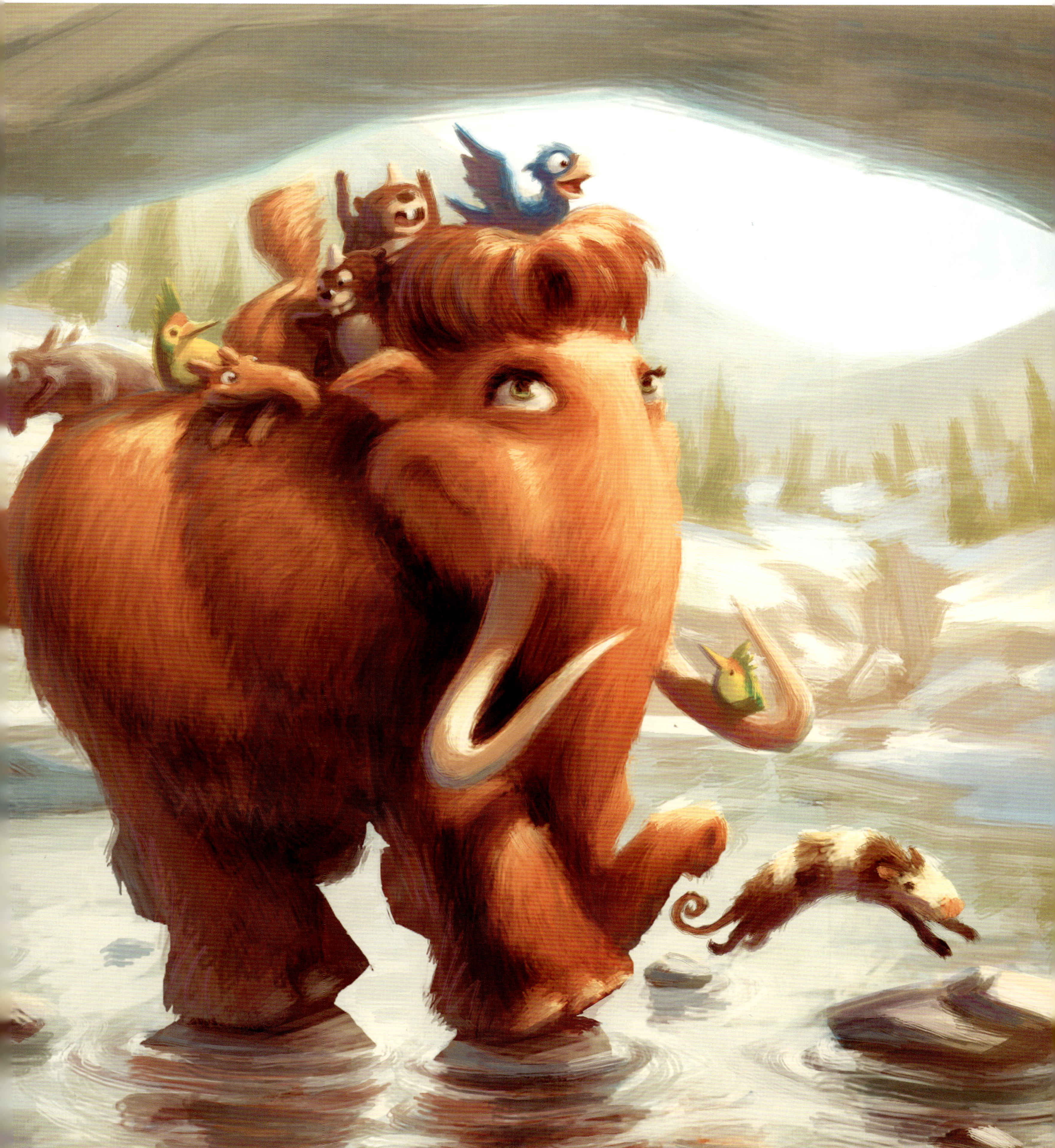

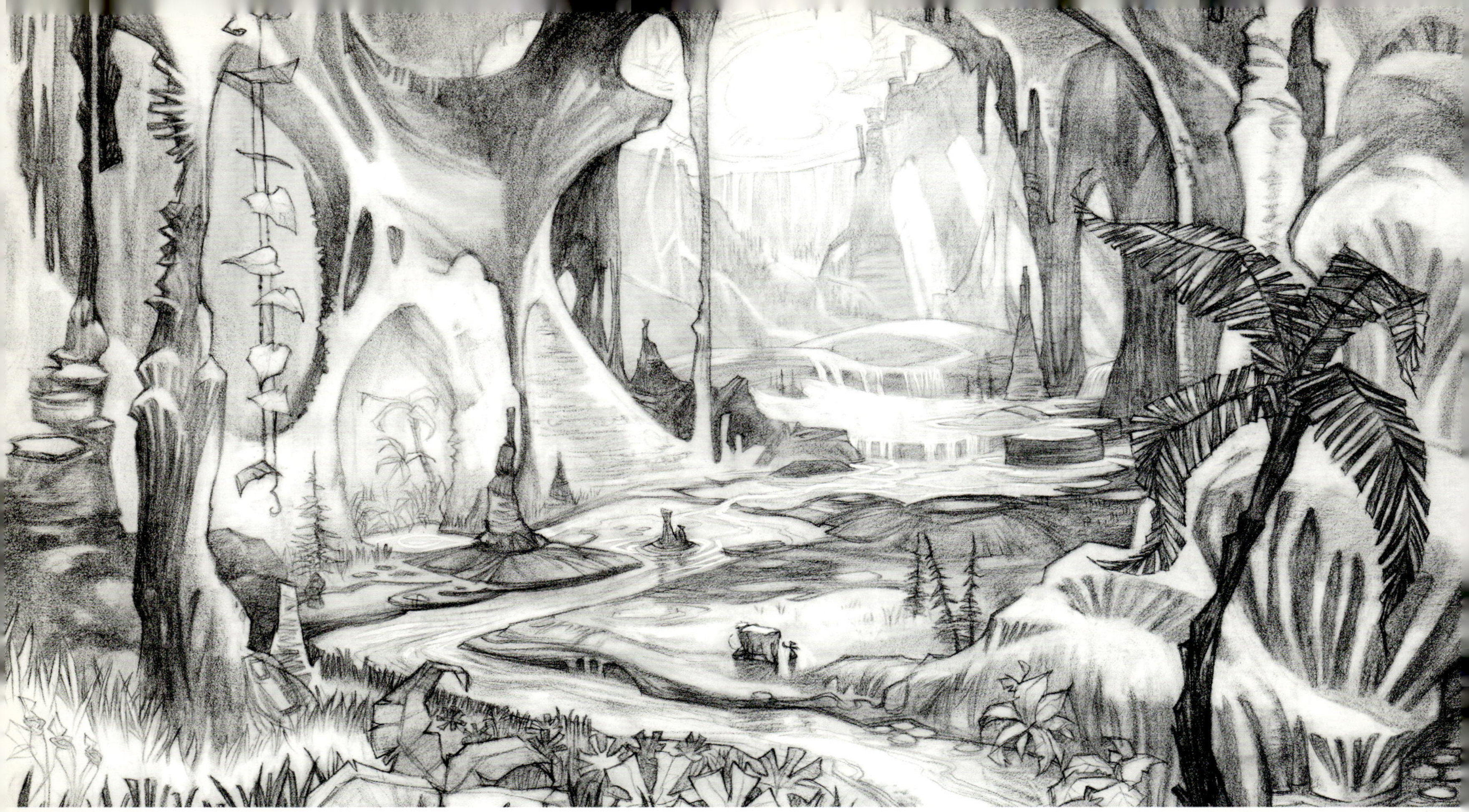

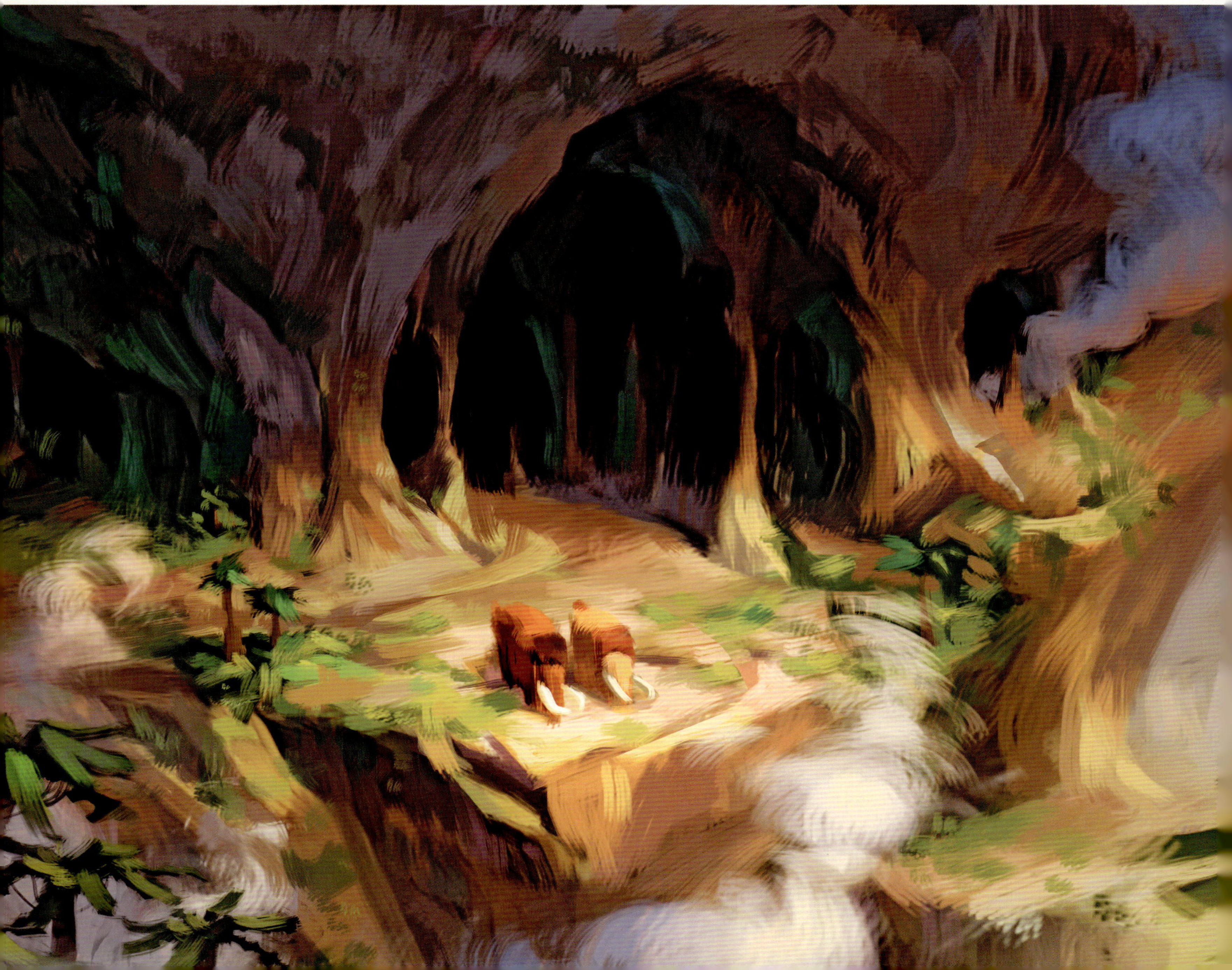

(Opposite top) **The Lost World** – concept art • Peter Clarke, *(Opposite bottom)* **Manny and Ellie explore the Lost World** – color key • Mike Lee, *(Top)* **Rudy** – character sculpt • Peter de Sève (design) and Michael Defeo (sculpt), *(Above)* **Lost World (three images)** – environment concept art • Jon Townley (design) and Robert MacKenzie (painting)

half of the movie, but needed to start to focus some of his attention on a newly green-lit project, a film that would eventually become *Rio* (see Chapter 7). Historically, Blue Sky has made room for additional directors as a means of shepherding new talent and bringing additional creative vision to a project. With Saldanha working on two films, Blue Sky approached staff animator Mike Thurmeier to codirect *Ice Age: Dawn of the Dinosaurs*.

Thurmeier grew up in the prairies of Ontario and was hired by Blue Sky immediately after graduating from Sheridan College's traditional animation program. He worked on every Blue Sky film after *Bunny*, first as a lead animator, then as a supervising animator, and finally as a senior supervising animator. He also built a rapport with Knapp, who was art director on the short film that Thurmeier codirected, *No Time for Nuts*. Thurmeier's familiarity with the property and characters made him a solid choice to codirect this feature film. "I love the original language of the first film," says Thurmeier.

In the original *Ice Age* movie, the glaciers on the surface would dwarf a character as large as Manny. In the jungle, Manny's scale is compromised even further by the towering dinosaurs at every turn. "In reality, there's not that much of a size difference between a mammoth and a dinosaur," says Saldanha. "But we wanted to push the proportions a little bit more to help our storytelling. Manny is used to being the biggest thing on the screen, and now we had to quadruple the scale of the elements around him so he felt small compared to the world we created."

The filmmakers devised a conceit to explain the Lost World: Heat from the earth's core warmed empty pockets under the ice, creating an enormous greenhouse. But being an underground jungle, the Lost World had its share of challenges. For instance, without a sun, a global light source was needed, and this became a puzzle to be solved. "We decided to use the icy ceiling of the Lost World as a giant scrim," says Knapp. "This allowed us to give it a hazy and tropical subterranean look—but not feel dark—while still getting a sense of the time of day outside."

ICE AGE: DAWN OF THE DINOSAURS 153

Color contrast was also a problem. Whereas before the characters were in front of a blank, white backdrop, now they were up against different shades of green. The fur of Sid and Scrat in particular were a challenge to keep in their normal hues or "local colors." Scrat is a neutral tan, and his fur reflects whatever color is around him. Sid is a warm yellow ochre, which skews a cool green in the shadow of the jungle. Knapp pushed the environment to a cooler hue so Sid's coloring could feel warmer and more recognizable. When a lush backdrop was required behind Sid, it often had to have a bluish hue.

"Every shot is definitely combed over in an unbelievable amount of detail that would probably drive the common person insane," says Thurmeier. "But every choice is deliberate and everything you see on screen was probably discussed and decided on and tried a couple of times before it was completed."

INTERSPECIES CASTING

Character designer Peter de Sève found the new setting inspiring as well. "The movie was refreshing; the palette, texture, and lighting were different," he says. "I'm very fond of the third film, and I had a lot of fun doing the new characters."

Scores of dinosaurs—and a handful of mammals—were created for the film, from the pack of googly-eyed *Troodons* to the feathered and flightless *Archaeopteryx*. Though characters like Sid and Buck address them as equals, the dinosaurs don't talk back. It recalls the humans in the original *Ice Age* who simply grunt and gesture. "The question came up of whether the dinosaurs should talk, because they were sort of the main creatures of the film," says Thurmeier. In the end the dinosaurs were designed to be sentient, but not at the same level as the *Ice Age* characters, so they remained speechless. "Can you imagine writing dialogue for Momma T. rex?" asks Thurmeier. "Sid's scenes with her were much more effective the way it was."

(Opposite top) **Momma Dino face-to-face with heroes** – character sketches • Peter de Sève, *(Opposite bottom)* **Chasm (three images)** – color keys • Peter Nguyen, *(Top)* **Momma Dino with Buck on tail** – concept art • Peter de Sève (design) and Sang Jun Lee (painting), *(Center right)* **Scrat in Momma Dino's nostril** – character sketch • Peter de Sève, *(Bottom left and bottom right)* **Scrat and acorn in ice** – character concept art • Peter de Sève

ICE AGE: DAWN OF THE DINOSAURS 155

(Above) **Manny and Sid in Lost World** – concept art • Lizette Vega (design) and Sang Jun Lee (painting)

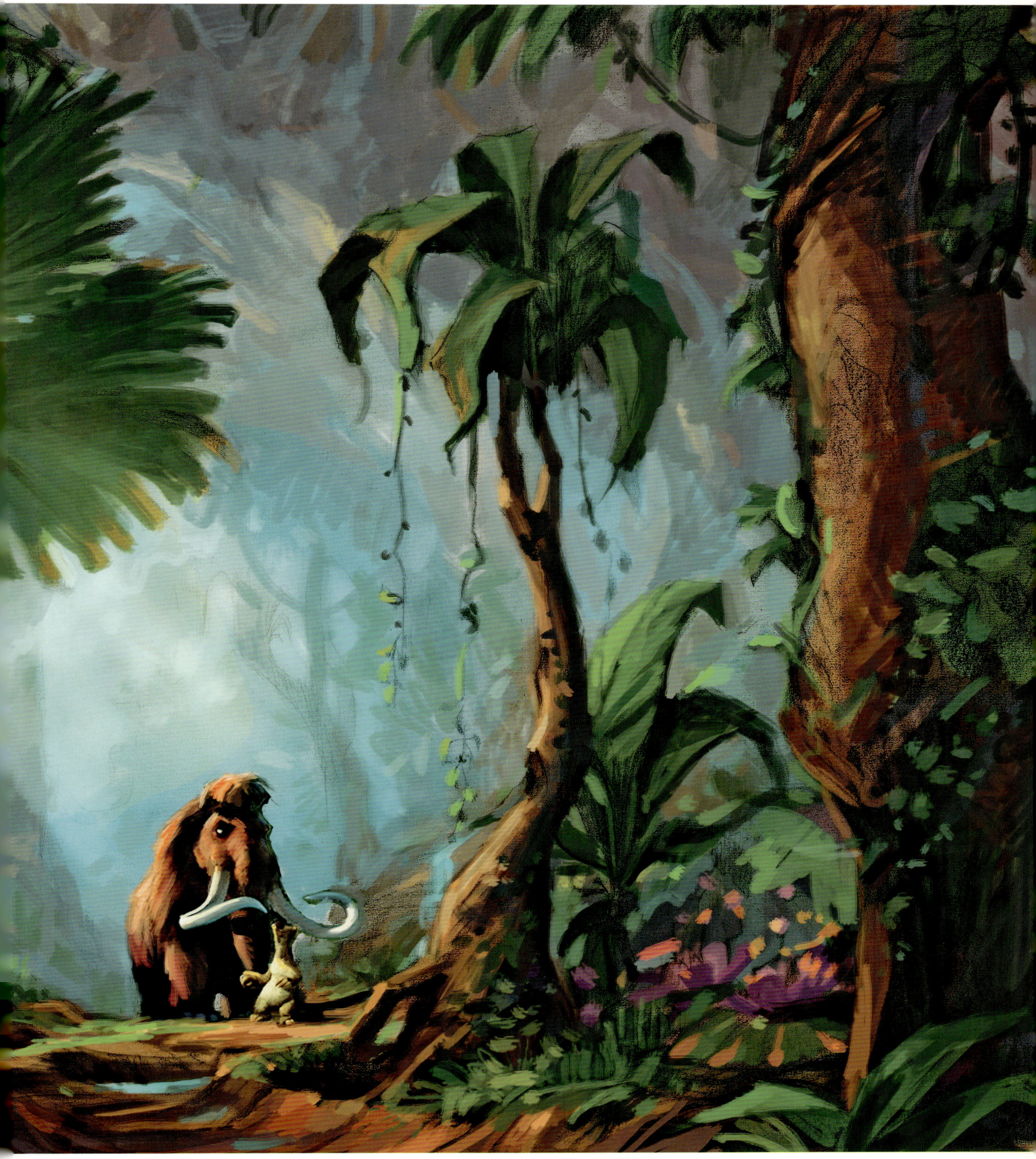

Buck the one-eyed weasel, on the other hand, is a character rich in expression both verbal and visual. His grasp on reality is dubious at best, and his body is as unstable as his sanity.

"He became more of this Captain Ahab character out in the wilderness," says Knapp. "He had lived among the dinosaurs, and he had mastered this world. Then he started going down this Colonel Kurtz route, where he'd been in the jungle just a little too long and started losing his mind, talking to trees and rocks and dinosaurs. And then he became like Tom Hanks and Wilson in *Cast Away*—at some point those moments started to coalesce and creep in."

Buck was voiced by Simon Pegg, who added his own twists to Buck's already twisted mind. For example, when Buck picks up a rock and starts talking into it like a cell phone, the lines are actually an improvisation by Pegg that were too good to cut: "All right, I love you, too, good-bye! Good-bye! Good-bye!"

(Above left) **Buck on pterodactyl** – final frame, *(Above right)* **Buck poses (three images)** – exploratory sketches • Peter de Sève, *(Opposite top left)* **Buck holding stick** – storyboard panel • Tony Maki, *(Opposite top right)* **Buck standing in shadow** – color key • Mike Lee, *(Opposite top right bottom)* **Buck with dagger in mouth** – color key • Peter Nguyen, *(Opposite middle)* **Buck and possums flying** – color key • Robert MacKenzie, *(Opposite bottom)* **Buck and friends** – final frame

158 THE ART OF BLUE SKY STUDIOS

ICE AGE: DAWN OF THE DINOSAURS 159

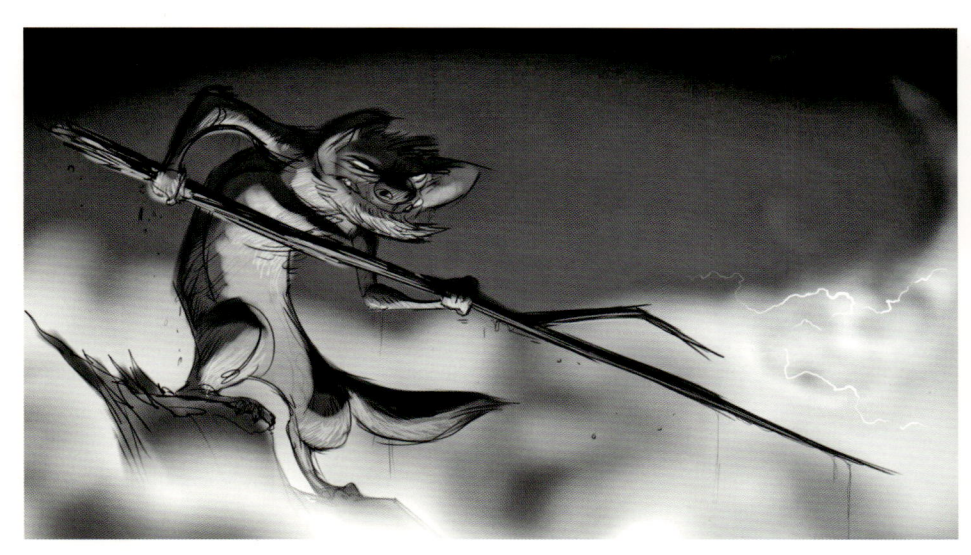

A LOOK INSIDE BLUE SKY

Set Design and Set Dressing

WHEN CREATING A WORLD RICH IN DETAIL, the Modeling department and the Camera & Staging department work closely with the artists who fill out the world, known as set dressers.

After the movie's environments are designed in 2-D with illustrations, the Modeling department builds the topography of the digital sets in the Maya program, creating the expansive areas where the characters will be performing. Then the Camera & Staging department does the camerawork, placing and moving the CG camera for the final film.

The Modeling department will also make smaller elements, such as a single type of tree or shrub. It is up to the set dresser to take that tree or shrub and place dozens, hundreds, or even thousands of that element in compositionally pleasing arrangements that make the world feel detailed, lived in, and robust.

"The set dressers are very aware of what will be on the screen," says Knapp. "They're working closely with the design department and with the cameras that Camera & Staging has created to arrange things and compose things to the final frame. It's the last artistic touch on the sets before things go to lighting."

(Above) **Mobile** – concept art • Jon Townley, *(Below)* **Playground tree** – concept art • Jon Townley (design) and Michael Knapp (painting)

160   THE ART OF BLUE SKY STUDIOS

(Top) **Lost World** – set design drawing • Tom Humber
(Above) **Lost World** – set dressing design • Tom Humber
(Left) **Roots on rocks** – set model asset • Arden Chan

ICE AGE: DAWN OF THE DINOSAURS 161

(Above) **Scrat and Scratte sequence** – color keys • Mike Lee, *(Opposite top)* **Various Scratte poses** – sketches • Peter de Sève, *(Opposite bottom)* **Scratte with acorn** – final frame

162   THE ART OF BLUE SKY STUDIOS

SCRATTE

The evolution of Scrat's character led to the creation of an adversary in the form of the beguiling femme fatale, Scratte. "It was an idea that was bouncing around for a while as something new and unique to play against," says Saldanha. "And I liked the idea of a flying squirrel, that she has something that Scrat doesn't have. Together with the nut, they would form a sort of love triangle." Torn between lust and greed, Scrat and Scratte show us the more manipulative and ultimately hilarious side of relationships.

Originally she was nameless. "I had labeled a drawing 'Scratte,'" says de Sève. "It was sort of a French female spelling, and they just ran with that. I was happy with the way she was modeled and animated. And to be fair, we never did come up with a better name than 'Scratte' (pronounced *scrat-tay*), though people tried."

ICE AGE: DAWN OF THE DINOSAURS

Scrat's New Love

AS ALWAYS, SCRAT'S STORY was told completely in pantomime. The script called for a sequence in which he and Scratte begin as adversaries and find themselves entangled in rapture. Karen Disher storyboarded the scene. "I thought, 'What if we did a musical number? A tango?'" recalls Disher. "It's really satisfying when you have an idea and you get to board it and shape it and choreograph it, and it gets into the movie. I really loved that sequence."

When an incomplete reel is presented in-house, temporary voices are needed to read lines from the script. Disher has long been a popular choice for temporary or so-called scratch tracks of dialogue, and for *Ice Age: Dawn of the Dinosaurs*, she did the scratch track for Scratte. The directors liked her rendition enough to cast her in the role, and she has been the voice of Scratte ever since.

As Scrat and Scratte's hate-love-hate relationship progresses, we get to see a whole new side of Scrat. His base animalism starts to be replaced with more human behavior. Influenced by Scratte, he begins to act more evolved, dancing and sitting upright. At the peak of Scrat's anthropomorphism, we find him pushing rock-furniture around a new tree hollow apartment he shares with Scratte. He is more evolved than ever but still the victim. At the last minute he opts to suffer by his acorn rather than at the hands of Scratte. He leaves her miles below the icy surface of his world, refusing to let a mate stand between him and his true love.

(Top) **Tug of war for acorn** – concept sketch • Peter de Sève, *(Above)* **Scratte feeding Scrat grapes** – color key • Robert MacKenzie, *(Opposite top)* **Scratte and Scrat inside tree trunk** – color key • Robert MacKenzie, *(Opposite bottom)* **Scrat and Scratte kiss** – color key • Robert MacKenzie

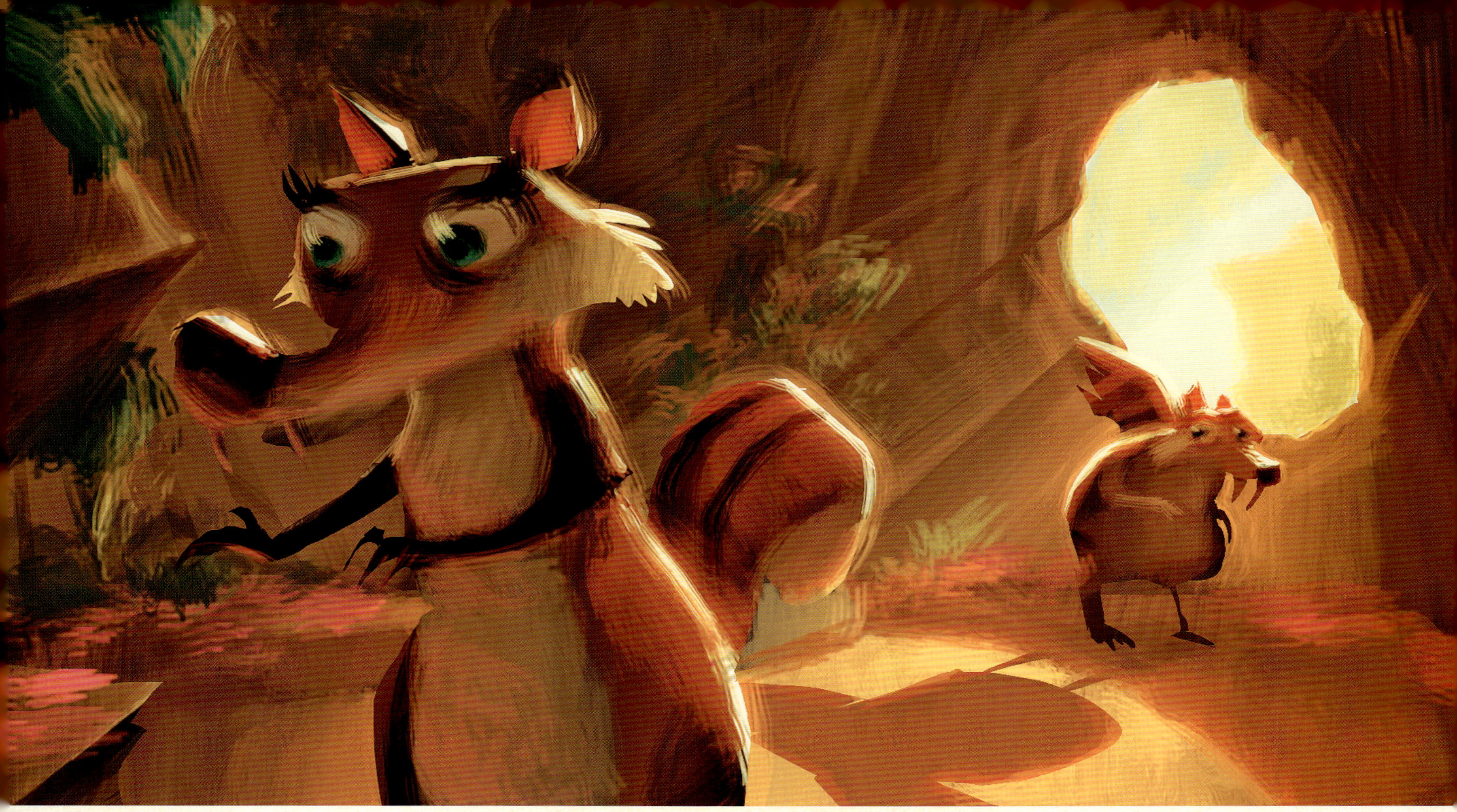

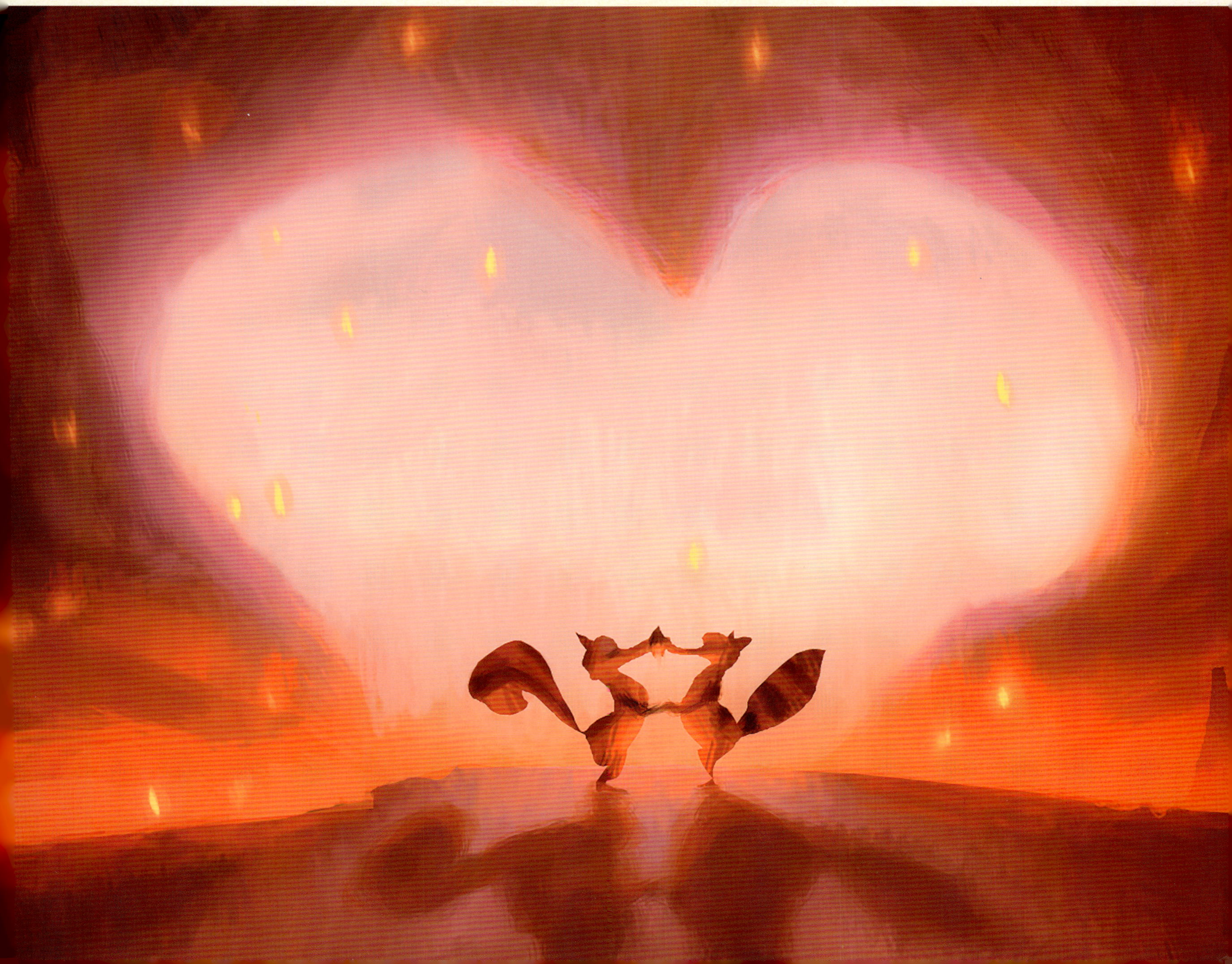

WATCHING THEM GROW

In *Ice Age: Dawn of the Dinosaurs*, the more familiar characters have begun their own evolution. Sid's compassion has developed into a desperate urge to mother. Diego's need for self-reliance causes him to turn his back on the herd. And emotionally guarded Manny has to embrace life with a new baby on the way. Producer Lori Forte continued to evolve the characters in the development of the script and considered the next step for Manny.

"Ellie's pregnant, and Manny is controlling, and he has to figure out how he's going to deal with that," says Forte. "To retain that protective element of Manny, you roll that into an experience for him—and that is protecting his wife in a Lost World, the worst environment he could be in. So we put them in new experiences, and their reactions can still be consistent, but they can grow. We know where their limits are, and we're pushing those limits all the time to see how they're responding to new situations."

Perhaps Manny has had his limits pushed more than any other character in the series. Having lost his mate and child to human hunters before the first movie even begins, he struggled with moving on with his life and accepting Ellie as a potential partner. Now he is safeguarding his pregnant wife like an overprotective father-to-be. Initially the filmmakers debated referencing Manny's traumatic past but ultimately decided that it was unnecessary. The fear of a first-time father is scary enough, let alone enduring the presence of ravenous dinosaurs.

"I consider Manny the heart of the series," says Thurmeier. "It's as if you're following this character through all these major points in his life. Sid and Diego offer interesting perspectives, but Manny's life is the spine of the storyline in all these movies."

Manny and the others are pushed to their limits during the final action scene. Ellie is giving birth to Manny's baby, but she is simultaneously attacked by a horde of carnivorous *Guanlongs*.

The climax itself is an all-out action-adventure extravaganza. "You have Manny and Diego trying to rescue Ellie, then you have Sid on the lava trying to escape Rudy, and you have Buck and the possums on the back of the pterodactyl," says Thurmeier. "It was an intercut action scene for about eleven minutes, and it was a challenge making sure the choreography of the scenes worked. You're cutting back to the right characters at the right time and not having too much time punching and fighting and kicking. It was a good education trying to make sure that the flow of the movie was great, that everybody's stories were being told at the right times."

(Opposite top) **Diego battles Guanlong** – color key • Ron DeFelice, *(Opposite bottom)* **Peaches** – concept art • Peter de Sève, *(Above)* **Diego and Guanlong sequence** – color keys • Ron DeFelice

ICE AGE: DAWN OF THE DINOSAURS 167

"I like that *Dawn of the Dinosaurs* spun the movies in a bit more of a wacky direction."

—MIKE THURMEIER

GARGANTUAN SUCCESS

The July 2009 release of *Ice Age: Dawn of the Dinosaurs* was hugely successful, becoming the highest-grossing animated film of all time internationally. The movie itself, and its use of 3-D, received high praise from fans and critics alike (including the legendary Roger Ebert) and also led to an attraction at the San Diego Zoo titled *Ice Age: Dawn of the Dinosaurs—The 4-D Experience*.

The third film also proved to be a paradigm shift for storytelling, giving Blue Sky more creative license within the *Ice Age* universe. "I like that *Dawn of the Dinosaurs* spun the movies in a bit more of a wacky direction," says Thurmeier. "It proved that it could be an adventure and include something a little odd, like dinosaurs in the Ice Age, but still make it fun and still get all the heart and the comedy like the first two did." The world of *Ice Age* would indeed become even more creative, but meanwhile, Carlos Saldanha's new project was coming to fruition.

(Above and right) **Various dinosaurs** – concept sketches • Peter de Sève
(Opposite) **Heroes running from Guanlongs** – concept art • Arden Chan (design) and Mike Lee (painting)

168   THE ART OF BLUE SKY STUDIOS

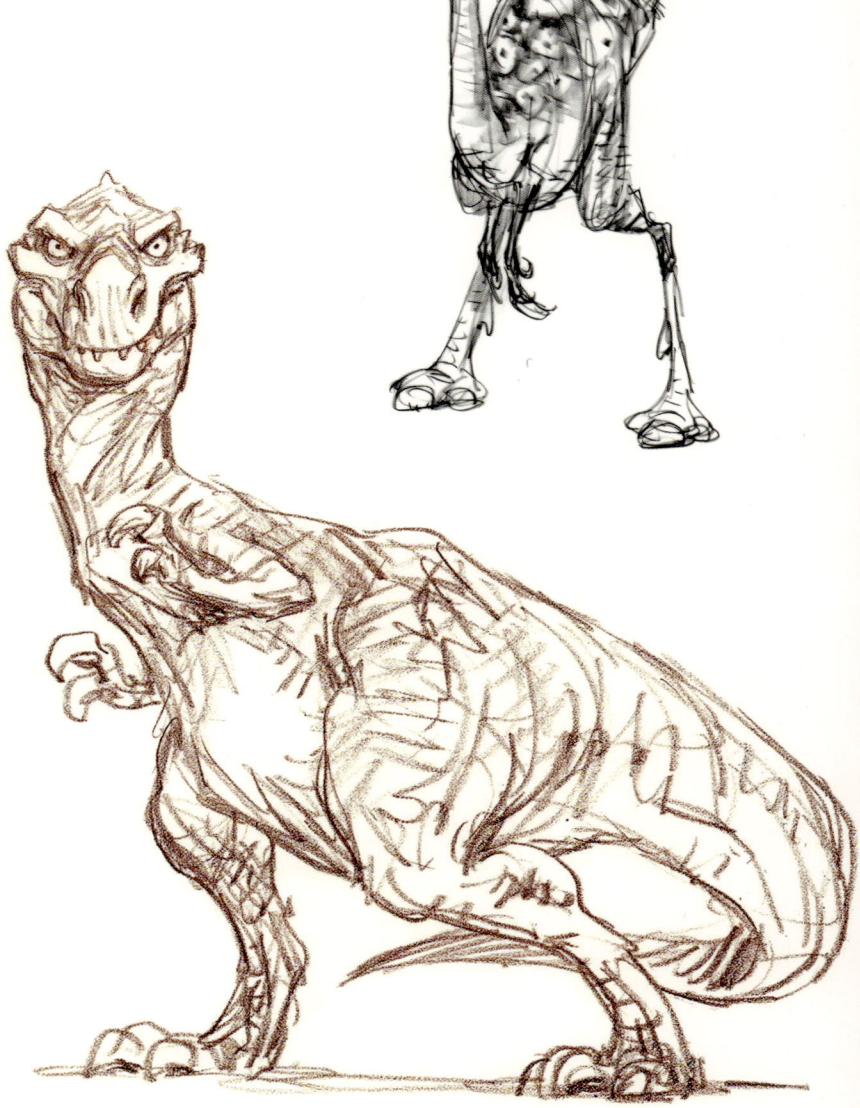

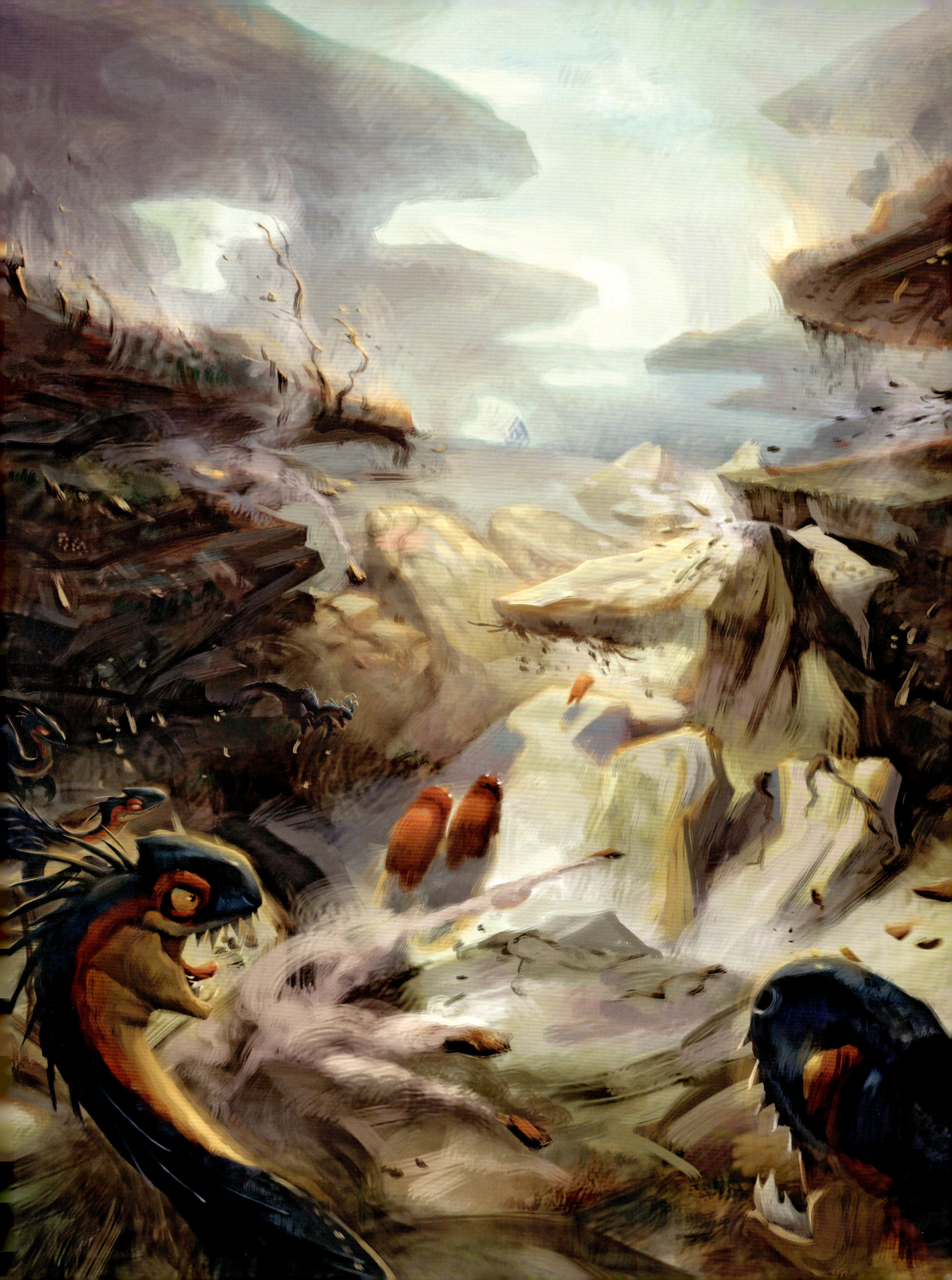

A LOOK INSIDE BLUE SKY

Camera & Staging Department

THE TEAM WHO COMPRISES the Camera & Staging Department could be considered the cinematographers of a Blue Sky film. The original label of the department was "Layout," named after its 2-D animation equivalent, because its members decide where the camera goes, how it's angled, and the way in which it moves. Camera & Staging works closely with every other department, weighing in on aspects like continuity, composition, staging, lens choice, and cutting, all to serve the viewers' complete immersion into the film.

In CG animation, cameras have zero limitations, which is not necessarily a good thing according to the head of Camera & Staging, Rob Cardone. "We can fly the camera through the eye of a needle if we want to," he says, "but just because we can do something physically impossible doesn't mean that we should."

Cardone (the younger brother of Blue Sky art director Tom Cardone) leads a team tasked with keeping the audience oriented and engrossed in the action. Their goal is to avoid creating shots that are so over-the-top they lose credibility with viewers. When his team plans their shots, they ask themselves, "How would we achieve this in live action?" This, says Cardone, helps base the scenes in reality, which feels more natural to the viewer: "Things like using camera-shake in reaction to an impact, or a zoom to achieve a certain feel, or a close-up reaction on a character to set up their point-of-view shot, or handheld movement—these all help to give the camera life and put the viewer in the moment with the character."

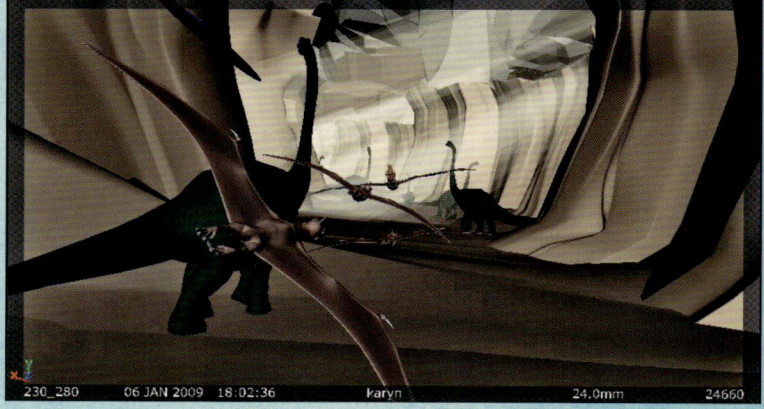

A sublime example of all these elements and more appears within the first six minutes of *Ice Age: Dawn of the Dinosaurs* in a chase scene between Diego and a gazelle. Different types of camera angles, shot-framing, and careful cutting build the tension and establish the distance between the two characters. As the chase ensues and the characters leap over a log, the camera is close enough to not only shake upon impact but also suffer mud splatter on its "lens."

(Top) **Soaring through canyon** – color key • Robert MacKenzie, *(Above)* **Soaring through canyon** – final camera • Karyn Monschein, *(Opposite top)* **Diego and Gazelle chase** – workbook cameras • Kevin Thomason *(top left)* and James Campbell *(adjacent three images)*, *(Opposite bottom)* **Diego and Gazelle chase** – final frame

170 THE ART OF BLUE SKY STUDIOS

ICE AGE: DAWN OF THE DINOSAURS   171

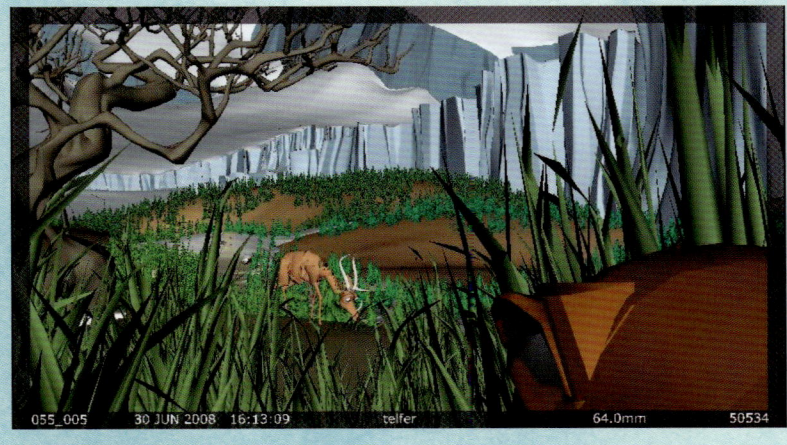

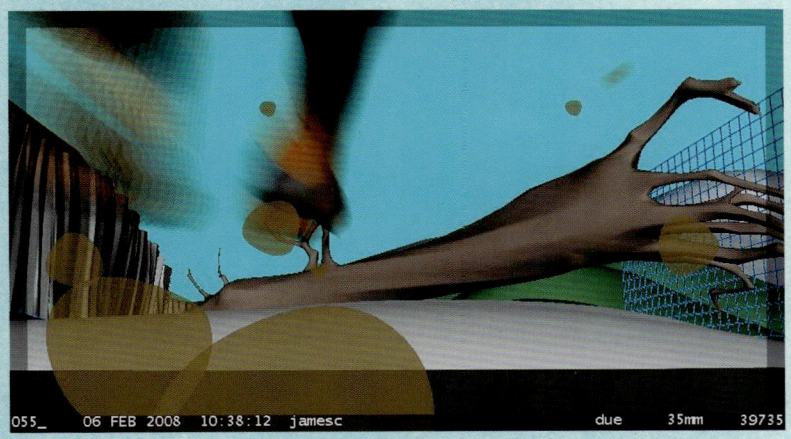

BLUE SKY SHORTS
Ice Age: A Mammoth Christmas (2011)

PRIOR TO THE RELEASE OF THE FOURTH *Ice Age* feature, *Ice Age: Continental Drift*, Fox commissioned this TV special for the holiday season. *Ice Age: A Mammoth Christmas* provided a narrative bridge between the birth of Peaches the Mammoth in the third film and her adolescence in the following film. It also delivered a breathless festive adventure where we meet Santa Claus and catch a glimpse at the origins of his workshop, while Prancer, the confident and generous flying reindeer, steals the show.

"Prancer was quite an evolution," says director Karen Disher. "In earlier versions he was bummed out because he thought being able to fly made him a freak, and he was conceived more as a Goth teenager. But then we realized that this character was no fun to watch at all. Besides, flying is awesome! If I could fly, I'd think it was the greatest thing in the world—who wouldn't? So we gave him a little more personality, which added a little more silliness and wackiness in the story, and I think it was a really good change."

Another element of silliness was provided in the form of the elves, who were created from the same models as the mini-sloths from

(Right) **Scrat on Christmas tree** –concept art • Peter Nguyen, *(Below)* **Sloth elves** –concept art • Peter Nguyen, *(Opposite top left)* **Santa** – character design • Peter de Sève (design) and Peter Nguyen (painting), *(Opposite top and bottom right)* **Santa and Prancer** – character sketches • Peter de Sève, *(Opposite center)* **Mammoth family** – color key • Peter Nguyen, *(Opposite bottom)* **Scrat with presents** – color key • Peter Nguyen

172　THE ART OF BLUE SKY STUDIOS

Ice Age: The Meltdown, but regroomed and recolored. Disher was glad to bring the popular troupe back to fill the role of the "Santourage."

"The theory was that before he meets the *Ice Age* characters, Santa's just a one-man show who makes toys and travels a five- or six-hundred mile radius around the North Pole every year on Christmas," says Disher. In the mini movie it's the *Ice Age* heroes who enable Santa to widen his reach to the entire world.

Putting Santa Claus back in the Ice Age required a few adjustments, however. He was dressed in a wardrobe befitting prehistoric times, a little rougher around the edges than the slick velvet Victorian coat we're used to seeing. "We wanted to keep him rooted in the *Ice Age* world," adds Disher. "We called him 'Neander-Santa.'"

This TV special premiered on Fox on Thanksgiving night in 2011. At the time it was the second-highest-rated program in its time slot and the most popular iTunes download during the week it premiered. It was released on DVD two days later.

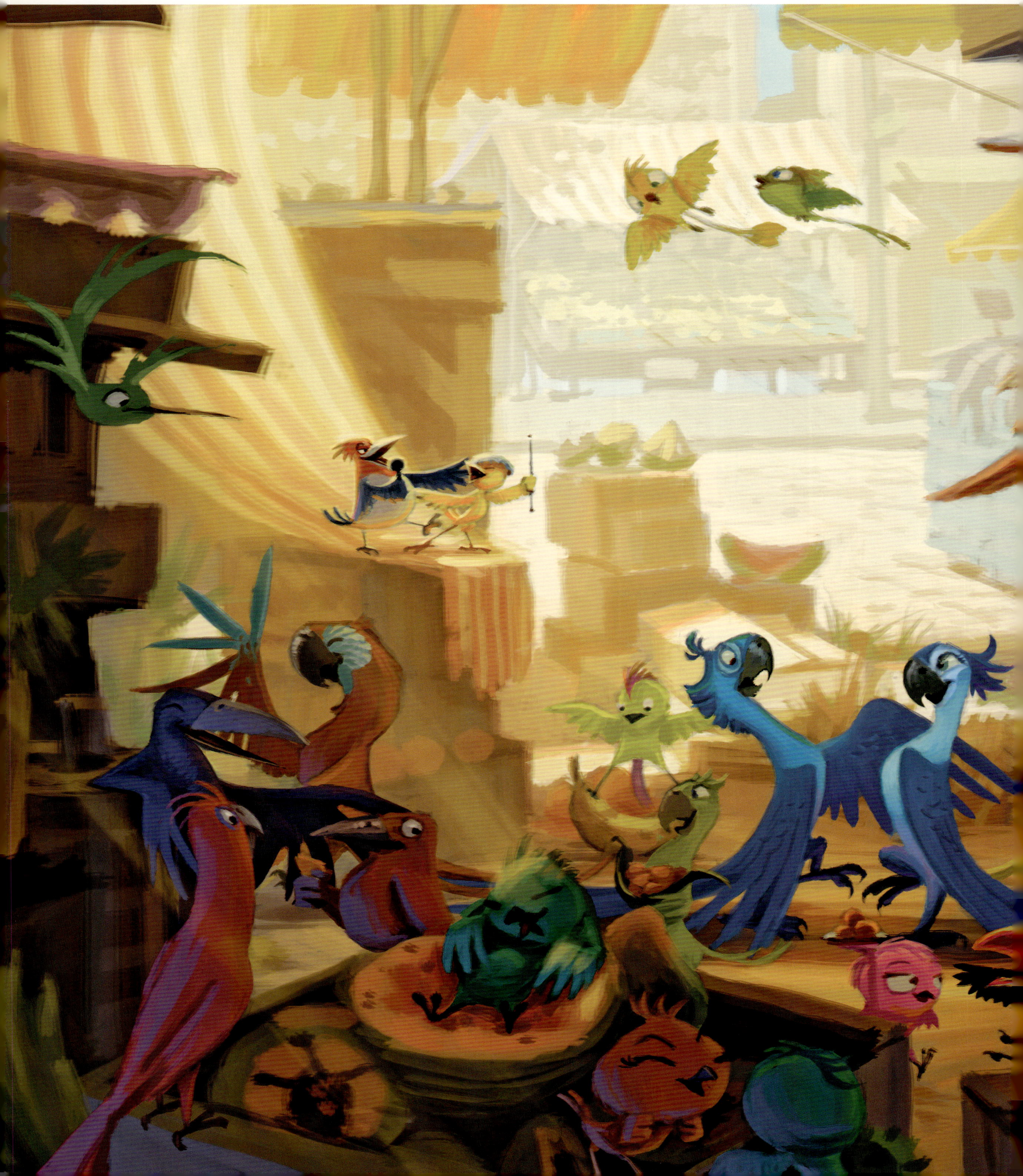

CHAPTER 6 • *Rio*

"Fly! It's not what you think up here, it's what you feel in here. And when you feel the rhythm of your heart, it's like samba. You fly!"

—RAFAEL THE TOUCAN

When you're the last of your kind, the fate of your entire species is resting on your shoulders. It takes great nobility, grace, and courage to heft such responsibility. Unfortunately, when we meet Tyler "Blu" Gunderson, aka Blu the macaw, he possesses none of these qualities. He only knows Minnesota weather and the inside of a bookstore. But he's sweet and friendly, if a little gawky. And we can hardly blame him for balking at a visit to exotic Rio de Janeiro.

What starts as a quick stay becomes an adventure through the landscape, music, and culture of the city. And just like Blu, the audience is helpless against the city's charms.

"I've felt that this is such a visually amazing place for animation," says director and Rio native Carlos Saldanha. "You have the music, the colors, the nature, the culture—so there are so many cool elements to the story. And I've always loved birds. I thought they would be a great animated element, and the story started from that."

Throughout the movie *Rio*, we travel by the famous beaches, between the crowded favelas, past local neighborhoods, and into the streets during Carnaval before completing the journey at the sanctuary in the lush forest in Rio. Every step is a tribute to a beautiful city and the bonds of friendship and romance it forges. Rio truly is the city of love.

HATCHING AN IDEA

Carlos Saldanha had begun developing *Rio* with the approval of then-president of Fox Animation, Chris Meledandri. However, during the production of *Ice Age: Dawn of the Dinosaurs*, Meledandri left to found his own company. Vanessa Morrison took over in the president's chair, and Saldanha had to pitch his movie all over again.

"I was afraid everything I had developed for *Rio* would go back to square one," he says. "But luckily Vanessa happens to be a fan of Brazilian culture and music and grew up listening to Sérgio Mendes and his Brazilian bands, and she said, 'I love this, we have to do it!' So I found myself working to finish up *Ice Age: Dawn of the Dinosaurs* and at the same time getting the characters and the script going for *Rio*."

(Previous pages) **Market party** – concept art • Kyle Macnaughton (environment), Marceline Tanguay (characters), and David Dibble (color), *(Above)* **Blu and Luiz** – character sketch • Sang Jun Lee, *(Opposite)* **Raphael** – concpet art • Sergio Pablos (design) and Randy Gaul (painting)

THE ART OF BLUE SKY STUDIOS

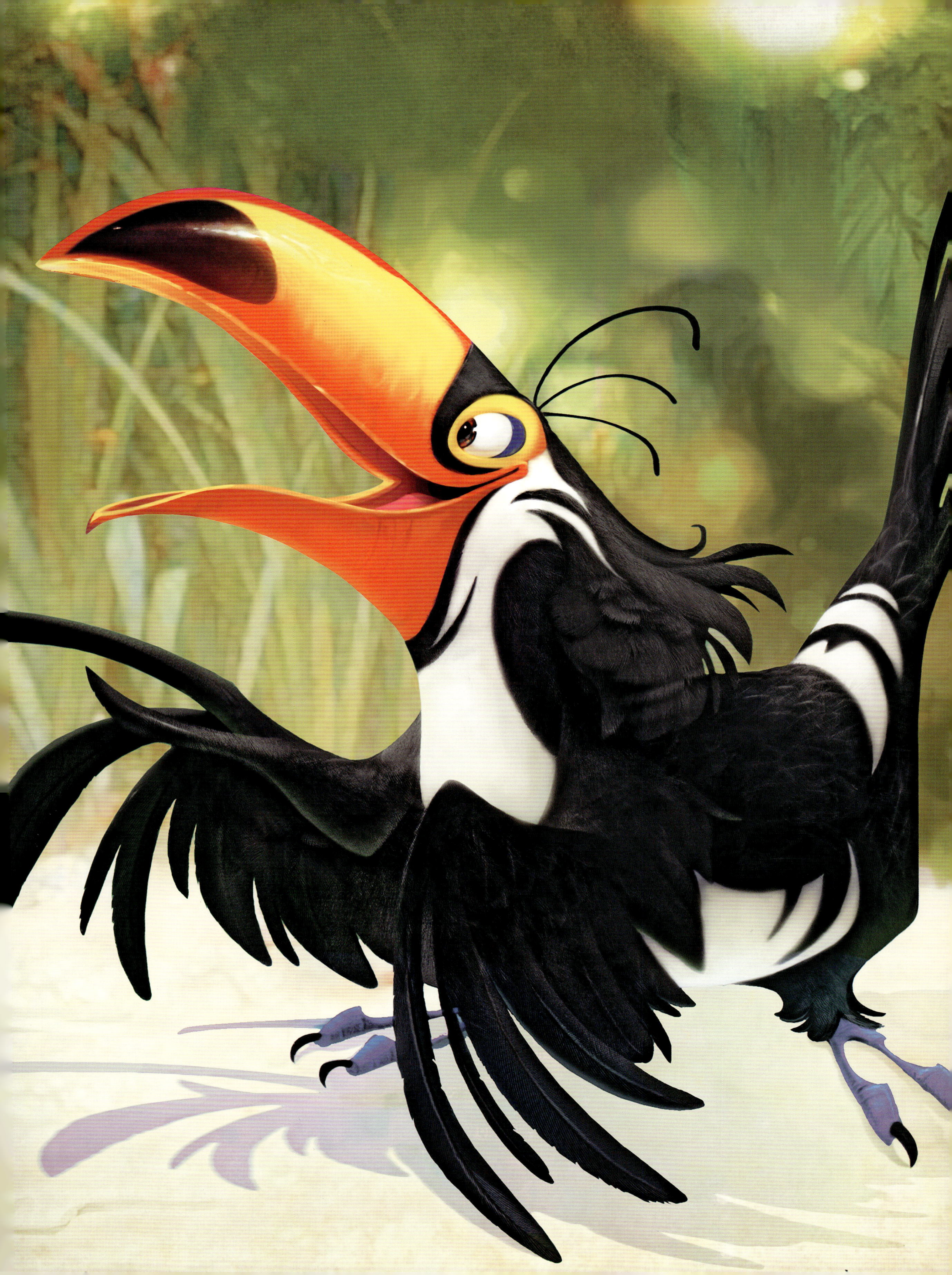

The story of *Rio* came from a bizarre fact: Every winter, penguins that have become stranded in Antarctic currents wash up on the beaches of Rio de Janeiro. Saldanha, who first came to New York from Rio when he was twenty-three, had originally framed the script around a penguin tourist arriving at Carnaval.

"Everybody loved the idea of somebody coming from a foreign place and then finding their heart and soul in Rio," says Saldanha, "and I tried to create a story that had all the elements I liked about the city. But there were a lot of movies about penguins out at that time. That's when we looked into macaws." Instead of a flightless bird, the film would star Blu alongside other tropical avians native to Brazil, and their love of flying would parallel the Brazilian free spirit.

This spirit is purely personified in Jewel, Blu's female Brazilian counterpart. The two macaws spend the movie trying to escape a gang of illegal smugglers, a horde of marmosets, and the embittered

178   THE ART OF BLUE SKY STUDIOS

cockatoo Nigel. The final script added the human characters Linda, Blu's Minnesotan companion; Tulio, a quirky Brazilian ornithologist; and Fernando, an orphan from a depressed part of town. Elsewhere, Rafael the toucan and Luiz the bulldog are friendly and helpful ambassadors, while Pedro the cardinal and Nico the canary represent the friendly competition between new and traditional Brazilian music. But the melodies of Rio de Janeiro are just one element of its culture, and Saldanha insisted on going deeper.

(Opposite top left) **Blu** – concept art • Sergio Pablos & Sang Jun Lee (design) and Randy Gaul (painting), (Opposite bottom) **Nico and Pedro fly over Guanabara Bay** – color key • Mike Lee, (Top) **Copacabana Beach as viewed from Sugarloaf** – concept art • Jake Parker, (Bottom left) **Nico and Pedro** – concept art • Sang Jun Lee (design) and Vincent Di Nguyen (painting), (Bottom right) **Luiz** – character design • Sang Jun Lee

180   THE ART OF BLUE SKY STUDIOS

(Opposite top) **Mocking Birds** – concept art • Peter Chan, *(Opposite center)* **Linda's bookstore exterior** – final digital art, *(Opposite bottom left)* **Moose Lake store signs** – concept art • Jake Parker, *(Opposite bottom right)* **Moose Lake Village founding father statue** – concept art • Peter Chan, *(Top)* **Linda** – early concept art • Sang Jun Lee, *(Left)* **Tulio in Linda's bookstore** – color key • Ron DeFelice, *(Bottom)* **Linda's bookstore** – concept art • Peter Chan (design) and Thomas Cardone (painting)

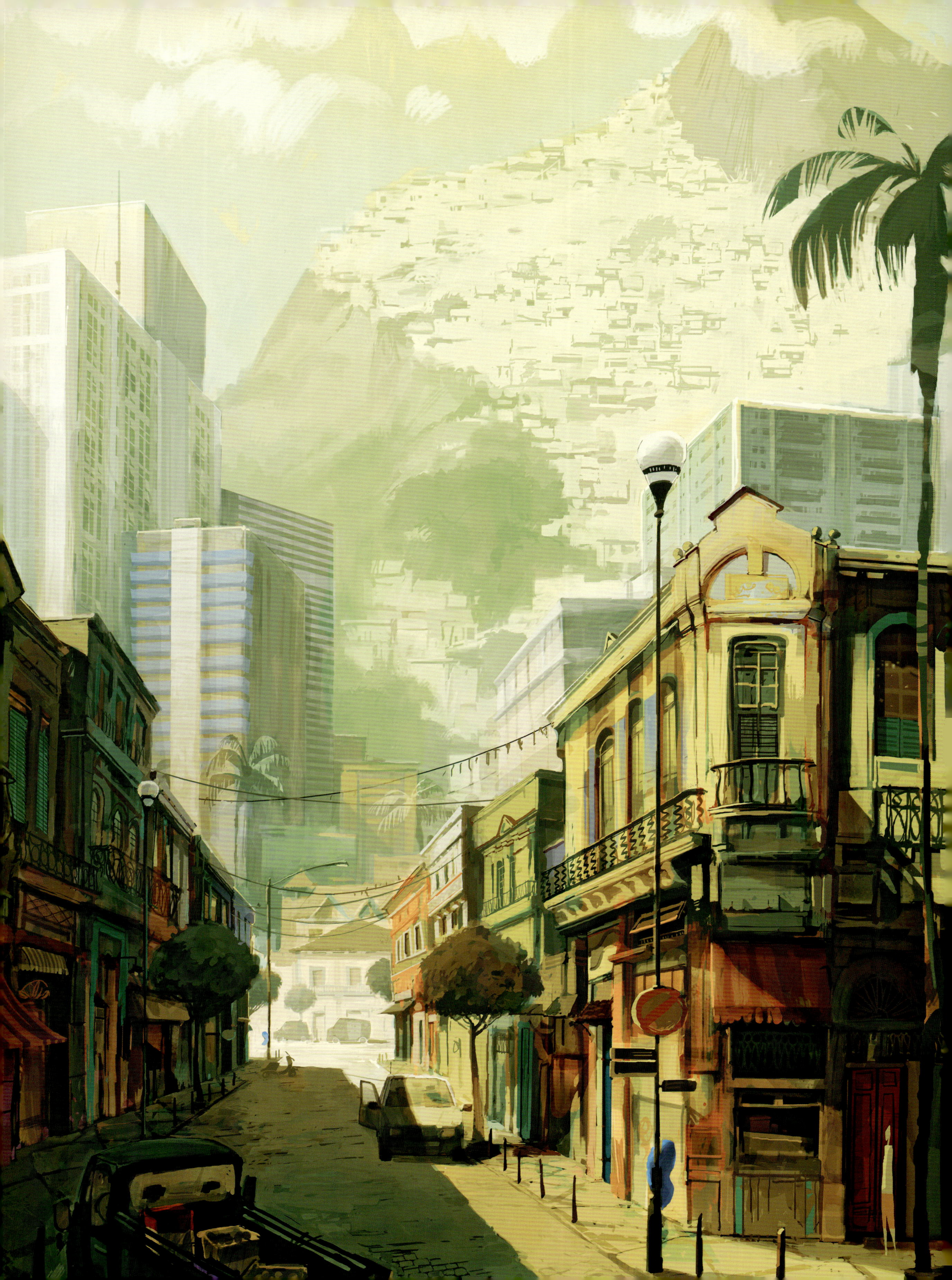

PAINTING THE TOWN

To help capture an authentic impression of Rio from the inside out, Saldanha and a small team traveled to the city during the week of Carnaval. Art director Tom Cardone was assigned to translate the sights for the screen.

"What we wanted to do was bring back our impression of the place, break it down, and capture it in our own style for the film," says Cardone. "The whole city is between the hills and the ocean. It's densely populated and pretty compressed, so within a couple of miles you can see the entire fabric of the city."

Cardone counted several types of architecture that would define the look and feel of Rio in the movie. In addition to the high-rises, the city's small and numerous favelas are an integral part of Rio's landscape. Built on public land with no building code, they seem to climb up the inclines of the mountains and over one another.

"The favelas have a very eclectic aesthetic," says Cardone. "From a distance they have a totally organic feel to them. There are terra-cotta cinder blocks, Portuguese tile work, corrugated metal for the roofs, and bright blue tubs on the roofs that collect water. All these things add character to the place."

(Opposite) **Colonial Rio street** – concept art • Kyle Macnaughton, *(Top)* **Fernando from early Rio scene** – concept art • Kyle Macnaughton (design) and David Dibble (color), *(Center)* **Favela** – concept art • Kyle Macnaughton, *(Above)* **Food stall** – concept art • Peter Chan, *(Right)* **Sneaking Fernando** – concept art • Sang Jun Lee

(Above) **Blu and Jewel above Guanabara Bay** – concept art • Arden Chan (design) and David Dibble (painting)

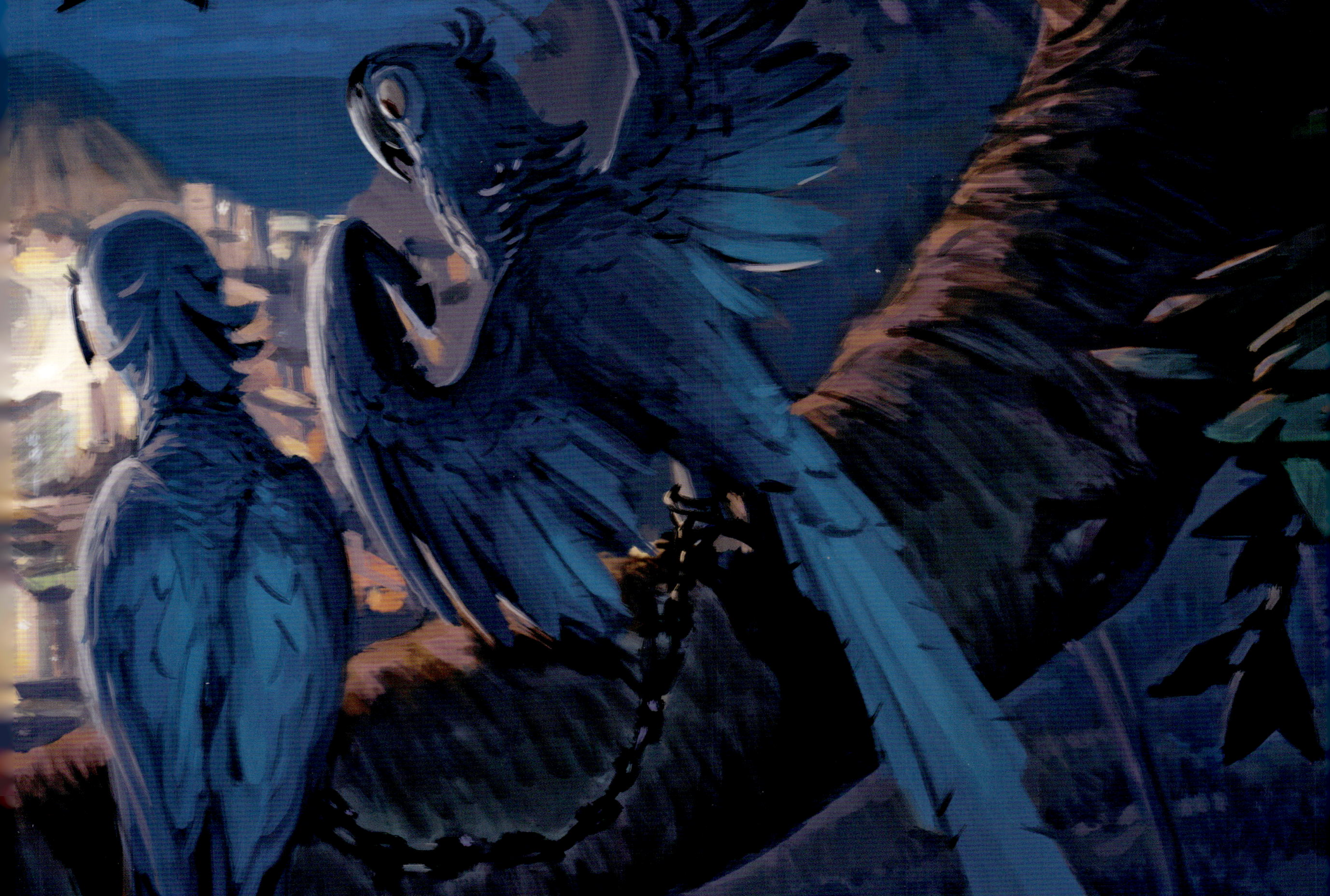

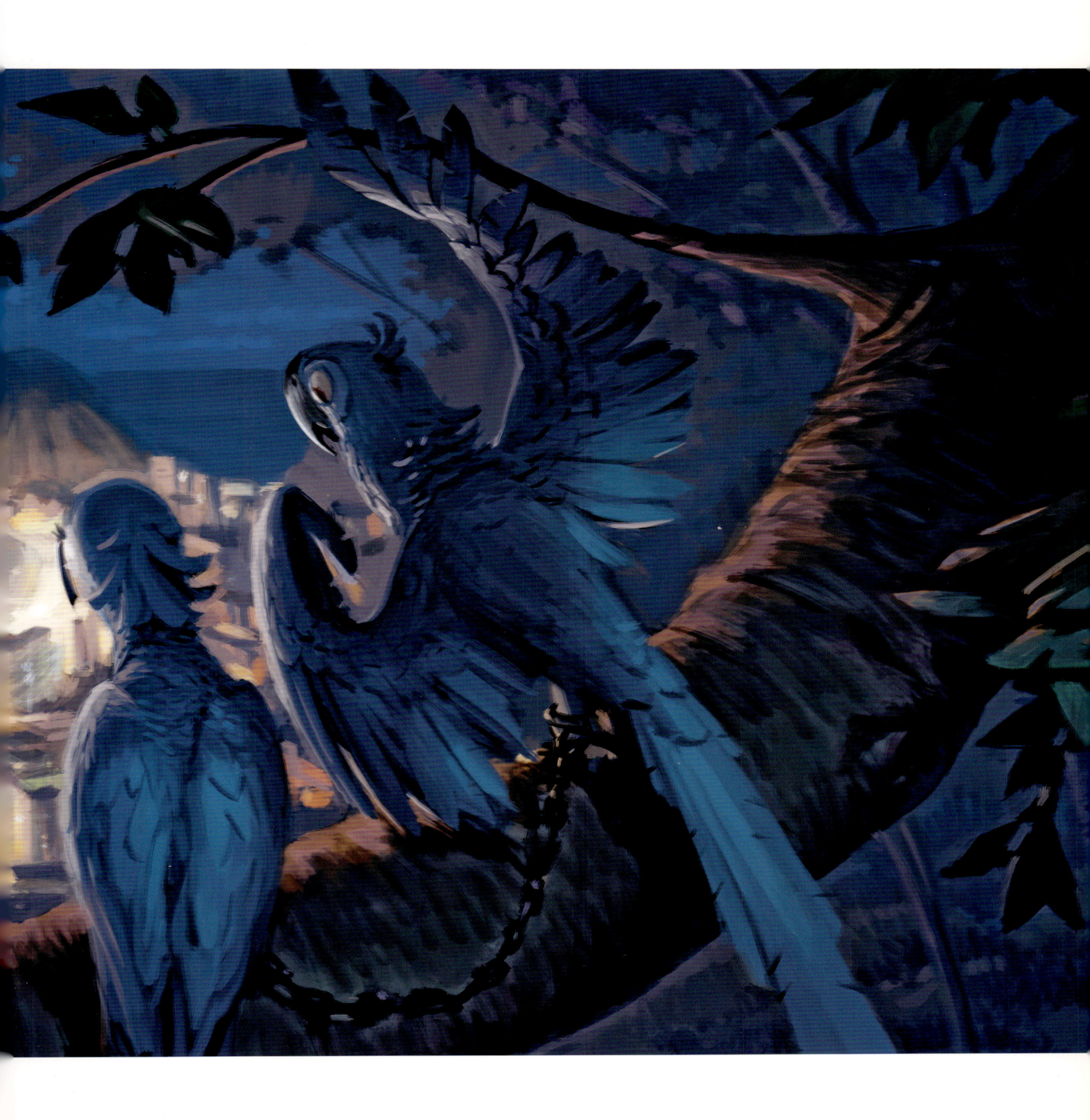

(Top) **Graffiti** – concept art • Willie Real, *(Above)* **Fruit market** – concept art • Greg Couch, *(Opposite top)* **Conservation center** – concept art • Peter Chan, *(Opposite bottom)* **Tram trolley** – concept art • Kyle Macnaughton

There were also colonial buildings with wrought-iron railings and ornate balconies. Cardone's team based the design of Tulio's bird sanctuary on a combination of architecture they saw at Rio's botanical gardens and zoo.

"It seemed like there was a lot of growth to the city in the sixties," adds Cardone, "so there's that mid-century modern feel to some of it, especially in places like Ipanema. There's an art deco period as well as more contemporary buildings. We wanted to tap into all those different styles when we assembled the buildings for the city, because it takes all those elements to make it feel like Rio."

Covering the city itself is famously illustrative graffiti art. All the graffiti seen in the film was designed in-house by Willie Real. The art is depicted in various styles that only enhance the film's visual landscape.

To push the graphic style of the movie, Cardone and his team settled on an "85 percent rule." Every object and person would have 85 percent realistic proportions and 15 percent stylized. It was a challenge finding that balance between realism and the movie's unique graphic style, but as Saldanha notes, "If you make the proportions too realistic, you lose a little bit of freedom, and we wanted to keep it more fun." Thus, the humans had larger-than-average heads, and the automobiles were likewise top-heavy over tiny wheels. Even the trolley that the characters ride is a little off, with bars that are not equidistant and a bottom that sags slightly. "It's not the first thing you notice," assures Cardone, "but we wanted you to feel the spirit and character of it."

(Above) **Blu on the Santa Teresa trolley** – concept art • Greg Couch

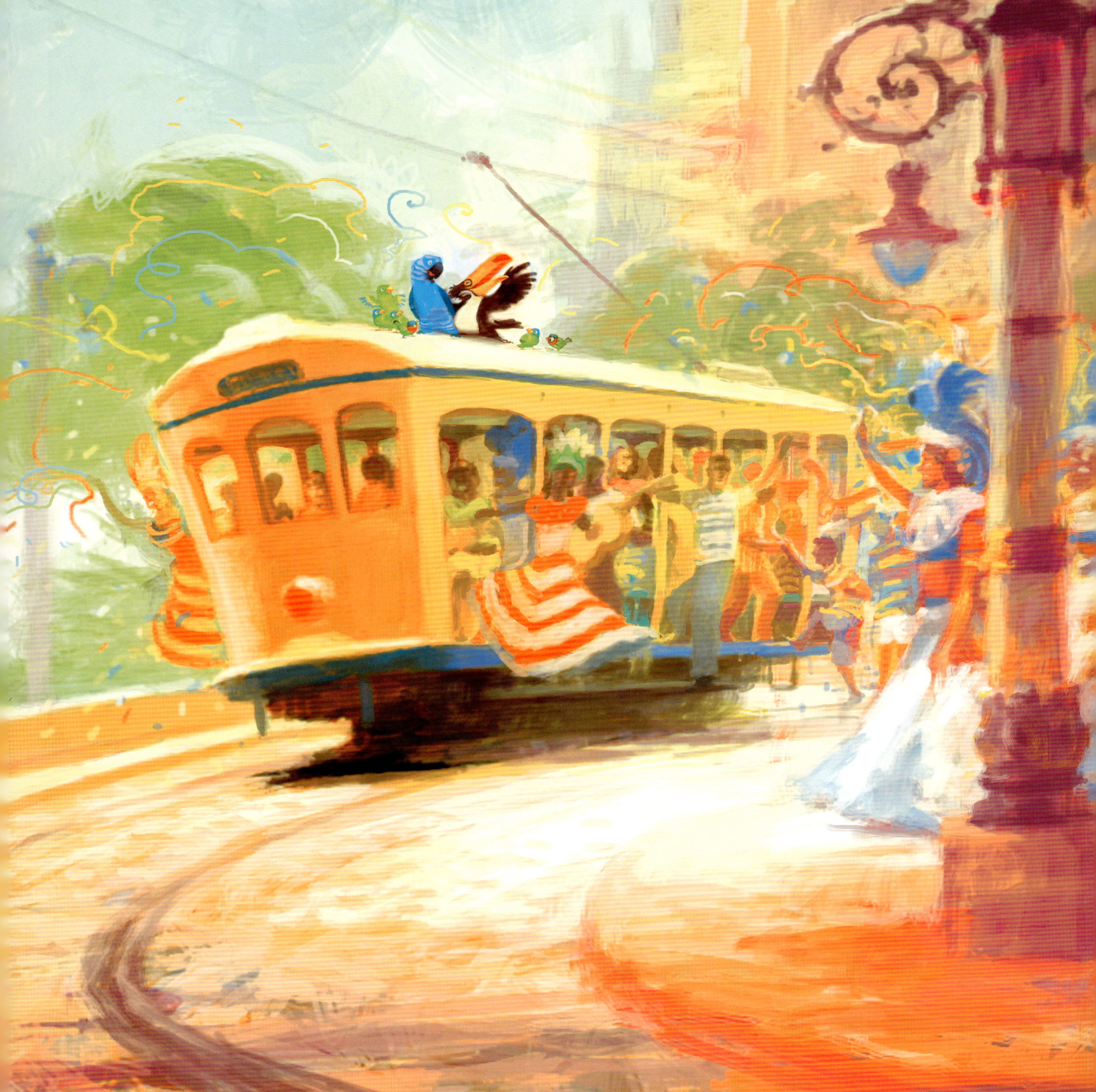

BIRDS OF A FEATHER

If the city of Rio is the star of the film, the characters themselves are an impressive supporting cast. The underlying plot that sees Blu and Jewel captured by bird traffickers is a veil for two concurrent love stories.

"One thing I love about macaws is that they're monogamous," says Saldanha. "Once they find a partner, they stay with that partner. That's very poetic. Part of the story is finding love and the complications and the explorations of the new environment. Trafficking birds is very much a reality in Brazil. Animals are still being poached and mistreated. There's nothing better to combat that backdrop than with love, and that's what the story ended up being."

Saldanha conceived Blu as an extension of his human companion, Linda. Both are fish out of water in Rio de Janeiro and have to learn to put their trust in others and themselves. They surpass their own limitations through the perils of the plot and the enchantment of Brazil. By the end of the film, little Linda from the bookstore races through the favelas on a motorcycle and dances atop a Carnaval float, whereas Blu finally embraces his own ability to soar.

The gestures of Blu and Linda reflect their own innate shyness, especially compared to Brazilian openness. "We had to figure out how to make the characters more Brazilian, more animated, to capture that flair," says Saldanha, "so we have them talking with their hands more and gesturing outward. Linda and Blu are a little more shy, so their body language for most of the film is very contained. It's a Brazilian stereotype, but a positive one, about having personalities that are fun, outgoing, colorful, and bright. There's a cultural essence of not being afraid of who you are—to put it out there."

(Opposite top) **Blu and Linda** – final digital art, *(Opposite center)* **Linda and Blu at breakfast** – concept art • Peter Chan, *(Opposite bottom left)* **Linda** – early concept sketches • Jason Sadler, *(Opposite bottom center)* **Linda with Blu in cage** – concept art • Jason Sadler, *(Opposite bottom right)* **Túlio and Linda** – concept art • Jason Sadler (design) and Vincent Di Nguyen (painting), *(Top left)* **Jewel** – early character sketch • Jason Sadler, *(Top center)* **Blu** – character sketch • Sang Jun Lee, *(Top right)* **Jewel poses** – character sketch • Sang Jun Lee, *(Center)* **Blu gestures** – concept art • Sergio Pablos, *(Bottom)* **Blu and Jewel** – concept art • Greg Couch

(Above) **Hang glider crash landing** – concept art • Willie Real (design) and Ron DeFelice (painting)

"It's a Brazilian sterotype, but a positive one, about having personalities that are fun, outgoing, colorful, and bright. There's a cultural essence of not being afraid of who you are—to put it out there."

—CARLOS SALDANHA

(Top) **Rafael and Blu** – concept art • Robin Joseph, (Top left and top right) **Blu poses** – character sketches • Sang Jun Lee, (Center left) **Blu and Rafael** – character sketches • Greg Couch, (Center right) **Blu with soccer ball** – character concept art • Sang Jun Lee, (Bottom) **Blu and Jewel** – final digital art, (Opposite) **Blu** – concept art • Robin Joseph

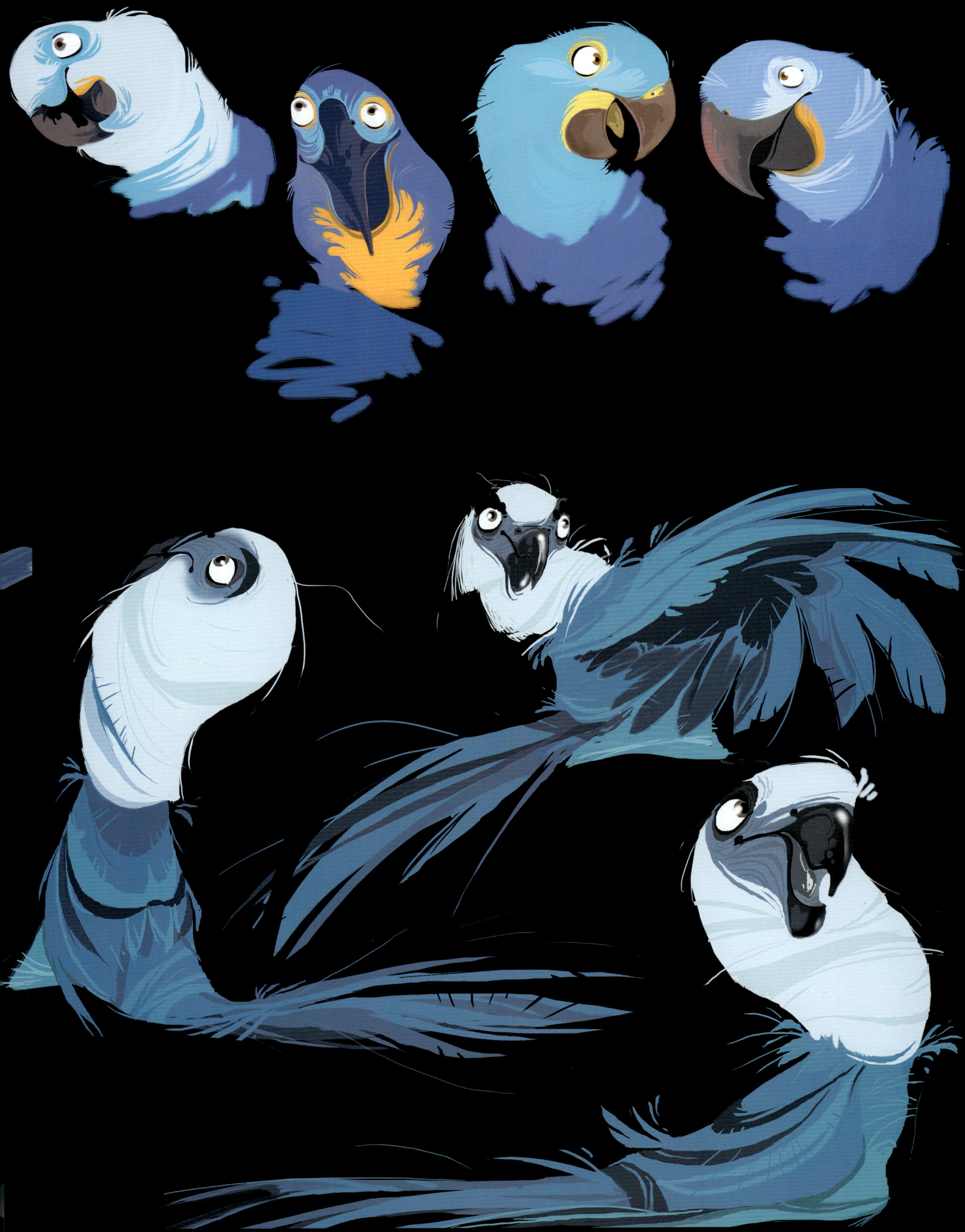

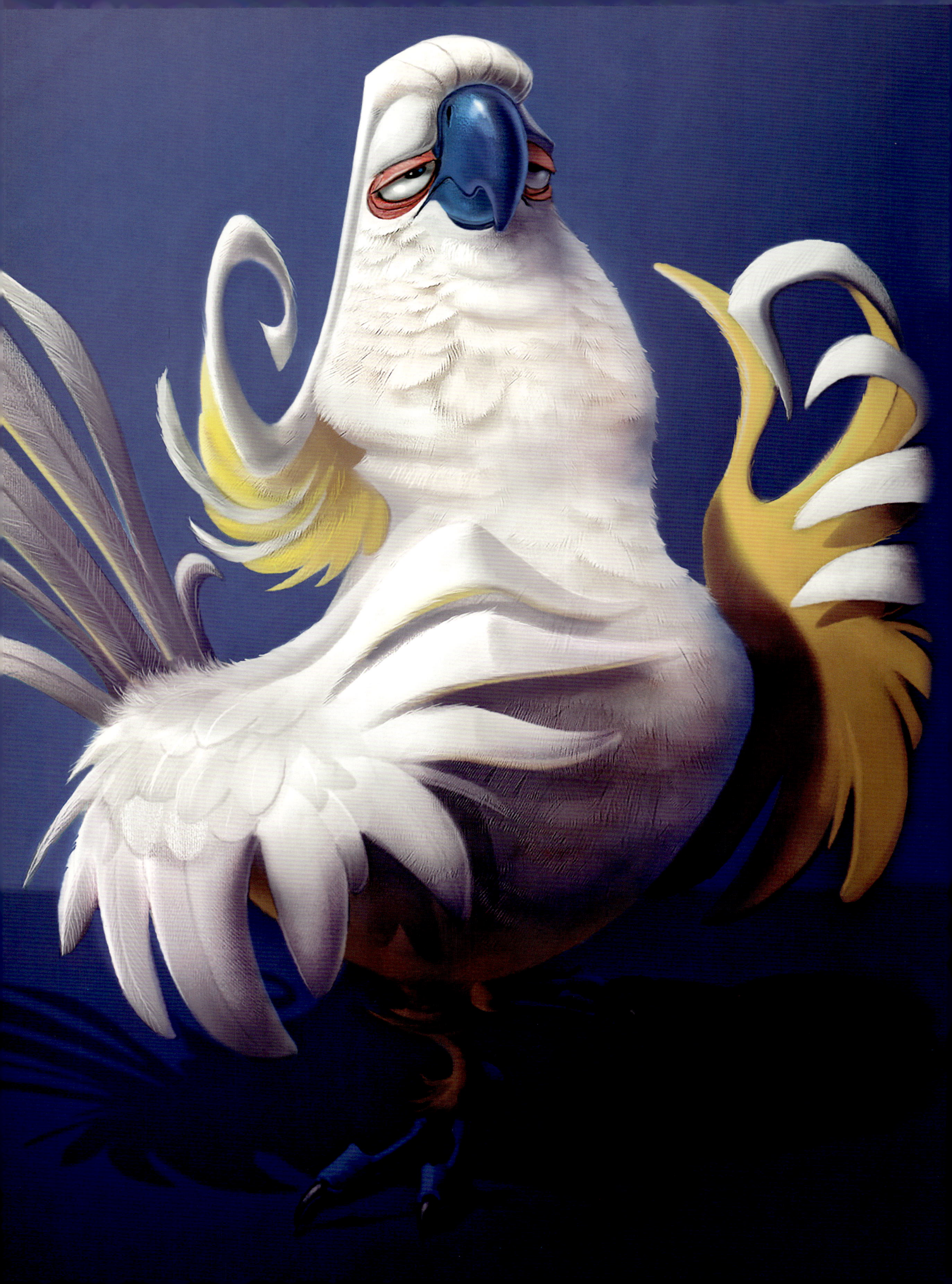

One distinctly non-Brazilian presence in the film is Nigel, a white Australian cockatoo with an Oceanian accent. "I always pictured Nigel as a cockatoo because they're from Australia and therefore would be a bit of an outcast," says Saldanha. "In Brazil you can actually import foreign birds in cages, but you cannot have native birds in cages. All these pretty native birds have got to have their freedom, so Nigel has a chip on his shoulder about that. Also, we made him mangy, a guy who isn't pretty anymore, as a way to give flavor to the character. It made him a villain, but he's still one of my favorite characters in the whole story."

If a character is going to elicit an emotional response from an audience, be it fear, laughter, or affection, the audience has to be able to relate to it somehow. "A big challenge in this film was that we needed to get the birds to act like birds, but also use their wings to gesture in an anthropomorphic way, too, more like humans," says Cardone. "A bird wing is very complex, so for about a year the studio worked on a prototype, and the technology they developed for the movement of the wings and feathers went into the final film." Each wing had to have feathers that represented fingers, as well as all the feathers that make up the different parts of the wing. The riggers and animators had to answer the ultimate question: What happens to each feather of a bird's wing when it's tucked inside or extended outward?

(Top) **Nigel** – concept art • Robin Joseph, *(Center right and bottom)* **Nigel gestures** – concept art • Sergio Pablos, *(Center left)* **Nigel and the marmoset** – concept art • Sang Jun Lee, *(Opposite)* **Nigel pose** – concept art • Sergio Pablos (design) and Randy Gaul (painting)

RIO 197

While working on the characters, the filmmakers wanted to make sure they were easy for the audience to register against a striking backdrop, whether it's the tropical jungle or the colors of the city. For instance, in the case of brightly colored tropical birds, attention had to be drawn to the face. In the case of Rafael, Cardone's team simplified a toucan's natural patterning on the beak, increased its saturation, and played up the concentric colors around the eyes. Blu and Jewel are already the only blue characters in the film, but their eyes are surrounded by concentric tones and are dotted with large and colorful irises.

"When an image comes up on screen," says Cardone, "we have a very short amount of time for the audience to read it. We want to direct the audience's eye so it's easily understood. We try to focus everything we do in the film, whether that's with the story, the character color, or the actual shot."

(Top left) **Rafael** – concept art • Sang Jun Lee, *(Top center)* **Toucan chicks** – concept art • Sang Jun Lee, *(Top right)* **Toucans in flight** – concept sketches • Jason Sadler, *(Bottom)* **Rafael with fruit** – concept art • Sang Jun Lee (design) and Ron DeFelice (painting), *(Opposite top and bottom)* **Rafael** – early concept art • Robin Joseph

198 THE ART OF BLUE SKY STUDIOS

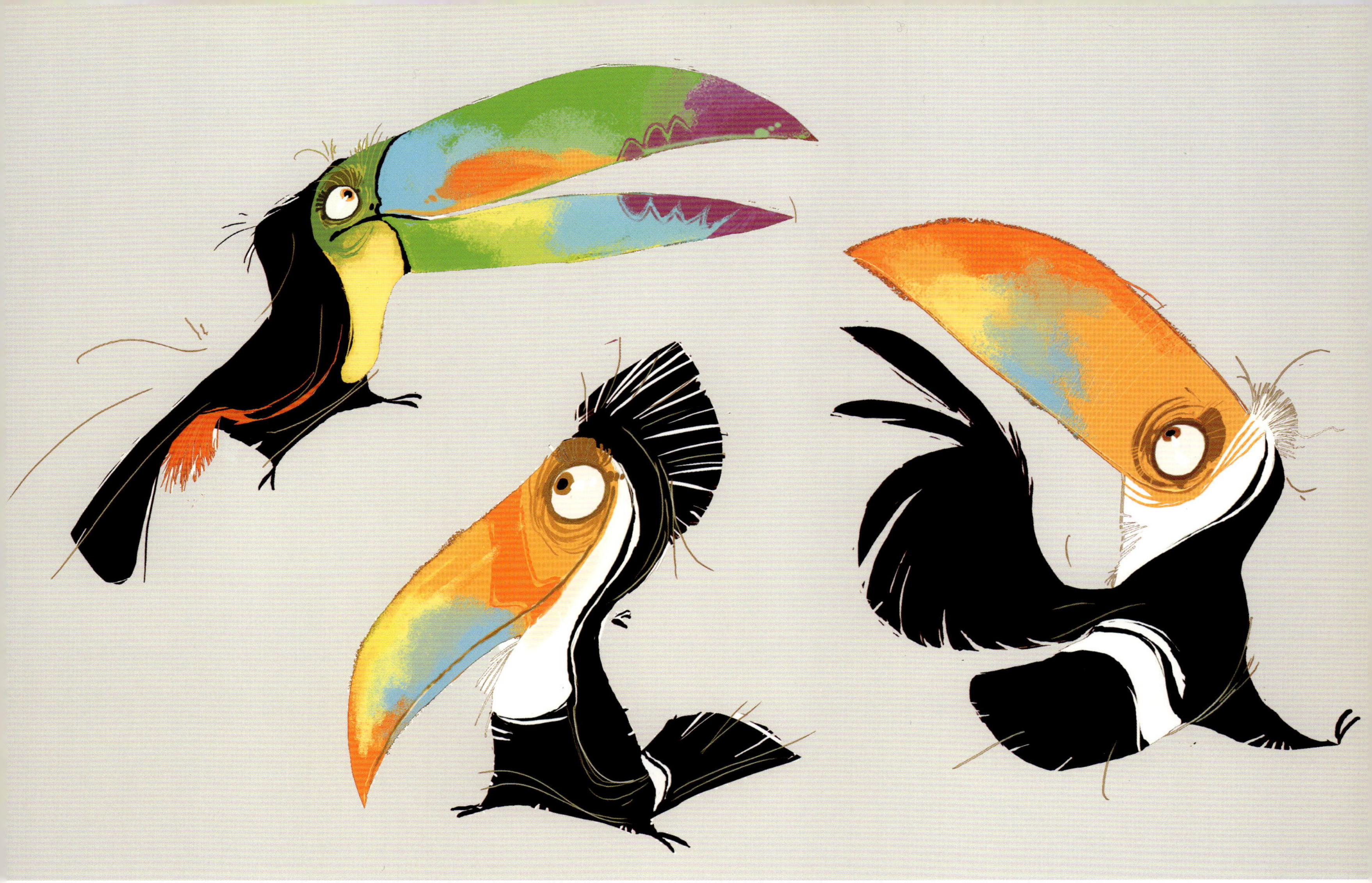

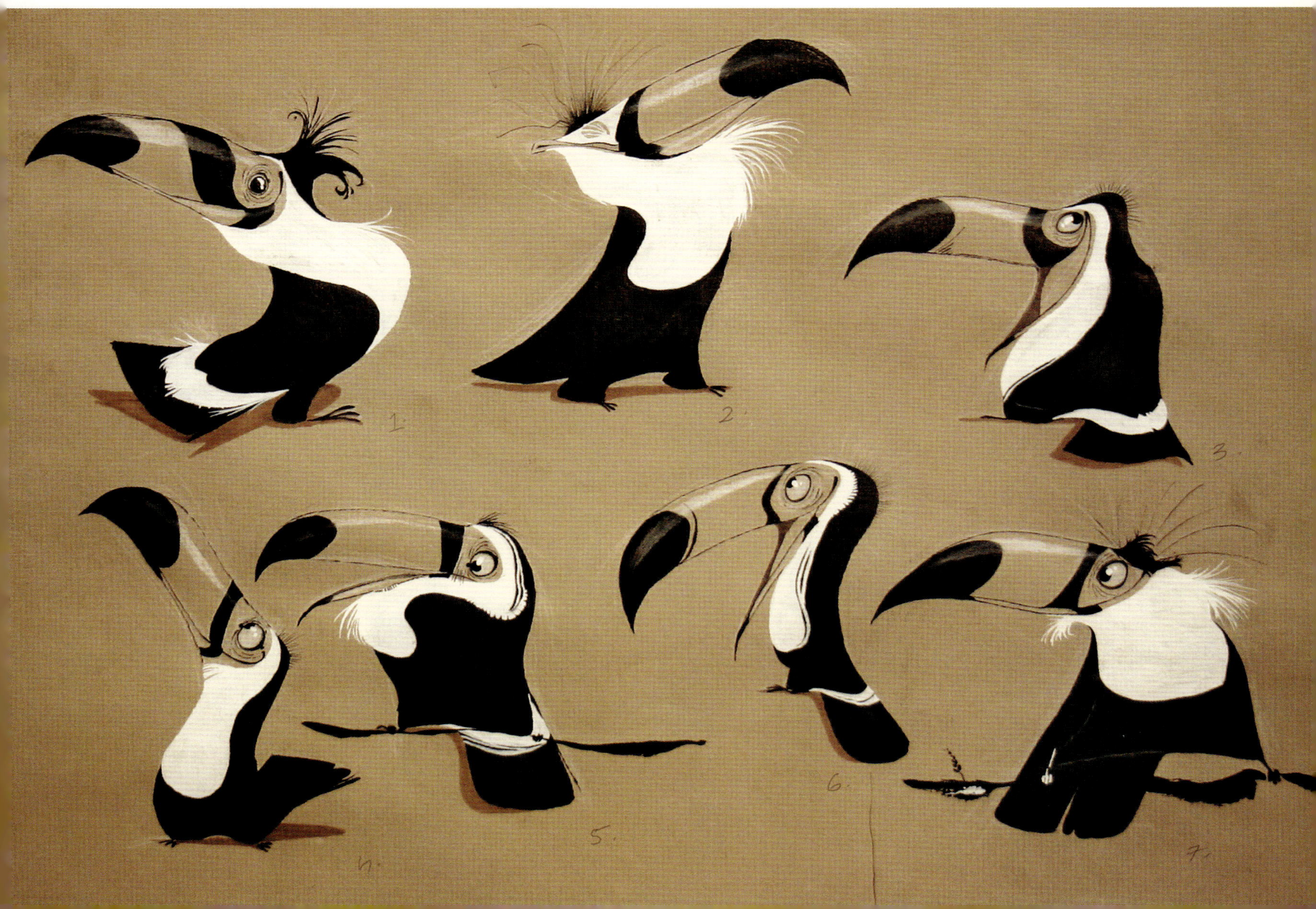
1.
2.
3.
4.
5.
6.
7.

TO DANCE AND SOAR

One of the most complicated sequences in the film was the portrayal of the Carnaval parade. From a graphic standpoint, it was a new visual experience for Cardone. "When we were at Carnaval in Rio," he says, "we could see all the floats and the choreography of the colors—how one flows into the next. It's just mind-blowing."

Cardone observed the parade from a second-story balcony directly over the parade itself. The whole team, including Saldanha, had secured feathery costumes from their local guide and joined in the parade. Like Linda and Tulio in the script, they would experience firsthand the music and rhythm of Carnaval.

After the trip, artists designed and modeled original floats and costumes for the Carnaval sequence, while the animators manipulated dozens of samba dancers with ornate, flowing outfits. "When we were creating the animation cycles for the samba, we tried to feel the elements of Brazilian dance," says Saldanha. "We wanted to make the movement authentic." The animators watched a lot of "How to Samba" videos online, and some even took lessons.

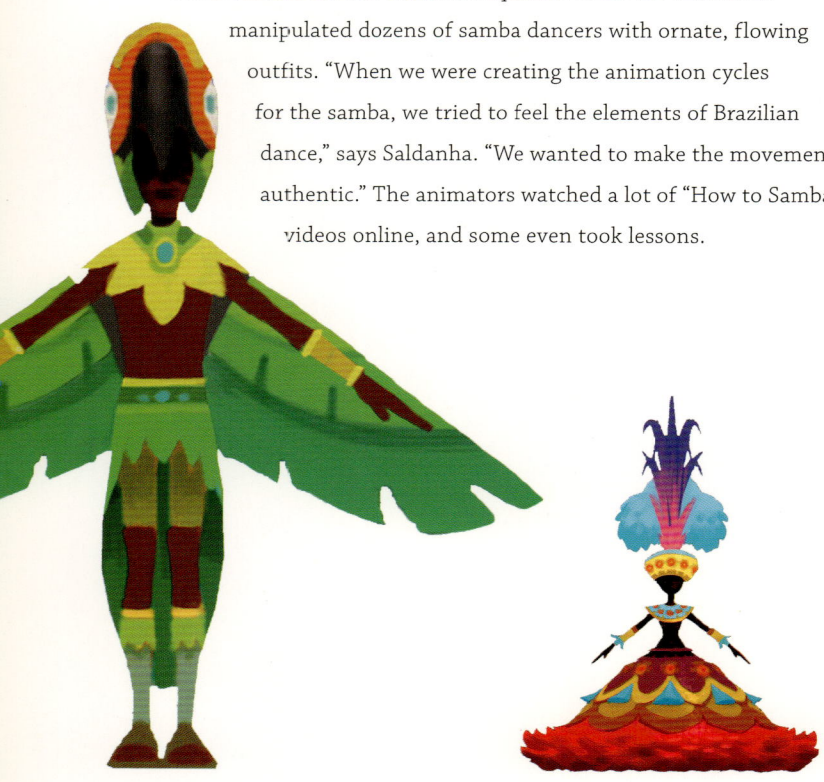

THE ART OF BLUE SKY STUDIOS

(Opoosite top) **Costume designs** – concept art • Jason Sadler, *(Opposite bottom)* **Costume variants** – concept art • Jason Sadler (design) and David Dibble (painting), *(Top)* **Carnaval float** – concept art • Greg Couch, *(Above)* **Dancers in parade** – concept art • Greg Couch

"Having no limits, that's what flying represents to me. That's what I went for."

—CARLOS SALDANHA

(Opposite top left) **Parade float** – concept art • Greg Couch, *(Opposite top right)* **Parade float** – concept art • Rachel Tiep-Daniels (design) and Mike Lee (painting), *(Opposite bottom)* **Carnaval float** – concept art • Greg Couch, *(Top)* **Parade** – final frame, *(Above)* **Lilypad float** – concept art • Arden Chan, *(Bottom left)* **Masks** – concept art • Willie Real, *(Bottom right)* **Chicken float** – concept art • Clayton Stillwell (design) and Jake Panian (painting)

The scene was a technical opus and a show-stopping narrative climax. However, the Carnaval segment was just one of many unforgettable moments in Rio, including the director's personal favorite.

"If there's something I have in common with Blu, it's that I'm afraid of heights," says Saldanha. "But the hand-gliding sequence is the kind of sequence that shows the elements of Rio that make it so unique. It's a very photogenic city, and a bird's-eye view makes it seem breathtaking. But also that sequence represents the essence of the movie, which is freedom and flying. It was the sequence that summed up all that I was trying to say in the movie."

TAKING OFF

Rio had its premiere in Rio de Janeiro in March 2011, to thunderous applause. After its US release in April, it went on to become the highest-grossing Blue Sky film outside the *Ice Age* franchise, with more than $484 million at the global box office. It also birthed the second franchise of the company, with a successful sequel just a few years away. Critics gave it glowing reviews, and the film made Saldanha a Brazilian national hero, all because of a little macaw who was afraid to spread his wings.

And as for what "flying" means to Saldanha? "For me it's the freedom to do what you love and to be who you are. Having no limits, that's what flying represents to me. That's what I went for."

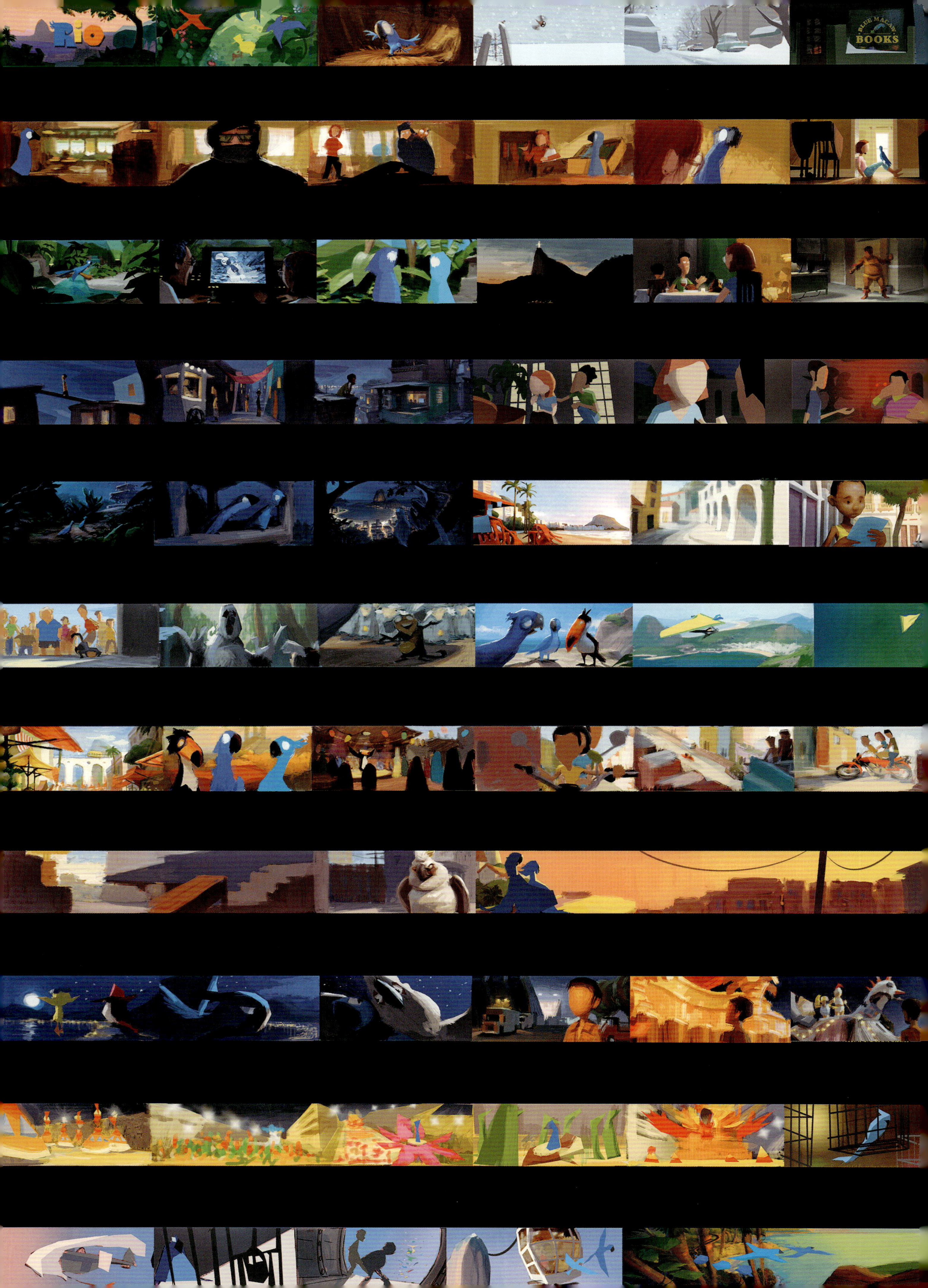
Rio
BLUE MACAW
BOOKS

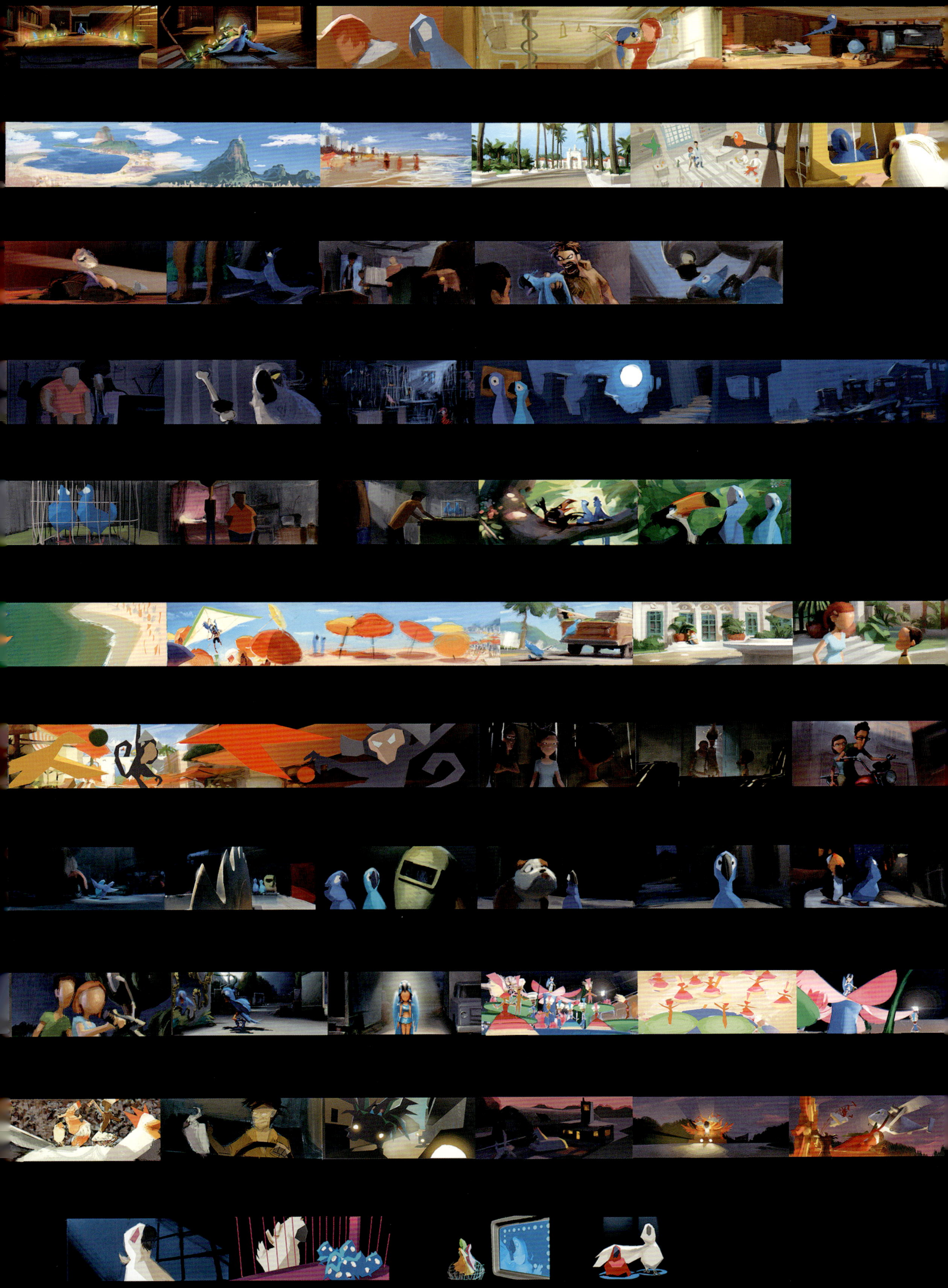

A LOOK INSIDE BLUE SKY

The Previs Department

PLANNING IS EVERYTHING IN FILMMAKING. CG filmmakers must first translate 2-D preproduction art—such as 2-D animatics (storyboard images spliced with sound) and concept paintings—into three dimensions. That initial 2-D art is delivered to the Previs department (short for "pre-visualization"), who figure out precisely how each scene will affect the Modeling, Rigging, Animation, Camera, and Lighting departments. It is in the Previs department that the images are first seen in 3-D, albeit in rough draft. The team produces very rough CG animations of complicated scenes, complete with an approximation of character placement and camera movements. These animations are viewed by all the departments to help them better understand what challenges lay ahead in production and how best to allocate their resources. *Rio* was the first Blue Sky film to have a fully fleshed-out Previs department, started and supervised by Brian Useo.

"The studio's final product is a 3-D movie, so it helps the directors and art directors to visualize the scenes in a more complete way than a 2-D design would," says Useo. "It's our job to translate those 2-D designs into 3-D for the first time, and we're literally creating everything from scratch. We do everything rough and fast and more 'proof of concept,' but we've ended up having more responsibility in helping people on the production side. So we do a rough modeling of the sets, rough materials, rough lighting, rough effects, rough animation camerawork—a little of everything—and we can get it done in an incredibly short amount of time. These Previs artists are like super-talented jacks of all trades."

(Previous pages) **Rio color script** • Thomas Cardone, *(Top)* **Bookstore** – previs frame • Sheng-Fang Chen, *(Opposite top)* **Bookstore shelves** – lighting frame • Svetla Gressak, *(Center)* **Moose Lake Village** – previs frame • Thomas Leavitt, *(Opposite center)* **Moose Lake Village** – lighting frame • Jeeyun Sung, *(Bottom)* **Smugglers' Warehouse** – previs frame • Thomas Leavitt, *(Opposite bottom)* **Smugglers' Warehouse** – lighting frame • Angel Camacho

RIO 207

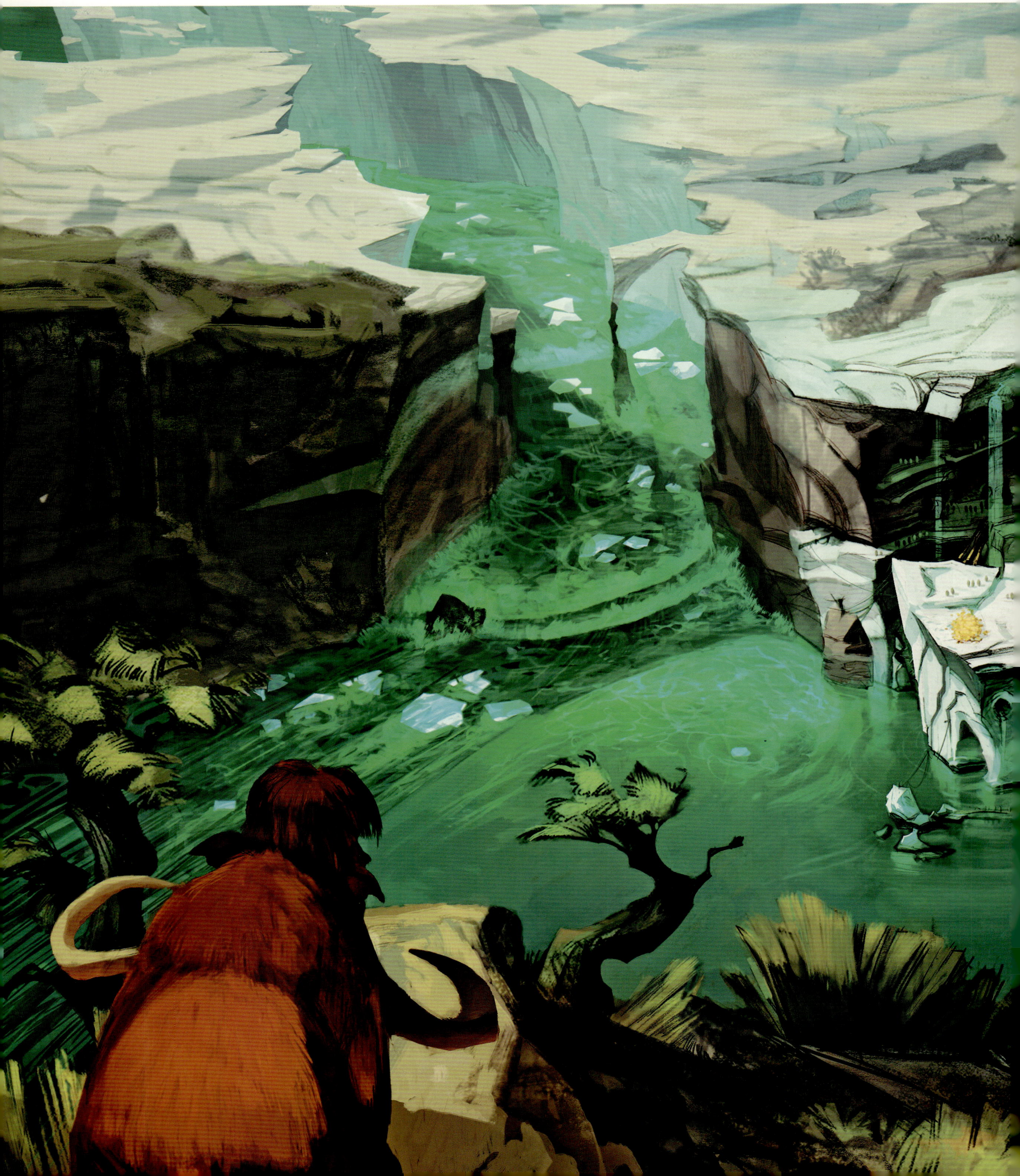

CHAPTER 7 • *Ice Age: Continental Drift*

> *"When this ends, I'll have a tiger skin hanging on my wall. I don't care whose. That mammoth has taken my ship, my bounty, and now the loyalty of my crew! I will destroy him and everything he loves."*
>
> —CAPTAIN GUTT

The *Ice Age* series was increasing in popularity with each successive film. Globally it was fast becoming one of Fox's most valuable properties. And there were still stories to tell, creatures to encounter, and natural phenomena to explore.

While *Rio* was being completed, the studio elected veteran directors Steve Martino and Mike Thurmeier to helm the fourth *Ice Age* film. Sharing directing duties would make a project this enormous considerably more manageable. Martino channeled his art directing experience into overseeing the look he envisioned for the film, while Thurmeier directed with an animator's sense of timing, honed by years of supervising teams on previous Blue Sky films.

What resulted was an adventure that managed to be more fantastical than any previous *Ice Age* story, while still staying true to the tone of the series. In *Ice Age: Continental Drift*, we find the characters have a slew of new challenges to overcome, from the romantic to the platonic, and from the familial to the nautical. We also meet our first true villains since Soto in the first film a decade before. Now the enemy has taken the form of Captain Gutt and his scurvy crew of prehistoric pirates, a group of colorful rogues who posed new problems for the animation and design teams. But much like the buccaneers in the film, the Blue Sky artists refused to stop until they came out victorious.

THE HEROES RETURN

Like everything *Ice Age*, the script began with longtime producer Lori Forte. "Lori came with some of the major bones of the story," says Martino. "She had read an article about a polar bear being separated from a pack and drifting on a piece of ice for hundreds of miles. She grabbed that little nugget and tucked it away for this film."

(Previous pages) **Manny overlooking beach** – concept art • Kyle Macnaughton, *(Top)* **Gutt with Sid** – early concept sketch • Peter de Sève (design) and Robert MacKenzie (painting), *(Opposite)* **Pirates** – concept art • Peter de Sève (design) and Robert MacKenzie (painting)

210 THE ART OF BLUE SKY STUDIOS

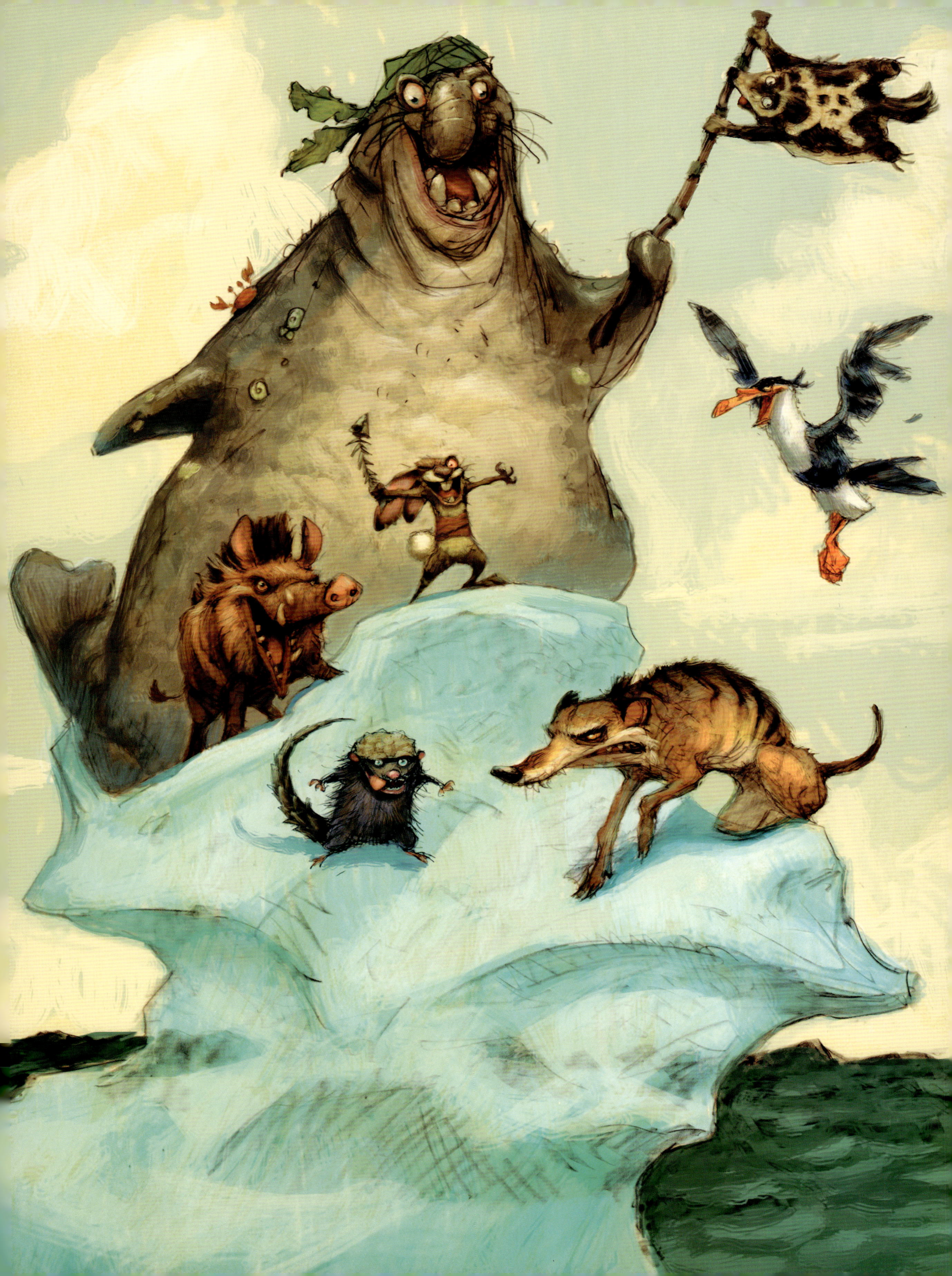

Within the *Ice Age* franchise, Forte is credited with developing stories from the universal aspects of family dynamics. For instance, this film introduces us to the adolescent Peaches, Manny and Ellie's rebellious teen daughter. The concept resonated with Martino, whose daughter would be about the same age, in mammoth years. "I was projecting onto Manny, because I was living that," he says. "I'm watching other parents trying to hold on too tight, and it seemed like we could mine comedy from this universal feeling that so many of us go through, either as parents or as kids trying to pull away."

On the other side of the coin are Sid's dysfunctional blood relatives, who abandoned him years before. The inspiration came from a scene in the original *Ice Age* in which Sid climbs down his tree looking for his family. He calls for them by name, including Uncle Fungus, only to find that they left him alone. Now they have returned, with aged sloth Granny in tow. They leave just as quickly as they come, ditching Granny on Sid. Although related to him, they don't accept him like Manny, Diego, and the others do. It's a reminder that family isn't necessarily defined by blood relations. "Sid's true family is the people he's with now," says Thurmeier. "So it's a different message, but an important one."

Both herd and family get split up when Manny, Diego, Sid, and Granny are set adrift in a tsunami, leaving Ellie, teenage Peaches, and the others on the mainland. Our heroes ride the waves atop their ice floe until they sail into Captain Gutt and his pirate crew. They are a ruthless bunch, but Shira the white saber-toothed tiger meets her match in Diego.

"Diego's been a lone tiger," says Forte. "He was ousted from his group, and he betrayed his pack, and he never really expected that other saber-toothed tigers would allow him to be part of their group because of what he has done. And here he finds Shira, who is just as rebellious as he is, and every bit as challenged, and suddenly he's found someone who melts his heart." Hard-boiled but empathic, Diego welcomes her to the herd—a community where everyone watches out for one another.

It takes the length of the film for Shira to turn her back on her fellow pirates. Scurvy as they are, they're characters you love to hate. And unfortunately for the *Ice Age* heroes, revenge is a dish they serve cold.

(Top) **Mountains with waterfalls** – concept art • Kyle Macnaughton, *(Opposite center)* **Island landscape** – concept art • Jon Townley, *(Opposite bottom left)* **Shira's island** – concept art • Andrew Hickson, *(Opposite bottom right)* **Scrat with acorn** – character sketch • Peter de Sève

ICE AGE: CONTINENTAL DRIFT 213

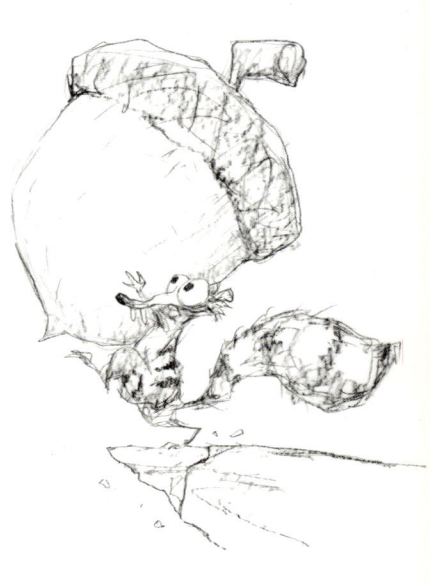

(Above) **Heroes coming ashore** – concept art • Kyle Macnaughton

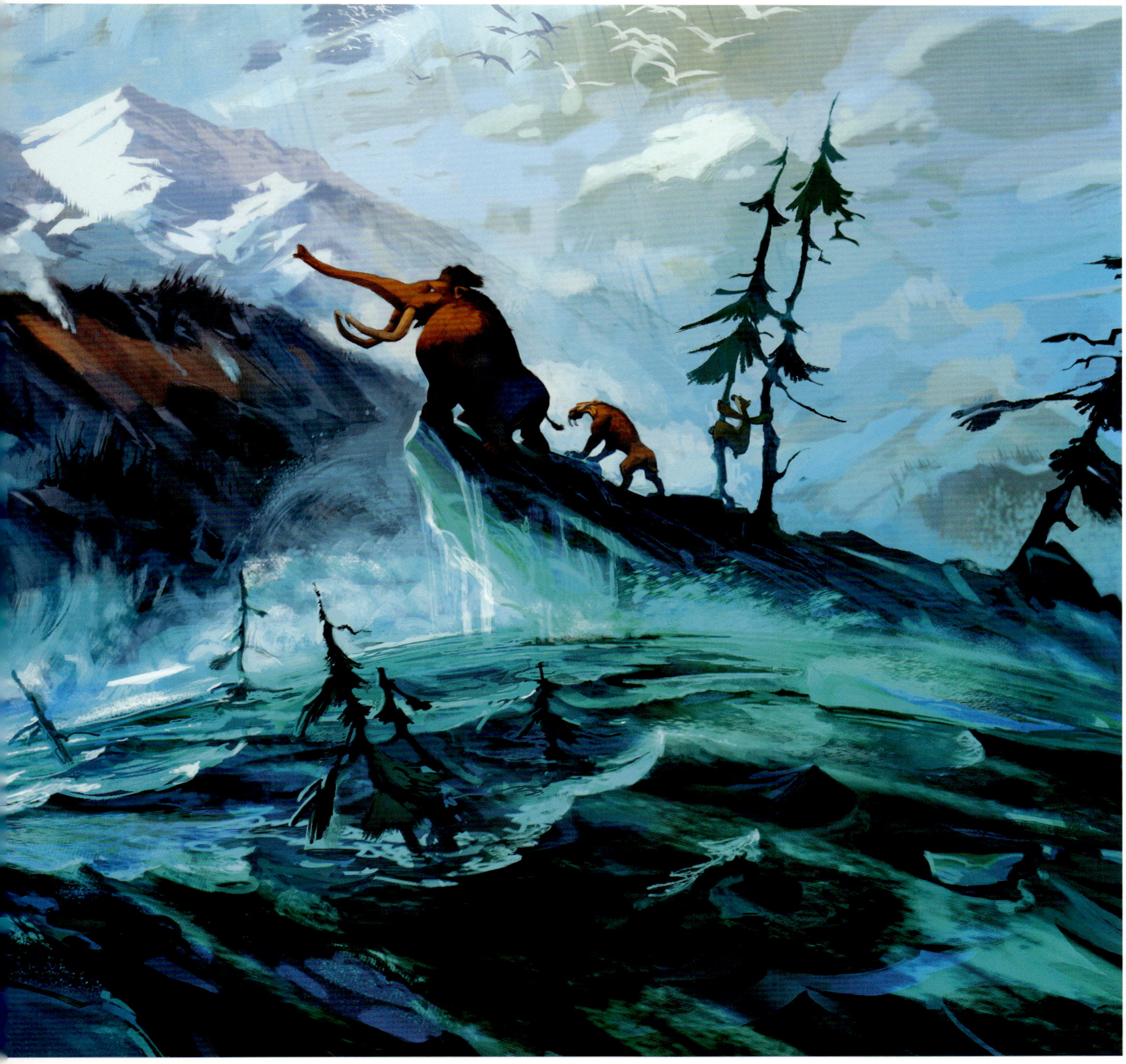

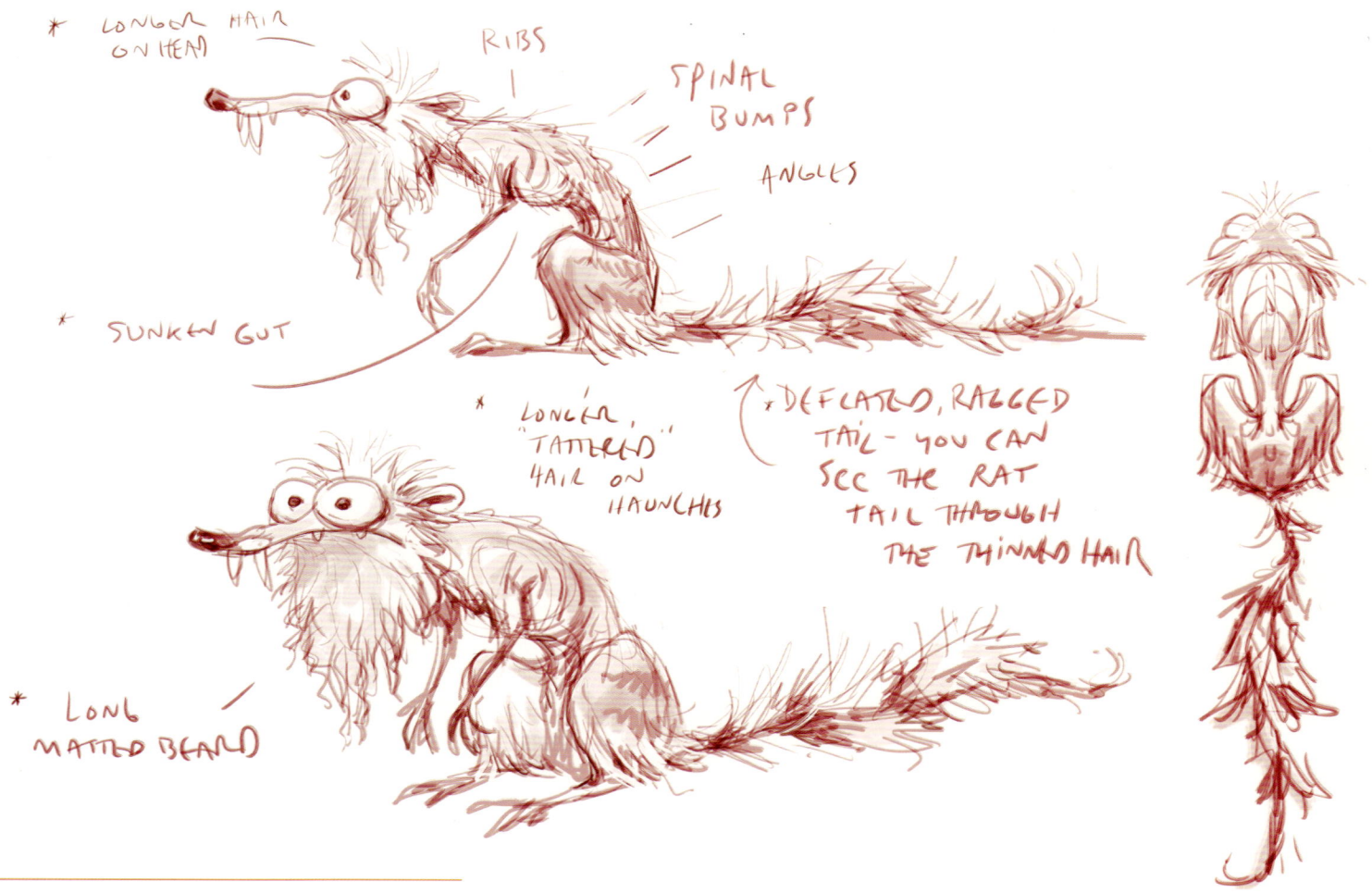

(Top) **Castaway Scrat art** – concept art • Peter de Sève,
(Above) **Castaway Scrat** – character designs • Peter de Sève

216   THE ART OF BLUE SKY STUDIOS

Granny & Precious

ORIGINALLY, GRANNY'S LOST PET, Precious, was going to be a giant squid before it evolved into the prehistoric whale that we see in the film, an animal that fits the characteristics of the extinct *Livyatan melvillei*. "I just knew I wanted to do a prehistoric whale and needed to 'prehistorize' it," says de Sève, "and those were the features I gave it. But I wanted paleontologists to see them and recognize the characters, to know that I've done due diligence."

The directors differed as to whether Precious is Granny's actual pet or not. Martino feels that Granny's missing pet was a whale all along, but Thurmeier objects.

"Just how *crazy is* Granny?" Thurmeier laughs. "I think Granny's pretty crazy. The whale saw that she was feeding it and became her friend, but my personal interpretation is she's never seen that whale before in her life."

(Top left and top right) **Granny poses** – concept art • Peter de Sève, *(Top center)* **Granny** – painting over sculpt • Peter de Sève (design), Ric Sluiter (painting), and Michael Defeo (sculpt), *(Above)* **Precious** – color key • Vincent Di Nguyen, *(Below)* **Sloth family** – character designs • Peter de Sève (design) and Ron DeFelice & Michael Knapp (painting)

PIRATICAL ENOUGH

The designs of Gutt and his motley crew began at the tip of Peter de Sève's pencil. One of the pirates is a diminutive rabbit known as Squint, but the filmmakers had once considered him for captain. Squint was designed with a peg leg made from a narwhal tusk but with the same compromised stature. "He was going to be a Napoleonic badass," says Martino, "but we realized that if Manny made just one misstep, he'd squash him. We needed something to go up against Manny that would be a tangible force."

That's when de Sève pitched the idea of a pre-orangutan known as a *Gigantopithecus*. "Immediately when I drew him, I thought, 'He's perfect,'" says de Sève. "He can swing from the yardarms and rigging of the ship like nobody else. He'd be fun to animate, and we've never seen an orangutan villain. It would be unique, and I think it turned out pretty cool."

"With Peter de Sève you don't just get a character designer, you get really valuable story ideas," says Thurmeier.

"He's always looking to make the presentations of characters funny," says Martino, "to show off not just their form but their personalities, too."

(Top left) **Flynn** – character design • Peter de Sève (design) and Peter Nguyen (painting), *(Top right)* **Silas** – character design • Peter de Sève (design) and Ric Sluiter (painting), *(Opposite top left)* **Dobson** – character design • Peter de Sève (design), Alena Wooten (sculpt), and Vincent Di Nguyen (painting), *(Opposite top right)* **Squint** – painting over sculpt • Peter de Sève (design), Peter Nguyen (painting), and Vicki Saulls (sculpt), *(Right)* **Rat poses** – early concept art • Peter de Sève, *(Opposite bottom)* **Iceberg ship** – concept art • Ric Sluiter

THE ART OF BLUE SKY STUDIOS

ICE AGE: CONTINENTAL DRIFT   219

The directors retained as much orangutan in the character as they could lest Gutt came to resemble *Tarzan*'s Kerchak or other gorilla movie villains. Thus, his orangutan fur had to look both naturalistic and distinct. Art director Nash Dunnigan was entrusted to nail down the visual tone of the film.

Dunnigan had studied art at the Virginia Commonwealth University before becoming a freelance illustrator in New York and then working for local TV animation studios. Luckily, a friend advised him to learn Maya if he wanted to break into features. He took the advice and landed a job at Blue Sky creating layouts for *Robots*. He segued into design and later art directed the short *Surviving Sid*. Despite his major experience, tackling Gutt and his crew proved to be a considerable challenge.

"We looked across the board at different types of simians with crazy hair displays," says Dunnigan, "and once we did, we thought it could work for Gutt, if we made it organic enough. We thought of how to get colorful and flamboyant fashion without making a costumed version of an animal."

Just as Gutt's matted dreadlock whiskers resemble those of Blackbeard, his shoulder tufts look like a sea captain's epaulets, while the hair on his head is moussed to resemble a pirate's signature tricornered hat. "Are the characters 'piratical' enough?" was a question de Sève would often ask the filmmakers.

220   THE ART OF BLUE SKY STUDIOS

Sticking to the rules of the *Ice Age* universe, only humans may wear textiles. But that doesn't mean that fur or found objects can't resemble a semblance of clothing. Squint the rabbit wears his ears down like the tail of a cap. The kangaroo Rasmussen's ("Raz") legs are groomed like pantaloons. "Initially she was a bar wench with almost a bustier," says Dunnigan, "but then she got tamed back to resemble tattered clothing. The way her legs are painted is meant to look like stockings with stripes on them."

Dobson the boar was given stripes as well. Gupta the badger resembles the Jolly Roger itself. Silas the blue-footed booby has bandana-like feathers. Flynn the elephant seal was designed by de Sève to have natural markings on his back recalling the ornate Maori facial art of Queequeg from *Moby-Dick*.

Shira the white saber-toothed tiger completes the scurvy group, with her earrings of brightly colored shells. The hue of that adornment was part of Dunnigan's color theory throughout the film.

"In developing the palettes for the characters," says Dunnigan, "we have warm earth tones for the good guys, and for the bad guys we went with grayed-out tones with flashes of color. So Shira got those earrings and her bright eyes. They're a nice flash of color against a colder palette. With Gutt, we put that flash of color in his pink face."

Side by side, the two groups look like natural enemies, and Gutt's menacing face is even more formidable against his ashen fur. Add to that a hypnotic tangle of bearded dreadlocks and he's as wild an enemy as we've seen on the ice.

(Opposite top) **Gutt and Granny** – color callout and size comparison • Peter de Sève (design) and Vincent Di Nguyen (painting), *(Opposite bottom)* **Gutt leaping** – design for sculpt • Peter de Sève, *(Top)* **Squint** – early concept art • Peter de Sève, *(Center)* **Raz** – character design • Peter de Sève (design) and Jake Panian (color), *(Bottom left)* **Dobson** – concept art • Marceline Tanguay, *(Bottom right)* **Shira** – color callout • Peter de Sève (design) and Nash Dunnigan (painting)

ICE AGE: CONTINENTAL DRIFT 221

That beard did not come easy. For a character so dynamic, a beard unlike any that had previously been animated was required. "We've had a lot of characters with fur on their surface," says Thurmeier, "but nothing that had to interact with the body or had that kind of simulated feel." It was a new hurdle for the effects team.

In previous CG animation, characters with beards required very stiff whiskers that move like a solid mass when a character turns his head. However, every time Gutt turned, the strands of his beard needed to collide separately and with different levels of entanglement. The Fur department groomed Gutt's beard, and the Sim (or Cloth) department simulated the way it would react to the momentum of his head turning and the interaction with his chest and shoulders.

"It had to feel organic, too," says Dunnigan. "The team built levels of scale on it, so around the edges it's not quite as gnarly and knotted up, but it gets more tangled when it gets into the center." The beard was a milestone for CG effects, no less so than the scenes that depicted the crumbling of the Earth or the storm at sea.

(Top) **Pirate crew** – concept art • Peter de Sève, *(Center)* **Gutt beard breakdown (two images)** – color key and fur guide • Ric Sluiter (painting) and Nash Dunnigan (guide), *(Below)* **Gutt** – final frame

222 THE ART OF BLUE SKY STUDIOS

(Top) **Fireside** – color key • Jake Panian, *(Middle left)* **Hyrax charging** – color key • Peter Nguyen, *(Middle right)* **Hyrax** – color concept art • Ric Sluiter, *(Middle)* **Hyrax** – color sketches • Peter de Séve, *(Bottom)* **Hyrax** – color callout • Peter de Séve (character design), Jake Panian (shield & weapon design), and Ric Sluiter & David Dibble (painting)

Hyrax

THE MAMMALIAN HYRAX LIVE alone on their peaceful island until Captain Gutt enslaves them. Leave it to Sid to be the only one capable of communicating with them.

The hyrax are an indigenous, peace-loving community of cuddly puffs of fur who, thanks to our heroes, are able to realize their full potential as cunning warriors. Once Sid partners with the chief of the hyrax, both groups team up to fight Captain Gutt. The adorable little creatures charge ahead in face paint like the Scots in *Braveheart*, riding other hyrax like warhorses, and save the day.

ICE AGE: CONTINENTAL DRIFT   223

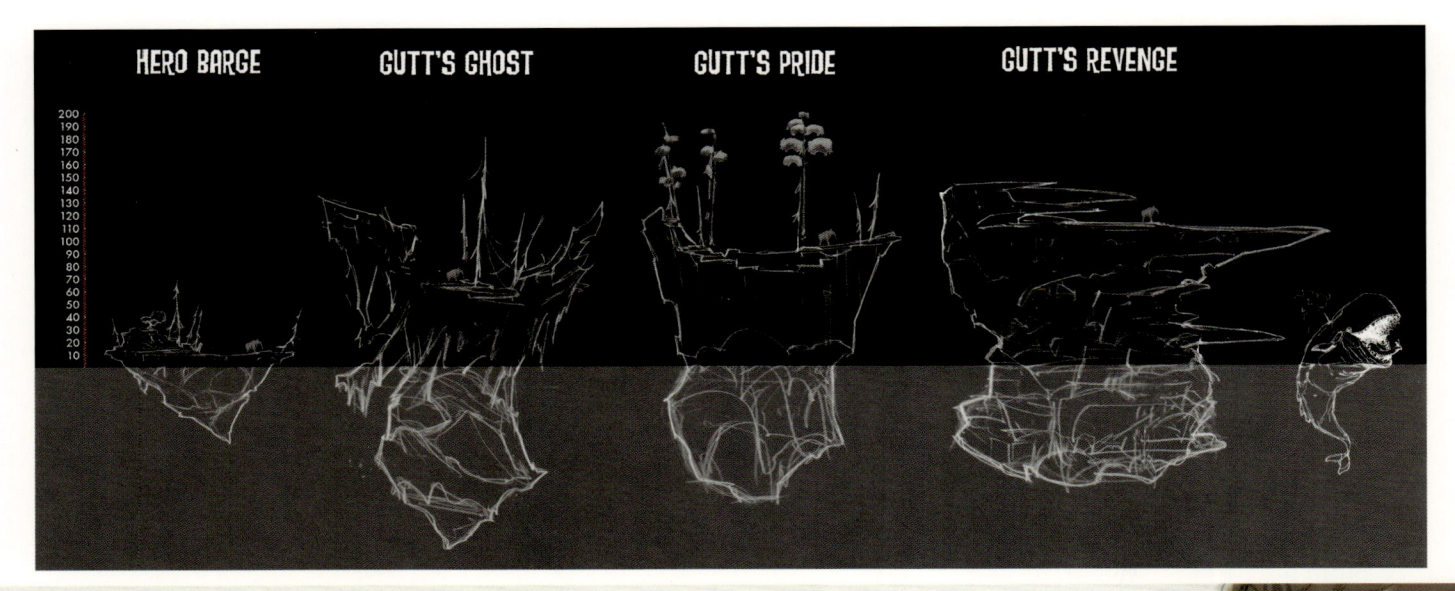

| HERO BARGE | GUTT'S GHOST | GUTT'S PRIDE | GUTT'S REVENGE |

224   THE ART OF BLUE SKY STUDIOS

(Opposite top) **Iceberg ship lineup** – concept art • Jason Sadler, *(Opposite bottom)* **Iceberg ship** – set design • Arden Chan, *(Top right)* **Hero barge** – set design • Clayton Stillwell, *(Center)* **Gutt's ship** – concept art • Clayton Stillwell (design) and Jake Panian (painting), *(Bottom left)* **Gutts's ship** – concept art • Jon Townley (design) and David Dibble (painting), *(Bottom right)* **Gutts's ship** – concept art • Arden Chan & Jason Sadler (design) and David Dibble (painting)

ICE AGE: CONTINENTAL DRIFT   225

(Above) **Trio separated on ice** – concept art • Michael Knapp

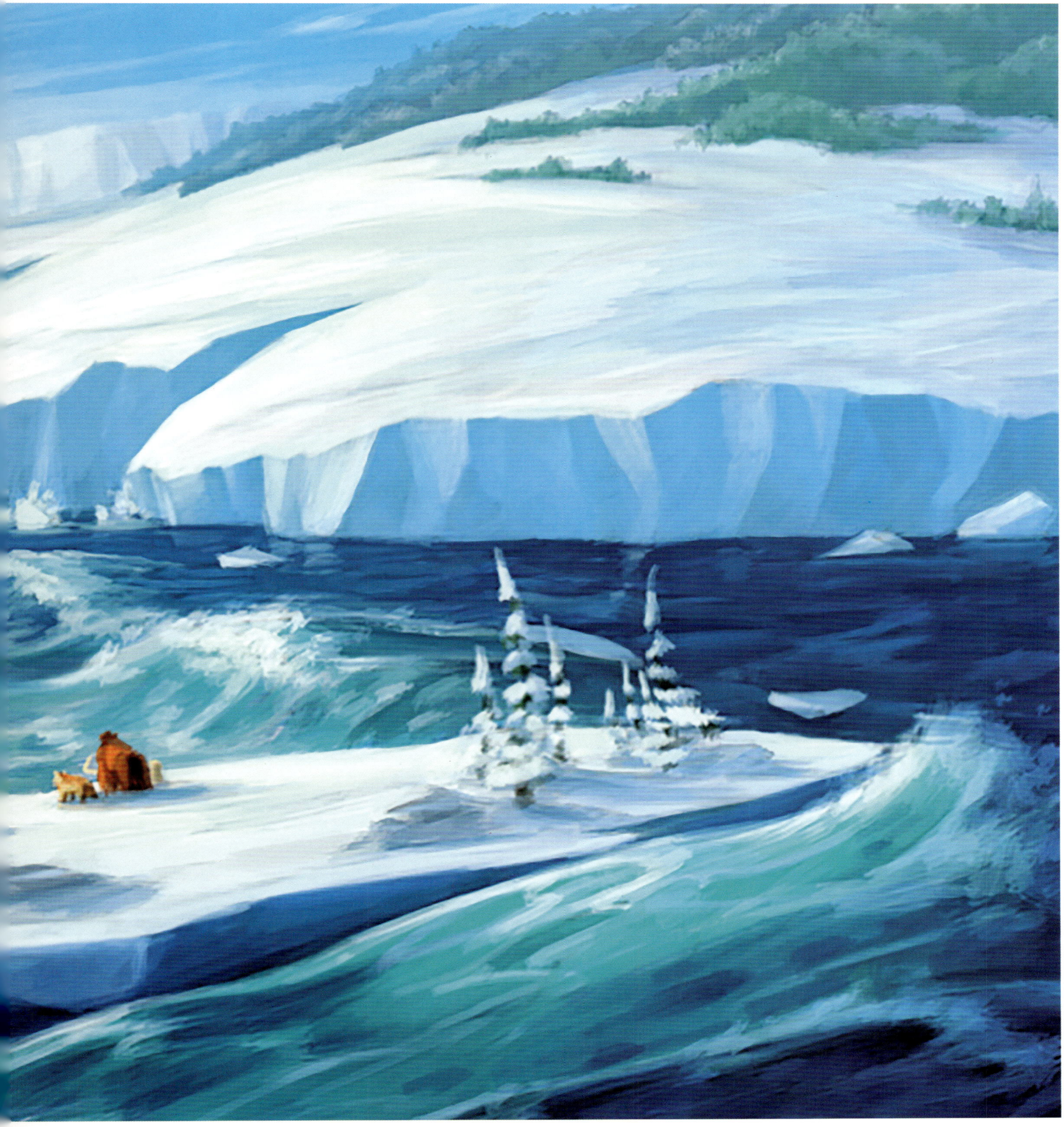

Scratlantis

AT THE FILM'S CLOSE, Scrat has followed a treasure map to an island oasis. It is filled with acorns aplenty and inhabited by a welcoming race of Scrats wearing togas.

"It's happened on every film I've worked on—you never know where the best or funniest idea is going to come from," says Martino. Blue Sky needed something to end the movie with a bang, a sequence that could rival the sequence in which Scrat causes the continental breakup. It was near the closing minutes of a brainstorming session when script supervisor Ed Corcoran blurted out the concept of Scratlantis. Everybody loved it.

"It's been a running joke internally that the Scrat character was designed early on with only three digits," says Martino, "and still he has to grab things all the time, so everyone really wishes he had a thumb." Hence, you might notice that the evolved Scratlantians possess the opposable thumb, long sought by any Blue Sky animator who worked on a Scrat scene.

John Powell's musical score plays underneath all of Scrat's scenes. He pays homage to Beethoven before reaching the choral swell of "Ode to Joy" when the intrepid saber-toothed squirrel arrives in Scratlantis. Powell changed the original German lyrics to the German translation of "nuts of Elysium" and other Scrat-related lines. But that's not all.

"In that sequence where Scrat pulls the plug and everything goes spiraling down into the earth," says Martino, "John Powell's idea was to take the 'Ode to Joy'—one of the fastest versions of 'Ode to Joy' ever played—and then record somebody singing that chorus. He then played it backward and phonetically wrote it out in reverse German. That's what the chorus got on their music stand. They sang 'Ode to Joy,' in reverse, phonetically, at this hyper pace."

"It was faster, it was in another key, and we re-orchestrated it in the style of the classic cartoons," says Powell, "which I'm sure Beethoven would have done if he had ever seen a cartoon."

228 THE ART OF BLUE SKY STUDIOS

(Opposite top) **Nut globe** – concept art • Marceline Tanguay, *(Opposite right)* **Scratlantians (four images)** – concept art • Marceline Tanguay (design) and Jake Panian (design & color), *(Top)* **Floor mosaic** – concept art • Marceline Tanguay (design) and Jake Panian (design & color), *(Bottom)* **Scratlantis plaza** – color key • Marceline Tanguay & Andrew Hickson (set design) and Ric Sluiter (painting)

230 THE ART OF BLUE SKY STUDIOS

(Top left) **Sunset behind islands** – concept art • Lizette Vega, *(Left)* **Scratlantis** – concept art • Marceline Tanguay, *(Above)* **Amphorae designs** – concept art • Marceline Tanguay

ICE AGE: CONTINENTAL DRIFT

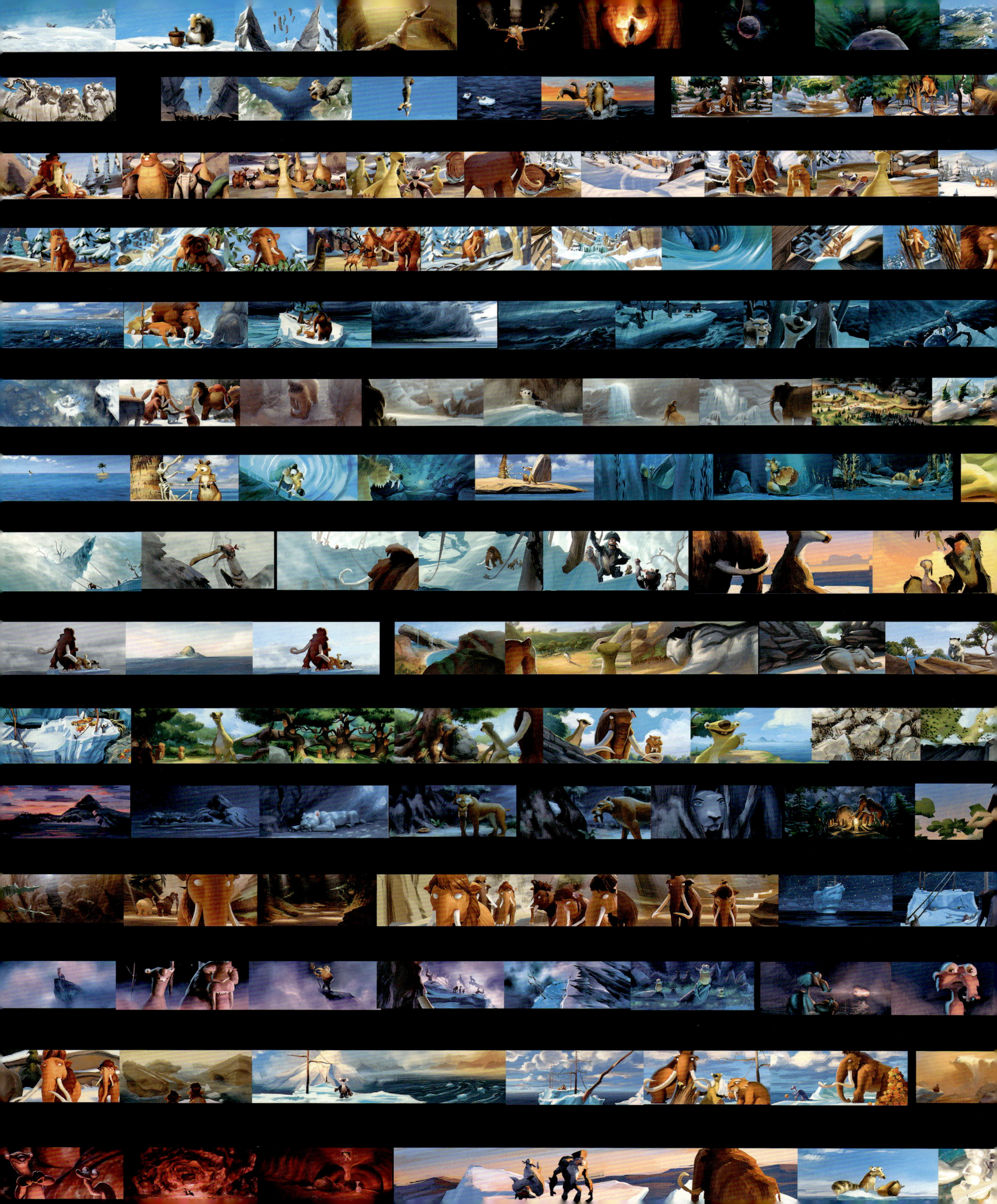

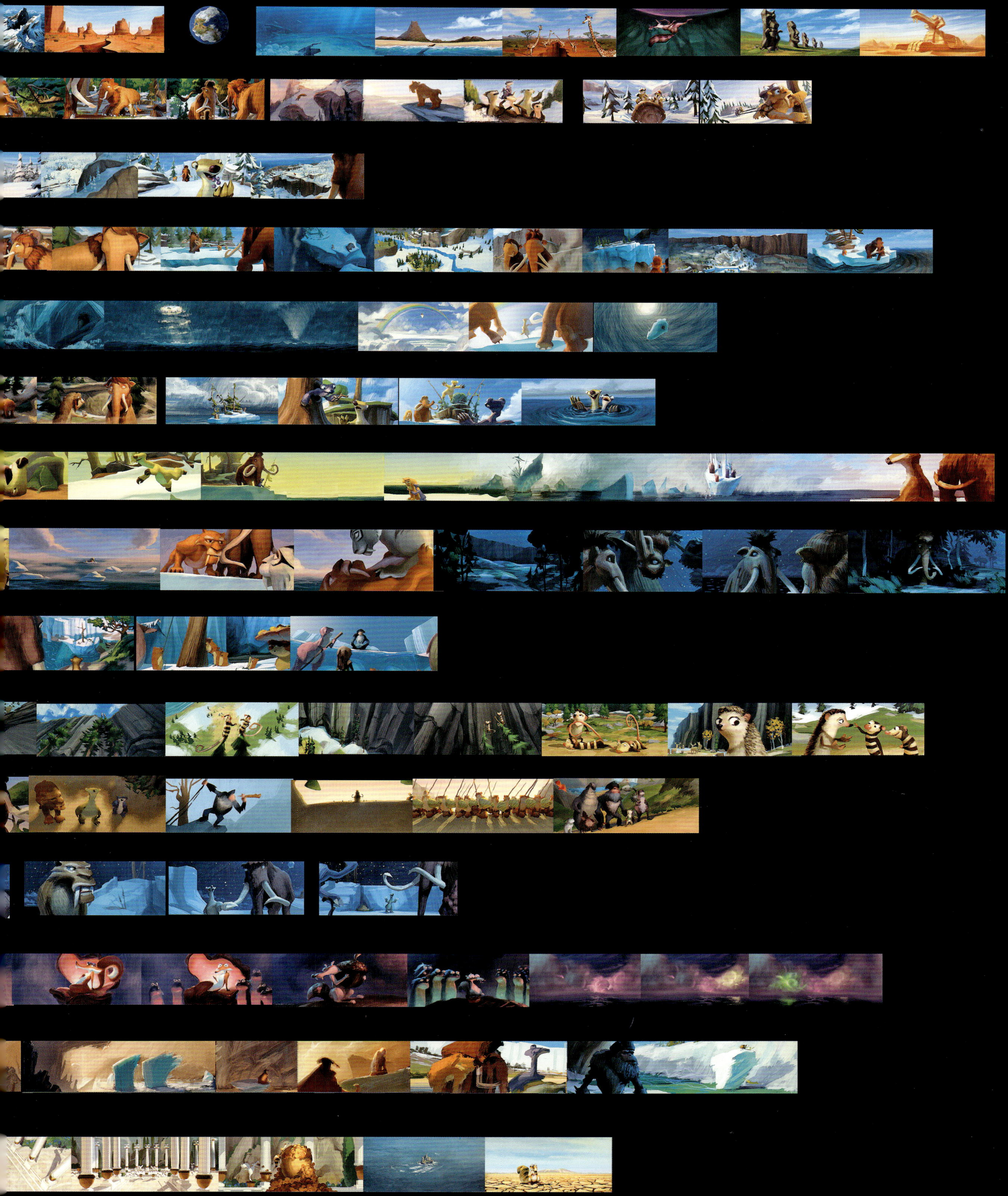

Sirens

THE DIRECTORS TOOK SOME artistic license in *Ice Age: Continental Drift* and added mythical creatures that they felt could fit within the tone of the series. "We're on a quest to get Manny and the characters home," says Martino, "so Homer's *Odyssey* was the inspiration for us."

With dinosaurs bending the rules of science fiction in the third movie and a spaceship appearing in a glacier in the first movie, a little twist of fantasy has become a staple of the *Ice Age* universe. Sticking solely to natural history would defeat the whimsy of a cartoon, and so the Sirens found their way into the film. "We don't take ourselves that seriously," adds Martino, "but our humorous take on Odysseus is our little educational nod."

The Sirens transition from sea serpents to sexpots at will. "I put their eyes on top of their heads because I wanted them to peek out of the water," says de Sève. He designed their mermaid alter egos and their rock perches after the drawings by Swiss symbolist artist Arnold Böcklin.

(Previous pages) **Ice Age 4 color script** • Ron DeFelice, Ric Sluiter, Nash Dunnigan, Dave Dibble, Vincent Di Nguyen and Jake Panian, *(Top)* **Sirens** – concept art • Peter de Sève, *(Bottom)* **Scrat peers at oyster** – color key • Jake Panian, *(Opposite)* **Scrat with sirens** – color keys • Jake Panian

THE ART OF BLUE SKY STUDIOS

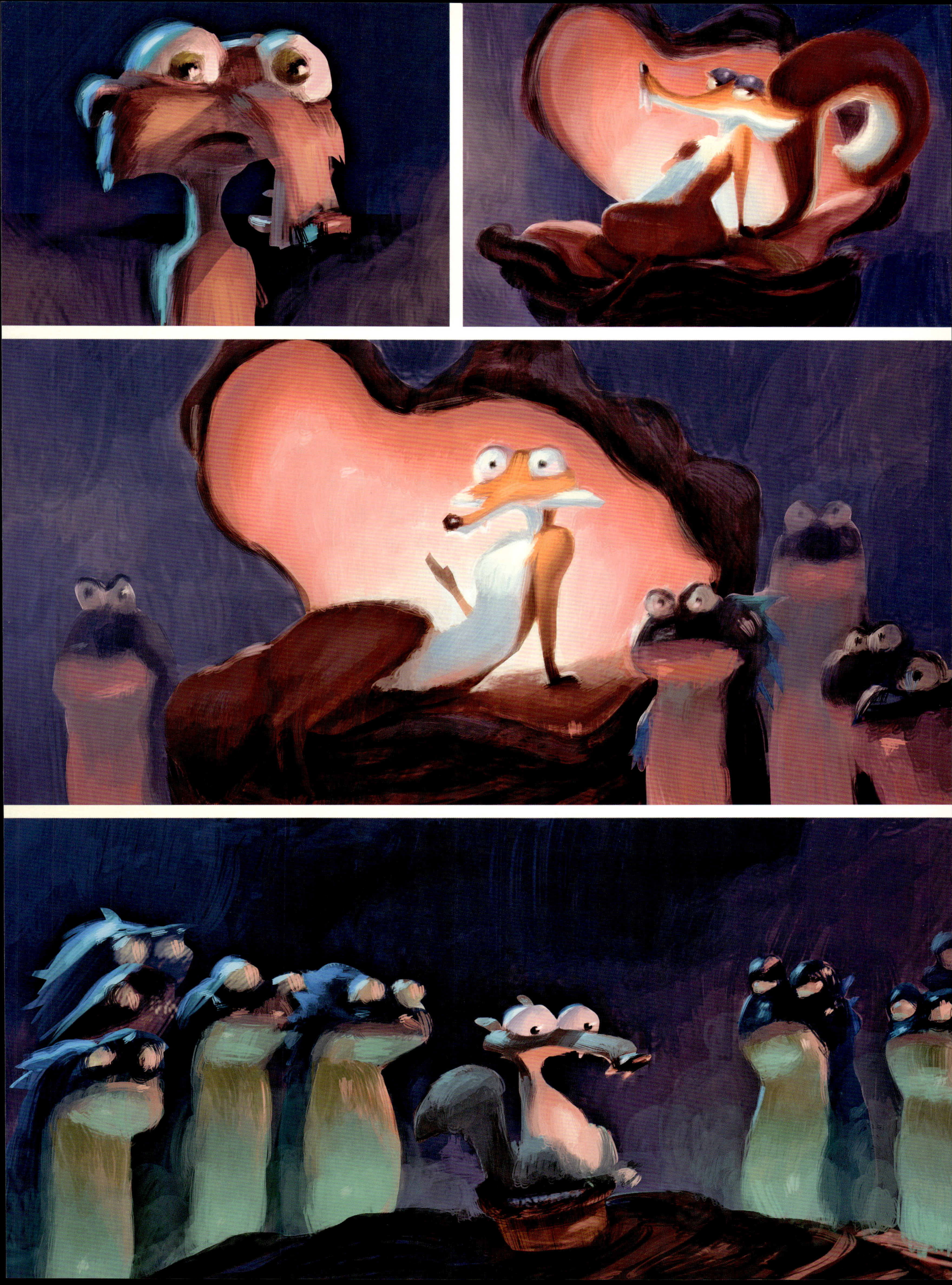

RIDERS ON THE STORM

When it comes to physical animation that is not character-related, the Effects department usually has a hand in it. They manipulate the water, wind, electricity, and other natural elements that interact with the other main elements of a scene. Normally, the production pipeline for a sequence sees the Effects department start their work close to the end, after the Animation department finishes the characters' performance. The "Schism" scenes, in which pieces of tundra break into the ocean, and the "Storm at Sea" scenes where our heroes almost capsize their ice floe, required heavy work from the Effects department at an early stage in order to pull off something so innovative and complex. As a result, the pipeline structure had to shift.

In the first render of the "Schism" scene, something about the earthquake looked askew. The cliff-side collapse seemed inauthentic, although the reason why was not immediately clear. The film needed a semblance of realism if the audience was to feel concern for the characters, and a CG earthquake that looked unrealistic would pull the viewers straight out of the story.

"Someone got the idea to put little tracking markers on everything in the scene," says Martino, "like a little speedometer reading, so everything in the scene had a printout as it was moving. And we were finding that big, heavy hunks of land were moving at an unlikely two hundred fifty miles an hour. It was way beyond what the physics of the real world would suggest, and it gives away the 'cheat' in a big way. We wanted the effects to have real gravity, so when the world crumbles, you feel the enormity of the weight."

"It's like video footage of glaciers crumbling," says Dunnigan. "From far away, they feel like they're falling in slow motion because they're so huge. So there's a sense of scale and believability you get in a camera, and if you fake it, [the audience will] know."

Once the Effects department monitored the scenes, they were able to perfect the physics of the animation. The "Storm" sequence offered its own difficulties that had to be overcome with technological innovation.

"The effects team wrote new software that enabled the layout artist to control the ocean dynamics in an accurate way," says Martino. "They could dial up the chop, or dial up the swells, and control all aspects of the water so it could be believable and be at the kind of scale we were looking for."

"Schism" and "Storm" were some of the most advanced effects shots Blue Sky had ever attempted, and they paved the way for other realistic and dynamic sequences that depicted the humbling power of Mother Nature. Nothing would make better use of the new software than Chris Wedge's next film, a project as organic in concept as *Robots* was mechanical and more ambitious than anything Blue Sky had attempted.

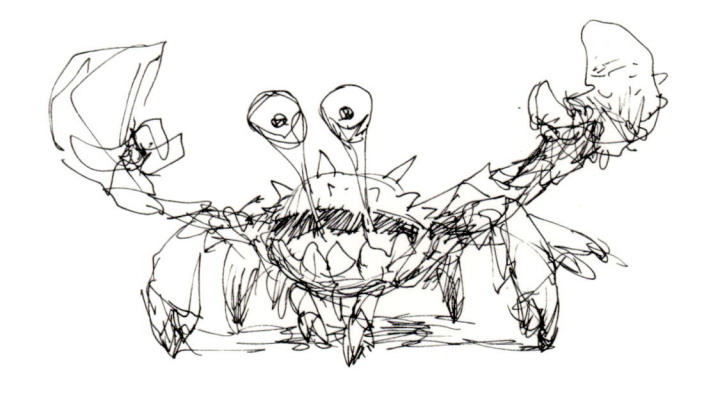

(Above) **Crab** – concept art • Peter de Sève, *(Right)* **Storm cloud** – concept art • Kyle Macnaughton, *(Bottom)* **Tidal wave** – concept art • Michael Knapp (design) and Robert MacKenzie (painting)

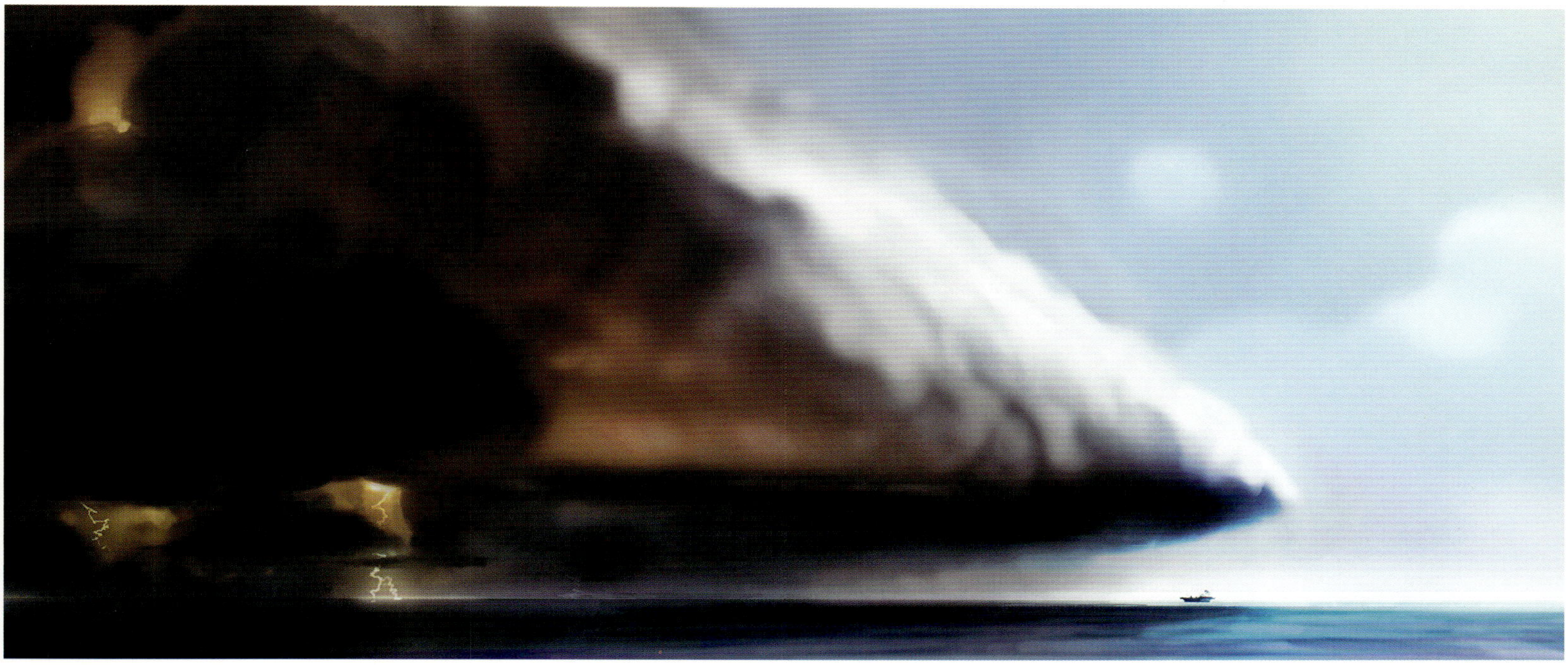

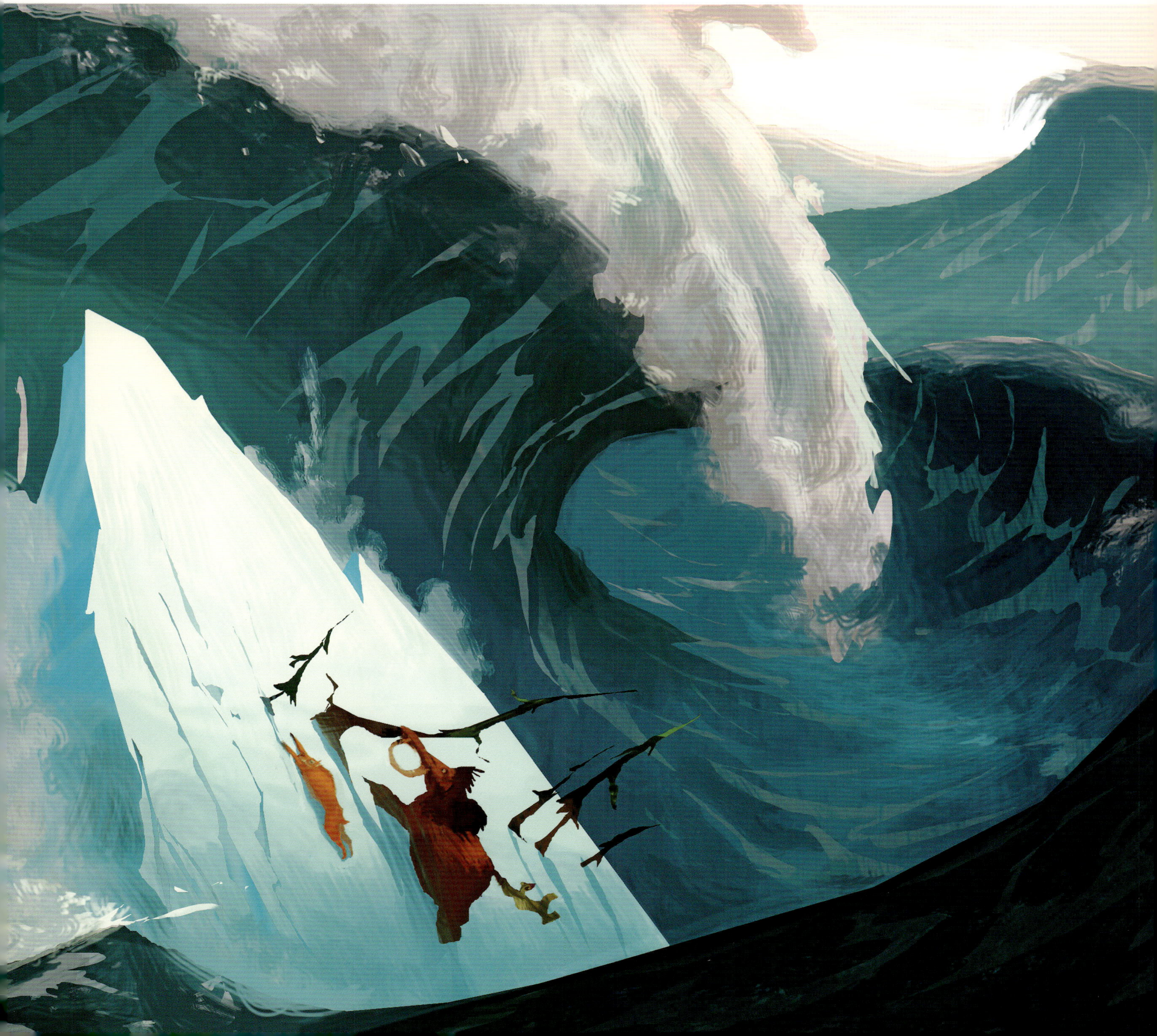

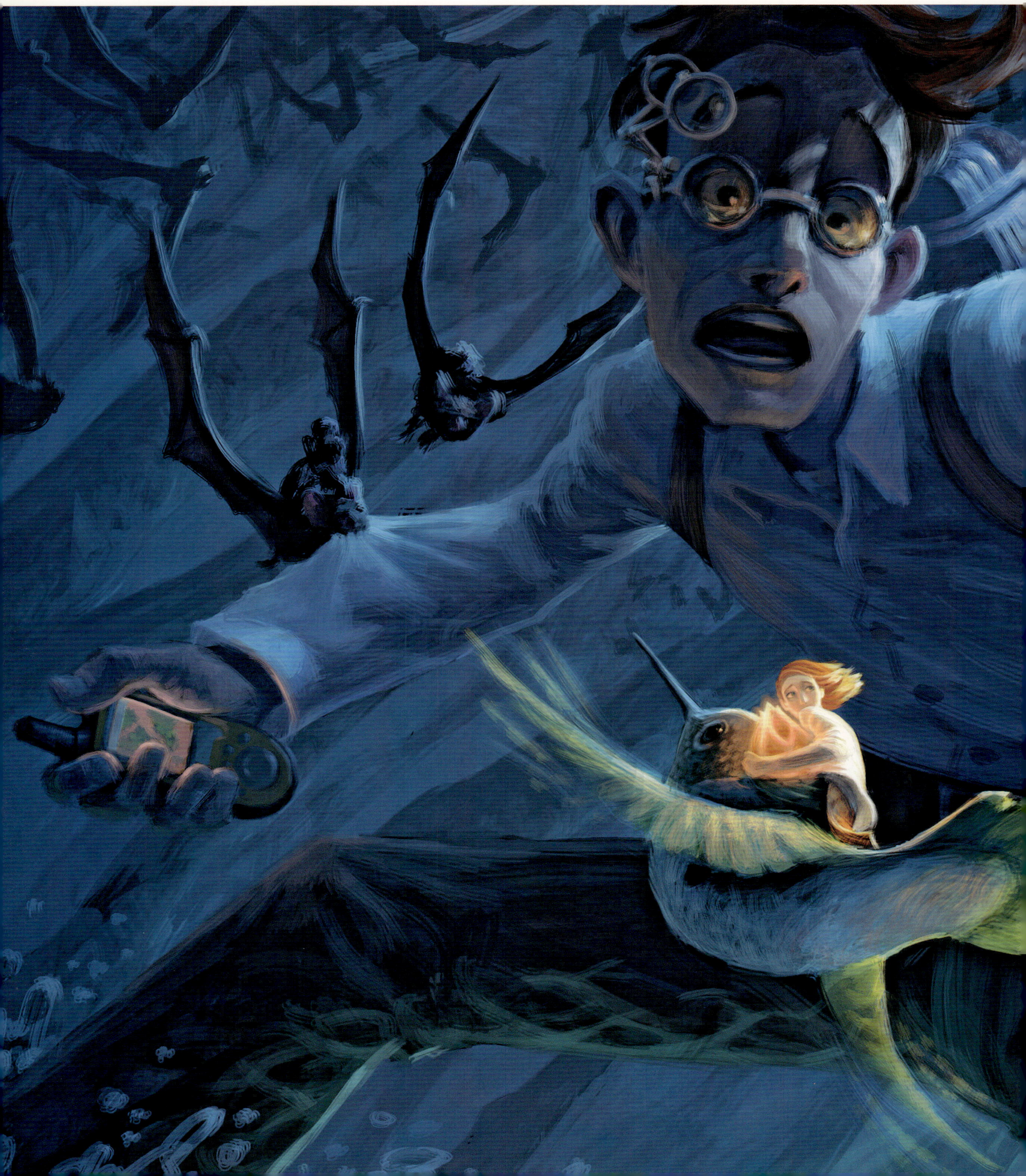

CHAPTER 8 • *Epic*

"Dad? I had the most messed up dream. There were talking slugs and tiny little soldiers and . . . aww, man!"

—MARY KATHERINE

The idea of fantastical creatures hiding in the woods is as old as legend. Chris Wedge and Bill Joyce were both struck by the meticulous history of European folklore, though North American woods hide just as many mysteries for those willing to look. What if, they wondered, there was something just as magical—but a little more contemporary—right here in our own backyard?

"I think *Epic* represents the most mature expression of thinking here at the studio, both technically and creatively," says director Chris Wedge. Although somewhat inspired by Victorian mythology, the vision for *Epic* and its characters is entirely original. "These are samurai who ride hummingbirds," continues Wedge. "People can die in this world, and there's a lot of big action and powerful emotion."

"We wanted to capture the spirit of cheerful adventure and wonder, but always in a style that made it more realistic," says Joyce.

Wedge and Joyce found further inspiration in an exhibit of Victorian paintings at Manhattan's Frick Collection. "It blew my mind," recalls Wedge. "The paintings were incredibly articulate, with astounding detail depicting civilizations in the forest with awesome clarity. Some were tiny mythical creatures cavorting, some were ceremonies of coronations or other activities. I thought, this is the movie to make!"

FROM THE TREES

"I wanted it to feel like the woods of upstate New York," says Joyce. Although Joyce's art studio is based in Louisiana, when he and Wedge were guiding the final stages of production on *Robots*, Joyce was staying in a house in Katonah, New York. "You can walk around up there, and there's an ancient Hawthorne feel," he says. "It's amazing."

At the house, Joyce hosted a dinner party that included Wedge and executive producer James Hart. "After a few drinks, I said, 'Come to the meadow and see your movie,'" recalls Joyce. He led them down a dirt path in the twilight to a field of the most luminous fireflies they had ever seen. The group stood in awe.

(Previous pages) **Battle for Moonhaven** – concept art • Michael Knapp, *(Top)* **M.K. and Mub** – concept art • BJ Crawford, *(Opposite)* **Leafman** – concept art • Michael Knapp

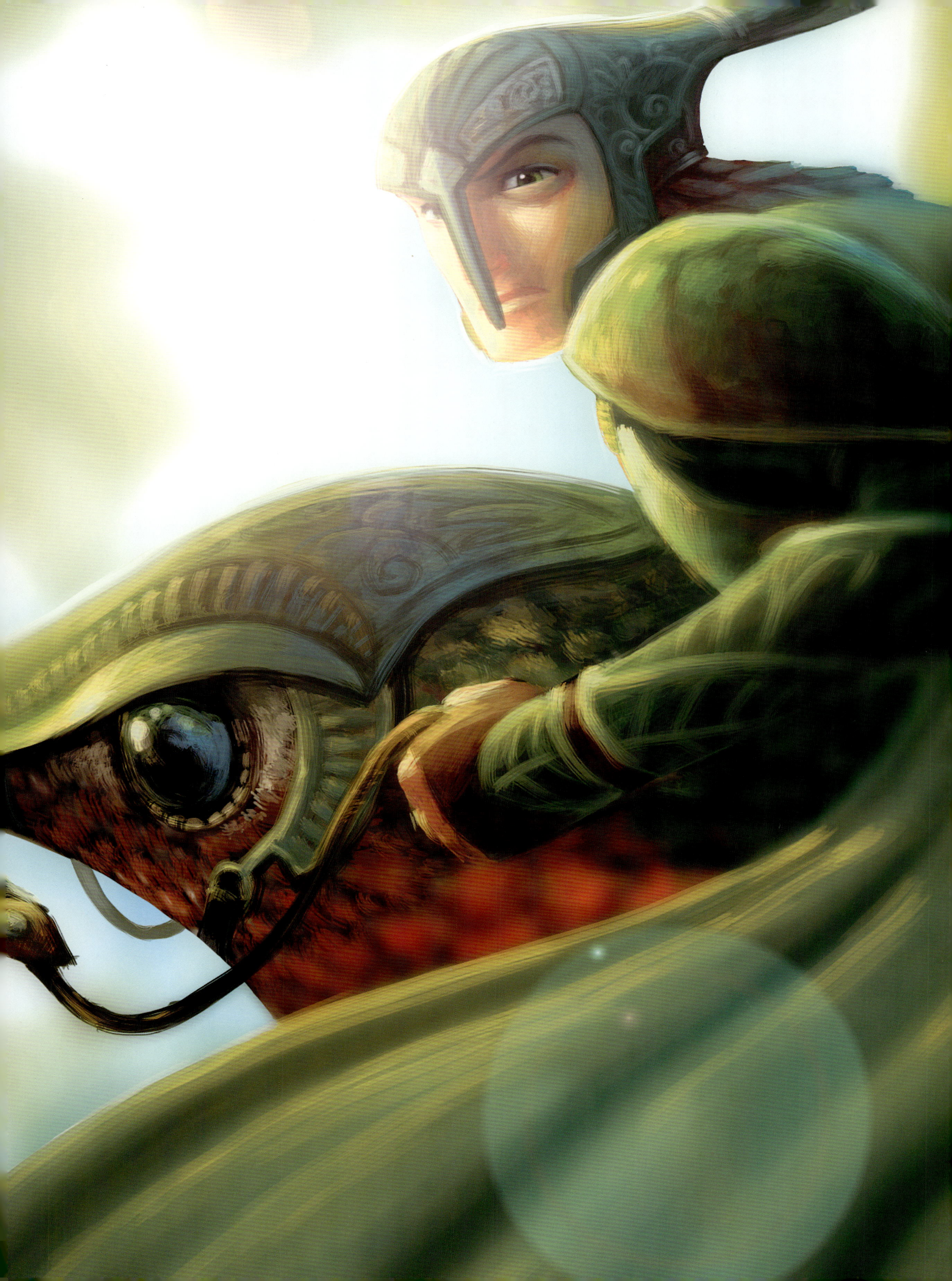

After several drafts, the story of *Epic* crystalized. Mary Katherine is a teenager sent to stay with her eccentric father, Professor Bomba, in his country home. Bomba is obsessed with a tiny civilization in the forest, but Mary Katherine, known as M.K., is incredulous—until she is shrunk down to the size of these tiny people by their monarch, Queen Tara. M.K. soon meets the bird-riding warriors called Leafmen, along with creatures called Boggans, which embody living decay, and the Jinn, beings that personify the flowers and undergrowth of the forest. Before being wounded, the queen of the forest entrusted M.K. with the forest's salvation in the form of a magic pod. Nim Galuu, the caterpillar oracle, unfurls the scrolls of wisdom to direct M.K. on her quest. And so M.K., along with rookie Leafman Nod, seasoned Leafman Ronin, Mub the slug, and Grub the snail, journey to deliver

(Right) **Bomba's house** – 3-D concept design • Rachel Tiep-Daniels, *(Bottom)* **Bomba in forest** – concept art • Kyle Macnaughton, *(Opposite)* **M.K. arriving at Bomba's house** – color key • David Dibble

"I think *Epic* represents the most mature expression of thinking here at the studio, both technically and creatively."

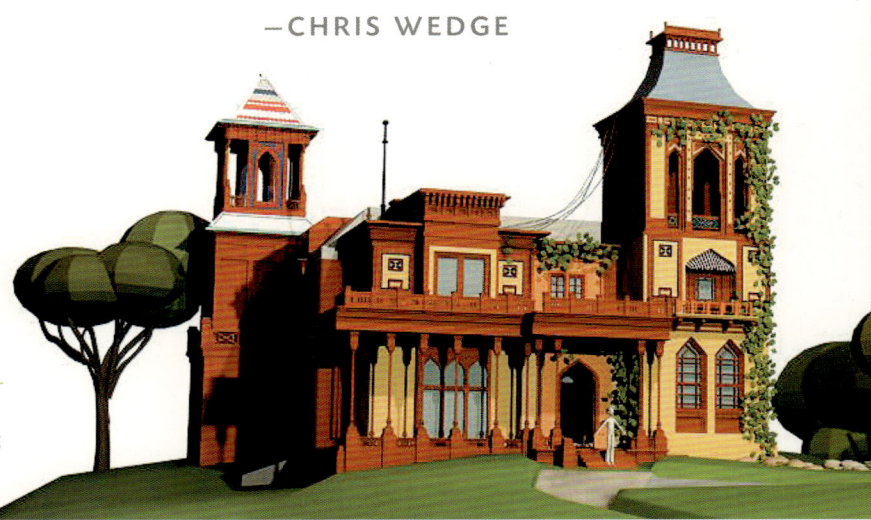

—CHRIS WEDGE

242 THE ART OF BLUE SKY STUDIOS

EPIC 243

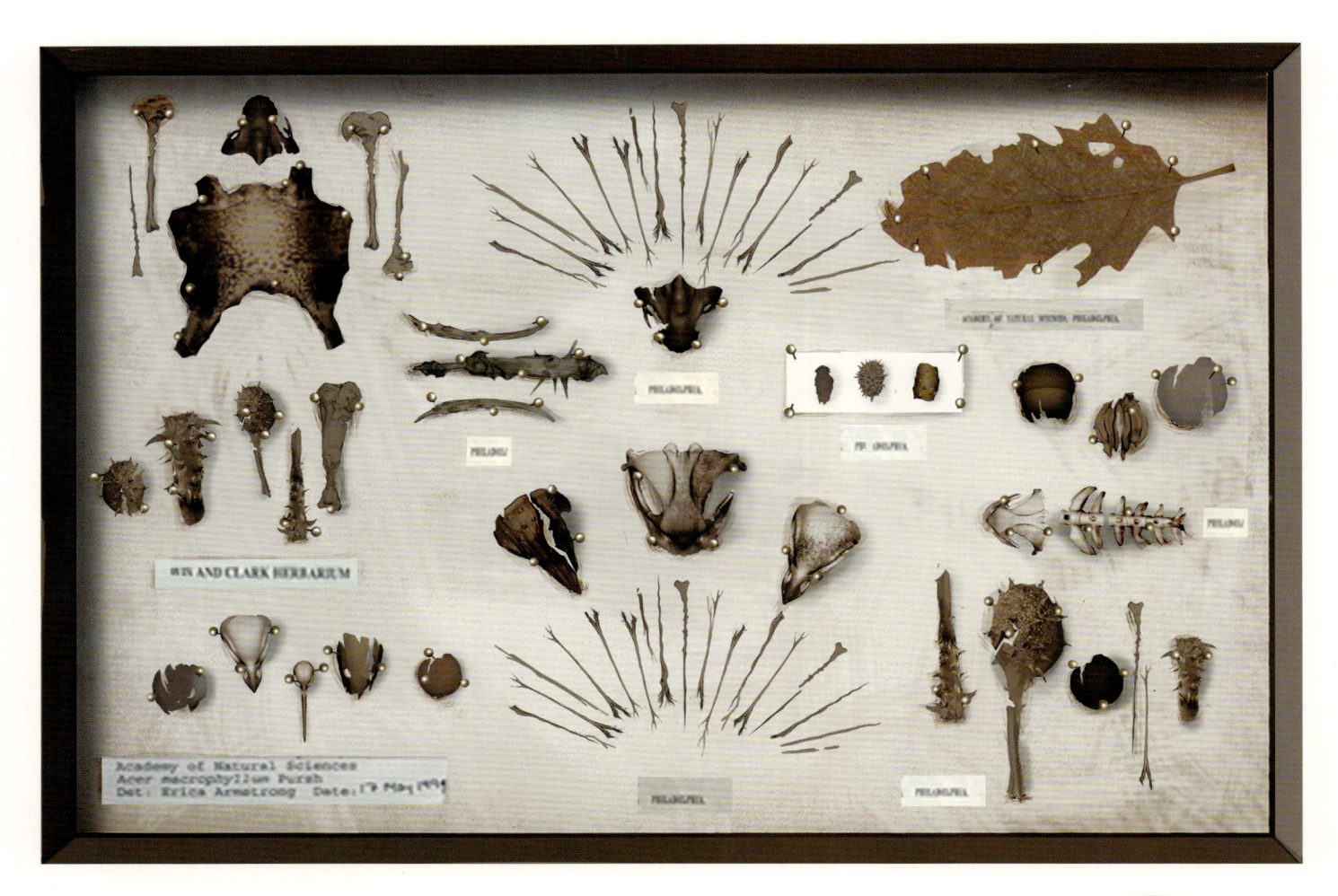

the pod to the rocky outcrop Moonhaven and ensure the forest's survival. Meanwhile, Mandrake, leader of the Boggans, will stop at nothing to foil their plan.

When Wedge and his crew pitched the idea to Fox, they brought with them actual items from Bomba's collection. In glass cases were the queen's tiny chariot, complete with tiny woven ropes, and a tiny saddle strapped to a sculpted hummingbird skeleton. Bomba's ultrasonic digital-magnifying helmet was also constructed at actual size, as if inviting the studio to join in the hunt for leafmen.

(Top) **Armor display** – prop concept • Sandeep Menon, *(Center left)* **Turtle barge** – sculpt • David Mei, *(Center right)* **Jinn skeleton display** – sculpt • Michael Defeo (sculpt) and David Mei (weathering), *(Bottom left)* **Bomba with magnifying glass** – concept art • Sang Jun Lee, *(Bottom right)* **Bomba's headgear** – color callouts • Jake Panian & Jake Parker (design) and Tyler Carter (painting), *(Opposite)* **Nim's Apothecary** – concept art • Greg Couch

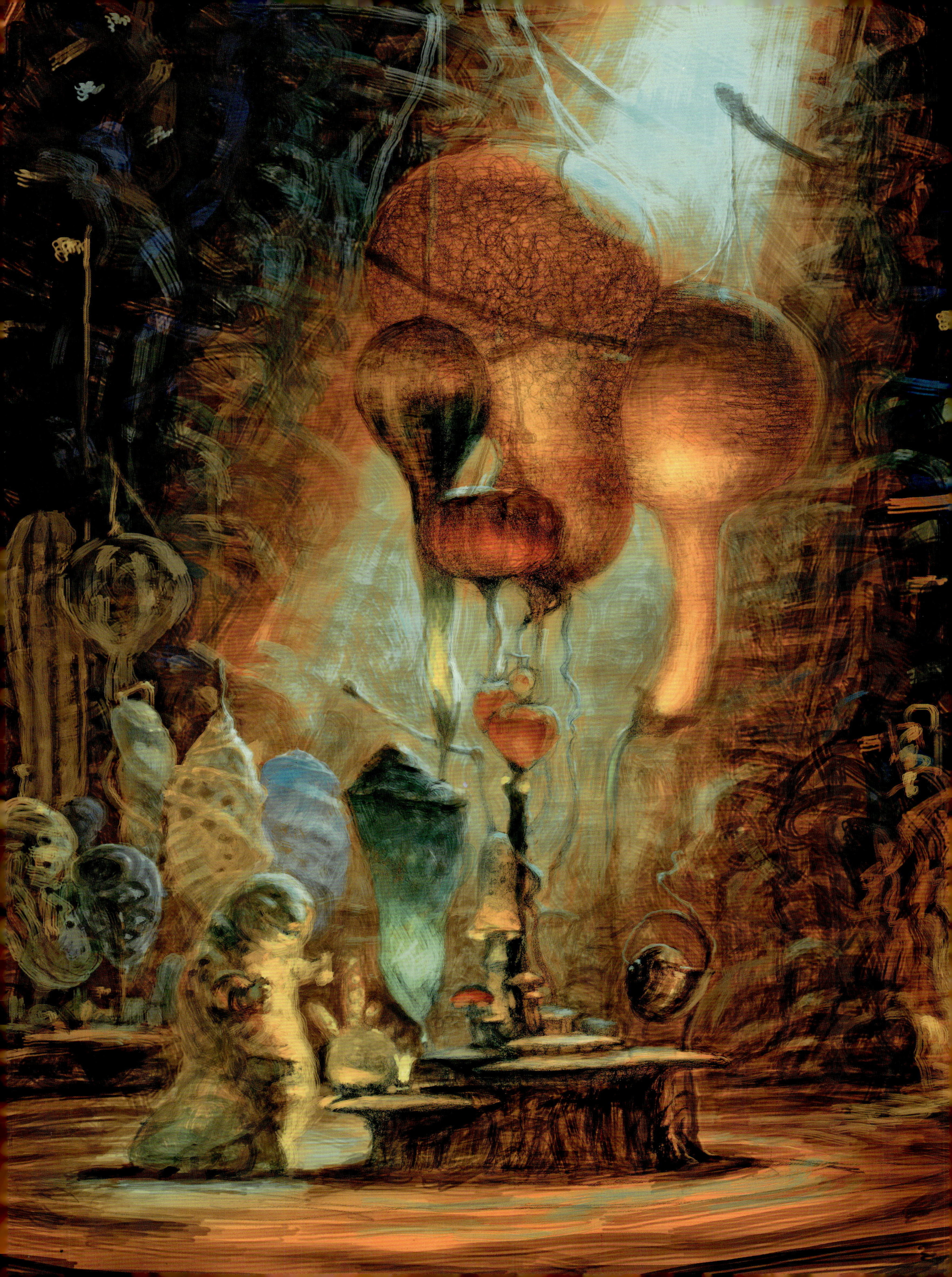

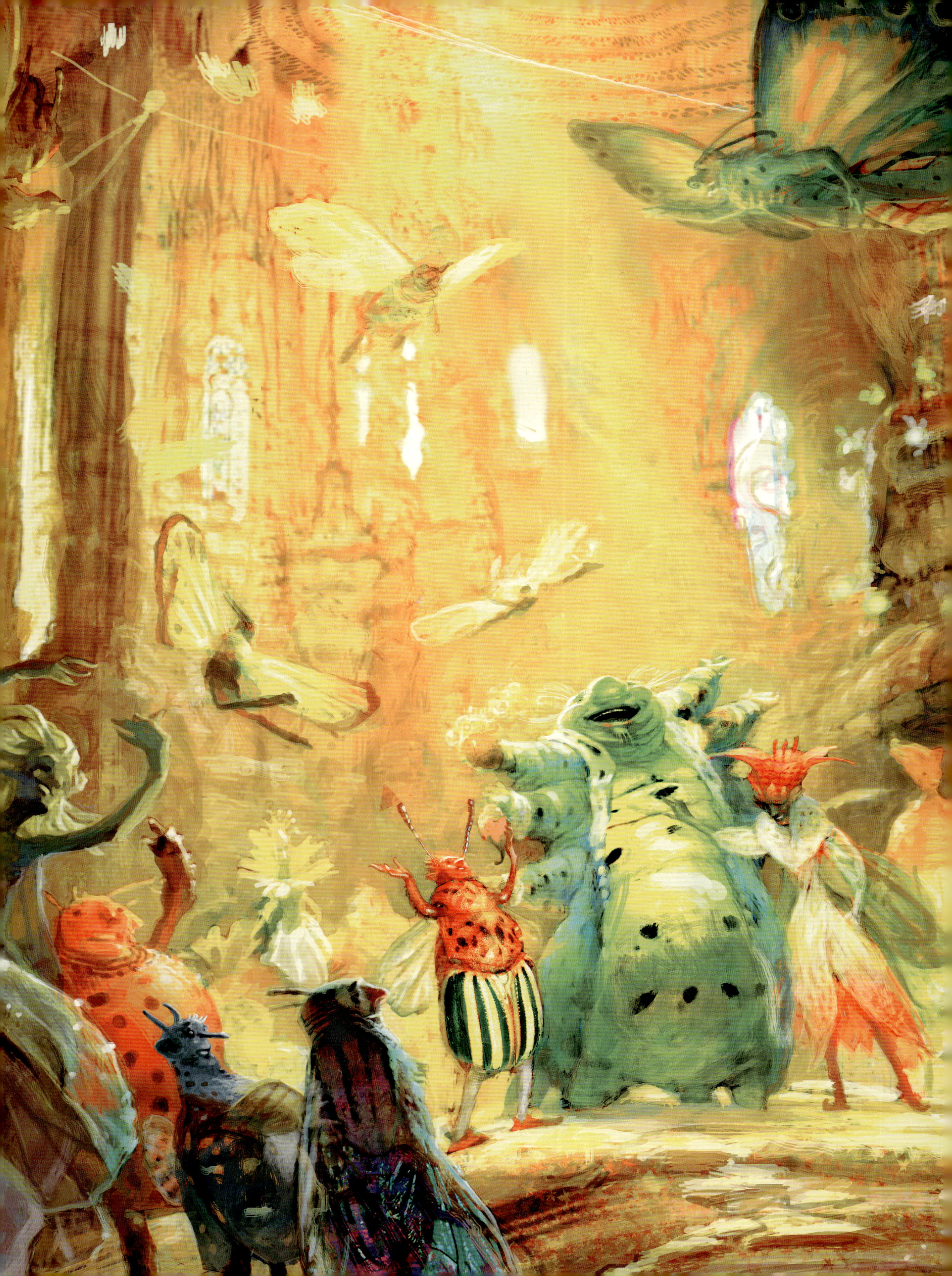

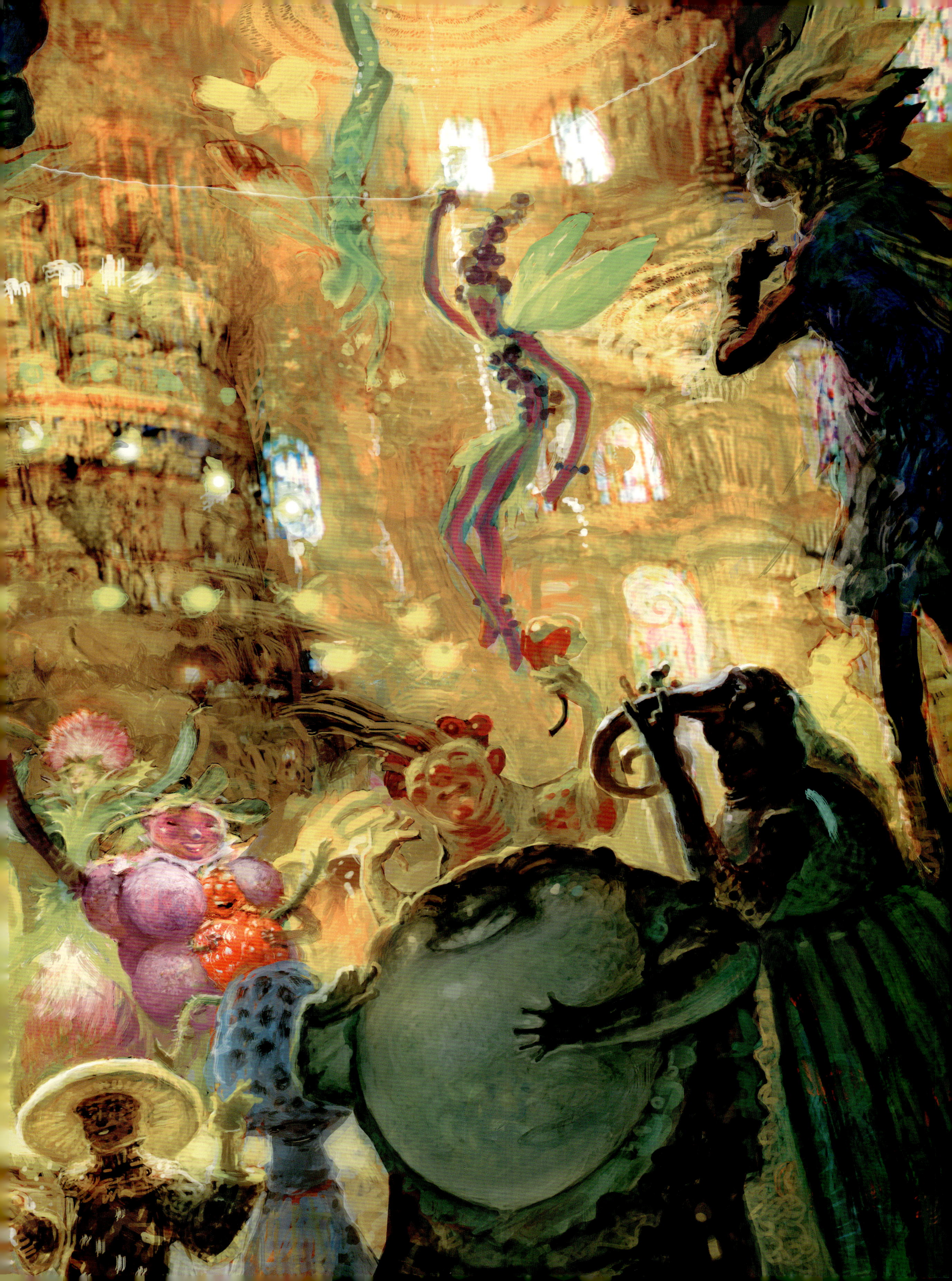

TINY HEROES

"We felt the story could have been done just as well as a kind of live-action, CG hybrid," says Wedge, "but at the end of the day, I think we were right to animate the whole thing, because it feels stylistically coherent and is more interesting to watch." Wedge knew that the film needed a forest environment that looked cinematic but naturalistic. In the years between conception and production, technology finally caught up with his aspirations. At long last, CG animation could replicate the subtle luminosity and semitransparent leaves of a living forest. The Leafmen, the Boggans, and the Jinn could now exist in a believable forest.

"There are a lot of characters whose lives intermingle," says Wedge. According to Wedge, Ronin, Nod, and Mary Katherine—the

(Previous pages) **Jinn party inside tree** – concept art • Greg Couch, *(Right)* **M.K. expressions (two images)** – character sketches • BJ Crawford, *(Far right)* **M.K. pose** – character sketch • Sang Jun Lee, *(Bottom)* **M.K. kneeling in forest** – concept art • Sang Jun Lee (design) and Mike Lee (painting), *(Opposite top)* **Nod and M.K. on leaf** – final digital art

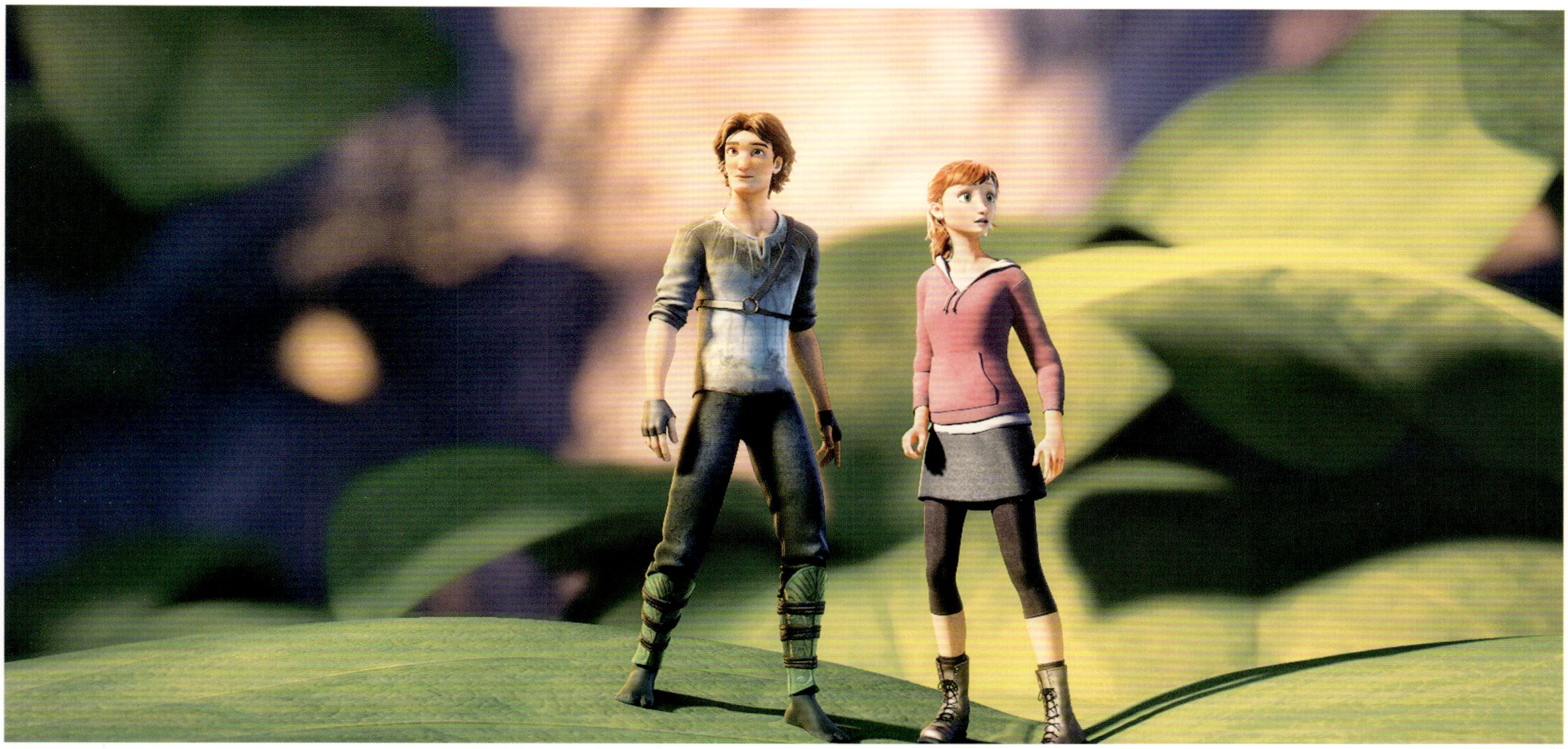

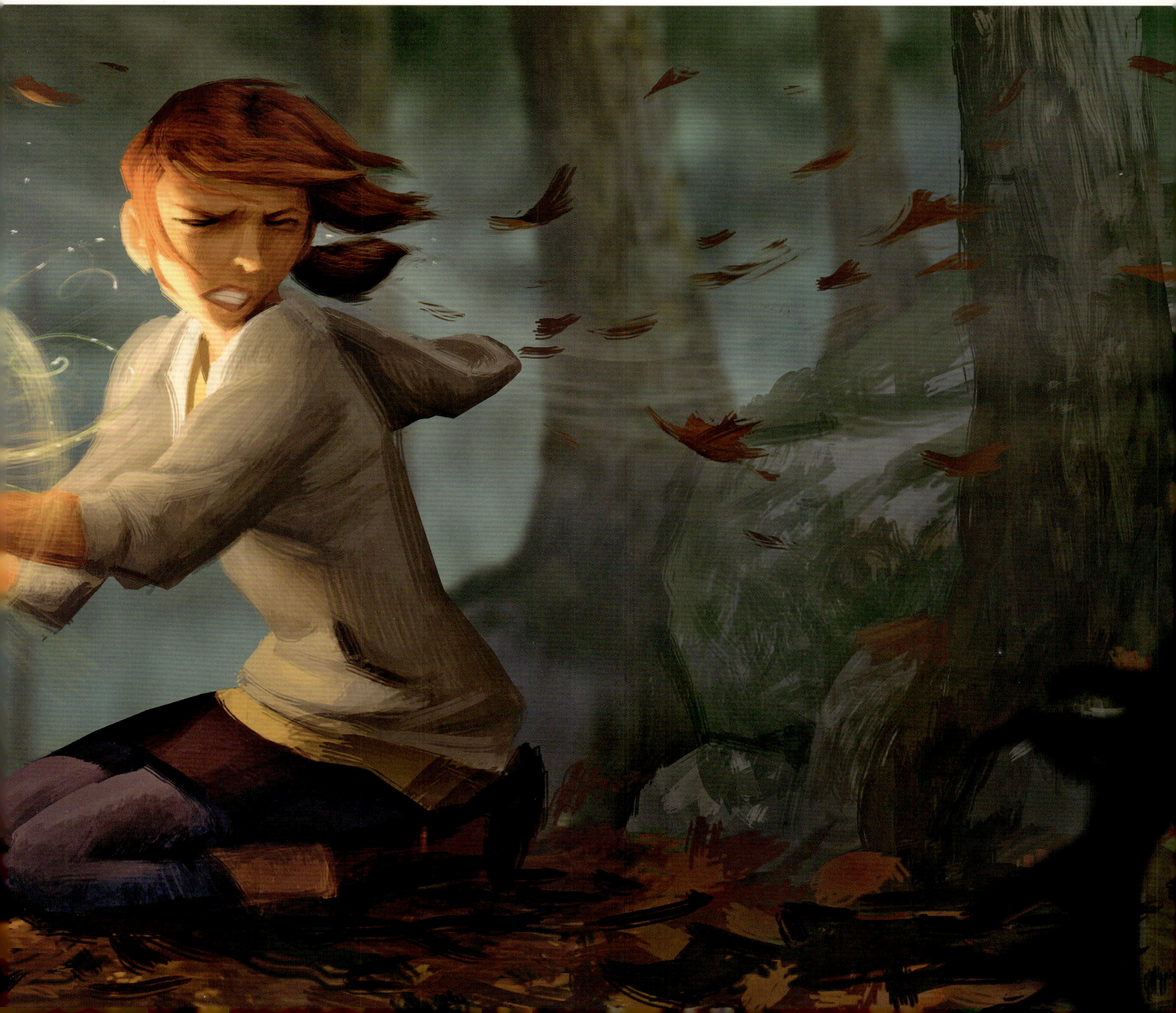

three lead characters—were the hardest to crack. Their growth from beginning to end had to be subtle but significant. Nod the novice must learn to work in a team; Ronin is tough as nails but is bound by love to his lost queen; and M.K. must learn how to come out of her shell and become a true hero. Her arc in particular is the most visual, represented by the way she wears her fuchsia hoodie. From beginning to end, her head, hands, and body gradually emerge from her hoodie like a chrysalis.

250 THE ART OF BLUE SKY STUDIOS

(This page) **Nod** – character concepts • Greg Couch, *(Opposite top)* **M.K. and Nod on hummingbird** – color key • David Dibble, *(Opposite middle left)* **Nod on hummingbird** – concept art • Sang Jun Lee, *(Opposite bottom left)* **Nod kneeling** – character sketch • BJ Crawford, *(Opposite right)* **Nod** – costume design • Clayton Stillwell

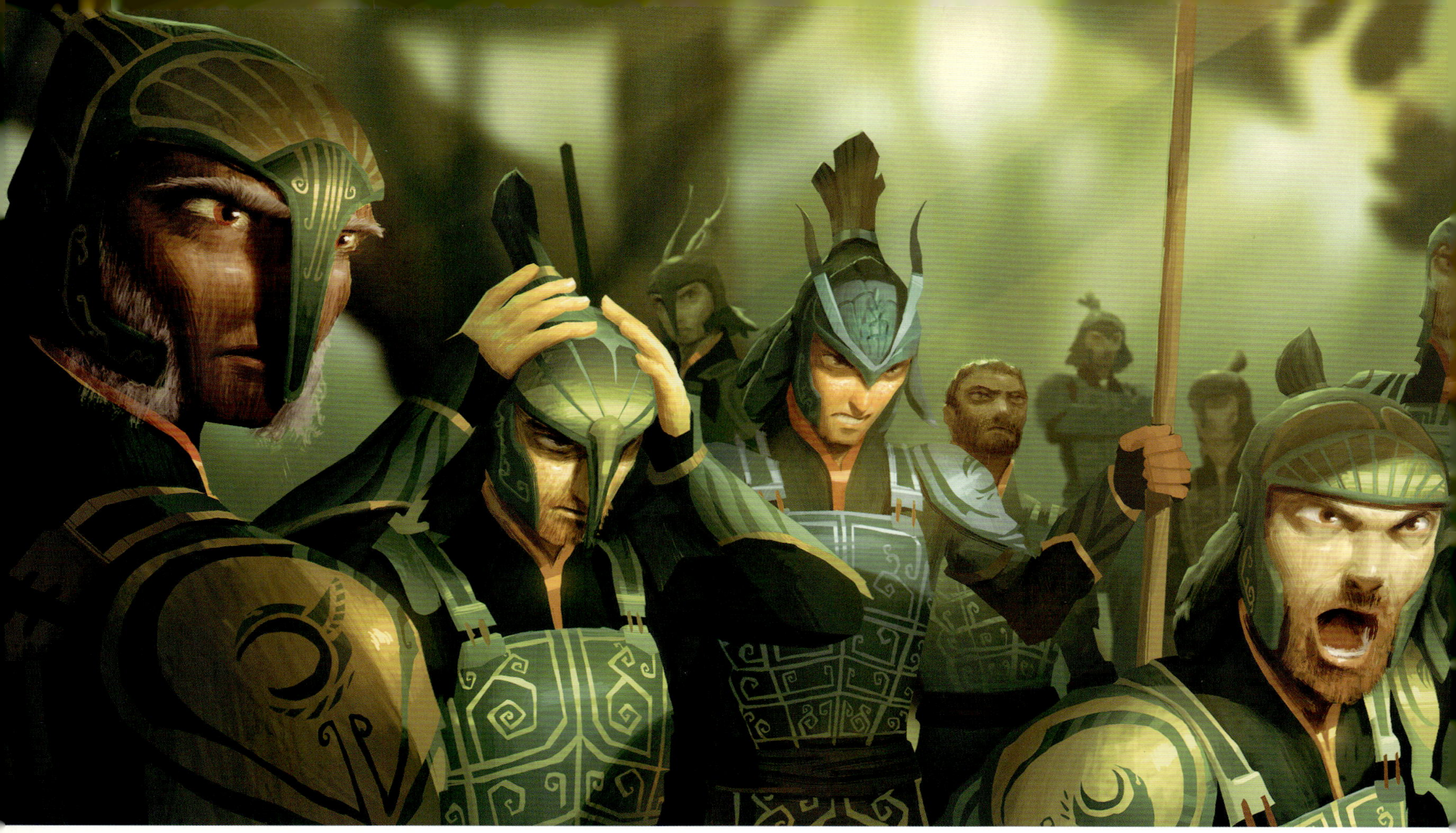
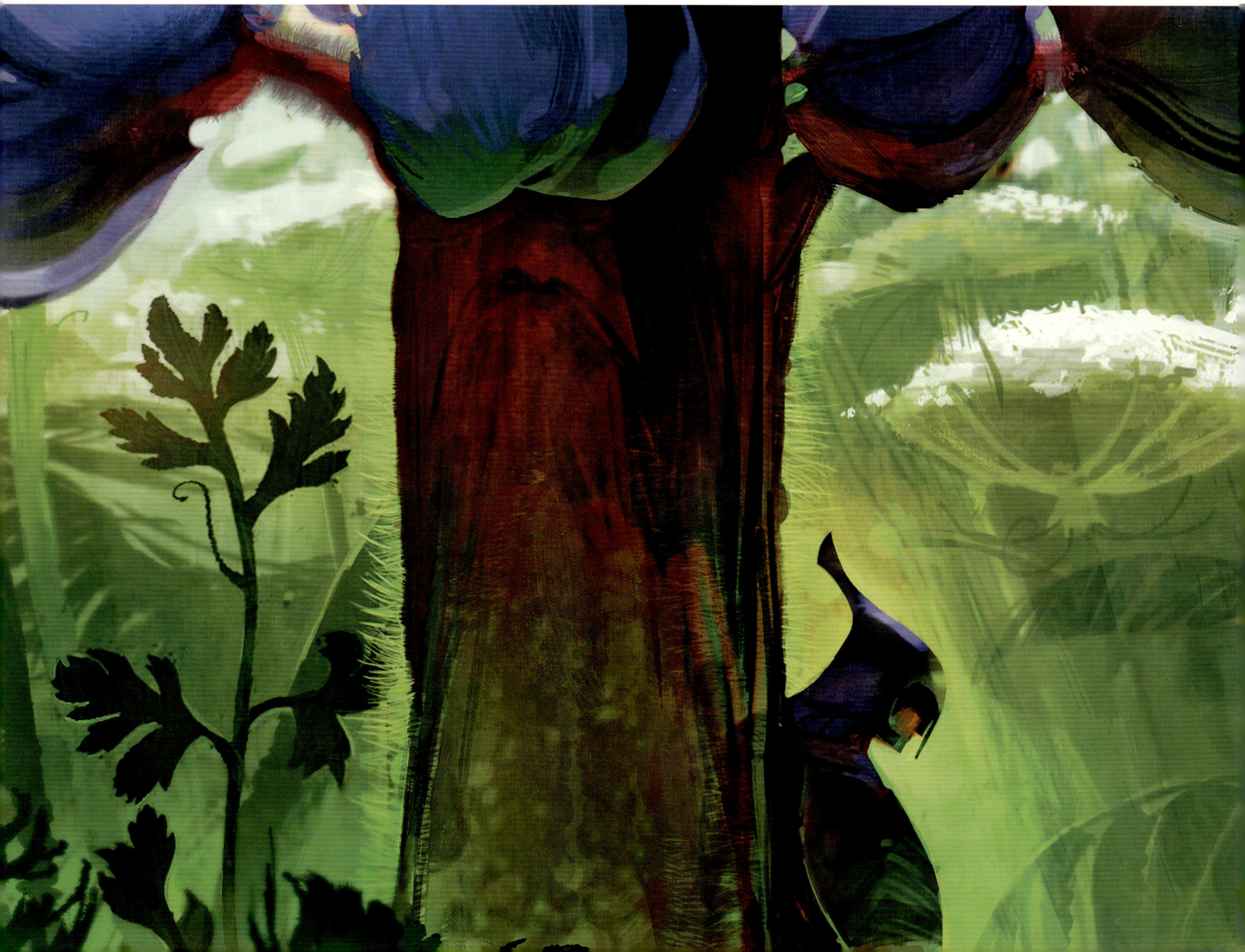

Mub and Grub, the invertebrate comic relief, are "your traditional animated flour sacks," says Wedge, recalling the standard animation exercise. This tried-and-trusted method for sharpening animation skills sees artists make an anthropomorphic bag gesticulate while still retaining its mass. Mub and Grub take that basic exercise to a new level, becoming scene-stealing characters in their own right. Before becoming a slug and snail, the two were designed as a species of plant-tenders called "Lowlies" by Joyce.

Joyce's initial art depicting the "Lowlies" was passed along to production designer Greg Couch. Couch redesigned the characters into Mub and Grub, two of the animal species that dwell in the forest. He also devised the three most fantastical species of the forest: the Leafmen, the Jinn, and the Boggans.

"The Leafmen are the most human," says Wedge, "and have as much facility with creating things out of different material as we do. The only difference is they do it on a molecular scale, so their stuff's a little coarser, but they can still weave and sew and work metal."

Originally the Boggans were more humanoid as well. "We decided to make them more like amphibious animals, reptiles, and the things that crawl under logs," says Wedge. "And Greg did a great painting nailing the look of the Jinn."

(Top) **Leafman on hummingbird** – concept art • Bill Joyce, *(Right)* **Podlings** – concept art • Greg Couch, *(Opposite top)* **Leafmen** – concept art • Justin Weg (poses) and Mike Lee (painting), *(Opposite bottom)* **Leafman against plant** – concept art • Kyle Macnaughton

EPIC 253

(Top) **Leafmen shield patterns** – concept art • Michael Knapp, *(Center and above)* **Ronin, Mub, Grub, and M.K. in forest** – color keys • Robert MacKenzie, *(Left)* **Ronin** – character sketch • BJ Crawford, *(Below)* **Ronin gestures** – character sketches • Sang Jun Lee, *(Opposite)* **Ronin** – concept art • Michael Knapp and Robert MacKenzie

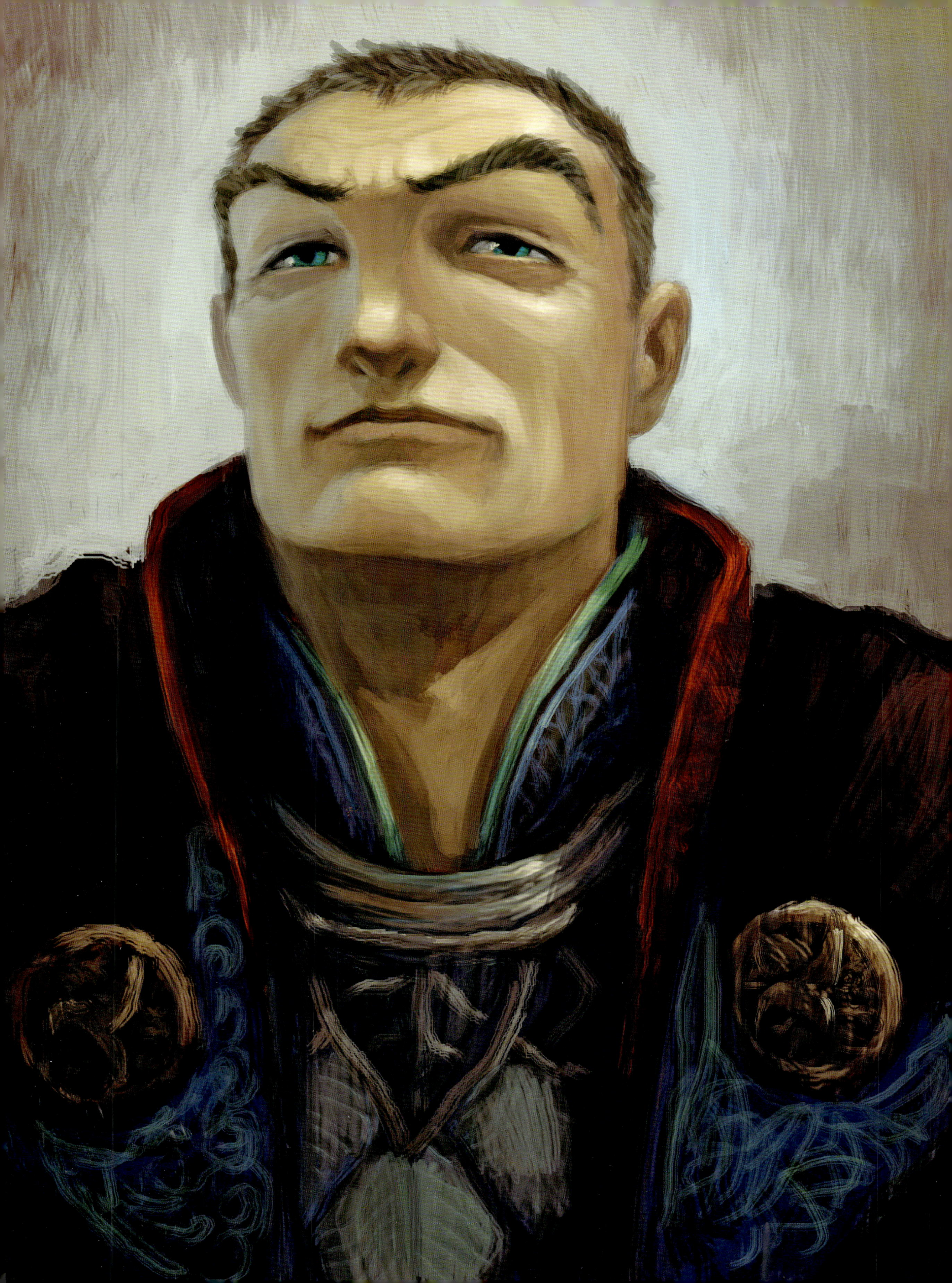

(Above) **Moonhaven** – concept art • Greg Couch

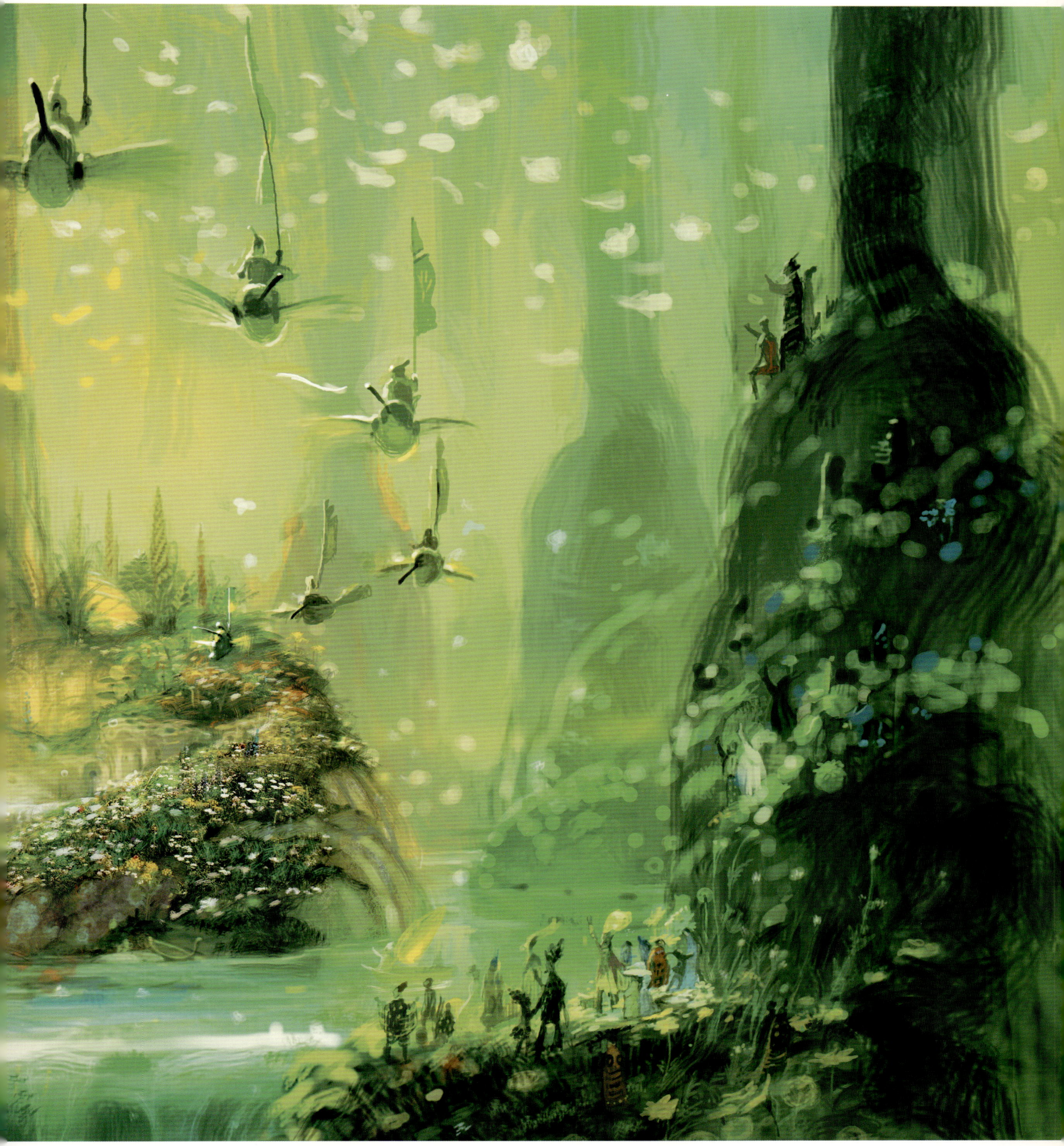

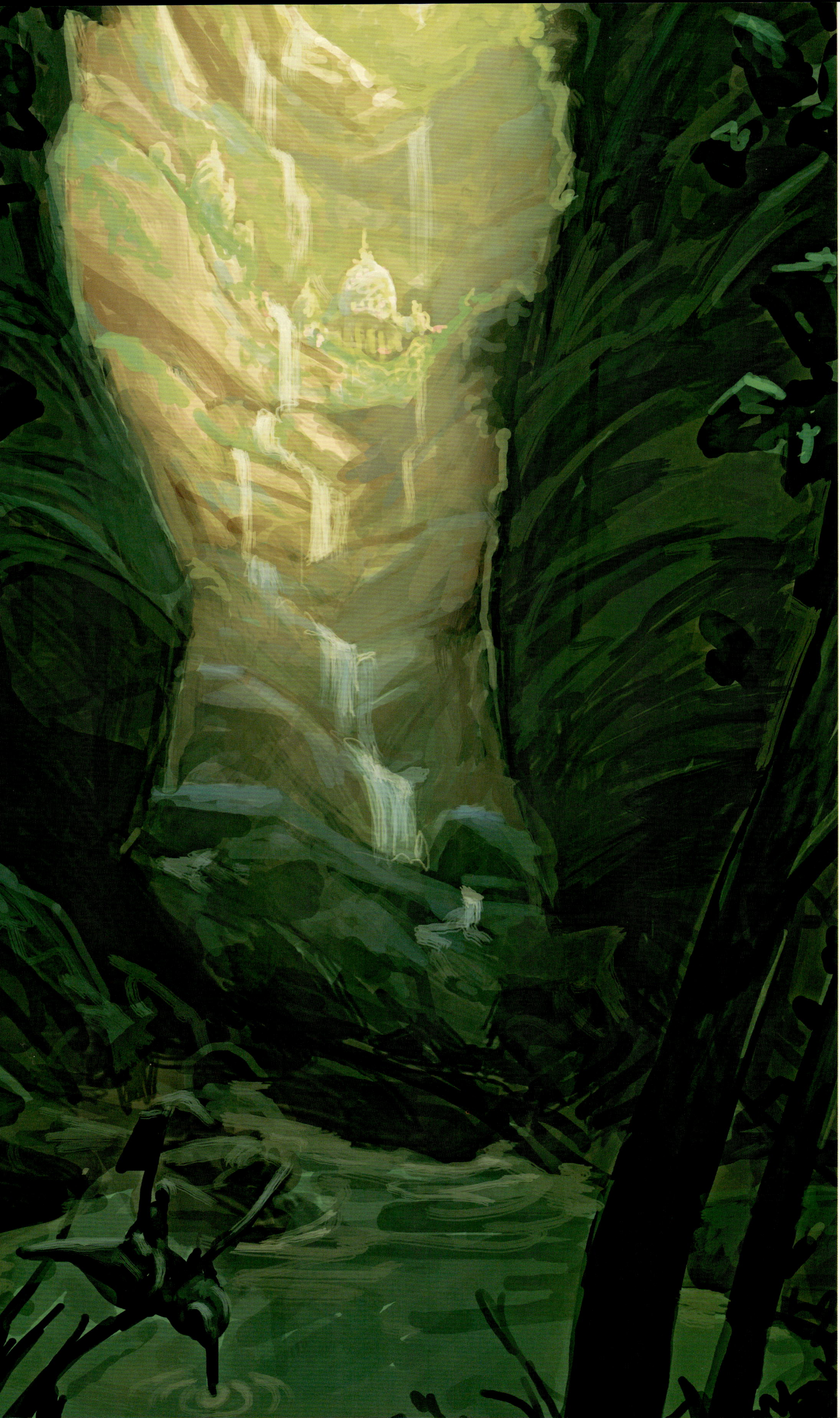

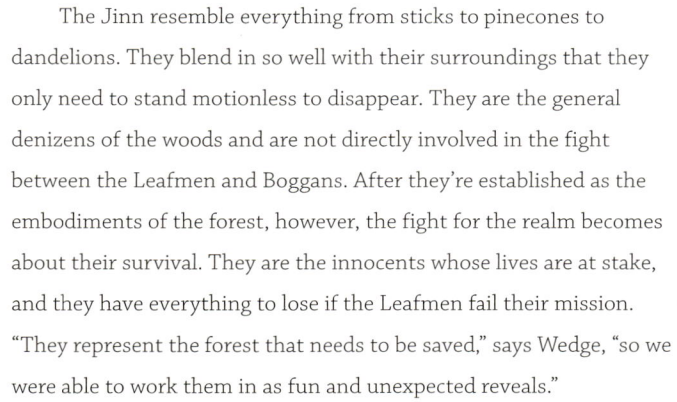

The Jinn resemble everything from sticks to pinecones to dandelions. They blend in so well with their surroundings that they only need to stand motionless to disappear. They are the general denizens of the woods and are not directly involved in the fight between the Leafmen and Boggans. After they're established as the embodiments of the forest, however, the fight for the realm becomes about their survival. They are the innocents whose lives are at stake, and they have everything to lose if the Leafmen fail their mission. "They represent the forest that needs to be saved," says Wedge, "so we were able to work them in as fun and unexpected reveals."

Couch explored what a personified embodiment of the forest might look like. He first drew tiny people wearing plant-clothes, but that was a dead end—it lacked authenticity. He was finally able to capture the image of the Jinn by approaching the assignment in a whole new way. "I finally realized it's not that they're people who wear plants," says Couch. "They're plants behaving like people. It's a change in how you look at things, turning it on its head. They weren't pinecones that behaved like people, or people wearing pinecones, they were a manifestation of pinecone, some sort of expression of the natural world. Sometimes you have to look at something the other way around. And that's when I love my job most."

(Opposite) **Moonhaven cliff** – concept art • Michael Knapp, *(Top left)* **Leaf mother and daughter** – concept art • Greg Couch, *(Top right)* **Flower girls** – concept art • Greg Couch, *(Center)* **Mushroom people** – concept art • Greg Couch, *(Left)* **Jinn mother and daughter** – final digital art

EPIC 259

"I finally realized it's not that they're people who wear plants. They're plants behaving like people."

—GREG COUCH

(Top) **Royal barge** – early concept art • Bill Joyce, *(Left)* **Queen Tara** – model • Cleveland Hibbert, *(Above)* **Queen Tara costumes** – concept art • Michael Knapp, *(Opposite top)* **Pod patch** – early concept art • Greg Couch, *(Opposite bottom)* **Queen Tara** – costume concept art • Greg Couch

260 THE ART OF BLUE SKY STUDIOS

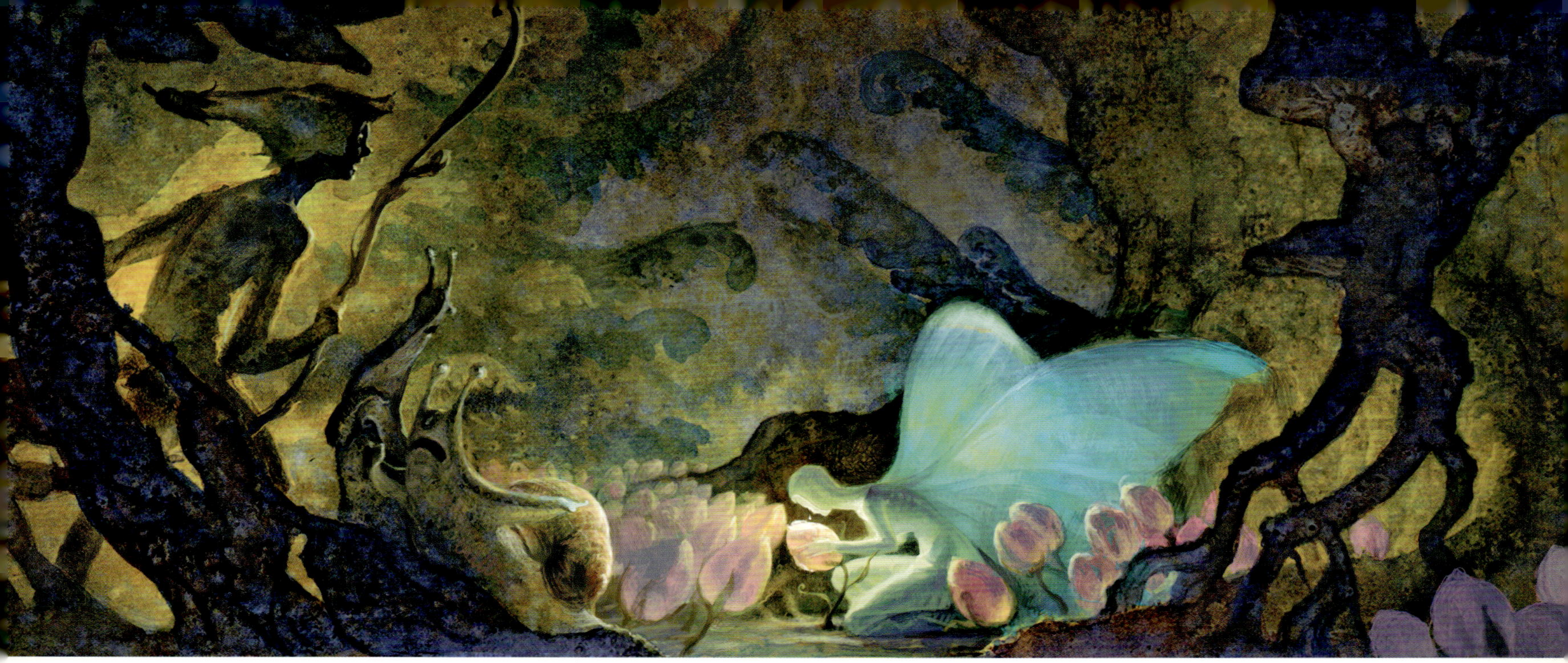

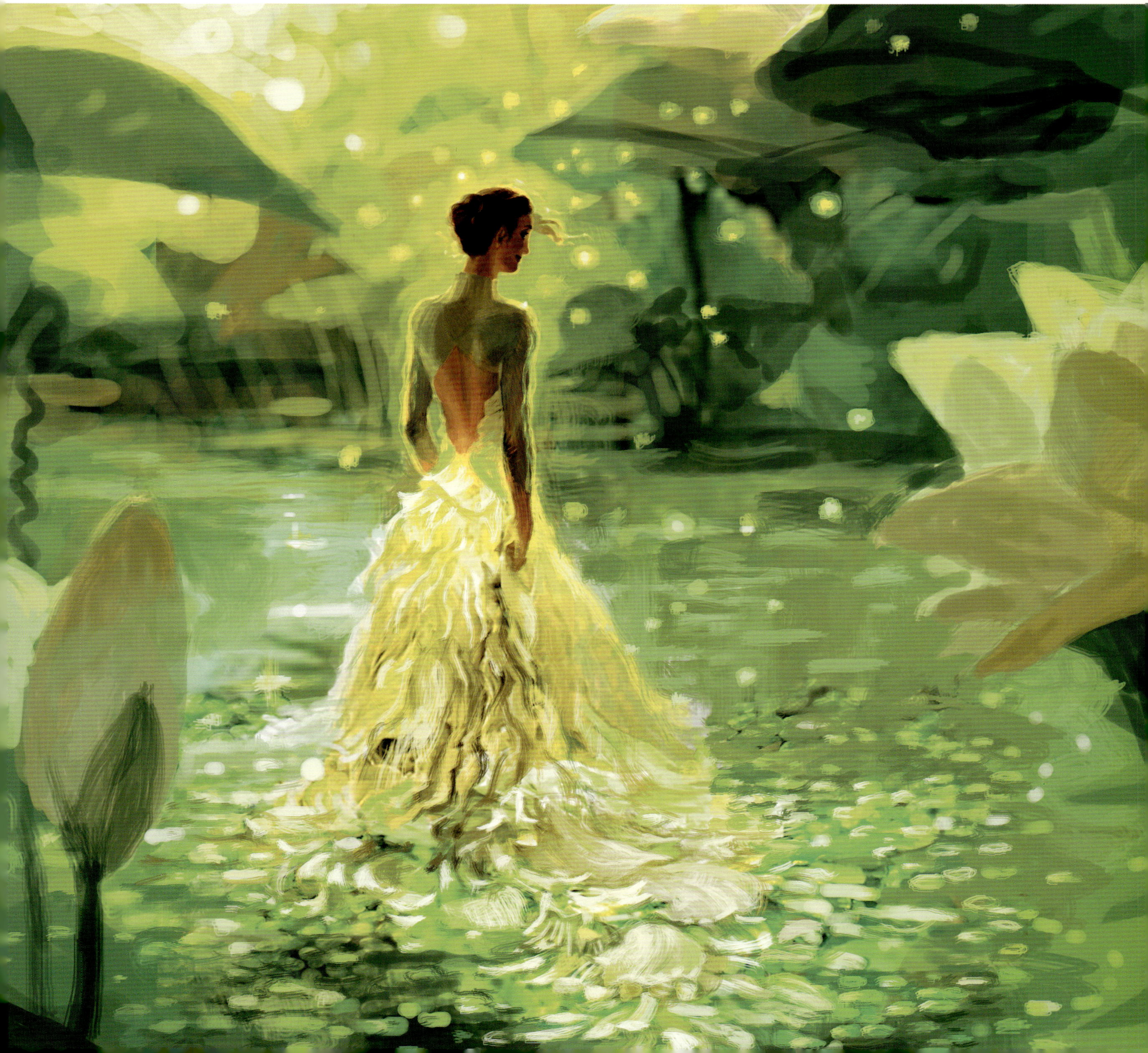

A LOOK INSIDE BLUE SKY

Animation Department

THE ANIMATION DEPARTMENT is the largest department at Blue Sky, numbering upwards of a hundred people. Overseeing it are several animation supervisors who manage the team and report to the film's director. While the director manages the entire project, the Animation department, using a variety of Maya plug-ins developed in house, works on delivering the character performances in the film.

"What people respond to is the belief that there's really a living, breathing character there," says supervisor Nick Bruno. Blue Sky animators follow in the shoes of the 2-D animators who came before them whose imagination—and character acting—was spun from the end of a pencil. "We never want to be held back by technology," continues Bruno. "In the past, CG animators were locked to really stiff, rigid models that were as cumbersome as blocks of wood. I think it's safe to say that every tool the industry developed tries to re-create the control an animator gets with a pencil."

To get maximum impact from the characters' movements, the animation team uses techniques as old as traditional animation. They may pose the character so the backbone makes an attractive flowing "S"-curve, or they might check the silhouette of the figure to see if, just by looking at its contours, the pose is visually clear and dynamic. The animators will stop at nothing to get the shape exactly right for the character, and sometimes that comes down to adjusting the CG model itself.

For instance, while working as an animation lead on *Dr. Seuss' Horton Hears a Who!*, Bruno made a thumbnail drawing—a small rough sketch by hand—of the Mayor with a stapler embedded in his face, his rubbery head caved in so the stapler was like a hot dog in a bun. "In order to get that, I had to model all the separate pieces of geometry of the Mayor's head, down to his teeth, moving it vertex by vertex," says Bruno. "It took a long time making what looks like a simple shot, but it wouldn't be as funny or as appealing if we didn't."

"Everyone was experimenting with how far they could push the animation," says animation supervisor Jim Bresnahan. "We were constantly looking for ways to get from pose A to pose B. We had time to explore that in *Horton*, which we needed for the zany animation style of the film. I think a lot of us here would admit to being inspired by Looney Tunes and animation of that era. We try to add those old-school tricks like smear frames and multiples whenever it's appropriate." The animators use "multiples" in *Ice Age: Continental Drift* when Scrat spins around the earth's core so fast that we see multiple versions of him at once. We see smears on Crash and Eddie in *Ice Age: The Meltdown* when they're moving so fast rolling down a hill or flying through the sky that their bodies appear to be in two points at once, with a streak of color in between. These and other tricks of the trade were throwbacks to the golden age of animated slapstick.

During the production of *Epic*, Bruno was on other assignments and animated only a single sequence featuring the quick-aging fruit fly. It's six seconds long, but the scene delivers one of the best laughs in the film. Bruno was directed to age the character using only pantomime, but he adjusted the model to change the size of the head, the softness of the legs, and the color of the eyes; so from child to adult to elder, it takes on three different appearances, and all before the camera cuts.

"When we have a good idea, we'll stop at nothing to make it come to life," adds Bruno. "Sometimes that means painting yourself into a corner and you need some late nights and some elbow grease to pull it off, but when you sit in a movie and people laugh at your shot, that's all you remember."

(Above) **Fruit fly ageing (three images)** – final frames, *(Opposite left)* **Ronin (two images)** – concept art • Michael Knapp, *(Opposite top right)* **Nod and Ronin** – BJ Crawford, *(Opposite bottom right)* **Ronin** – final frame

262 THE ART OF BLUE SKY STUDIOS

Sometimes that extra effort is toward making the animation subtle. In *Ice Age: Dawn of the Dinosaurs*, Momma Dino is surrounded by crazy, hyperactive characters. "You can see what's going on in her eyes and gestures," says Galen Chu, an animation supervisor on the film. "That character really shows how much you can express with so little."

Chu was also animation supervisor on *Epic*, a film rife with subtle character performance. None of the humans or Leafmen were animated through motion-capture. Typically, animators may act out a scene and film themselves for video reference. This may be inspiration for the timing of a movement, but is by no means a direct source of the animation. In the end, the scene still has to come from the imaginations of the animation team. An animator's instinct is often to push the movement toward something more exaggerated, and it gets tricky when some characters are subtle by their very nature.

"It was very hard to make Ronin look right," says Chu. "We were asking animators to restrain themselves from going too far, especially in his facial animation, and to make those boundaries smaller and tighter. So when shots of Ronin worked well, *we* looked at them closely."

Making the Leafmen look human was as challenging as making a woolly mammoth look elephantine. Although there's a human voice and personality coming out of Manny, he still has the musculature of a mammoth. When he moves, he does so in a way true to his anatomy.

"Elephants don't gallop," says Chu. "They're so heavy, they need to lock their legs, like the body mechanics of a pole-vaulter hurdling forward. They couldn't put a leg down, keep it bent, and support their weight—they don't have enough muscles for that. So when they move quickly, they have to walk fast. It feels like a stiff run."

To get the animation just right, the animators present different stages of their work to the director in testing or "sweatbox" sessions, named after the method established in the 1930s at the Disney studio. An animated shot first goes through the Blocking stage, in which the basic actions are roughed out and the character pops from pose to pose, holding each for a few beats. These poses are called "storytelling poses" or "extremes" because they describe the performance of the character. The movements between the extreme poses get fleshed out during the Spline stage (named after an element found in the Maya 3-D animation software package). It is here that the animators figure out the best way to connect one gesture to another. Still, the timing may not be perfect, and the shot may need some further tweaking in the final polish stage. This could be to help the poses read better, give the character more personality, or push the expressiveness of the gesture, but this is all done with the intent to honor each individual frame. And with twenty-four frames in a single second of a Blue Sky film, that's a lot of work.

The integrity of the animation team comes through in every scene, whether the animation is realistic or extremely exaggerated. Every shot is watched and rewatched in a loop and goes through several drafts before it's finally complete. Some shots are hugely emotional or comedic moments, while others are the transitional moments—the glue that holds those big scenes together. All are essential in telling the story and following the director's vision. After several sessions of reviewing the animation, a shot will finally earn the director's approval. It will make its way "downstream" through the production pipeline, until it is ready to be cut into the finished movie.

(Above) **Ronin and Queen Tara in Moonhaven** – concept art • Greg Couch (design) and Michael Knapp & David Dibble (painting)

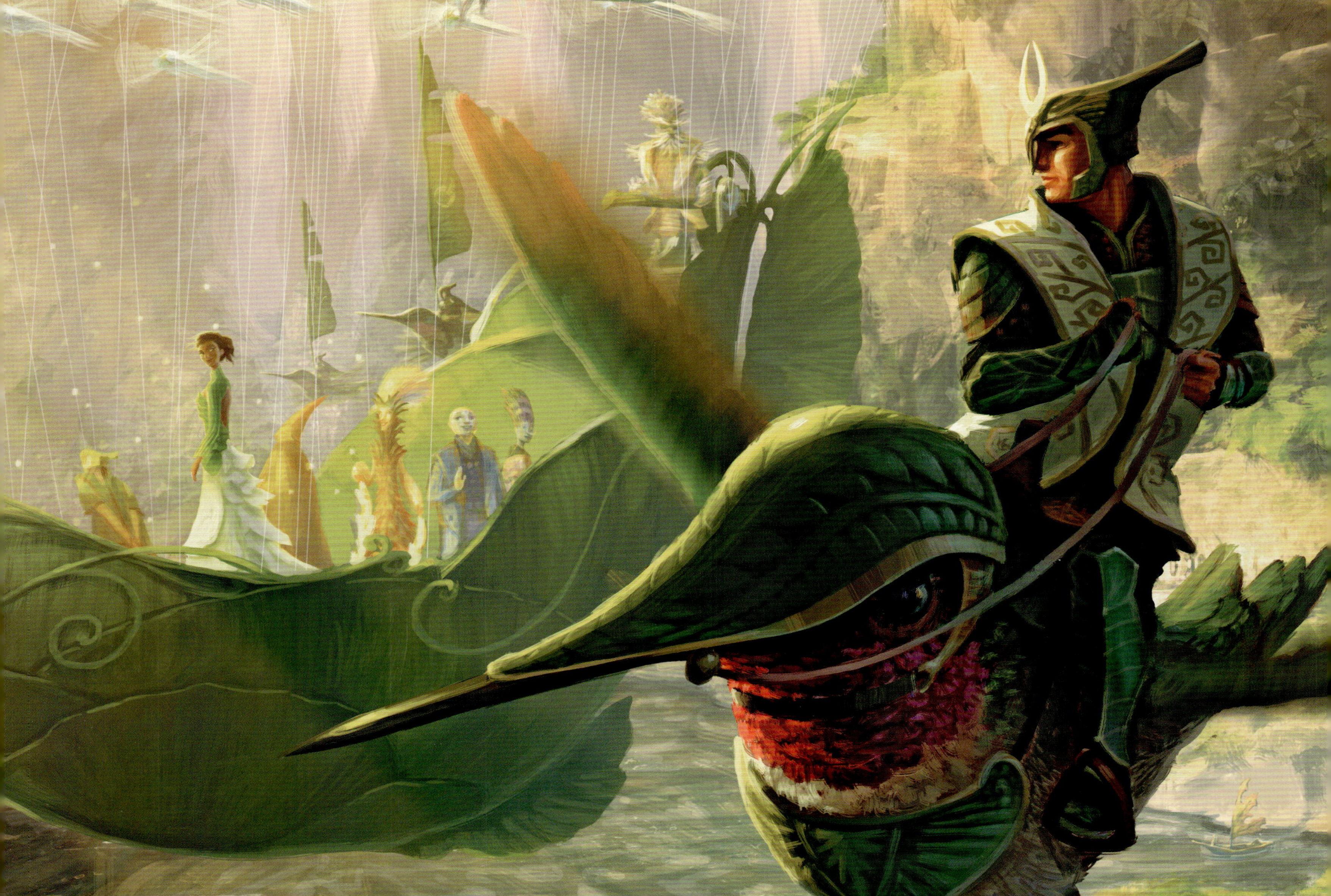

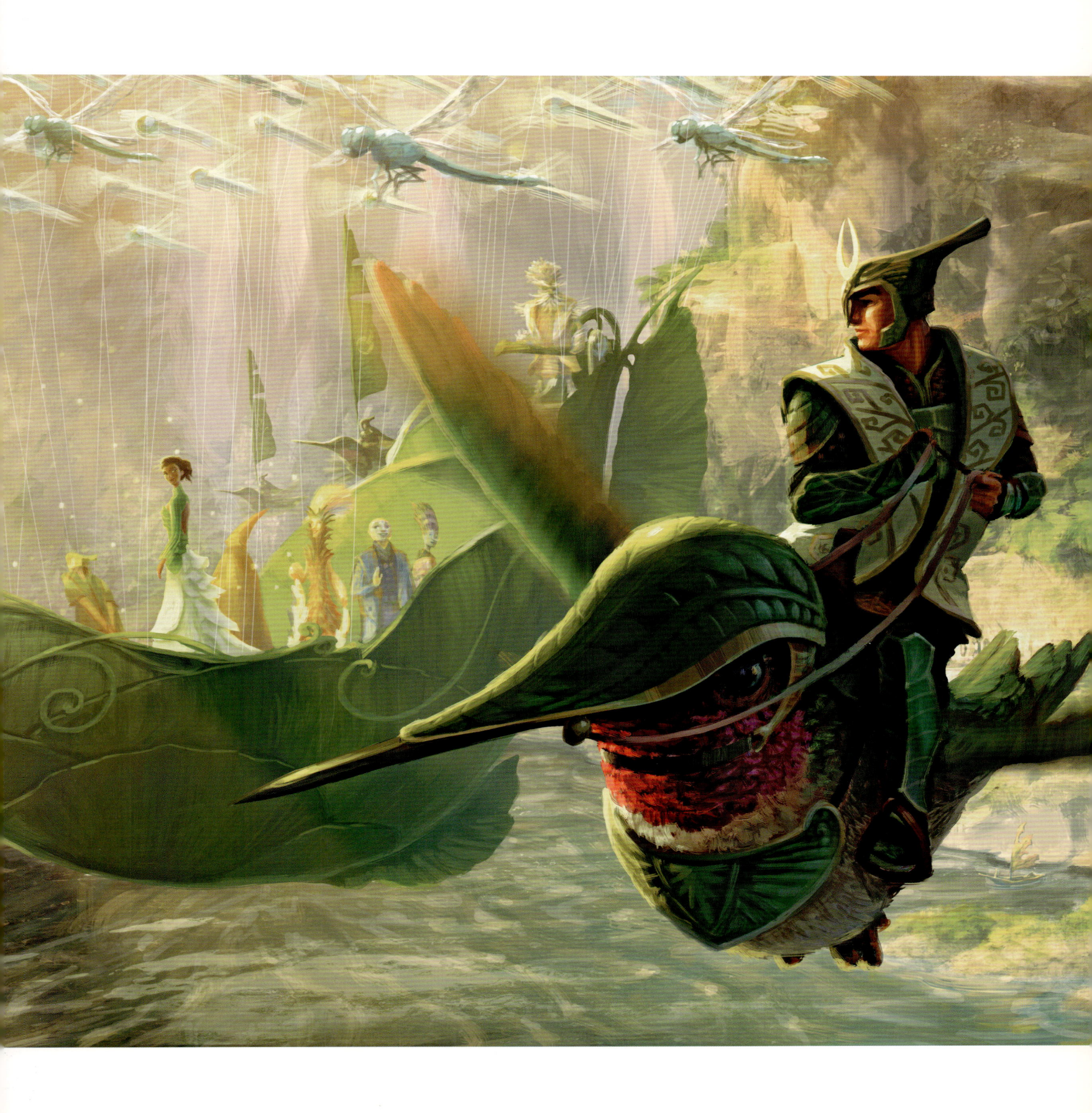

THE NATURE OF TECHNOLOGY

While Couch created drawings and paintings that evoked the sentiment of the film, art director Michael Knapp was tasked to implement those ideas and shepherd them through all the various stages of production. It required both creative and technical understanding. The Boggans' home of Wrathwood, for instance, was a rotted tree trunk comparable to a hollow skyscraper. It contained cliffs, bridges, ledges, and tunnels that, to the characters, were enormous.

"We wanted Wrathwood to be a spectacular, huge environment that the Boggans live in," says Knapp. "It was always based on the idea that they lived in a hollowed-out stump, and from a logistical standpoint it's a very complex thing to pull off."

The studio could spend millions of dollars and several years building a single set piece, but that really wouldn't be a responsible allocation of resources. Instead they planned how to cheat the illusion of a single enormous environment. They would have to build only select sections of Wrathwood's interior, and this planning took part in Previs.

Knapp worked closely with the Previs department to break up the set into modular chunks. "There were only a handful of well-planned larger pieces that we used to create the bridges and walls, and we constructed them out of highly detailed smaller chunks. We were then able to hide any repetition by turning off some of the smaller chunks and rearranging them to create 'new' structures. The material treatment tied it all together. The audience is never aware of it, and it looks great."

By planning in advance, the artists were also able to limit the file size of each shot, making for a faster render and saving precious time. Those modular chunks of the set that were not in front of the camera could have their visibility turned off in the computer—thus saving precious processing time. Planning how to build the set in chunks was essential to a movie as visually complex as *Epic*. The film had plenty of effects-heavy scenes that needed their share of valuable time and manpower. And anything that didn't serve the film had to be scrapped.

One such scene saw a crown bloom from little seedpods atop Queen Tara's head. "But that was way too effects-heavy and ultimately didn't fit her character," says Knapp. The scene remained unproduced, and resources were instead allotted to more pivotal scenes, like the sequence in which Queen Tara is ambushed by Boggans at the pond.

(Opposite top and bottom) **Wrathwood** – concept art • Jake Panian, *(Top left)* **Mandrake** – concept art • Bill Joyce, *(Top right)* **Mandrake** – concept art • Sang Jun Lee, *(Above)* **Dagda** – concept art • Robert MacKenzie, *(Bottom)* **Mandrake and Dagda** – concept art • BJ Crawford

(Above) **Nim's tree** – concept art • Simon Varela

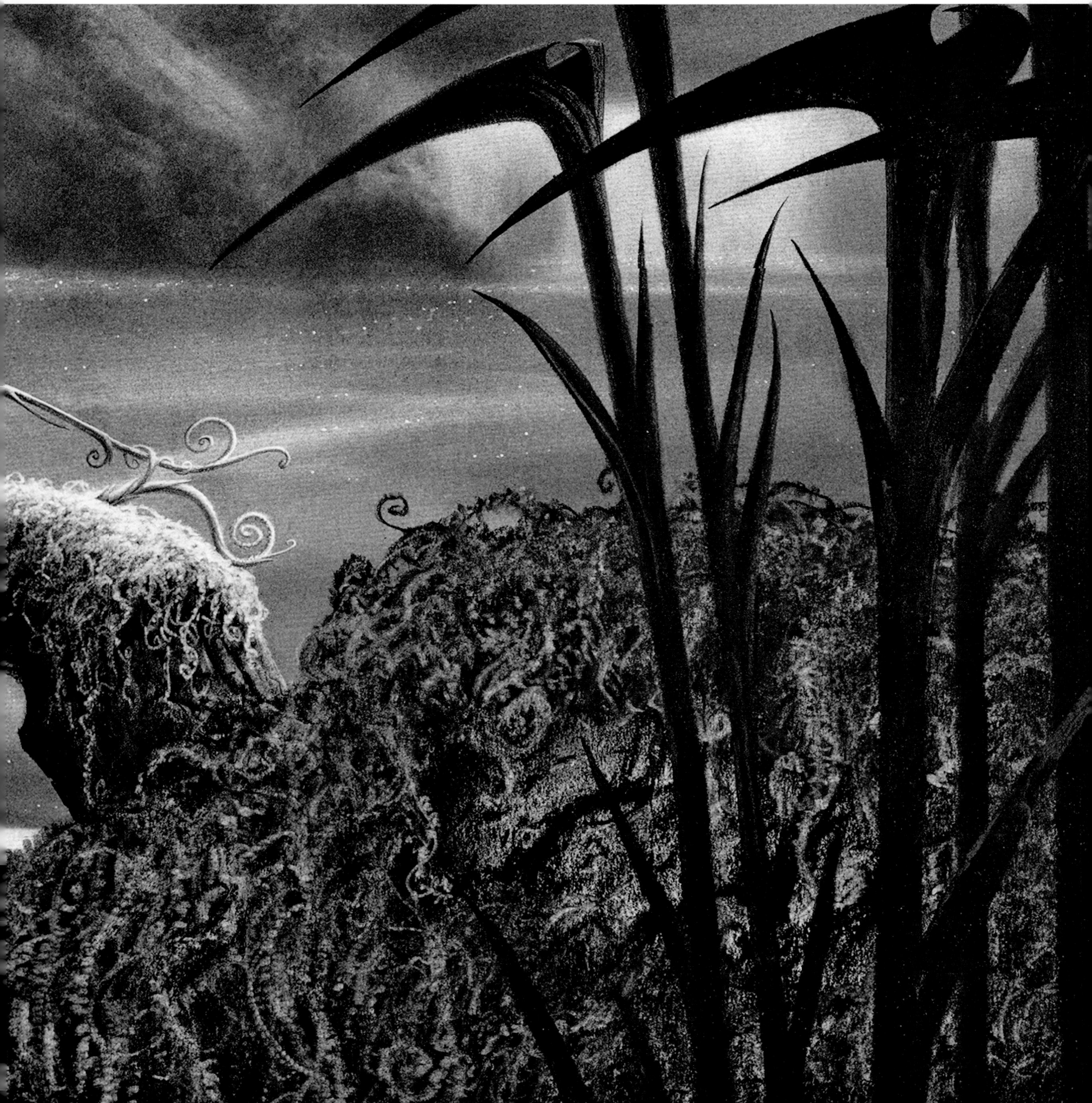

"Greg Couch is responsible for one of the most time-consuming elements in the movie," says Wedge. "The ambush scene at the lily pond took two years to complete. And the surprise location we had for the battle helped make it a very powerful scene." Storyboard artist Adam Van Wyk conceived of the thousands of Boggans hiding beneath the tree bark, and Couch created an inspirational painting of their reveal. Rendered in tremendous detail, the painting even highlighted every last little weapon and the manner in which the light would hit each one. "The painting sat there and people just looked at it, shaking their heads," says Wedge, "but we made sure everyone knew that this was a very integral part of the story and that we had to do it."

The animated scene, with its horde of Boggans throwing off their camouflage and swarming with their weapons drawn, was key to the plot and to the believability of the environment. The tree bark they discard looks like real tree bark; the light behind them looks like actual forest light, and each of them is animated independently. This level of realism makes the Boggans seem like a real threat, but it's just one example.

The entire film is composed of scenes staged in believable digital environments. The team at Blue Sky has always held the belief that if the locations look real, the audience will become immersed in the story that much more. Forests in particular have always been a challenge to create using CGI, for instance, in the distinctive way that light shines through a leaf.

This effect (known as "transmittance") also applies to human skin, which we can see through to a certain degree if there is a light source behind it. In *Epic*, a character's ear that is backlit may glow because some of that light shows through. The level of transparency visible in our skin—or in a leaf—has never been better resolved in CG animation.

"The movie has some of the most beautiful animation, lighting, and imagery that ever was in CG," says William Joyce. "I think *Epic* got everything right. It got the tone just right—fun, dark, heroic, and enchanting—the true spirit I hoped the movie would be."

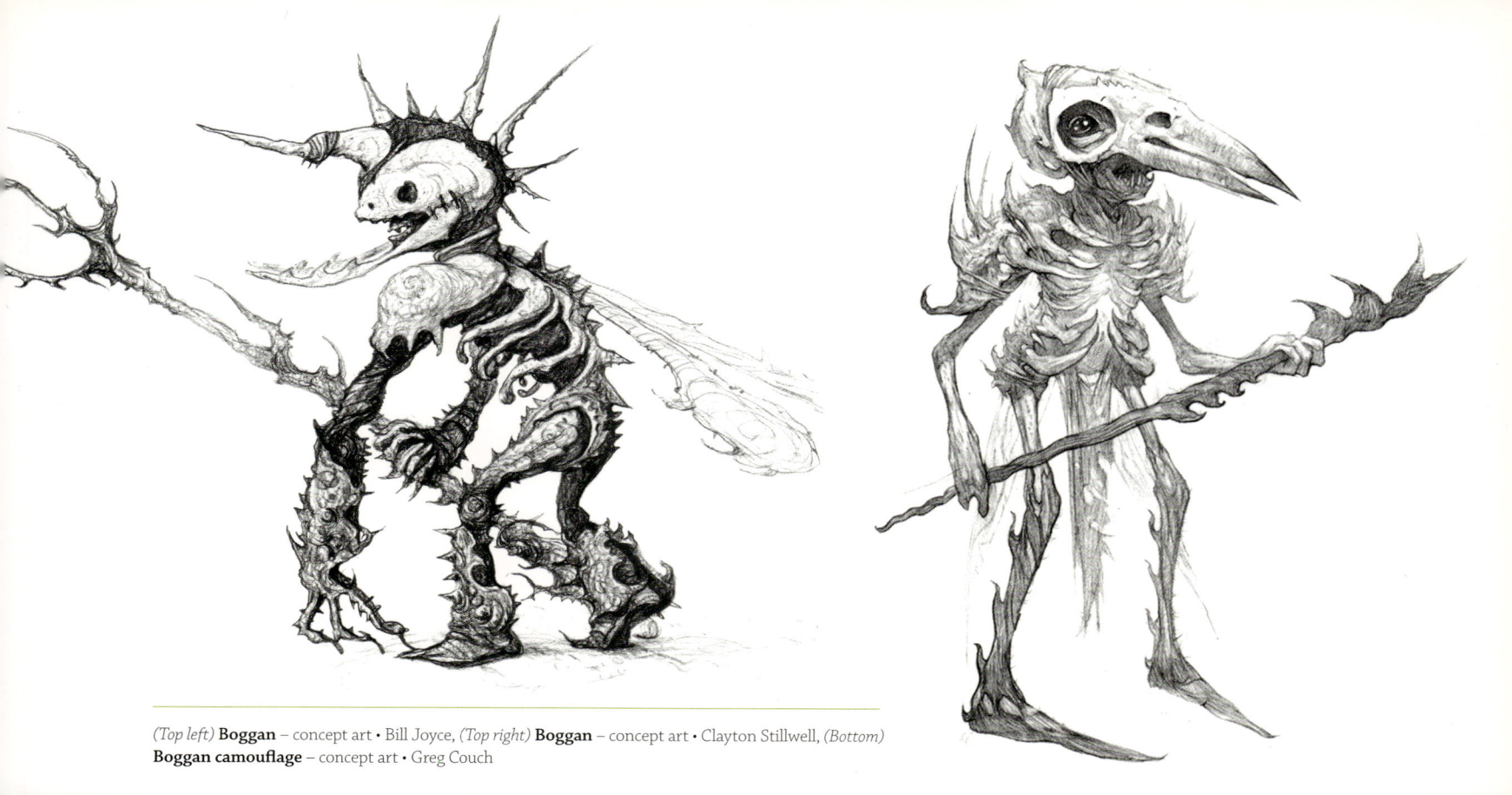

(Top left) **Boggan** – concept art • Bill Joyce, *(Top right)* **Boggan** – concept art • Clayton Stillwell, *(Bottom)* **Boggan camouflage** – concept art • Greg Couch

A LOOK INSIDE BLUE SKY

Lighting Department

THE WORK THAT BLUE SKY'S LIGHTING DEPARTMENT carries out is the final major stage in the production pipeline and makes use of Blue Sky's proprietary software. Headed by Haji Uesato and Jeeyun Sung, the department sees the two lighting supervisors alternate between films, taking turns managing a team of thirty to fifty lighting artists. While a supervisor is completing scenes on one film, the other is working on the subsequent film, lighting "camera tests" on character models and "diorama tests" on backgrounds. In either case, they do much more than simply flick on a light switch.

"We're composing," says Uesato. "It's part of cinematography. We're guiding the eye within each frame throughout the entirety of each sequence. We're creating emphasis and hierarchy, all the time trying to further the narrative of the story. The lights are tools we use to help tell the visual story."

Lighting has the ability to direct the audiences' attention so subtly that they don't even realize it. After a scene is animated and approved, it still looks very flat before it reaches the Lighting department, and it's up to those artists to light it in very particular ways.

For instance, in *Epic*, there are several scenes that take place in Bomba's house, and each one is lit differently. When M.K. meets him at the start of the film, the characters are lit from underneath to evoke a sense of mystery. There is something amiss, the lighting tells us, and the audience is unable to feel completely at ease. In the closing scene, as M.K. and Bomba work together in his home, the two are cast in soft, friendly, open light. It's the same environment but with substantially different lighting, and it reinforces the arc of their relationship and the film's happy ending. A place that was once strange and intimidating is now warm and inviting.

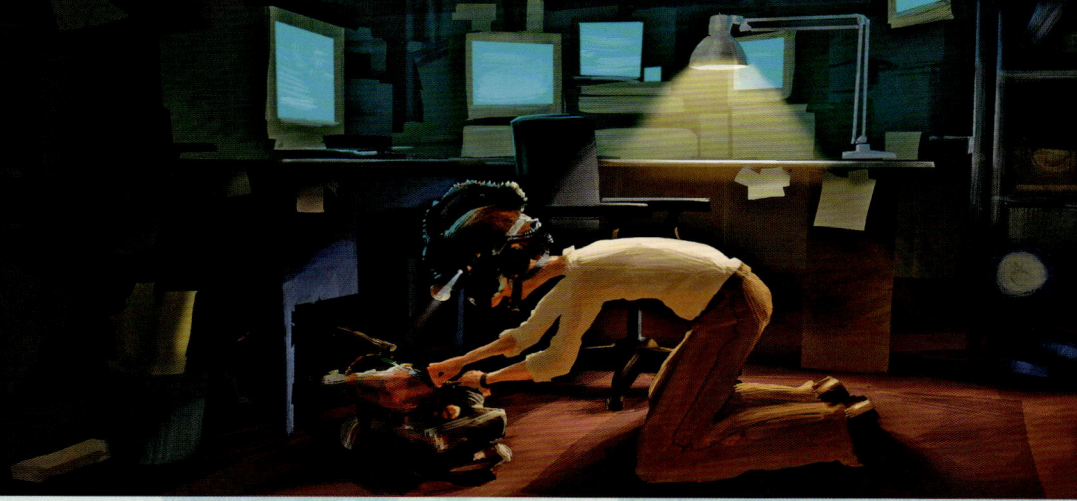

But putting the lights in after the animation is a little backward compared to regular filmmaking. "In live-action filmmaking, the camera and the lighting go together," says Uesato. "So when a shot is being prepared in a live-action shoot, the director of photography sees the lighting setup, can sculpt it with the camera, and can get blocking for the performance, too. It's 'Lights, Camera, Action.' But in CG it's 'Camera, Action, Lights.' There is no lighting on a CG set to add layers of emphasis or counter-balance to the visuals. So we kind of have to figure out what the intentions were and make sure the right story is being told."

To keep those intentions consistent from start to finish, the art department creates "color keys" in Photoshop. These beautiful digital paintings are designed to illustrate what a sequence of the final film will look like with the proper color and lighting applied. As lighting supervisor on *Epic*, Uesato was responsible for making sure the finished film matched the color keys, and Sung offered support when able.

"*Epic* is everyone's pride in the Lighting department," says Sung. "Chris Wedge was pushing for really realistic lighting, and it obviously looks the most like real life of all our films. He wanted you to feel like you were immersed in that world."

"Every shot has a story to tell," adds Uesato, "and every shot has a trajectory that feeds into the shots around it that move the story somewhere. Lighting is all about making decisions and biasing your answer one way or another. This could be making something lighter or darker, or making something read more or less. Hopefully it's subtle. You're not hitting anyone over the head with it, but that's what we do."

The artists of the Lighting department are some of the unsung heroes of an animation studio. The better they do their job, the less likely you are to notice it.

(Top row) **Nim's speech** – color key *(left)* by Mike Lee; lighting & compositing *(middle & right)* by Dan O'Brien, *(Bottom row)* **Bomba in lab** – color key *(left)* by Ron DeFelice; lighting & compositing *(middle & right)* by Angel Camacho

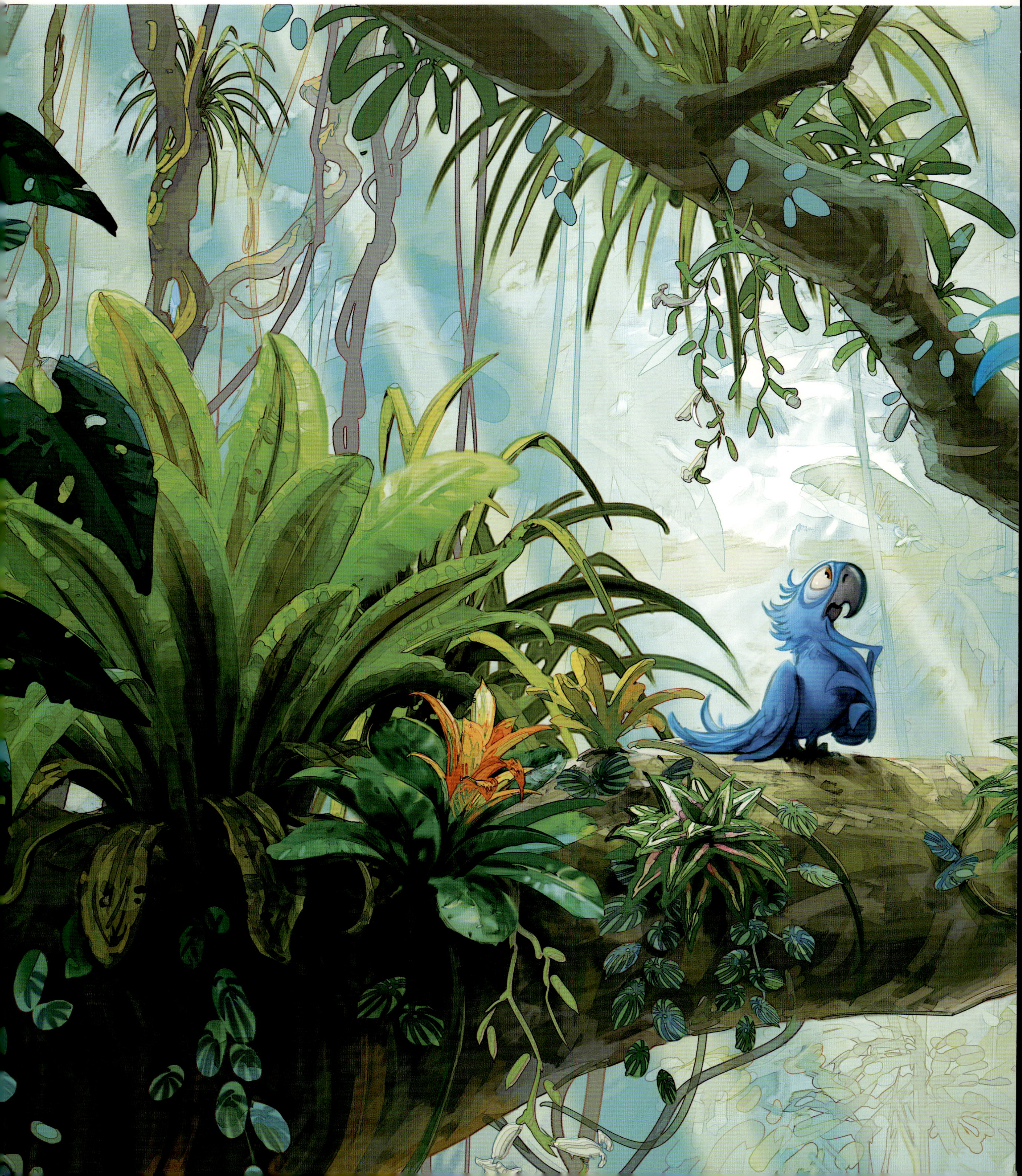

CHAPTER 9 • *Rio 2*

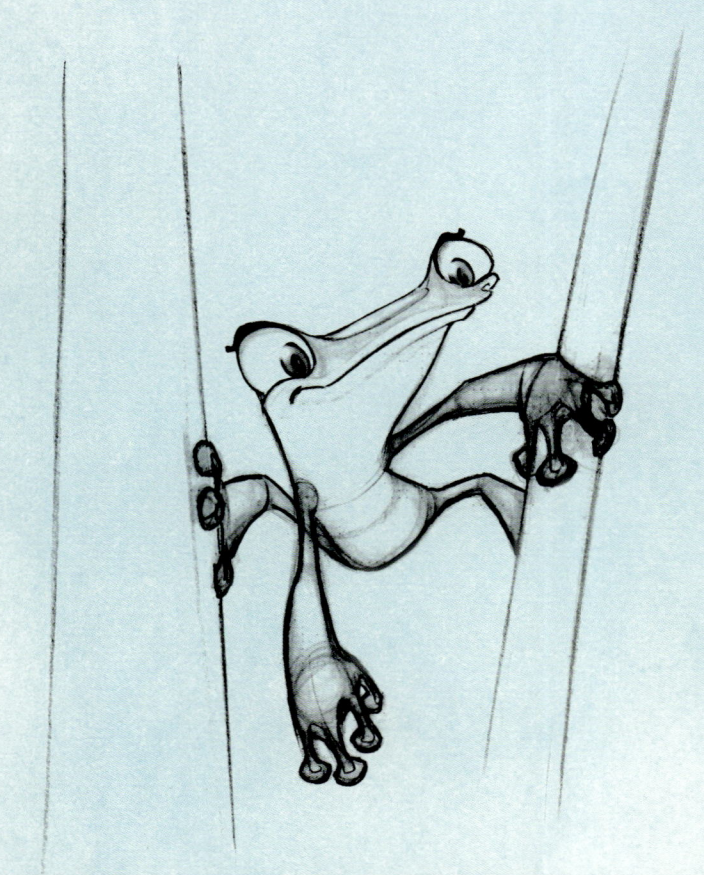

"We're not people, we're birds! We have to get out into the wild and be birds, Blu."

—JEWEL

Being Blu is hard enough. He may be the only introverted tropical bird living in the world's samba capital. Despite relocating from Linda's Minnesota bookshop to the wilderness of Brazil, he was able to build a family with Jewel, the blue Spix's macaw. And although they have their wings full with their three hatchlings—

Bia, Carla, and Tiago—he thinks that's where his difficulties end. But when Blu meets a distrustful tribe of wild Blue Macaws, discovers the threat of loggers to their habitat, and reencounters a homicidal cockatoo, he once again has to spread his wings and rise to the occasion.

"The good thing about sequels is that people want to see your characters, and they like the story you told in the first place," says director Carlos Saldanha. "But by the same token, the challenge is to feel fresh and unique, and you add new characters, and that creates complications."

Saldanha and his team looked to a natural development in Blu and Jewel's story. We watched them fall in love, in the original film, and now their relationship has progressed toward family life. What took Blu to Rio was the fear that he was the last male of his kind. What takes him and his family to the Amazon is the news that an entire flock of Blue Macaws live there. And they have no clue what's waiting for them on their journey.

SOMETHING BORROWED, SOMETHING BLU

Saldanha regrouped with art director Tom Cardone for this sequel. This time the characters travel across Brazil into the city of Manaus and throughout the densest parts of the Amazon to discover that they are not the last of their kind. In fact a secret community of blue Spix's macaws has been thriving far away from any human contact.

The filmmakers had to reconstruct the Amazon rainforest to fit the style and storytelling of the movie. It's one thing to caricature Rio's architecture to evoke the culture. It's another to caricature nature

(Previous pages) **Blu and Jewel with epiphytes** – concept art • Jon Townley (background painting) and José Manuel Fernández Oli (character poses & painting), *(Top)* **Gabi** – character sketch • Jason Sadler, *(Opposite)* **Blu and Jewel by waterfall** – concept art • Nathan Fowkes

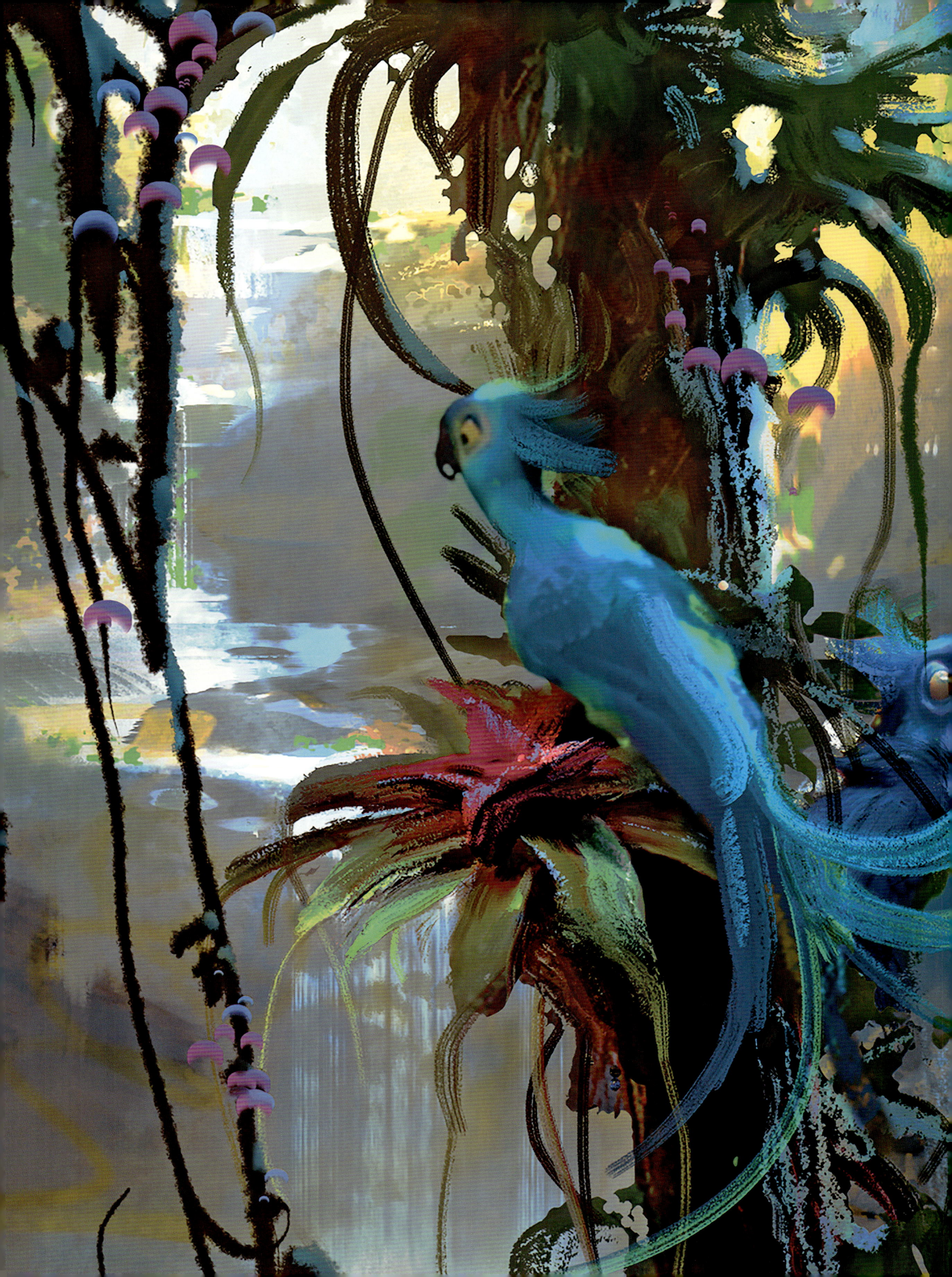

itself. Blue Sky reconstructed the Amazon rainforest in an immersive and believable yet highly stylized way.

"When searching for a way to caricature the forest, we looked hard at style cues from the culture," says Cardone. "We love the black-and-white tile patterns on the sidewalks, the wave pattern of Copacabana, and the signature sidewalks of Ipanema. Even though these are very old designs, there is something about them that makes you think of the textiles and design sensibility of the late sixties and early seventies. It seemed to stand out to us, and I wanted to key in on that and find ways to influence our plants with that design language. You think of textile prints from that era, how things were exaggerated and simplified. A good example is the flower stickers that they used to put on slippery surfaces. We found plants that would lend themselves to that and leaf shapes that we could push very easily into popular shapes from that era."

Once you look for it, you can spot the organic interpretation of floral print patterns popular in the 1960s. Simplified and exaggerated designs of that style appear throughout *Rio 2*'s rainforest as exotic leaves and blossoms. The visuals create a stylized version of the jungle that pushes reality just enough to fit in with the tone of the film.

But since such a large portion of the movie takes place in a single environment, different backdrops were required to keep it interesting and varied. That's where Cardone focused on different motifs.

(Top) **Jungle floor** – concept art • Aidan Sugano, *(Right)* **Jungle tree with Blu and Jewel** – concept art • Arden Chan, *(Bottom)* **Blu on jungle floor** – concept art • Andrew Hickson, *(Opposite left)* **Credits** – concept art • Aidan Sugano, *(Opposite top right)* **Blu with map** – concept art • José Manuel Fernández Oli (design) and Peter Nguyen (painting), *(Opposite bottom right)* **Map** – concept art • David Dibble

278 THE ART OF BLUE SKY STUDIOS

Pop-Up Travel Scene

"WE READ THE SCRIPT and identify possible locations," says Cardone, "and then try to figure out what we might have in our toolbox in terms of how we can push the design of the various locations to feel different with things like light, color, shape language—and then we see what suits the story best."

The depth of Blue Sky's toolbox contains motifs as unexpected as a pop-up book style. When Blu and Jewel travel across Brazil, each city on their flyover map emerges like a pop-up page and cross-dissolves into a fully three-dimensional set piece.

"It was really fun because we were able to push the look of those sequences to be very stylized," says Cardone. "So we're in and out of this graphic world. It was another way to bring some fun and variety into the movie."

(Above) **Macaw village area** – concept art • Nathan Fowkes

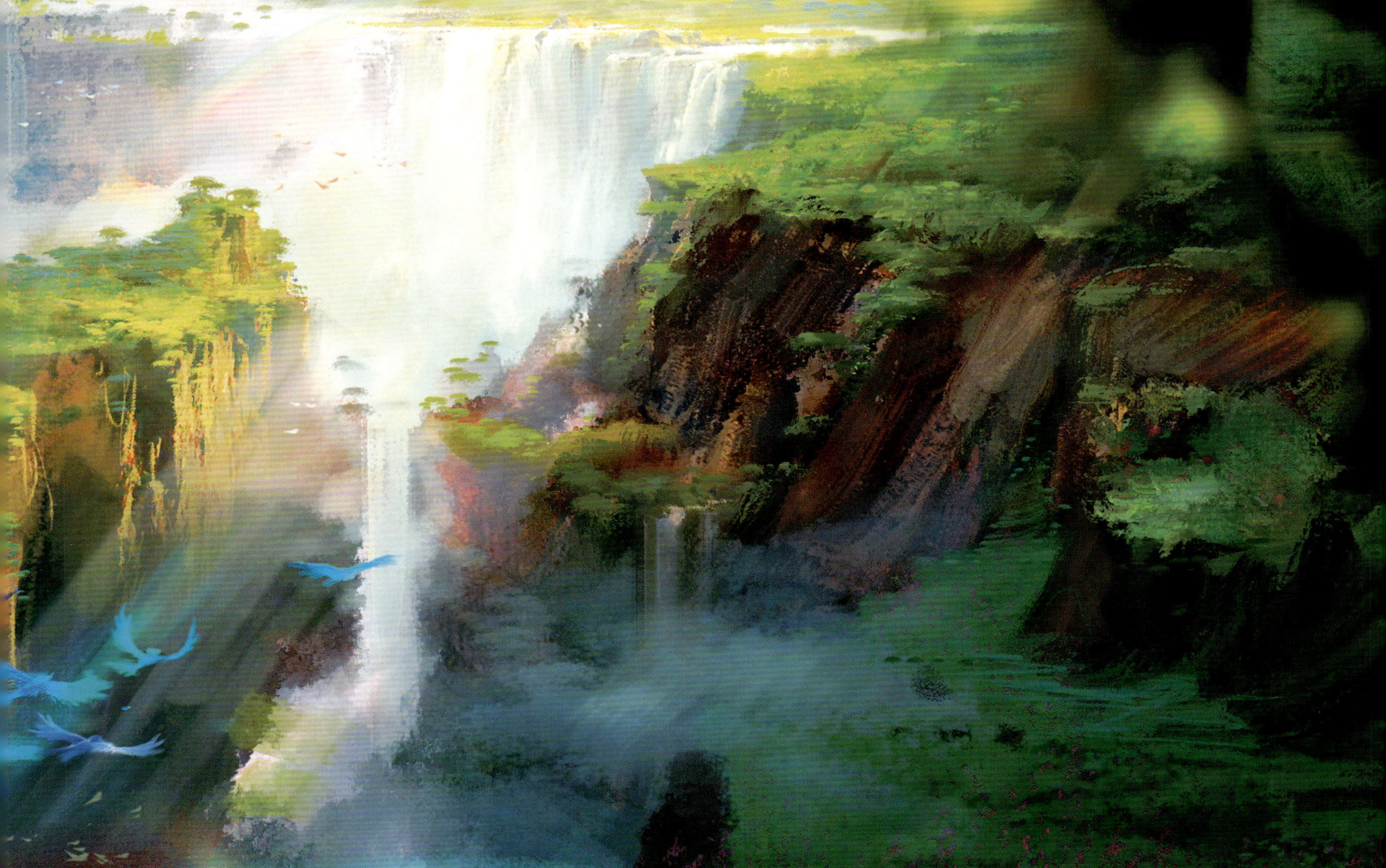

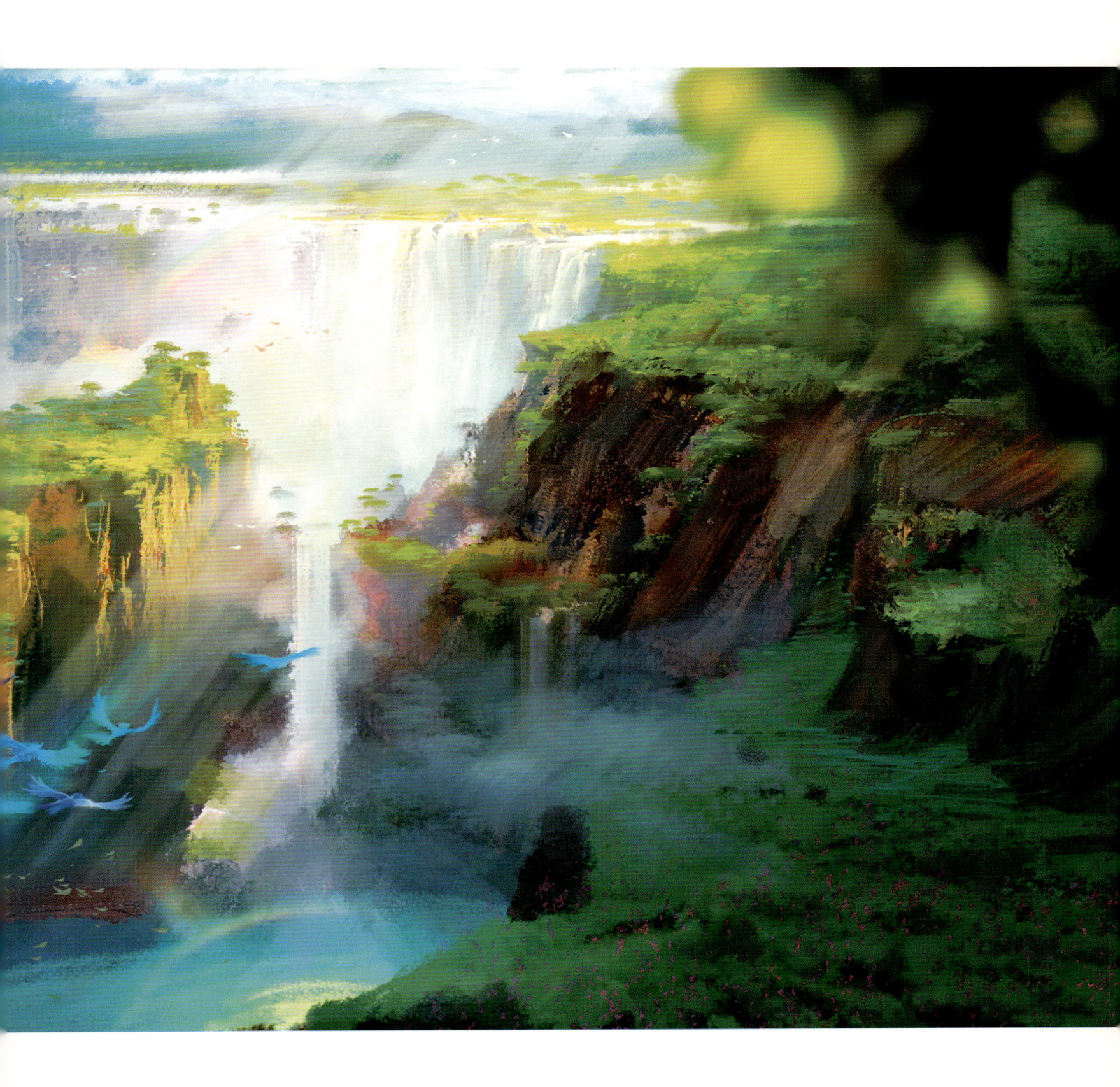

"Within the jungle," says Cardone, "we might have an area with a lot of rounded, moss-covered rocks and rapids in the river, so the motifs would be very spherical and less about the vertical of the trees. And we found other places where some of the trees had fallen down naturally, which creates diagonals, so maybe for the right sequence we would go for a motif like that. An aerial view of a bunch of cut logs on a winding river looks like matchsticks, and we thought of that in terms of a graphic pattern. We know that, because the rainforest is so dense, there's less light low on the ground that gets filtered through the canopy of the trees. When you get higher up, it becomes brighter, so we tried to plan sequences with that in mind."

Lighting plays a significant, if subtle, role in these jungle scenes, and it required an innovative touch. Normally when a character is in front of scenery as complex as a wild jungle, the backdrop might steal the audience's attention. These jungle scenes needed special consideration from the lighting team to keep the characters the main focus of each shot. Cardone pushed for a colored and very atmospheric backdrop that bent the laws of physics that normally guide Blue Sky's renderer, CGI Studio.

To support the staging of a character in a jungle environment, the lighting department normally adds atmosphere like a sun haze, which gives the illusion of a distant and unfocused background. To keep the background colorful and simplify the contrast and detail behind the characters, the lighting team—headed by Jeeyun Sung—implemented a colored atmosphere, skewing toward blue/green. Thus the filmmakers are able to focus our attention on the characters against a lush rainforest canopy.

(Bottom) **Carla, Bia, and Tiago settle into their new home** – concept art • José Manuel Fernández Oli (design) and Nathan Fowkes (painting), *(Left)* **Capybara baby** – concept art • José Manuel Fernández Oli (design), *(Opposite top)* **Jewel's family** – final digital frame

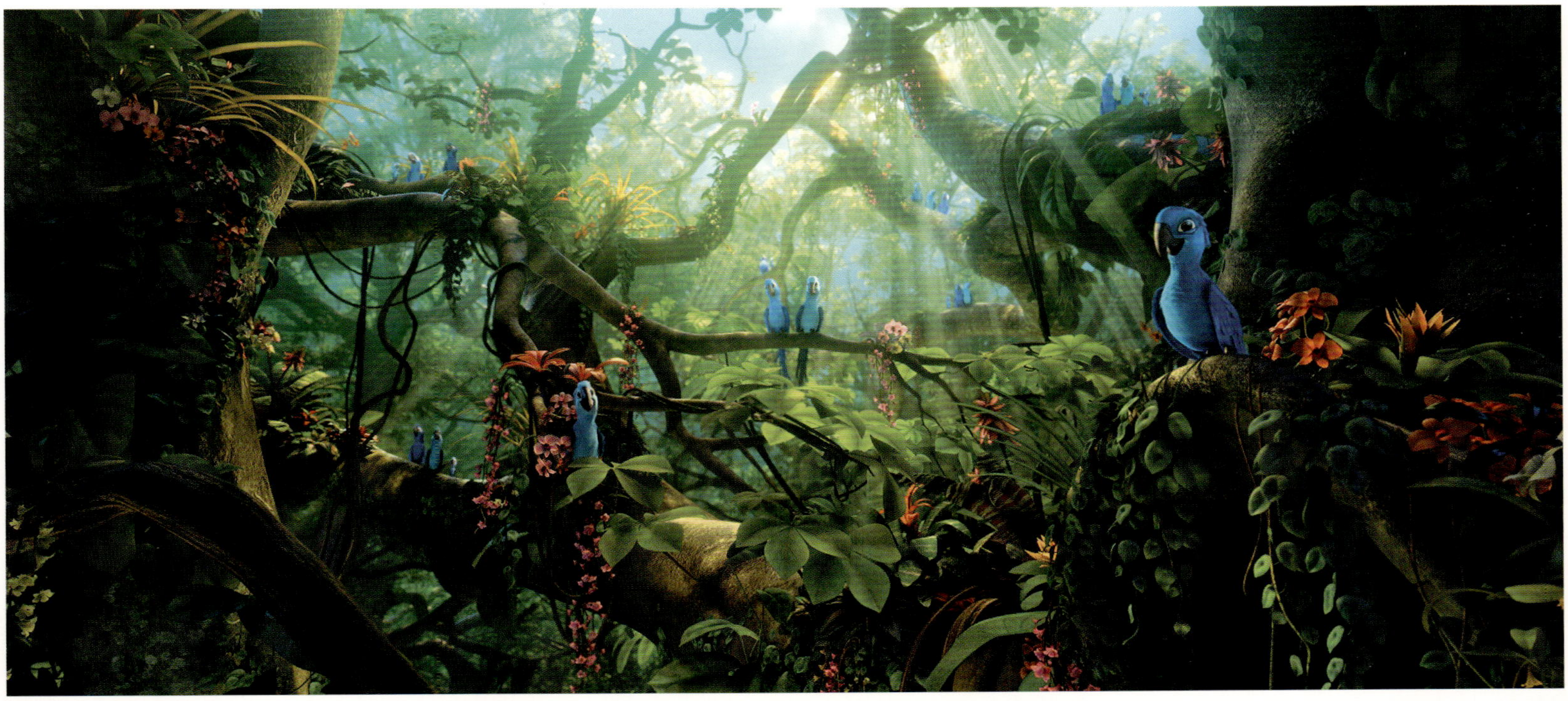
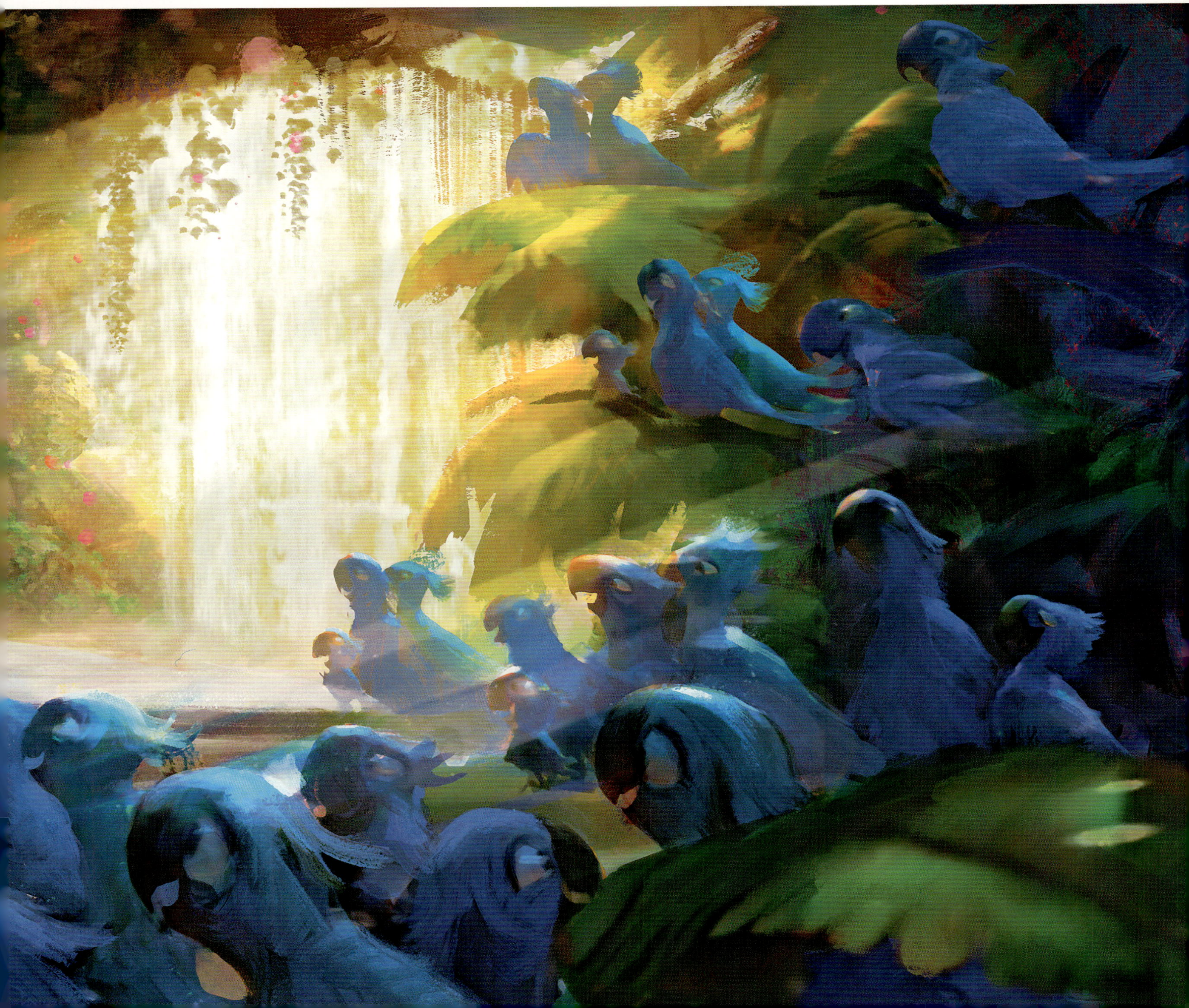

(Top) **Nigel and Charlie cross the river** • Peter Chan (design) and Ric Sluiter (painting), *(Opposite top)* **River boat (three images)** – paintings over models • Aidan Sugano (design), Dinis Morais, Jonathan Lin & Christian Haniszewski (models), and Jake Panian (painting), *(Opposite center)* **Blu and Jewel's river boat** – concept art • Thomas Cardone, *(Opposite bottom)* **River boat on the Rio Negro** – concept art • Aidan Sugano

"Growing up in Brazil, I had felt that we've got to protect these beautiful creatures, because once you destroy them they're gone forever. Like me, the characters feel that nature needs to be protected."

—CARLOS SALDANHA

284 THE ART OF BLUE SKY STUDIOS

RIO 2 285

A JUNGLE OUT THERE

The movie's design sense extends toward the characters as well. "You start your character design based on the personality pitched to you by the director and portrayed in the script," says Cardone. "Then you try to find the clearest way to make each character distinct from one another."

For the little blue triplets, variation was key. Bia, Carla, and Tiago emerge as Blu and Jewel's precocious kids, and they couldn't be more different. "These characters had to look similar enough to be the same species, but still be recognizable as individuals," says Cardone. "Some of the strongest tools to make characters distinct are shape and color. Jason Sadler, who designed the kids, starts his design process in silhouette." Bia, the book-smart child, resembles Jewel, whereas Carla, the outgoing child full of life, is a bit stockier and full-figured. Tiago's disheveled feathers aren't fully formed, and he acts like a little wild man.

A whole clan of macaws had to be modeled to look distinct from one another, especially Eduardo, Jewel's domineering father with an indefatigable distrust of humans.

"He's a wild bird," says Saldanha, "and he believes that birds need to be separated from humans because humans tend to destroy them." Ultimately there's sympathy for Eduardo's outlook when we see the extent of his habitat's destruction at the hands of the villainous loggers.

"Growing up in Brazil, I had felt that we've got to protect these beautiful creatures, because once you destroy them they're gone forever," says Saldanha. "Like me, the characters feel that nature needs to be protected."

HOME TWEET HOME

286 THE ART OF BLUE SKY STUDIOS

(Top) **Macaws with dolphins** – concept art • Greg Couch, *(Bottom)* **Tree home moment** – concept art • José Manuel Fernández Oli (design) and Peter Nguyen (painting), *(Opposite top)* **Blu and the kids make breakfast** – concept art • José Manuel Fernández Oli (design) and Ric Sluiter (painting), *(Opposite center)* **Embroidered welcome mat** – graphic • David Dibble, *(Opposite bottom left)* **Macaw kids** – character sketch • Jason Sadler, *(Opposite bottom right)* **Macaw kids** – concept art • Jason Sadler (design) and Peter Nguyen (painting)

RIO 2   287

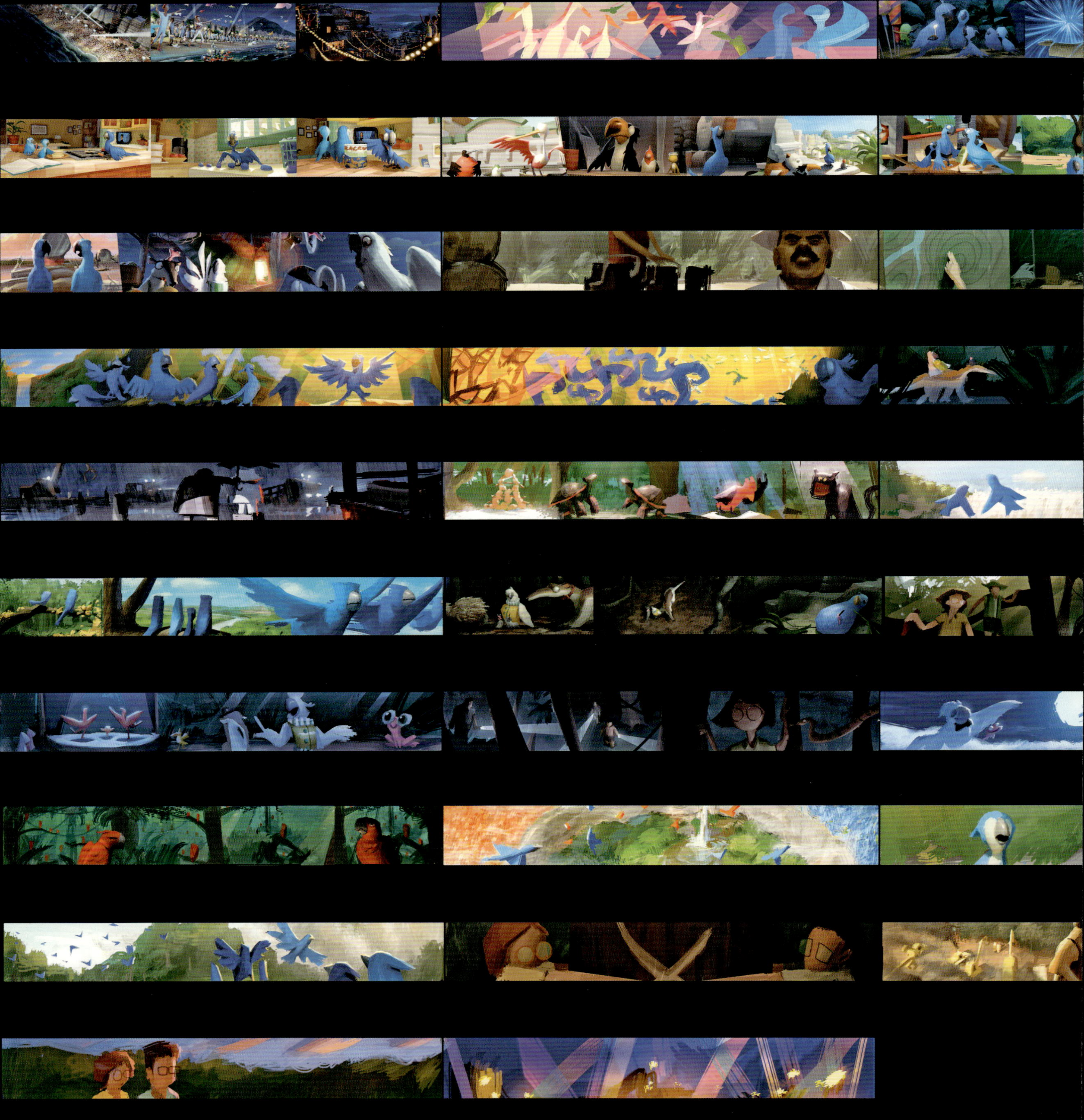

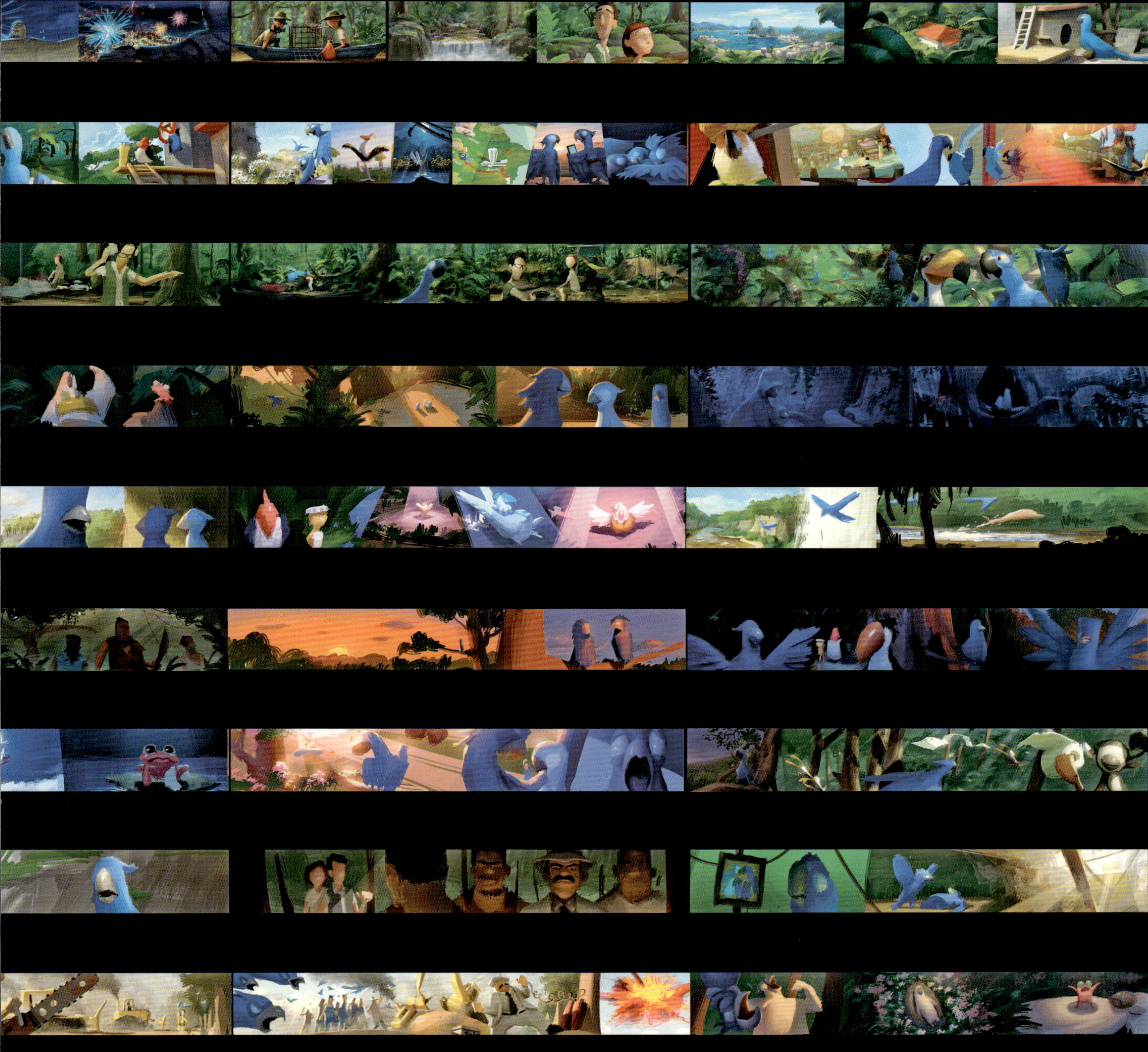

"The head of the logging company is a mysterious and frightening character," says Cardone, "so we staged him in ways that are intimidating. When you first see him, he's under the shadow of a canopy. Our first impression is his alligator boots and that his fedora darkens his face."

Accompanying him is an emperor tamarin monkey, one of the many new characters who appear in the film. As with the real wild simians and their natural handlebar mustaches, the designers took the original characteristics of the local animals and used them as launch points for new ideas. The natural colors adorning a giant anteater could be seen to resemble a vest, so for Charlie the anteater, the designers gave him a bow tie and bowler hat to complete the look.

(Previous pages) **Rio 2 color script** • Mike Lee, *(Top)* **Charlie eating** – final frame, *(Bottom left)* **Charlie (two images)** – sketches • BJ Crawford, *(Bottom right)* **Charlie** – concept art • José Manuel Fernández Oli (design) and Aidan Sugano (painting), *(Opposite top)* **Gabi** – concept art • BJ Crawford *(left & right)* and Jason Sadler *(middle)*, *(Opposite center)* **Gabi** – concept art • Jason Sadler (design) and Aidan Sugano (painting), *(Opposite bottom)* **River sideshow** – concept art • Aidan Sugano

290   THE ART OF BLUE SKY STUDIOS

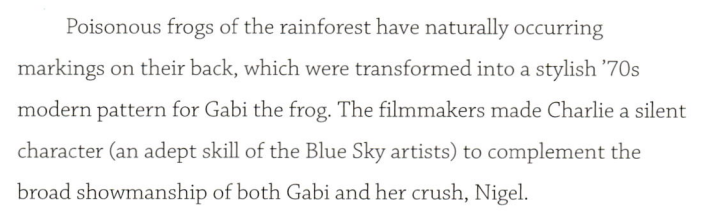

Poisonous frogs of the rainforest have naturally occurring markings on their back, which were transformed into a stylish '70s modern pattern for Gabi the frog. The filmmakers made Charlie a silent character (an adept skill of the Blue Sky artists) to complement the broad showmanship of both Gabi and her crush, Nigel.

"Can you imagine a bird and a frog in love?" asks Saldanha. "There's a lot of potential for comedy there. A poisonous frog can never be touched, so nobody wants to be close to it, and Nigel is a repulsive villain who doesn't feel love and doesn't feel that he has a place in this world. They're two outcasts, so naturally Gabi thinks they're perfect for each other."

However, Nigel's story is more than a plot device in this film. True to the events of the previous film, we find him at rock bottom, defeated, demoralized, and defeathered. His heart blackens against Blu and Jewel, whom he blames for his condition, but Gabi possesses only unconditional love for him. She sees the beauty in Nigel that is missed by everyone, including himself.

"Understanding the weakness of characters and trying to overcome their challenges is something I enjoy exploring," adds Saldanha. "I think I always look for characters with heart that you could tell good stories with; stories about family, love, and friendship. I have a large family, and I come from a family-driven environment, so those are all types of stories that mean something important to me."

(Top) **Birds watching forest's destruction** – concept art • Andrew Hickson (design) and Nathan Fowkes (painting), *(Bottom)* **Blu's confrontation with loggers** – concept art • Nathan Fowkes, *(Opposite bottom)* **Macaw flock with loggers** – concept art • Greg Couch

292   THE ART OF BLUE SKY STUDIOS

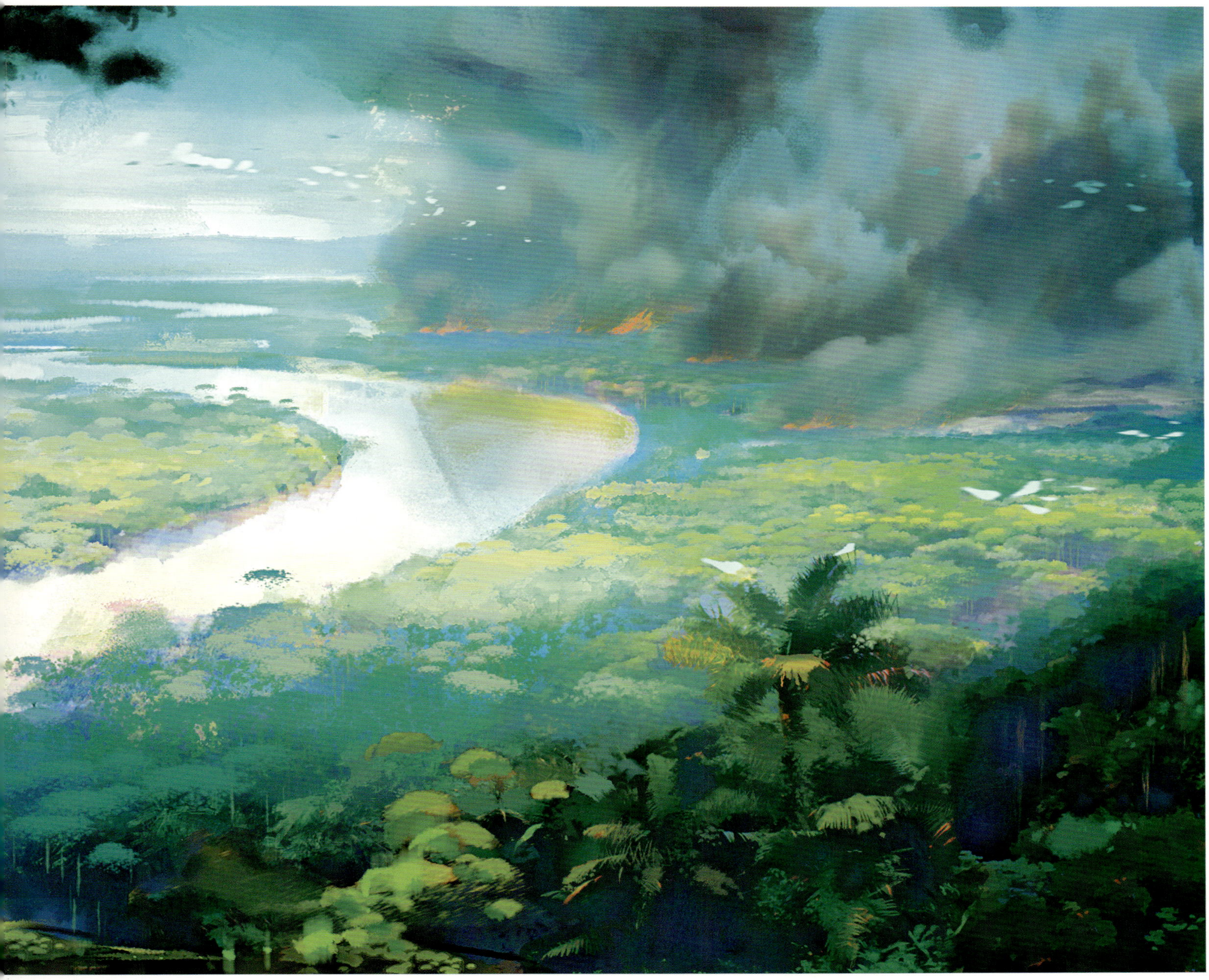

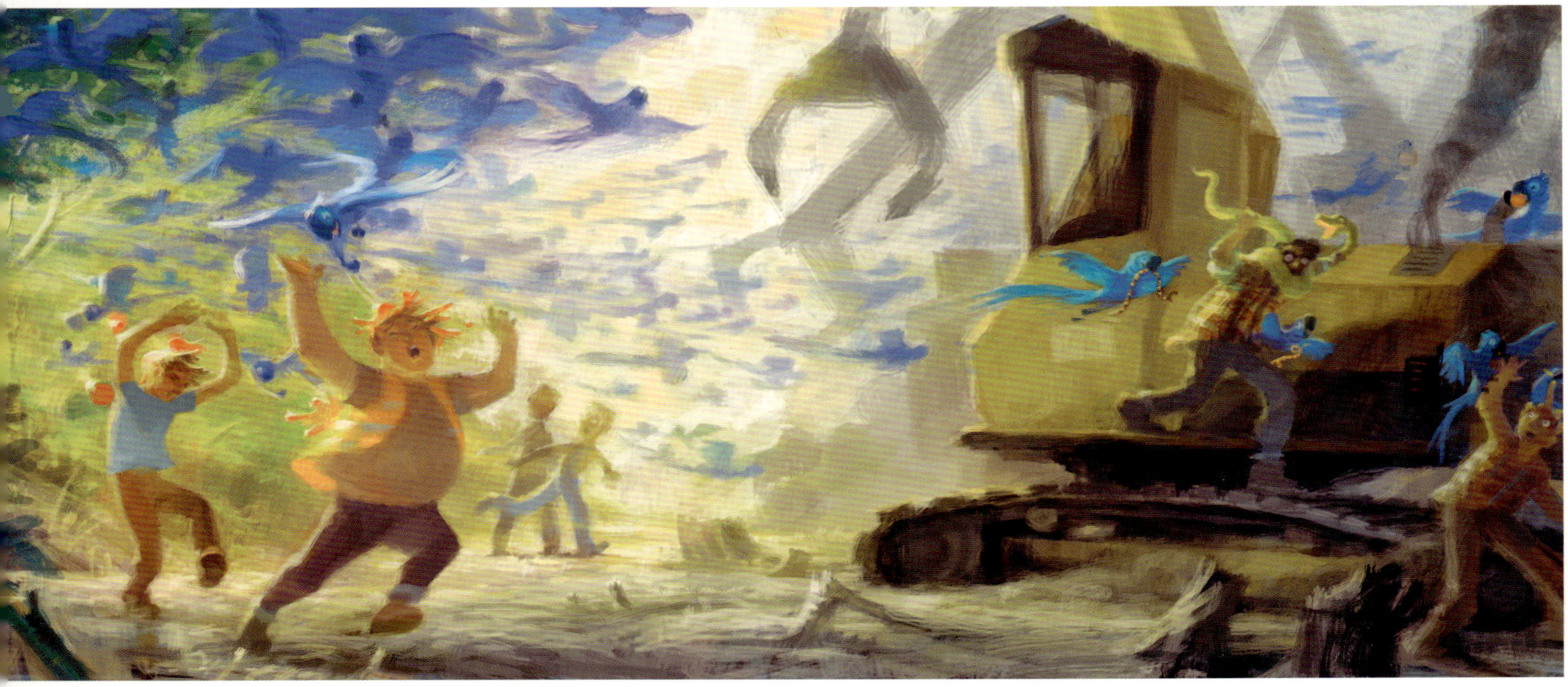

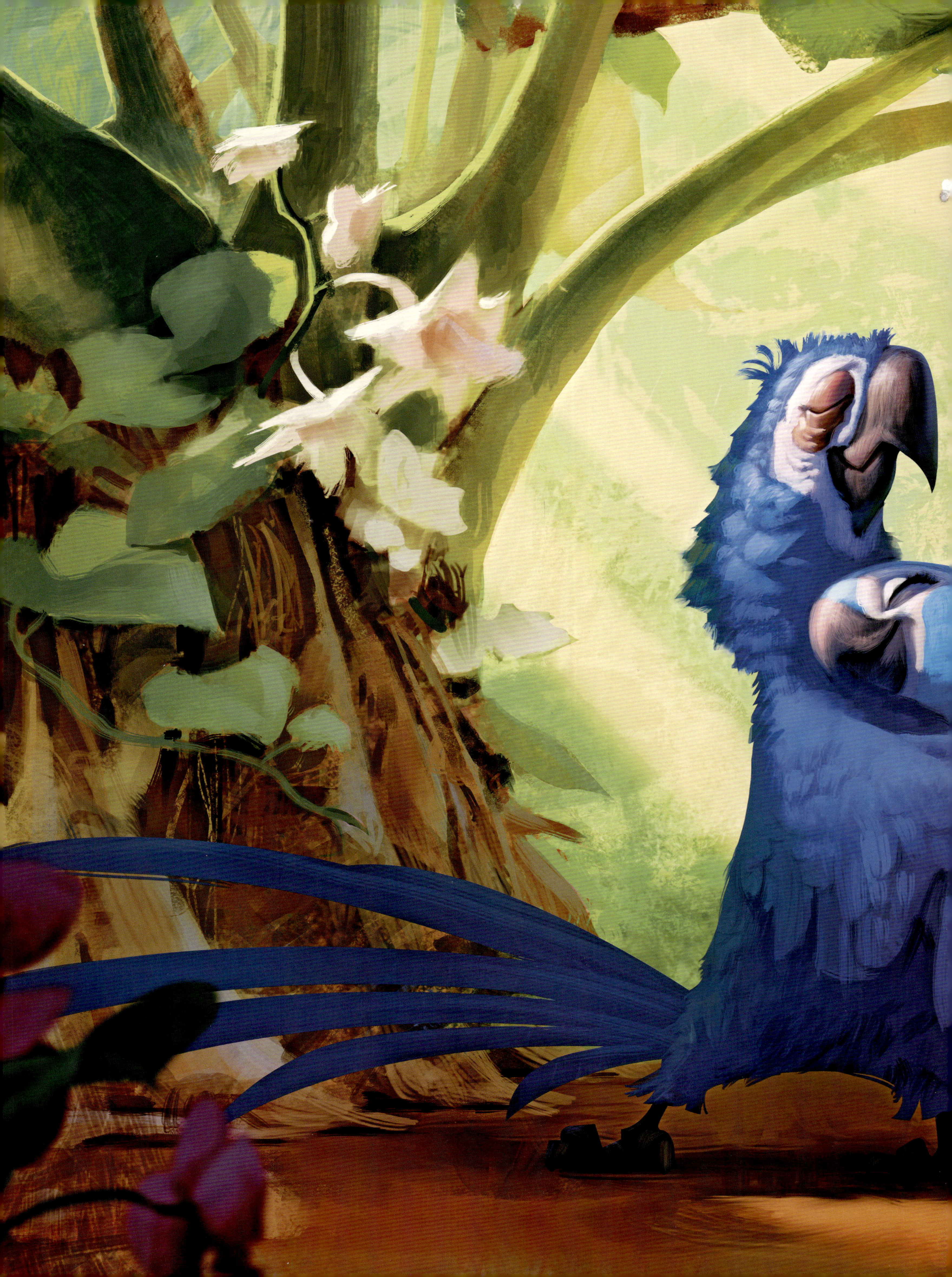

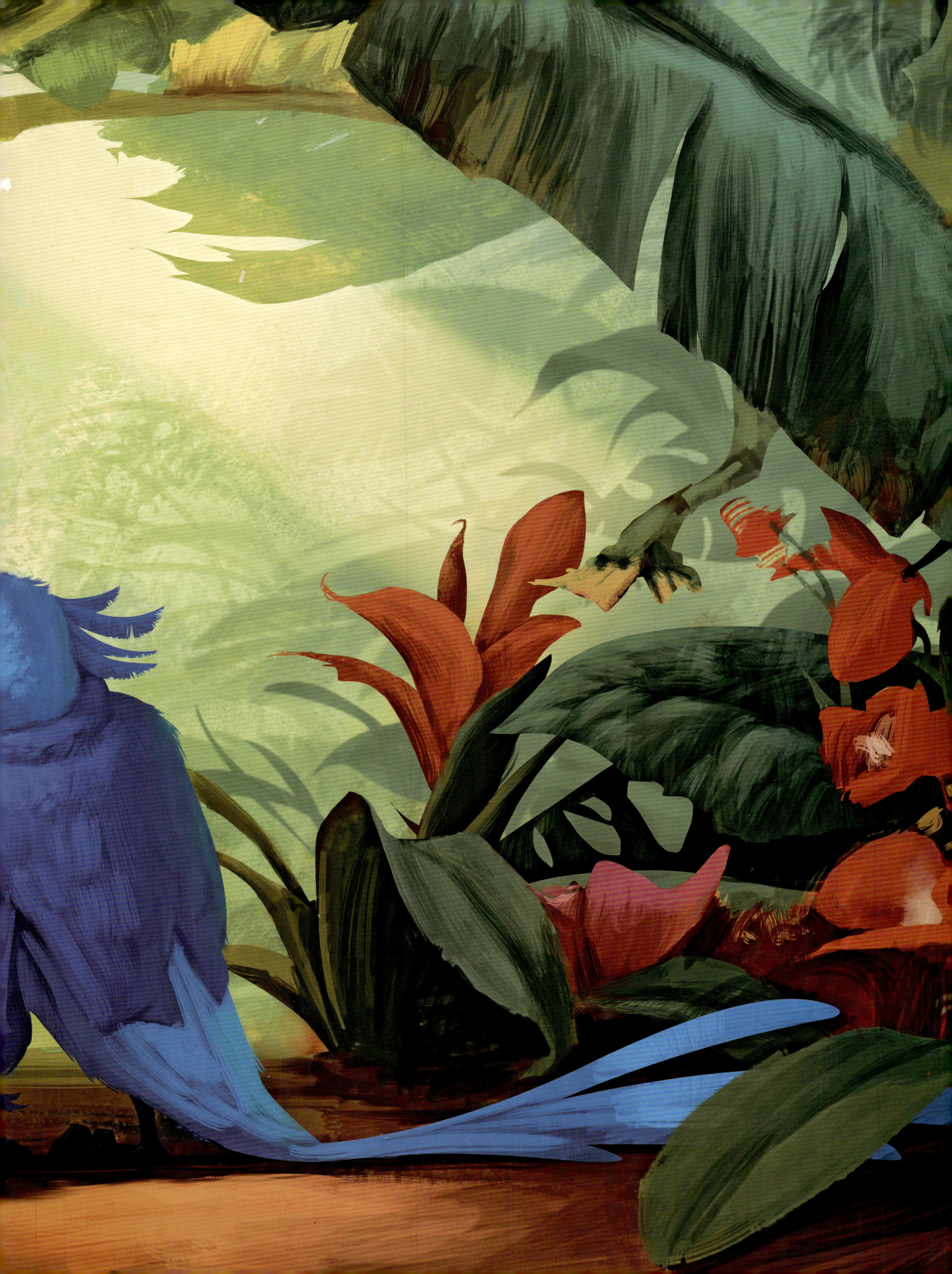

A LOOK INSIDE BLUE SKY

The Music of Blue Sky Films

THE MUSIC BEHIND A BLUE SKY FILM sometimes tells as much of the story as the characters themselves. Composer John Powell has written the musical scores for *Robots, Ice Age: The Meltdown, Dr. Seuss' Horton Hears a Who!, Ice Age: Dawn of the Dinosaurs, Rio, Ice Age: Continental Drift,* and *Rio 2*. His portfolio also includes animated films for Disney and DreamWorks and live-action films as action-packed at the *Bourne* trilogy and as emotionally gripping as *United 93*.

A film aimed at all ages like those in the *Ice Age* or *Rio* series has its own challenges that set it apart from adult-skewed live-action genres. "The difference between animated and other films is that you have a more balanced view of comedy, adventure, and action," says Powell. "Whereas a live-action film is more about being only a thriller or only an action film, an all-ages film allows you to be much more broad in your approach to music. You can have grand scale like *Ice Age: Continental Drift*, as grand as has ever been done in a live-action film, and then there's comedy like you would have in a live-action comedy. It has more styles in a way because it's the nature of the audience and the storytelling."

Powell carefully considers the storytelling when he prepares to score a film. A rough cut of the film is complete before he begins composing, and he works closely with the directors to determine what musical themes can be used. Particular characters may have their own leitmotifs (or short musical phrases), and broader musical themes can be used to link the film together.

Part of this method, appropriately enough, is inspired by the zany cartoons of animation's golden age. "I loved those Warner Bros. cartoons and [composer] Carl Stalling," says Powell. "They were very influential. Today there's always the comedic element to animated movies that leaves room to do more comedy music—and that's what we think of as classic cartoon music. But with these movies, you also have to score a lot of it as if it were live-action."

In order to make the melodies of *Rio* and *Rio 2* sound as sophisticated as those found in a live-action movie, legendary Brazilian bandleader Sérgio Mendes was enlisted, as well as musical contributor Carlinhos Brown. In Mendes's vast professional career, these projects mark the first time he has worked on a feature film. "It's been a wonderful experience," says Mendes. "Rio is where I grew up, so the movies are about a place I know very well."

According to Mendes, director Carlos Saldanha was already a fan of the 2006 album *Timeless*, a contemporary reinterpretation of classic bossa nova songs by Mendes and rapper will.i.am. Saldanha reached out to Mendes to be executive music producer of *Rio*.

The original *Rio* evokes the city and the Carnaval celebration, while *Rio 2* required something that matched the more tropical settings. "Now the birds fly to different parts of Brazil, and they go to the Amazon," says Mendes, "so it allows us to bring all the other beautiful facets of Brazilian music that aren't only related to Rio. Brazil has so much musical diversity, not only rhythmically but melodically, so it gave us a possibility to bring in some other sounds and songs that are very different from the first movie."

The movie contains music inspired by the jungle itself, like from the band Uakti, a favorite of Mendes. The members use handmade instruments to create a contemporary sound with a mysterious and beautiful quality that echoes the wild Brazilian rainforest.

Although Mendes focused more on the songs while Powell focused on the score, both musical elements had to unite seamlessly in the film.

"You try to work in coordination with a film like this," says Powell. "Some of the score comes out of the songs, and some of the songs come out of the score. It's kind of a mixed process. Sérgio and I have been spending a lot of time trying ideas out for songs, and out of that sometimes comes the score, so hopefully it's all integrated and smoothly locked together in a kind of logic."

The director monitors the whole process, so at the end of the day it's his vision that guides the film. "Carlos is such a brilliant director," says Mendes, "so if you look at the film, you'll see his sensitivity to the colors, the people, everything. He captured the essence of the soul of Brazil—one that is warm, generous, happy, sunny, sensual, and romantic."

(Previous pages) **Jewel and Eduardo reunion** – concept art • Aidan Sugano, *(Top)* **Capybaras** – concept art • José Manuel Fernández Oli (design) and Vincent Di Nguyen (painting), *(Center)* **Nigel and Bia** – concept art • Peter Chan (design) and Aidan Sugano (painting), *(Left)* **Rafael, Pedro, and Nico** – concept art • José Manuel Fernández Oli (design) and Aidan Sugano (painting)

(Above) **New Year celebration** – concept art • Greg Couch

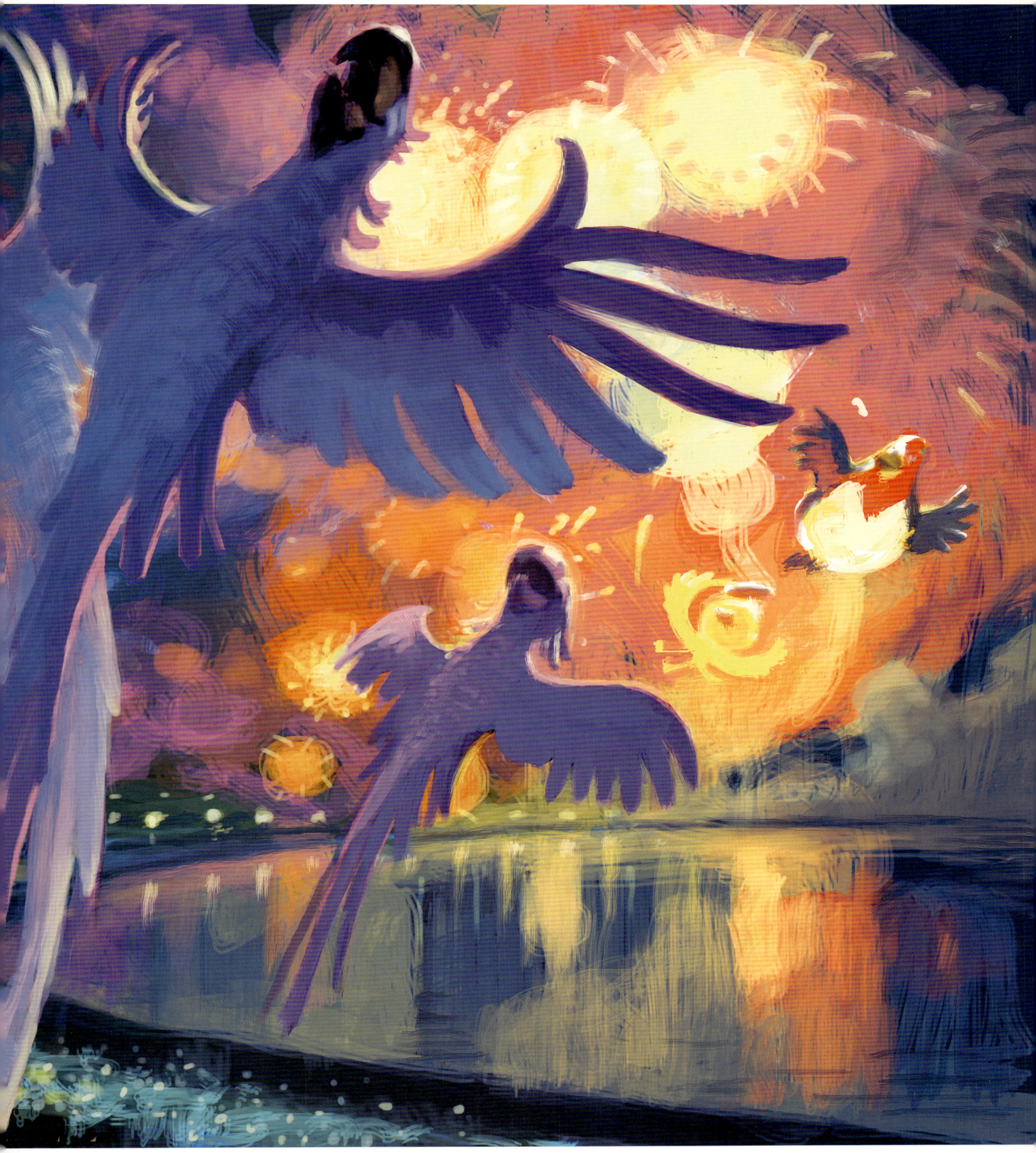

300 THE ART OF BLUE SKY STUDIOS

EPILOGUE

◆

It is an exemplary feat for a company like Blue Sky Studios to thrive in an ever-changing tide of taste and technology. Over time, audiences have grown more sophisticated, and they now have greater access to an increasing number of entertainment options.

Maintaining a high level of success in such a fast-moving environment is not an easy task; it takes growth and courage for Blue Sky to continually push the limits of what is possible in animation.

The studio began with a novel way to replicate light rays and has gone on to design whole worlds that enthrall and delight audiences. Each new film reveals a unique visual approach—from the jagged shapes of the prehistoric *Ice Age* universe to the lush picture-postcard lands of *Rio* to the realistic natural wonders in *Epic* and the Rube Goldberg towns of *Robots*. It's staggering that a single studio has produced all these vastly different films and that, from the get-go, the company has managed to reinvent itself with each project.

But Blue Sky is nothing without the people inside the studio. Every person at Blue Sky possesses a level of creativity and dedication that makes these films extraordinary, imbuing each with a level of warmth and humanity that captures the hearts and minds of audiences throughout the world.

In the years ahead, the studio will continue to create new adventures for the characters we love, as well as surprise us with diverse new worlds that rival our own reveries, such as that of the upcoming *The Peanuts Movie*. They will do what they do best: bring into existence characters, worlds, and stories that stay with us for years and become part of our collective consciousness. Future audiences will emerge, and new dreams will be inspired, affecting generations to come. That, in essence, is the art of Blue Sky Studios.

(Left) **Charlie Brown and Lucy** – conceprt art • Jon Townley (design) and José Manuel Fernández Oli (character poses & painting), *(Following pages)* **Pilot Snoopy** – conceprt art • José Manuel Fernández Oli

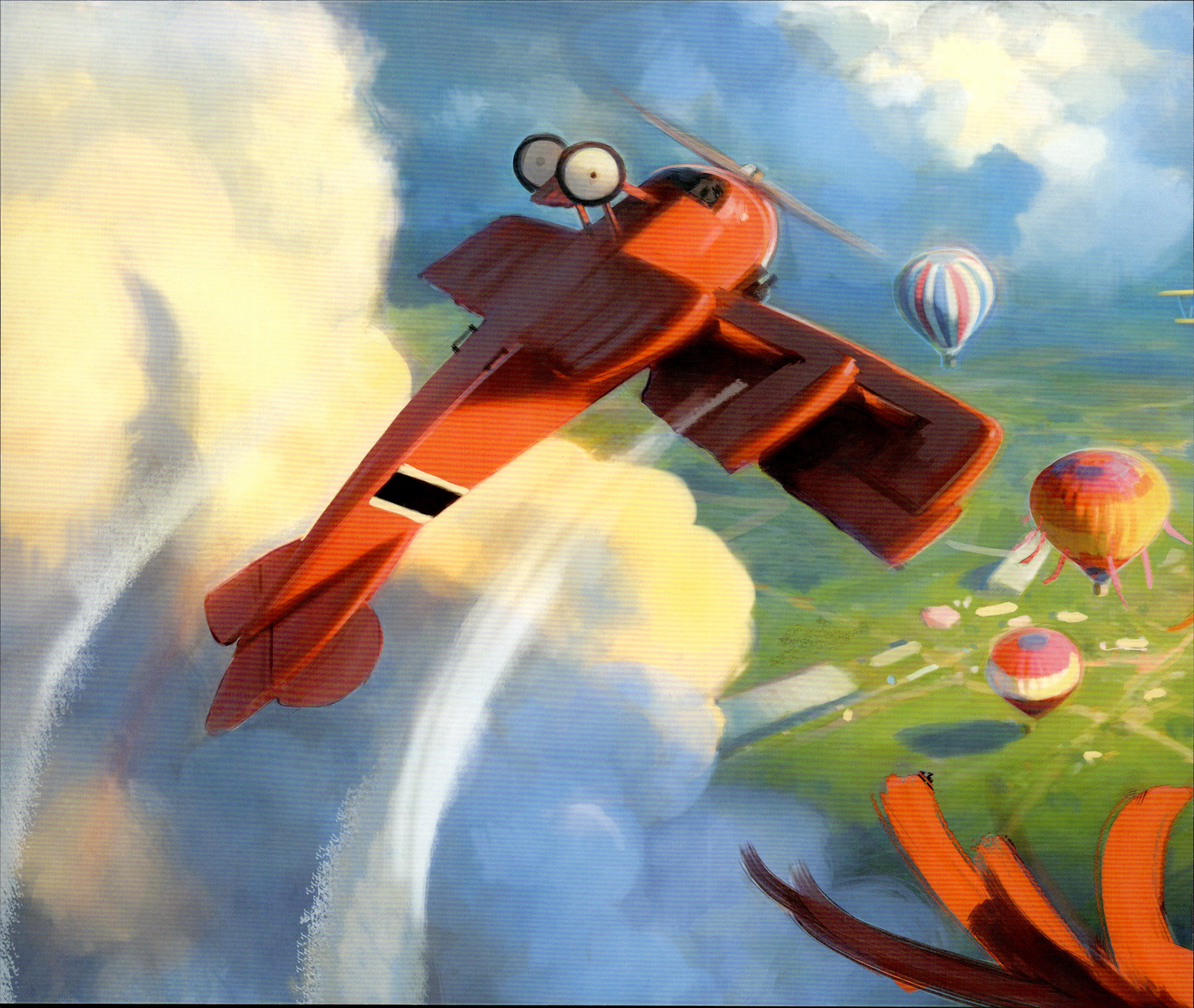

Ice Age, Ice Age 2: The Meltdown, Ice Age: Dawn of the Dinosaurs, Ice Age: Continental Drift TM & © 2014 Twentieth Century Fox Film Corporation. All Rights Reserved. RIO, RIO 2 © 2014 Twentieth Century Fox Film Corporation. All Rights Reserved. EPIC © 2014 Twentieth Century Fox Film Corporation. All Rights Reserved. Robots TM & © 2014 Twentieth Century Fox Film Corporation. All Rights Reserved. Horton Hears a Who! - © 2014 Twentieth Century Fox Film Corporation. All rights reserved. Dr. Seuss, Horton Hears A Who! and Dr. Seuss Characters TM & © 1954, 2014 Dr. Seuss Enterprises, L.P. All Rights Reserved. Dr. Seuss Properties TM & ©2014 Dr. Seuss Enterprises, L.P. All Rights Reserved. The Peanuts Movie - © 2014 Twentieth Century Fox Film Corporation. All rights reserved. PEANUTS © Peanuts Worldwide LLC.

All rights reserved. No part of this publication may be reproduced, stored in a retrieval system, or transmitted, in any form or by any means without the prior written permission of the publisher, nor be otherwise circulated in any form of binding or cover other than that in which it is published and without a similar condition being imposed on the subsequent purchaser.

A CIP catalogue record for this title is available from the British Library.

ISBN: 9781783293544

Find us on Facebook: www.facebook.com/titanbooks
Follow us on Twitter: @TitanBooks

REPLANTED PAPER Insight Editions, in association with Roots of Peace, will plant two trees for each tree used in the manufacturing of this book. Roots of Peace is an internationally renowned humanitarian organization dedicated to eradicating land mines worldwide and converting war-torn lands into productive farms and wildlife habitats. Roots of Peace will plant two million fruit and nut trees in Afghanistan and provide farmers there with the skills and support necessary for sustainable land use.

Published by Titan Books, London. Published by arrangement with Insight Editions, P.O. Box 3088, San Rafael, California 94912, USA. www.insighteditions.com

Manufactured in China by Insight Editions

Titan Books
144 Southwark Street
London SE1 0UP
www.titanbooks.com

AUTHOR ACKNOWLEDGMENTS

My gratitude to all the generous people involved in film production who contributed to this book: Jim Bresnahan, Nick Bruno, Rob Cardone, Tom Cardone, Rob Cavaleri, Galen Chu, Greg Couch, Peter De Sève, Karen Disher, Nash Dunnigan, Chloe Esposito, Lori Forte, Bill Frake, Kirk Garfield, Jimmy Hayward, Bill Joyce, Mike Knapp, Carl Ludwig, Steve Martino, David Mei, Sérgio Mendes, John Powell, Aaron Ross, Carlos Saldanha, Vicki Saulls, John Siczewicz, Chris Siemasko, Jeeyun Sung, Melvin Tan, Mike Thurmeier, Mike Travers, Eugene Troubetzkoy, Haji Uesato, Brian Useo, and Chris Wedge. Enormous gratitude to my editor, Chris Prince, at Insight Editions and to Melanie Bartlett and Stephanie Swengel at Fox. I owe a huge debt of thanks to my friend Jerry Beck and to John Culhane and my parents.

INSIGHT EDITIONS

Publisher: Raoul Goff

Acquisitions Manager: Robbie Schmidt

Executive Editor: Vanessa Lopez

Senior Editor: Chris Prince

Art Director: Chrissy Kwasnik

Designer: Jenelle Wagner

Production Editor: Rachel Anderson

Production Manager: Anna Wan

Editorial Assistants: Elaine Ou and Kathryn DeSandro

Insight Editions would like to thank Josh Izzo, Lauren Winarski, Jennifer Birmingham, Justina Wong, Carlee Weinbaum, Melanie Bartlett, Michael Knapp, Brian Keane, Angela Macias, Susan Brandt, Melissa Menta, Craig Herman, Leah Bloise, Megan Greene, and the many people at Fox Animation and Blue Sky Studios who helped make this book possible.

(Above) **Ice Age: Dawn of the Dinosaurs: Scrat and Scratte** – concept art • Peter de Sève, *(pp. 2-3)* **Rio 2: Driftwood celebration** – concept art • Arden Chan (design) and Aidan Sugano (painting), *(pp. 6-7)* **Ice Age: Dawn of the Dinosaurs: Lost World** – concept art • Michael Knapp, *(pp. 8-9)* **Dr. Seuss' Horton Hears a Who!: Whoville** – concept art • Kyle Macnaughton (design) and Xiangyuan Jie (painting)